Peacemaking and the Canon Law of the Catholic Church

Law and Religion

Volumes published in this Brill Research Perspectives title are listed at *brill.com/rplrs*

Peacemaking and the Canon Law of the Catholic Church

By

Charles J. Reid, Jr.

BRILL | NIJHOFF

LEIDEN | BOSTON

Library Congress Control Number: 2023949916

Typeface for the Latin, Greek, and Cyrillic scripts: "Brill". See and download: brill.com/brill-typeface.

ISSN 2667-3398
ISBN 978-90-04-68144-6 (paperback)
ISBN 978-90-04-54574-8 (e-book)
DOI 10.1163/9789004545748

This book is printed on acid-free paper and produced in a sustainable manner.

To the memory of Professor James A. Brundage, mentor, friend, and inspiration

Contents

Preface

The popular conception of the author is someone solitary and isolated, working hours a day at a desk, uninterrupted by human interaction. That may be the experience of some authors, but that certainly does not describe mine. I know from experience that the writing of books requires supportive colleagues and friends. And this is the place to acknowledge debts to those persons who rendered aid, insight, and sometimes even just moral encouragement.

I would like to begin with a group of people I know at Emory Law School, most of whom have an association with the Center for the Study of Law and Religion. I should like to begin by acknowledging Lee Ann Bambach. It was Professor Bambach who extended to me an invitation to participate in a conference she was organizing on alternative dispute resolution and the law. "Could I please submit a paper?" She asked. I did as she requested and that paper became the early, first draft of this book. I should also like to thank Dr. Courtney Freer. Dr. Freer chaired the panel at which I presented my paper, and asked good and important and thoughtful questions. Then there is Silas Allard, the managing editor of the Journal of Law and Religion, who helped steer an early version of this book in the right direction. Finally, of course, there is John Witte. John has been a valued friend for over thirty years. And he concluded that this text should find a fitting home in the book series he helps to edit. I hope you like the book!

I must also thank some persons at my home institution, the University of St. Thomas School of Law in Minnesota. First, I must thank the University administration for granting me a sabbatical in the spring of 2022. It was during that sabbatical semester that I wrote and delivered the paper that became this book, and it was also during that time that the outlines of this larger project became clear. I would also like to thank Professor Mariana Hernandez Crespo Gonstead, who was the first person to suggest to me the theme of "peacemaking" as the central unifying principle of the volume. I must thank the University of St. Thomas Library staff. There is Michael Robak, the Library Director of the Schoenecker Law Library of the University of St. Thomas. Michael is a friend, a supporter, and a very generous and warm colleague. I must also acknowledge a debt to the Law Library's staff, particularly Stefanie Hollmichel, who is always quick to fill even the most challenging interlibrary loan requests. And Niki Catlin, research librarian, who also provided much needed assistance.

And since this work is interdisciplinary, I must indicate my appreciation for the great support I have received from the staff of the Archbishop Ireland

Memorial Library, who always graciously answered even the most obscure questions. In particular I should like to thank Betsy Polakowski, who has recently stepped down as Director of the Ireland Library, and Mason Mitchell, who has recently assumed that mantle. Finally, I should state my gratitude for the wonderful support I have received from the Law School's administration. There is Joel Nichols, whom I have known for a quarter century, and who has been an enthusiastic friend and colleague, now serving in the role of Interim Dean of the Law School. And I should also thank Lisa Schiltz, the Law School's Associate Dean, who is always quick with a warm-hearted word. Thanks! And there are my many colleagues. I shall single out two – Rob Kahn and Julie Jonas – for their wonderful conversations on scholarship and much else.

I must also thank my wife, Cheryl Thorgaard Reid, who must put up with the idiosyncracies of an author at work. Cheryl has been a loving, supportive, devoted, and wonderful human being in the more than forty years that we have known each other. She tolerates my eccentricities with humor and fondness. Cheryl, thanks so very much!

Finally, I must thank James Brundage, to whose memory this book is dedicated. I first became acquainted with Professor Brundage in the 1970s, while I was an undergraduate at the University of Wisconsin-Milwaukee. Over the years he became a mentor, a friend, and an inspiration. I hope that this book repays the early confidence he showed in me.

Peacemaking and the Canon Law of the Catholic Church

Charles J. Reid, Jr.
University of St. Thomas, School of Law, Minneapolis, Minnesota, USA
CJREID@stthomas.edu

Abstract

At the level of both theology and praxis, the Catholic Church has long had a commitment to peacemaking. This volume explores the range of the Church's commitment to establishing peaceful relations among contending parties by focusing on three discrete areas of concern. These include: the use of papal diplomacy to resolve international conflicts; the utilization of the tools of arbitration and alternative dispute resolution as a means of promoting the amicable settlement of private litigation; and the development of the tools of reconciliation to restore good relations between ecclesiastical superiors and those subject to their authority. The book concludes with an appendix that proposes a variety of ways in which the Church might use its good offices to repair breaches among persons and nations.

Keywords

canon law – arbitration – reconciliation – diplomacy – papacy – Second Vatican Council – international law – Pope Francis – St. John Paul II – Pope Leo XIII – Hundred Years War – Alternative Dispute Resolution

Part 1: Introduction

This book is about peacemaking and the canon law of the Catholic Church. The mention of the word "peacemaking" presents a seemingly vast array of possibilities. The word "peace," after all, may mean many things.

Thus Christians know that peace begins with a properly formed mind and soul. There is an absence of anxiety and a feeling of closeness to God. One has a sense of wholeness, well-being, self-understanding. Peace flows from a willing acceptance of one's duties. It is an openness to accept the will of God. Peace, thus understood, might be attained through prayer and meditation.

 | DOI:10.1163/9789004545748_002

But while this sense of interior peace is important, indeed, indispensable to an integral life, it is not the subject of this book. Peace, for purposes of this book, should be understood as the absence of conflict. So what is conflict? Imagine two sides that are at loggerheads. One side believes itself to be justly aggrieved. Someone or something has done them a terrible wrong. The other side believes its cause to be just and its motives pure. This is conflict. Conflict of this sort may involve the great and the mighty, the powers that be which control world events. Or it may involve persons, ordinary, everyday persons, going about their business, who find themselves drawn into a dispute through no fault of their own.

If we are speaking about sovereign powers, then there is the danger of war. Or of reprisals, or acts of blank hostility. Hundreds of thousands, perhaps millions of persons can suffer irreparable harm because of the unresolvable conflict between two sovereign powers. On the other hand, if we are speaking about individuals who are in conflict with one another, and they have the means and the motives to seek justice in a court of law, then we might be confronted with a lawsuit. "See you in court," is a favorite taunt, but it can carry real meaning when we are dealing with parties who have the deep pockets to see through on the threat of litigation.

But these are not the only forms of conflict that can arise. There is also the silent conflict that can percolate beneath the surface when parties of widely divergent power come to clash. The stronger party, who may occupy a position of hierarchical superiority, inadvertently, or thoughtlessly – or perhaps deliberately – never notices the harm that is implicit in the decisions that he makes. The weaker party, the party with less bargaining power, or financial resources, or even just less skill in managing interpersonal disputes might, as a result, experience not only a keen sense of helplessness or anger, but also come to the conclusion that nothing can be done and that the powerful will have their way.

Broadly speaking, these are the three types of conflict with which this book is concerned. It would seem that canon law ought to be uniquely adapted to bring peace among persons. And we will discover – through our examination of history, of language, and of legal structure – that the canon law is, indeed, better equipped for peacemaking than even many canonists appreciate.

The first of the three great themes that this book investigates is the relationship of the papacy and sovereign power. What role specifically can the papacy play in negotiating an end to international disputes? That the papacy has come to play such a role is the result of historical contingencies traceable back in time for better than a millennium and a half. If one had to identify a starting point for this function of the papacy, one might locate it in the tumultuous circumstances of mid-fifth century Rome.

Pope Leo the Great (reigned 440–461) not only arbitrated disputes among other leading churchmen, he led a delegation to meet with Attila, often called Attila the Hun, following that nomadic warrior's conquest and sacking of the City of Aquileia in 452. Prosper of Aquitaine, the theologian who served as Leo's secretary, left only the briefest of accounts of the Pope's meeting with Attila.[1] Attila was puffed up with "savagery" (*saevitia*) and "cruel desire" (*cupiditas*). But Leo, relying only upon the help of the Lord, met with the warrior king, and so deeply impressed him that he instructed his army to refrain from war, promised to keep the peace, and retreated across the Danube River.[2]

The record of the meeting resonated across the centuries. Thus Raphael painted the scene for a fresco that remains to this day in the apostolic palace in Rome. Leo and his entourage fill the left side of the painting, looking not only in command but even, if that is possible, somewhat serene. Overhead, Sts. Peter and Paul, armed with swords, watch vigilantly. Attila and his forces fill the center and the right of the canvas, greater in number, but in a state of disorder, even somewhat confused. The twofold message is clear: first, that where there is conflict, strife, or disorder, the Church is prepared to bring harmony, concord, and, in a word, peace; and, second, that there is no situation so grim, so devoid of prospects for peace, that one can only surrender hope of a peaceful solution. If Attila could be persuaded to abandon war and keep the peace, then anyone might.

The fact of the meeting, and its artistic recollection a thousand years later, evinces the long institutional commitment the papacy has had to the peaceful resolution of disputes among nations. In two parts, this volume cannot hope to recapture the breadth and depth of this history. One would need volumes to tell the story comprehensively. But we can sample it. Thus a large portion of Part 2 is devoted to Pope Martin v's effort to arbitrate an end to that interminable series of medieval conflicts between France and England which we know today as the Hundred Years War. Part 3, then, brings the story forward in time, to the modern papacy. We encounter a series of popes – Leo xiii, Benedict xv, John Paul ii, and Pope Francis – who use their good offices to avert conflict among nations. These popes have understood peace to include not only the cessation of hostilities, but the creation of substantively just outcomes.[3] And we shall see that on occasion they are even successful.

---

1 Prosper of Aquitaine, *Epitoma Chronicon*, 1367, *Monumenta Germaniae Historica, Auctores Antiquissimi*, vol. 9, p. 482; cf., Bronwen Neil, *Leo the Great* (New York, 2009), pp. 8–10 (summarizing both sources and scholarship on this meeting).

2 Prosper, *Epitoma, supra*, 1367, p. 482.

3 Kenneth Himes, "Papal Thinking About Peace Since *Pacem in Terris*: The World Day of Peace Messages, 1967–2013," *Journal of Catholic Social Thought* 11 (2014), pp. 9–32.

If the clash of sovereign powers is one type of conflict that the Church seeks to avert, then another is contentious litigation. Canon lawyers were pioneers in creating a dense and sophisticated body of rules for the proper adjudication of trials and appeals.[4] Scientific evidentiary standards had been widely adopted,[5] and it was even the case that a professional canonical bar of expert lawyers had come into being.[6]

But not every dispute led to a contentious trial. Indeed, litigators, legislators, and even the Roman pontiff himself had occasion to resort to and to recommend alternative dispute resolution as a viable means of settling conflicts. This was the case as early as the twelfth and thirteenth centuries, and it remains true today. Alternative dispute resolution, in other words, has a long and deep history within the Catholic Church.

When we address the non-judicial settlement of contentious cases, we shall build upon two sets of axioms. The first concerns the nature of litigation. Private litigation, in most systems of law, is adversarial. This is so even in those European legal orders popularly called "inquisitorial" because of the investigative role of the judge in criminal cases.[7] Indeed, if one takes seriously J.A. Jolowicz's observations about the origins of civil procedure as the search for a substitute for the violent settlement of disputes, a certain adversariness is hard-wired into every legal system.[8] But an adversarial process is not without costs, even where justice is done. Parties may harbor deep and lasting animosity towards one another. They may be psychologically or emotionally scarred by the proceeding.

Litigation, furthermore, carries not only a psychic but a financial price, and one or the other of the parties might face economic ruin because of the expense. It may even be the case that the ruination of one's opponent is the objective of the better-situated litigant, since litigation is often deeply unequal.

4 See, for example, Kenneth Pennington, "The Jurisprudence of Procedure," in Wilfred Hartmann and Kenneth Pennington, eds., *The History of Courts and Procedure in Medieval Canon Law* (Washington, DC, 2016), pp. 125–159.

5 James A. Brundage, "Full and Partial Proof in Classical Canonical Procedure," *The Jurist* 67 (2007), pp. 58–71; Richard M. Fraher, "Conviction According to Conscience: The Medieval Jurists' Debate Concerning Judicial Discretion and the Law of Proof," *Law and History Review* 7 (1989), pp. 23–88; and James Q. Whitman, *The Origins of Reasonable Doubt: Theological Roots of the Criminal Trial* (New Haven, CT, 2008), pp. 51–90.

6 See generally, James A. Brundage, *The Profession and Practice of Medieval Canon Law* (New York, 2004).

7 J.A. Jolowicz, "Civil Procedure in the Common and Civil Law," in Guenther Doeker-Mach and Klaus A. Ziegert, eds., *Law, Legal Culture, and Politics in the Twenty-First Century* (Stuttgart, 2004), pp. 55, 59.

8 J.A. Jolowicz, "Adversarial and Inquisitorial Models of Civil Procedure," *International and Comparative Law Quarterly* 52 (2003), pp. 281, 282.

The party with the greater resources might thus prevail not on the merits, but because the other side discovers that it cannot compete.

Our second set of axioms focuses upon our ideals. It is preferable, wherever possible, to find a system of dispute resolution that achieves justice between the parties but that carries less cost than litigation. A system that does not create enduring hatred between the parties is to be preferred over a system that stimulates and fosters such antipathy. The search for justice, furthermore, should never leave one financially insolvent. A system that can promise that the parties will have their dispute fairly and appropriately resolved and that both sides should still remain fiscally sound afterwards ought to be considered a superior system. A system that does not deter the disadvantaged or the economically vulnerable from pursuing their claims because they reasonably believe that their adversary has privileged access to deeper pockets or better lawyers is preferable to one in which such inequalities are a sad fact of life.

If the first two-thirds of this book is concerned respectively with the papal mediation of international disputes and with the settlement of private litigation, the volume's final part looks to reconciliation as a tool for resolving the harm sometimes caused by administrative decision-making. What do I mean by that? The explanation must begin with the recognition that the Catholic Church is hierarchical. There is the Pope, of course, who stands supreme as legislator, judge, and authoritative teacher. But there are also bishops. Worldwide, there are some 3,000 dioceses and other ordinariates that exercise jurisdictional power.

The hierarchical authorities, as will be explained in Part 5, enjoy the power of executive decision-making. Their decisions, in other words, constitute a species of administration. Administrative decision-making, furthermore, is not always pain-free. Persons might have their rights infringed. Thus, for example, the decision to close a school (or, for that matter, to expel a student) might deprive someone of access to a Catholic education. Similarly, parties might lose access to important ecclesiastical benefits, including access to the sacraments. Such decision-making, in other words, might particularly harm those who are most loyal to the Church, and those who are least capable of defending their prerogatives under the canon law.

As shall be seen, the 1983 Code of Canon Law has included provisions that seek to remedy precisely these sorts of situations. The remedies that are offered are far from perfect, but they represent a major shift in canonical thinking prompted by the practical implementation of the teachings of the Second Vatican Council.

It should be mentioned that this book partly takes inspiration from Professor James Brundage's keynote address to the Canon Law Society of America in

1983.[9] Professor Brundage was primarily an historian of medieval canon law, and the audience he had been invited to address was composed principally of modern practitioners of canon law. He challenged his listeners: canon lawyers had become reduced in significance, both in the larger society, and within the Church, where their principal workload consisted of the resolution of matrimonial matters.[10] But an avenue was open to canonists to break out of these narrow confines. They could offer their services as mediators and arbitrators of disputes not only, or even primarily, to ecclesiastical institutions, but within the larger secular society. There was certainly a need. Litigation is "too slow," and "the justice system is seriously overloaded."[11] Drawing upon long-standing principles of equity, deeply embedded within the canonical legal order, contemporary canonists could become ministers of justice in meaningful ways.[12] Indeed, Brundage closed, the performance of such a service "is at the very heart of the Gospel message and thus central to the Church's mission."[13]

This volume is written and informed by the spirit of Professor Brundage's recommendations. The three large themes explored in this volume – the peaceful settlement of international conflict, the arbitration of private disputes, and the reconciliation of parties wounded by heedless administrative decision-making – are united by a single insight. And that is that justice is best arrived at through good-faith compromise, through genuine efforts to see matters as the other side does, and through a willingness to abandon intransigence in favor of flexibility.

This volume takes inspiration from Professor Brundage's work in a second respect as well. Like Professor Brundage, I see canon law as a unity. Contemporary canonists stand in an unbroken line with the medieval creators of the discipline, the great early modern commentators, and the law-makers and legal interpreters of the nineteenth and twentieth centuries.

One might do well, therefore, to review this history briefly. The founding texts of canon law can be traced to the patristic authors and the popes of Late Antiquity – to St. Ambrose (*c.*339–397), St. Augustine (354–430), to Leo the Great, and to St. Gregory the Great (reigned 590–604), among others.

Some seven hundred years later, in the eleventh and twelfth centuries, the many writings that these authors produced came to be excerpted, edited, and analyzed, systematically arranged, and given normative effect by emerging schools of learned jurists. This process of retrieval, which had its culmination

9 James A. Brundage "Canon Law as an Instrument for Ecclesial Reform: An Historic Perspective," *Canon Law Society of America Proceedings* 45 (1983), pp. 1–17.

10 *Id.*, p. 15.

11 *Id.*, p. 16.

12 *Id.*, pp. 16–17.

13 *Id.*, p. 17.

in the canonical text known as Gratian's *Decretum* (c.1140), was followed by a period of intense papal legislative activity, which continued through the high and late middle ages (for the sake of simplicity, from the time of Pope Innocent III (reigned 1198–1216) to the Fifth Lateran Council (1512–1517). This large swathe of papal legislation was, furthermore, collected, edited, and published in a series of compilations. These compilations included the *Liber Extra*, published in 1234 by Pope Gregory IX; the *Liber Sextus*, published in 1298 by Pope Boniface VIII; the *Clementine Collection*, published in 1317 by Pope John XXIII; the *Extravagantes Ioannis XXII*, published in 1484; and finally, the *Extravagantes Communes* (1501). Taken as a whole, the body of texts from Gratian's *Decretum* to the *Extravagantes Communes* comprise the *Corpus Iuris Canonici* – the "Body of Canon Law."

The production of canon law, however, did not cease in 1501. The three great ecumenical councils of the post-Reformation period also represent important stages of development in the law. These include the Council of Trent (1545–1563); the First Vatican Council (1868–1870); and the Second Vatican Council (1962–1965). The latter two Councils, furthermore, were followed by the promulgation of codes of canon law. The codifications of the early and latter twentieth century, it must be added, differ fundamentally from the medieval decretal collections in ways that will be explored in later parts of this book.

The historical scope of this project is deliberately spacious and wide-ranging. Still, taken as an ensemble, the parts of this book are meant to correspond to three distinct jurisprudential "moments" within the history of the Catholic Church. The first such "moment" involves the Church as international actor. It harkens back to a time when popes were themselves politically influential players on the international scene, and had the authority and credibility to intervene in conflicts and controversies with some hope of bringing those disputes to peaceful resolution. The second "moment" – of which the First Vatican Council and the 1917 Code of Canon Law were the crowning achievements – is the final attainment, the summit, the climax of the papacy as centralized, absolute monarchy. It was the First Vatican Council, after all, which dogmatically defined the doctrine of papal infallibility. The third such "moment," representing today's Catholic Church, is shaped and molded by the Second Vatican Council, and the expectations for a more horizontally-organized, participatory church that were given life at that Council.

We shall find that a commitment to conciliation, arbitration, and other forms of alternative dispute resolution remained a constant feature of each of these moments, even as the subject-matter susceptible to arbitration shifted in scope and content, and the justification for arbitration changed in character. The dedication to the peaceful, non-contentious settlement of disputes, in other words, has been a constant feature of canonical history. This is a commitment that can be identified not only in the narrative of Church history, but in the consistent linguistic choices of canonical law-givers over centuries. It is that story that we shall now review.

Finally, standing behind this book, animating it as it were, is a belief that the Catholic Church, at its best moments, can be a force for peace and reconciliation in the world. To be sure, the Catholic Church has not always been a force for peace. The historical record makes this plain whether we look at the political role assumed by the Holy See in medieval or even in more recent times, or whether we examine the Church's litigation strategy in certain high-profile cases. Still, the dominant message of the Gospel has been irenic. Christ, after all, is entitled "The Prince of Peace," not "The God of War." Society is better served when the Church lives up to its call to carry its message of reconciliation to the world. And, as this volume makes clear, there actually have been times when the Church has succeeded in bringing peace to a shattered world.

The Church can live out this peacemaking mission in at least two ways. First, the world is confronted with geopolitical breakdown. We are living in a world in which nations have gone to war with nations. Wars and rumors of wars are more than just biblical prophecy. It is therefore a good thing to have an entity like the Catholic Church, that can intervene, that can negotiate, and that can call on its diplomatic good offices to bring stability, hope, and, yes, finally peace to a deeply conflicted planet.

And, second, not only the world, but civil society is faced with discord and strife. There are divisions in civil society that threaten to cause breaches among persons and groups. Litigation is yet another source of strife, even if the dispute is limited to private persons alone. Again, as this volume demonstrates, the Church long ago developed the mechanisms that can assuage and heal deep divisions among contending parties. It is hoped that a book like this one – that explores the many ways in which popes and canonists grappled with the problems of peacemaking in a broken world, from the twelfth century to the present moment, – might advance this process in at least small and incremental ways.

Part 2: The Hundred Years War and Papal Diplomacy

2.1 *High Papalism*

Our story commences with the medieval papacy at the zenith of its power, say, from the pontificate of Pope Innocent III (1198–1216), through Pope Innocent IV (1243–1254), to Pope Boniface VIII (1294–1303). These were popes who regularly immersed themselves in the affairs of secular realms. Thus on the occasion of the factional fighting that accompanied the death of the German Emperor Henry VI, Innocent III played a game of power politics. This can be seen clearly, for instance, in the complicated dealings he had with Otto, Duke of Brunswick, whom he crowned Otto IV, Holy Roman Emperor,[14] only in turn to cause him to be excommunicated and deposed from that office.[15] Pope Innocent had similarly convoluted relations with King John of England. He variously had John excommunicated and placed the nation of England under interdict,[16] only to grant John the favor of invalidating *Magna Carta* upon his request.[17] Yes, Innocent III might have been the Vicar of Christ and he might have stood in a line of succession traceable to Peter the Apostle, but he was still a major participant in the tawdry sport of geopolitics and grand strategy.

Similarly, Innocent IV famously waged a years-long campaign to remove Frederick II from the imperial throne that ended with the Emperor's death in 1250. Nor was that the only political action Innocent IV took. In 1245, in the decree *Grandi non immerito*, he denounced King Sancho II of Portugal (describing him as an "imbecile"), and called upon the leadership of that Kingdom to remove him from office in favor of his brother Afonso III.[18] Sancho was, Innocent alleged, a "useless king," a *rex inutilis*, someone wholly inadequate to the demands of the office.[19] Deprived of the monarchy, Sancho died in exile two years later,[20] while Afonso enjoyed a long and effective reign, dying in 1279.[21] Maybe Innocent IV was correct in his judgment about the relative talents of Sancho or Afonso, but we are nevertheless given the unseemly picture of a

---

14 Francesco Renzi, "The Crisis of Power: Otto IV, Kings of Léon-Castile, the Cistercian Order," in Flocel Sabaté, ed., *Life and Religion in the Middle Ages* (Newcastle-Upon-Tyne, 2015), pp. 103, 106.

15 Stefan Stantchev and Benjamin Weber, "'*In Coena Domini*:' A Hierocratic Weapon or a Pastoral Staff?" *Bulletin of Medieval Canon Law* 38 (2021), pp. 361, 384; Stephen C. Neff, *Justice Among Nations: A History of International Law* (Cambridge, MA, 2014), p. 55; and Peter D. Clarke, *The Interdict in the Thirteenth Century: A Question of Collective Guilt* (Oxford, UK, 2007), p. 104.

16 Felicity Hill, *Excommunication in Thirteenth-Century England: Communities, Politics, and Publicity* (Oxford, UK, 2022), pp. 127–128.

17 Richard H. Helmholz, "Pope Innocent III and the Annulment of *Magna Carta*," *Journal of Ecclesiastical History* 69 (2018), pp. 1–14; and Morris B. Hoffman, *The Punisher's Brain: The Evolution of Judge and Jury* (Cambridge, UK, 2014), p. 249, note 36.

18 Brett Edward Whalen, *The Two Powers: The Papacy, the Empire, and the Struggle For Sovereignty in the Thirteenth Century* (Philadelphia, 2019), p. 270, note 77.

19 Edward Peters, *The Shadow King: Rex Inutilis in Medieval Law and Literature, 751–1327* (New Haven, CT, 2010), pp. 139–140.

20 H. Salvador Martínez, *Alfonso X, the Learned: A Biography*, Odile Cisneros, tr. (Leiden, 2010), p. 380; Stephen Lay, *The Reconquest Kings of Portugal: Political and Cultural Reorientation on the Medieval Frontier* (New York, 2009), p. 255.

21 Afonso's reign corresponded with "an important phase of centralization and affirmation of royal power." Armando Norte, "Literati in the Court of King Afonso III of Portugal (1248–1279)," *Royal Studies Journal* 2 (2015), pp. 1, 1.

pope arranging the political affairs of Europe according to his best lights of what the moment required.

Pope Boniface VIII, on the other hand, enjoyed less success in his intrusions into the royal realm. His encyclical *Unam sanctam*, promulgated in 1302, can be understood as the most expansive statement of high papal ideology in the Middle Ages, teaching as it did papal supremacy over the temporal world, including its rulers.[22] Still, Boniface was unable to make good on its contents in the real world of power politics. Locked in conflict with King Philip IV ("the Fair") of France, it was now the Pope who was treated badly – kidnaped by French forces, roughed up, dying only one month later.[23]

The point in all of this was that popes saw themselves as empowered to judge kings on their fitness for office and to declare them deposed where found to be unworthy. This was a power that was exercised from time to time, and was bound to leave monarchs with at least some uneasiness in their dealings with the Holy See. Even if the kings and crowned heads of Europe did not accept high papalist ideology – perhaps especially if they rejected the fullness of papal claims – it would seem reasonable for them to refuse to grant to popes the power to arbitrate royal disputes.

This plausible assumption, however, must be modified in light of the historical record. For it is also the case that popes sometimes did arbitrate disputes among kings. Thus in 1177, Pope Alexander III helped to broker a peace agreement – The Peace of Nonancourt – "with reference to Auvergne, Chateauroux, and other fiefs."[24] "Honorius III (1216–1227) arbitrated a peace treaty between Pavia and Milan and prevented a French invasion of England (1216)."[25] Pope Gregory IX (1227–1241) mediated disputes between England and France, and between Genoa and Venice.[26] And Pope Gregory XI negotiated the Treaty of Villeneuve, bringing to an end the conflict between Naples and Sicily.[27]

---

22 Brett Edward Whalen, *Dominion of God: Christendom and Apocalypse in the Middle Ages* (Cambridge, MA, 2009), p. 206.

23 On different aspects of this relationship, see, for instance, Joseph Strayer, *The Reign of Philip the Fair* (Princeton, NJ, 1980), pp. 237–279; Tomaž Mastnak, *Crusading Peace: Christendom, the Muslim World, and Western Political Order* (Berkeley, CA, 2002), pp. 229–241; John Marrone and Charles Zuckerman, "Cardinal Simon of Beaulieu and Relations Between Philip the Fair and Boniface VIII," *Traditio* 31 (1975), pp. 195–222; Elizabeth A.R. Brown, "Moral Imperatives and Conundrums of Conscience: Reflections on Philip the Fair of France," *Speculum* 87 (2012), pp. 1, 9–10.

24 Jackson H. Ralston, *International Arbitration From Athens to Locarno* (Stanford, CA, 1929), p. 183.

25 Ronald G. Musto, *Catholic Peace Tradition* (New York, 2002), p. 100.

26 Jean Gaudemet, "Le role de la papauté dans le réglement des conflits entre états aux XIIIe et XIVe siécles," *Recueils de la Société Jean Bodin* 15 (1961), pp. 79, 93.

27 Elizabeth Casteen, *From She-Wolf to Martyr: The Reign and Disputed Reputation of Johanna I of Naples* (Ithaca, NY, 2015), p. 147.

Still, at least during the twelfth and thirteenth centuries, the papacy struggled to establish a role for itself as an arbitrator of disputes among states. Mileta Novakovitch has asserted that this was because heads of state viewed with suspicion (*méfiance*) papal motives, and feared the possibility of bad-faith dealing. The papacy, after all, remained a powerful player on the European stage and, as such, other parties always harbored the concern that the popes were looking first after their own interests.[28] But by the fifteenth century, as we shall see, the situation was ripe for an audacious attempt by a pope to settle the most prolonged and troublesome conflict of the Middle Ages – the Hundred Years War.

2.2 *The Great Western Schism*

Pope Gregory XI, who settled the conflict between Naples and Sicily, was also the last of the Avignon popes. For it was the case that for much of the fourteenth century, the Catholic Church was governed by popes who ruled from Avignon, in Provence, in southern France, and not from Rome. Pope Clement V, a Frenchman, a native of Aquitaine,[29] and the Bishop of Bordeaux, was crowned pontiff in Lyon in 1305, and made the decision to relocate the papal court to Avignon in 1309.[30] The relocation was the product of French politics and French domination of the papal court, and it was not well received in many quarters of Europe.

There were many calls for the papacy to return to Rome – that place which had witnessed the martyrdom of St. Peter and that City over which the popes traditionally presided as bishop.[31] Petrarch famously denounced the papacy's relocation in enduring terms – the Avignonese papacy was the "Babylonian Captivity" of the Western Church.[32] In the 1370s, Birgitta of Sweden implored Pope Gregory XI to return the papacy to Rome[33] – a call that was renewed by Catherine of Siena following Birgitta's death.[34] And in 1377, shortly before his

28 Mileta Novacovitch, *Les Compromis et les arbitrages internationaux du XIIe au XVe siécle* (Paris, 1905), p. 28.

29 Sophia Menache, *Clement V* (Cambridge, UK, 1998), p. 52.

30 David Morrow Bryson, "Clement V and the Road to Avignon, 1304 to 1309," in Helen J. Nicholson, ed., *On the Margins of Crusading: The Military Orders, the Papacy, and the Christian World* (London, 2016), pp. 61–73.

31 Stefan Weiss, "Luxury and Extravagance at the Papal Court in Avignon and the Outbreak of the Great Schism," translated by Charlotte Masemann, in Joëlle Rollo-Koster and Thomas M. Izbicki, eds., *A Companion to the Great Schism (1378–1417)* (Leiden, 2009), pp. 67, 85.

32 Marjorie O'Rourke Boyle, *Petrarch's Genius: Pentimento and Prophecy* (Berkeley, CA, 1991), pp. 74–82.

33 "Birgitta's Reply to Pope Gregory XI's Request for a Sign," February 1373. In *The Revelations of St. Birgitta of Sweden*, Denis Searby tr. (Oxford, 2008), vol. II, pp. 256–257.

34 Unn Falkeid, *The Avignon Papacy-Contested: An Intellectual History From Dante to Catherine of Siena* (Cambridge, MA, 2017), p. 146).

death early the following year, Gregory XI, at least partly prompted by these calls, relocated the papacy to Rome.[35]

Gregory's demise so soon after returning the papacy to Rome had unfortunate consequences. Many doubted the move was anything more than a temporary expedient and that the papacy would once again swiftly decamp for Avignon. Thus the papal conclave of April, 1378, proved to be unruly. The election was now to take place in Rome, and the stakes were high. Mobs surrounded the palace where the election was to take place, demanding the election of an Italian pope.[36] Fearing for their safety, the cardinals elected Bartolomeo Prignano, who was Archbishop of Acerenza and Bari but not a member of the college of cardinals.[37] He assumed the name of Urban VI,[38] and quickly irritated a number of the cardinals who had selected him.[39]

In September, 1378, a group of cardinals, who had decamped from Rome and sought refuge in central Italy, repudiated the election of Urban VI on the basis of duress, declared the papal office vacant, and proceeded to elect Robert of Geneva, who took the name of Clement VII.[40] Urban VI, however, refused to budge from his version of the papal throne, and Europe was now presented with the sorry spectacle of two competing popes, each with plausible claims of legitimacy.

Thus commenced the Great Western Schism. The nations of Europe backed one or the other of the claimants. France naturally adhered to the Avignon pope and so England, its great rival, found itself compelled by geopolitics to align with Rome.[41] Castile gave its support to Avignon though its enthusiasm for

---

35 Carol M. Richardson, *Reclaiming Rome: Cardinals in the Fifteenth Century* (Leiden, 2009), p. 15; and Gerald Parsons, *The Cult of Saint Catherine of Siena: A Study in Civil Religion* (Aldershot, UK, 2008), p. 8.

36 Joëlle Rollo-Koster, "Civil Violence and the Initiation of the Schism," in Rollo-Köster and Izbicki, eds., *Companion to the Great Schism*, *supra*, pp. 9–65.

37 Joseph Canning, *Ideas of Power in the Late Middle Ages, 1296–1417* (Cambridge, UK, 2011), p. 165.

38 G.H.M. Posthumus-Meyjes, *Jean Gerson – Apostle of Unity: His Church Politics and Ecclesiology* (Leiden, 1999), p. 16.

39 Daniel Williman, "Schism Within the Curia: The Twin Papal Elections of 1378," *Journal of Ecclesiastical History* 59 (2008), pp. 29, 31 (the cardinals found Prignano, now Urban VI, "a reformer, bent on depriving them of their honours and perquisites, and mentally erratic besides").

40 Joëlle Rollo-Koster, *Avignon and Its Papacy, 1309–1417: Popes, Institutions, and Society* (Lanham, MD, 2015), p. 242; and Daisy Delogu, *Theorizing the Ideal Sovereign: The Rise of the French Vernacular Royal Biography* (Toronto, 2008), p. 190, note 42.

41 Philip Daileader, "Local Experiences of the Great Western Schism," in Rollo-Koster and Izbicki, *Companion to the Great Western Schism*, *supra*, pp. 89, 90–96.

the Avignonese cause waned as the decades rolled on.[42] "The Empire, Hungary, Tuscany, Lombardy, Bohemia, Poland, Denmark, Sweden [and] Norway ... recognised Urban VI."[43] "Savoy, Naples [and] Lorraine" sided with the Avignonese Clement VII, as did Scotland.[44]

Not only the nations, but saints and other religious leaders variously supported one or the other of the contending popes. St. Vincent Ferrer (1350–1419) was a Dominican friar from Valencia, an incisive theologian, and a popular preacher.[45] He concluded that Urban VI had been invalidly elected, and authored a treatise on behalf of the Avignon line of popes.[46] Blessed Ursulina of Parma (1375–1408) was a visionary[47] who was instructed in a dream to travel to Avignon to convince Clement VII to renounce his position in favor of the Roman line of popes.[48] Clement heard her out, but remained firmly ensconced on his version of St. Peter's throne.[49] Christine de Pizan (1364–1430) was born in Venice but brought up in France where her father held a position as court physician.[50] She was a prominent poet, writer, and visionary,[51] who lamented the Schism in a series of writings. She deplored it all, and placed blame on the intransigent rivals who stood in the way of a unified Christendom.[52]

---

42 *Id.*, pp. 97–98.

43 A. Francis Steuart, "Scotland and the Papacy During the Great Schism," *Scottish Historical Review* 4 (1907), pp. 144, 144–145.

44 *Id.*, p. 145.

45 His reputation is mixed, at best, today. Although he was the author of leading works of theology, he was also known as an ecstatic who conducted anti-Semitic campaigns in Spain. See Susan L. Aguilar, "Jewish-Christian Relations in Teruel, Aragon: 1391 and its Aftermath," in Kim Bergqvist, et al., eds., *Conflict and Collaboration in Medieval Iberia* (Newcastle-upon-Tyne, 2020), pp. 249, 259–260. He was also among the most prominent logicians of his time. Philip Daileader, *Saint Vincent Ferrer, His World and Life: Religion and Society in Late Medieval Europe* (New York, 2016), pp. 12–16.

46 Renate Blumenfeld-Kosinski, *Poets, Saints, and Visionaries of the Great Schism, 1378–1417* (University Park, PA, 2006), p. 78.

47 Gwenfair Walters Adams, "Visions of the Otherworlds in the Late Middle Ages, *c.*1300–*c.*1500," in Richard Matthew Pollard, ed., *Imagining the Medieval Afterlife* (Cambridge, UK, 2020), pp. 115, 126 (Ursulina frequent recipient of visions of the saints).

48 Blumenfeld-Kosinski, *Poets*, *supra*, pp. 86–90.

49 *Id.*, pp. 87–88.

50 Dallas G. Denery, II, "Christine de Pizan on Gossip, Misogyny, and Possibility," in Jason Glenn, ed., *The Middle Ages in Texts and Texture: Reflections on Medieval Sources* (Toronto, ON, 2011), pp. 309, 309.

51 Jacqueline Broad and Karen Green, *A History of Women's Political Thought in Europe, 1400–1700* (Cambridge, UK, 2009), pp. 10–37.

52 Blemenfeld-Kosinski, *Poets*, *supra*, pp. 150–161.

The situation seemed hopeless. Theologians began to argue that only a church council – the so-called *via concilii* – could resolve the impasse.[53] In 1409, an ecumenical council – the Council of Pisa – was convoked to resolve the crisis.[54] The Council ordered the two competing pontiffs deposed and elected in their places Pietro Filargo, who took the name of Alexander V.[55] Alas, the Council of Pisa only muddied matters further, since the Roman and Avignonese popes declined to go along with its decrees and refused to resign.[56] Thus the Pisan Council succeeded only in creating a third claimant to the papal throne, making the resolution of the Schism seem even more remote.

The so-called conciliarists – the advocates for resolving the Schism by an assembly of the universal Church – were not, however, deterred, and just a few years later, in 1414, a second Council – the Council of Constance – was convened. This Council was not without its dismaying, controversial moments. Thus at the invitation of the Council, Jan Hus, the Bohemian reformer, traveled to Constance to explain himself only to have his safe conduct pass revoked and be burnt at the stake for heresy.[57] Still, the Council did succeed in obtaining the resignation or deposition of each of the three rival popes and in 1417 elected a successor who would preside over a newly-reunited papacy.[58]

2.3 *Pope Martin V*

That successor was Pope Martin V, elected Pope in November 1417, not by the College of Cardinals, as canon law had long required, but by a conclave involving both cardinals and other participants in the Council of Constance.[59] He came from one of the oldest noble families of Rome – the Colonna dynasty. The family possessed great wealth and influence within the Papal State, but some members were associated with the so-called "Ghibellines" – the anti-papal faction that enjoyed substantial strength in a number of Italian cities and

53 Francis Oakley, *The Conciliarist Tradition: Constitutionalism in the Catholic Church, 1300–1870* (Oxford, UK, 2008), pp. 60–110; Paul Avis, *Beyond the Reformation: Authority, Primacy, and Unity in the Conciliar Tradition* (London, 2006), pp. 73–83.

54 John B. Morrall, *Gerson and the Great Schism* (Manchester, UK, 1960), pp. 76–93.

55 Alison Williams Lewin, *Negotiating Survival: Florence and the Great Schism, 1378–1417* (Madison, WI, 2003), pp. 160–161.

56 C. Colt Anderson, *The Great Catholic Reformers: From Gregory the Great to Dorothy Day* (New York, 2007), p. 131.

57 Pavel Soukup, *Jan Hus: The Life and Death of a Preacher* (West Lafayette, IN, 2020), pp. 145–158.

58 Stefan Bauer, *The Invention of Papal History: Onofrio Panvinio Between Renaissance and Catholic Reform* (Oxford, 2020), p. 124.

59 Gene Brucker, *Living on the Edge in Leonardo's Florence: Selected Essays* (Berkeley, CA, 2005), p. 70.

communes. Thus Sciarra Colonna, a Roman general, in good Ghibelline fashion, was among those commanders who assisted King Philip the Fair in his conflict with Pope Boniface VIII.[60]

Still, it was often the case that the Colonna family allied itself with ecclesiastical power. Indeed, many members of the family became leaders within the Church. "Thus in the late thirteenth century five of the seven sons of Stefano Colonna il Vecchio were clerics."[61] And these clerics were accustomed to holding and exercising the highest authority. Giovanni Colonna (ca. 1170–1245) had been made a cardinal by Pope Innocent III in the first years of the thirteenth century.[62] Giacomo Colonna (ca. 1250–1318) followed in Giovanni's cardinalatial footsteps.[63] Landolfo Colonna (1250–1331) was not a cardinal, but he was an historian and a lawyer, the author of a history of the world, and a friend and patron of Petrarch.[64]

Margherita Colonna (ca. 1254–1280) was a Franciscan nun and visionary who was beatified by Pope Pius IX in 1847.[65] Then there was Giles of Rome (ca. 1243–1316). A fourteenth-century biography gives his name Egidio Colonna.[66] Very likely a student of Thomas Aquinas's,[67] Giles was a professor, a scholar, a member of the Augustinian Order, as well as the Archbishop of Bourges. he wrote on physics, biology, and political theory.[68] His *De Regimine Principum* – "On the Governance of Princes" – was among the most successful works of its kind in the middle ages.[69] Giles, however, unlike his

60 Strayer, *Philip the Fair, supra*, p. 278.

61 Ronald G. Musto, *Apocalypse in Rome: Cola di Rienzo and the Politics of the New Age* (Berkeley, CA, 2003), p. 95.

62 Erik Leland Saak, *High Way to Heaven: The Augustinian Platform Between Reform and Reformation, 1292–1524* (Leiden, 2002), p. 47.

63 David Burr, "History as Prophecy: Angelo Clareno's *Chronicle* as a Spiritual Franciscan Apocalypse," in Michael F. Cusato and Guy Geltner, eds., *Defenders and Critics of Franciscan Life: Essays in Honor of John V. Fleming* (Leiden, 2009), pp. 119, 124.

64 Marc Laureys, "Antiquarianism and Politics in Fourteenth-Century Avignon: The Humanism of Giovanni Cavallini," in Jan Papy and Karl A.E. Enenkel, eds., *Petrarch and his Readers* (Leiden, 2006), pp. 31, 40; and "Colonna, Landolfo," *Treccani Enciclopedia online*).

65 Bianca Lopez, "Between Court and Cloister: The Life and Lives of Margherita Colonna," *Church History* 82 (2013), pp. 554–575.

66 Although his relationship with the Colonna family has been disputed. See Roberto Lambertini, "Giles of Rome," *Stanford Encyclopedia of Philosophy* (online).

67 Charles F. Briggs, "Life, Works, Legacy," in Charles F. Briggs and Peter S. Eardley, eds., *A Companion to Giles of Rome* (Leiden, 2016), pp. 6, 8.

68 Lambertini, "Giles of Rome," *supra*.

69 Roberto Lambertini, "Political Prudence in Some Medieval Commentaries on the Sixth Book of the *Nichomachean Ethics*," in István P. Bejczy, ed., *Virtue Ethics in the Middle Ages: Commentaries on Aristotle's Nichomachean Ethics, 1200–1500* (Leiden, 2008), pp. 223, 233–234.

probable relation Sciarra, was among Pope Boniface VIII's staunchest intellectual defenders.[70]

Odo Colonna, the future Pope Martin V, was born in 1369 and was a scion of this long noble line. He likely studied at the University of Perugia, but no record of his degree can be found.[71] He was made a cardinal in 1405, and took an active role in prosecuting Jan Hus, ordering him excommunicated in 1411, in an early stage of the judicial process against him.[72] Odo Colonna was a man, in other words, already accustomed to using power to real and sanguinary effect. He was also a creature very much of his age. He relied on his lay relatives in the governance of the Church and has been described by historians as a notable practitioner of papal nepotism.[73]

But as Pope Martin V, his assignment called not for blunt force, or the enrichment of his network of family and friends, but for the sophisticated use of all of the tools diplomacy had at its disposal.[74] Martin moved delicately in the beginning because it had been years since a single pope was in a position to take decisive action. Indeed, for the first two years of his pontificate, Martin resided not in Rome but in Florence.[75] When he arrived in Rome in 1420, he discovered the Eternal City to be in a state of shambles.[76] He involved himself deeply in Rome's rebuilding and was hailed by contemporaries as "a third Romulus, a third founder of the city."[77]

If the urban landscape of Rome required attention, so, too, did its political institutions. There were still issues lingering from the Council of Constance. Martin had to overcome the resistance of the Anti-Pope Benedict XIII – who had been deposed by the Council of Constance but who resisted removal

70 Briggs, "Life, Works, Legacy," *supra*, pp. 21–22.

71 François-Charles Uginet, "Martin V," in Phillippe Levillain, ed. *The Papacy: An Encyclopedia* (New York, 2002), vol. II, p. 974.

72 Thomas A. Fudge, *The Trial of Jan Hus: Medieval Heresy and Criminal Procedure* (Oxford, UK, 2013), 143.

73 Jennifer Mara Desilva, "Articulating Work and Family: Lay Papal Relatives in the Papal States, 1420–1549," *Renaissance Quarterly* 69 (2016), pp. 1, 7, 10–12.

74 "Martin V," *Brittanica Academic*, academic-eb-ezproxy.stthomas.edu/levels/collegiate/article/Martin-V/51150.

75 Brian Jeffrey Maxson, "Visual and Verbal Portraits of Cardinals in Fifteenth-Century Florence," in Piers Baker-Bates and Irene Brooks, eds., *Portrait Cultures of the Early Modern Cardinal* (Amsterdam, 2021), pp. 69, 74–75.

76 Ted Byfield, *The Christians: Their First Two Thousand Years*, vol. VIII, *The Renaissance: God in Man, AD 1300–1500* (Edmonton, AB, 2010), p. 61.

77 Elizabeth McCahill, *Reviving the Eternal City: Rome and the Papal Court, 1420–1447* (Cambridge, MA, 2013), p. 24.

from office until his death in 1423, at the age of ninety-four.[78] Within the Italian Peninsula, he had to deal with itinerant *condottieri* – "mercenaries" – who threatened political and social stability.[79] In 1429, he "crushed by force of arms" a revolt by the City of Bologna.[80] A scholar has written that "[t]he fifteenth-century papacy was engulfed in a crisis of legitimacy."[81] Pope Martin meant to alter this judgment of history to the best of his abilities.

The papacy had suffered enormous reputational injury during the Great Schism.[82] Indeed, there were many Church leaders – the so-called Conciliarists – who wished to see Church Councils become the primary means of ecclesiastical governance, in a power-sharing arrangement with the papal office.[83] And if Martin hoped to succeed, he needed to accommodate these interests as well. Thus he convoked Council of Pavia-Siena in 1423,[84] and the Council of Basle in 1431, just weeks before he died.[85]

It is not our purpose, in what follows, to judge Martin V's success or failure as pope. We mean only to indicate that he believed that one of his more effective tools in asserting the legitimacy of his rule was reliance on papal diplomacy, and more specifically on the arbitration of disputes among kings. In particular, Martin proposed to bring to bear the good diplomatic offices of the Holy See on that most intractable of medieval conflicts – the Hundred Years War.

2.4 *Pope Martin V and the Hundred Years War*

We must acknowledge that no one in the fifteenth century used an expression like "The Hundred Years War." That title was made famous by the French historian Jules Michelet in the nineteenth century.[86] To contemporaries, however, it

78 Francis Oakley, "History and the Return of the Repressed in Catholic Modernity: The Dilemma Posed by Constance," in Michael J. Lacey and Francis Oakley, eds., *The Crisis of Authority in Catholic Modernity* (Oxford, UK, 2011), 29, 34–35.

79 Niccolβ Capponi, *The Day the Renaissance Was Saved: The Battle of Anghiari and Da Vinci's Lost Masterpiece* (Brooklyn, NY, 2015), pp. 25–26.

80 J.N.D. Kelly and Michael Walsh, *A Dictionary of the Popes*, 3d ed. (Oxford Reference), www.oxfordreference-com.ezproxy.stthomas.edu/display/10.1093.acref/9780191795459.001.0001/acref-978191795459-e-241.

81 Emily O'Brien, *The "Commentaries" Of Pope Pius II (1458–1464) and the Crisis of the Fifteenth-Century Papacy* (Toronto, 2015), p. 19.

82 Kevin Madigan, *Medieval Christianity: A New History* (New Haven, CT, 2015), p. 378.

83 Simon Ditchfield, "Catholic Reformation and Renewal," in Peter Marshall, ed., *The Oxford Illustrated History of the Reformation* (Oxford, UK, 2015), pp. 152, 171.

84 William Patrick Hyland, Book Review [reviewing Walte Brandmüller, *Das Konzil von Pavia-Siena, 1423–1424*], *Catholic Historical Review* 89 (2003), pp. 770–771.

85 Carter Lindberg, *The European Reformations*, 2d ed. (Malden, MA, 2010), p. 47.

86 Nicholas Wright, *Knights and Peasants: The Hundred Years War in the French Countryside* (Rochester, NY, 1998), p. 117.

was the seemingly interminable series of wars, cease-fires, and broken treaties that extended from 1337, when King Edward III of England laid claim to the French throne by reason of his close blood relationship to the reigning French monarch's predecessor,[87] through to the expulsion of the English from most French territory at the Battle of Castillon (1453).[88]

It was a War, in other words, that had begun long before Martin V's birth and that would continue another two decades after his death. But his mediation nevertheless helped to bring about a major turning point in the conflict. The context was the aftermath of the Battle of Agincourt, fought on St. Crispin's Day (October 25, 1415). The English army had seemed to be outmatched, but relying on archery and superior tactics, King Henry V scored an absolute rout.[89] The French nobility was decimated in combat, and a path was seemingly opened to bringing the hostilities to a favorable close.[90] Combat continued to take place after Agincourt, but not at the same intensity. Thus the year 1416 saw the inconclusive Battle of Valmont, and in the following year, English forces took Caen, after a bloody siege.[91] In 1418, Henry sought to starve the City of Rouen of resources during yet another bloody siege.[92] The English, in other words, looked like they were slowly succeeding on the battlefield, with strangulating effect, and so it appeared to some like the time might be ripe for a negotiated peace.

Thus in February, 1418, only a few months after his election as Pope, Martin V chose to involve himself diplomatically in trying to arrive at a final settlement of the conflict. Perhaps he thought that Henry's seeming advantages augured well for a negotiated solution. Thus Martin dispatched as his personal representatives to the French and English crowns two cardinals. To the French, he sent Guillaume Fillastre (1348–1428), an eminent figure, a scholar who had "translated several works of Plato and wrote an influential treatise on usury."[93]

87 Geoffrey Templeman, "Edward III and the Beginnings of the Hundred Years War," *Transactions of the Royal Society* 2 (1952), pp. 69–88.

88 Nigel Hunt, *Landscapes of Trauma: The Psychology of the Battlefield* (London, 2020), p. 79.

89 Colm McNamee, "Britain (Narrative) (1300–1500)," in Clifford J. Rogers, ed., *The Oxford Encyclopedia of Medieval Warfare and Military Technology* (Oxford, UK, 2010), vol. 1, pp. 223, 234.

90 A.W.B. Simpson, "The Agincourt Campaign and the Law of War," *Michigan Journal of International Law* 16 (1995), pp. 653, 661–662; and Wayne Morrison, "Atrocity and the Power of the Image," *Social Justice* 36 (2009/2010), pp. 61, 69–72.

91 John Matusiak, *Henry V* (London, 2013), pp. 173–177.

92 Craig Taylor, "Henry V, Flower of Chivalry," in Gwilym Dodd, ed., *Henry V: New Interpretations* (York, UK, 2013), pp. 217, 236.

93 Kenneth R. Bartlett and Margaret McGlynn, *The Renaissance and Reformation in Northern Europe* (Toronto, 2014), p. 3.

Moved by scientific curiosity, he tried – not very successfully – to reconcile Ptolemaic geography with what was then known of the larger world.[94] Fillastre had also played an instrumental role at the Council of Constance. He had kept a diary of the proceedings that survives as one of our principal sources for the rub of personalities and politics that comprised the inner workings of that world-historic event.[95]

To the English there was sent Giordano Orsini, a member of an Italian noble family virtually the equal of the Colonna. Pope Celestine III (reigned 1191–1198) had been a member of the Orsini family.[96] So also had been Pope Nicholas III (1277–1280).[97] Giordano (ca. 1360–1438), now the bearer of the Orsini name, was a splendid specimen of a Renaissance cardinal, a patron of Leonardo Bruni, Nicholas of Cusa, and Lorenzo Valla.[98] Masolino da Panicale painted frescoes on his behalf.[99] He was a voracious book collector, who donated much of his library to the Holy See.[100] His palace was spacious and beautiful – an opulent edifice that could accommodate meetings and assemblies in grace and comfort.[101] His life typified, indeed, it embodied, the expression "Renaissance cardinal," in all of its exalted grandeur.[102] But Orsini was also politically astute,

---

94 John Larner, "The Church and the Quattrocento Renaissance in Geography," *Renaissance Studies* 12 (1998), pp. 26, 29.

95 "The most complete single account of the Council of Constance is the narrative history written by Guillaume Fillastre, Cardinal of St. Mark." Joseph Gill, "The Representation of the *Universitas Fidelium* In the Councils of the Conciliar Period," in G.J. Cuming and Derek Baker, eds., *Councils and Assemblies: Papers Read at the Eighth Summer Meeting and Ninth Winter Meeting of the Ecclesiastical History Society* (Cambridge, UK, 1971), pp. 177, 184.

96 Blake R. Beattie, *Angelus Pacis: The Legation of Cardinal Giovanni Gaetano Orsini, 1326–1334* (Leiden, 2007), p. 58.

97 Nick Havely, *Dante and the Franciscans: Poverty and the Papacy in the 'Commedia'* (Cambridge, UK, 2004), p. 51.

98 Oren Margolis, *The Politics of Culture in Quattrocento Europe: René of Anjou in Italy* (Oxford, UK, 2016), p. 113.

99 Carol M. Richardson, "The Allure of Rome," in Carol M. Richardson, ed., *Locating Renaissance Art* (New Haven, CT, 2007), pp. 25, 25; and Robert L. Mode, "Masolino, Uccello, and the Orsini 'Uomini Famosi,'" *The Burlington Magazine* 114, no. 831 (June, 1972), pp. 368–378.

100 Christopher S. Calenza, "The Will of Cardinal Giordano Orsini," *Traditio* 51 (1996), pp. 257, 268–286.

101 Patricia Waddy, "Cardinals' Palaces: Architecture and Decoration," in Mary Hollingsworth et al., eds., *A Companion to the Early Modern Cardinal* (Leiden, 2020), pp. 351, 352.

102 W.A. Simpson, "Cardinal Giordano Orsini (+1438) as a Prince of the Church and a Patron of the Arts: A Contemporary Panegyric and Two Descriptions of the Lost Frescoes in Monte Giordano," *Journal of the Warburg and Courtald Institutes* 29 (1966), pp. 135–159.

and enjoyed warm relations with Henry V, and, before him, with his father, Henry IV.[103]

In other words, as judged by the stature and significance of the negotiators Pope Martin dispatched, this was a serious diplomatic initiative. Fillastre and Orsini were among the most important power brokers in the Church, and it was plainly hoped that their intervention might pay real dividends.

"In April and May, 1418, Fillastre talked diligently to the French, while Orsini finally came to meet Henry V before Louviers on 21 June."[104] A preliminary peace plan was hammered out, but it was met with rioting on the streets of Paris.[105] There then ensued three-sided negotiations, brokered by Cardinal Orsini, and involving Henry V, French representatives, and envoys of the Duke of Burgundy that extended into 1419.[106] The interlocutors were careful in keeping their secrets and the substance of many of their exchanges can only be guessed at today.[107] Later that year, Martin V sent yet another papal negotiator to France, Henry Grenfels, to meet with the parties.[108] Eventually, the Pope became personally involved in the negotiating, when he met with French and Burgundian representatives.[109]

The combatants eventually agreed to terms that were formalized in the Treaty of Troyes of 1420.[110] As reduced to writing, the Treaty amounted to a victor's peace. While the Treaty is obscure on this point, it can be plausibly read as recognizing Henry V's claim to the French throne.[111] Key to the Treaty was Charles VI's – the reigning French monarch's – agreement that his own son, the future Charles VII, should be disinherited of all regnal rights in favor of Henry V's descendants.[112] Thus the Treaty was clear that the future Henry VI – Henry V's

103 Margaret Harvey, "Martin V and Henry V," *Archivum Historiae Pontificiae* 24 (1986), pp. 49, 54.

104 Margaret Harvey, *England, Rome, and the Papacy, 1417–1464: The Study of a Relationship* (Manchester, UK, 1993), p. 132.

105 Harvey, "Martin V," *supra*, p. 55.

106 *Id.*, pp. 56–58.

107 *Id.*, p. 56.

108 *Id.*, pp. 58–59.

109 *Id.*, p. 61.

110 Donald E. Queller, *The Office of Ambassador in the Middle Ages* (Princeton, NJ, 1967), p. 221.

111 Anne Curry, "Two Kingdoms, One King: The Treaty of Troyes and the Creation of a Double Monarchy of England and France," in Glenn Richardson, ed., *The Contending Kingdoms: France and England, 1420–1700* (Burlington, VT, 2008), pp. 23, 25. Cf., E. Cosneau, ed., *Les Grands Traités de la Guerre de cent ans* (Paris, 1889), pp. 102–115 (providing the French original of the Treaty).

112 Curry, "Two Kingdoms," *supra*, pp. 23, 30–32. Cf., Theodor Meron, "The Authority to Make Treaties in the Late Middle Ages," *American Journal of International Law* 89 (1995), pp. 1, 11–13 (further evaluating the Treaty of Troyes' provisions).

young son – would succeed to the thrones of both England and France. To be sure, the Treaty did not contemplate the absorption of France by England. As Anne Curry has put it, the Treaty intended to leave French institutions intact, creating a single monarch to rule a double kingdom.[113] But this would have been small comfort to Charles VI's biological offspring or to those French men and women who desired an independent French realm.

Henry V and Charles VI were eager to obtain ratification of the Treaty by as many institutions as they could. Thus they "required it be ratified by the estates of both kingdoms and proclaimed in both countries."[114] Why such a public campaign? Theodor Meron suspects that the principals had good reason to believe that the Treaty was unacceptable to certain important constituencies. Henry and Charles therefore hoped that the momentum of the ratification process would forestall challenges. If this was their intent, the two kings would soon find their hopes dashed.

In fact, one very important personage refused to give his assent to the Treaty's final text – Pope Martin V.[115] The English side did not react well. John, Duke of Bedford, Henry V's brother, informed the Pope that the convocation of a new Church Council might be a welcome development, indirectly threatening the security of Martin's position.[116] The canon lawyers who formed Martin's closest circle of advisors, however, provided the legal support Martin required to hold fast to his position. Ludovicus de Garsiis, for instance, wrote that "a living king lacked the capacity to deprive his heir of the kingdom," adding that only the Pope could do that.[117]

Why was the Treaty so extraordinarily one-sided? Yes, to be sure, French forces had suffered some notable military setbacks. But there was also every reason to believe that Charles VI (1368–1422) had lost his mind. His mental illness is well-documented in the records, and had already been apparent for some decades. The sources speak of him being as insane as the Babylonian King Nebuchadnezzar, whose madness drove him to live like the beasts of the field.[118] Charles imagined that he was made of glass and feared that he might shatter upon hard contact.[119] It is estimated that Charles suffered some forty

113 Curry, "Two Kingdoms," *supra*, p. 26.

114 Meron, "Authority," *supra*, p. 11.

115 Anne Curry, *The Hundred Years War Revisited* (London, 2019), p. 94.

116 Thomas M. Izbicki, "The Canonists and the Treaty of Troyes," in Stephan Kuttner and Kenneth Pennington, eds., *Proceedings of the Fifth International Congress of Medieval Canon Law* (Vatican City, 1980), pp. 425, 431.

117 *Id.*, p. 433, note 24 ("Rex vivens non habet facultatem ipsum privandi successione Regni".

118 Julie Singer, *Representing Mental Illness in Late Medieval France: Machines, Madness, Metaphor* (Woodbridge, UK, 2018), pp. 180–194; cf., *Daniel* 4: 25–31.

119 Amelia Soth, "The French King Who Believed He Was Made of Glass," *JStor Daily*, March 29, 2018, daily.jstor.org/french-king-who-believed-made-glass.

psychotic episodes, some lasting for months, extending over the last thirty years of his life.[120] Modern diagnosticians suspect strongly that Charles suffered either from bi-polar disorder or from schizophrenia.[121] Needless to say, Charles' court swirled with intrigue – with well-placed individuals alternately enabling his rule, or taking advantage of his shortcomings.[122]

The Treaty was, unsurprisingly, soon challenged – Charles' son, the future Charles VII, was entirely unprepared to have his inheritance thus bargained away. When Henry V and Charles VI both died in 1422, Pope Martin again offered his services in negotiating a second, more balanced treaty.[123] Dialogue, however, soon broke down, war broke out, and Charles VII soon found himself seated upon a much-diminished French throne,[124] where he was mocked as the "King of Bourges" for the shrunken territory he did control.[125] But Charles would rally his kingdom. Still to come were such iconic events as the siege of Orléans, the career, conquests, and fiery climax of Jeanne d'Arc – St. Joan of Arc (ca. 1412–1431), and Charles finally crowned in Reims Cathedral in 1429.[126]

Martin's intervention had halted the War, at least temporarily, and had given the promise of a peaceful settlement, but in the end, the lopsidedness of the Treaty of Troyes was a squandered opportunity. Another chance at peace would not come again. The War thus resumed its baleful trajectory. Peace, in other words, remained as elusive as ever.

Was Martin wise to have withheld his assent to the Treaty? Or, to put the question differently, could his assent have averted the renewal of hostilities?

---

120 Anne D. Hedeman, "Constructing Memories: Scenes of Conversation and Presentation in Pierre Salmon's 'Dialogues,'" *Journal of the Walters Art Gallery* 54 (1996), pp. 119, 119.

121 Rachel Gibbons, "'The Limbs Fail When the Head Is Removed:' Reactions of the Body Politic of France to the Madness of Charles VI (1380–1422)," in Sean McGlynn and Elena Woodacre, eds., *The Image and Perception of Monarchy in Medieval and Early Modern Europe* (Newcastle-Upon-Tyne, 2014), pp. 48, 63–65.

122 See generally R.C. Famiglietti, *Royal Intrigue: Crisis at the Court of Charles VI, 1392–1420* (New York, 1986). Martin V's canonists stressed that this was another reason the Treaty was suspect. "It was made by a sick king in the hands of his foe." Izbicki, "Canonists," *supra*, p. 433 and note 25.

123 Margaret Harvey, "Martin V and the English, 1422–1431," in Christopher Harper-Bill, ed., *Religious Belief and Ecclesiastical Careers in Late Medieval England: Proceedings of the Conference Held at Strawberry Hill, Easter, 1989* (Woodbridge, UK, 1991), pp. 59, 60–62.

124 Tracy Adams, "Christine de Pizan and Jehanne d'Arc: Above All the Heroes of the Past," in Cecile Thérèse Tougas and Sara Ebenreck, eds., *Presenting Women Philosophers* (Philadelphia, 2000), pp. 187, 196.

125 Deborah A Fraioli, *Joan of Arc and the Hundred Years War* (Westport, CT, 2005), p. 80.

126 Karen Green, *Joan of Arc and Christine de Pizan's Ditié* (Lanham, MD, 2021), p. 24.

Probably not. Although Charles VII had been formally disinherited, he was not without resources. With nothing left to lose, he was prepared to resist, and so were those around him.

2.5 *The Significance of Martin V's Negotiations*

Why should we be concerned with what amounted to a failed attempt by a pope to negotiate an end to the Hundred Years War? He failed, didn't he?

At least three points ought to be made in rebuttal. First, one must note the trust and faith that all of the parties placed in arbitration. Pope Martin V, his cardinal-delegates, and their royal interlocutors – on the French, English, and Burgundian sides – genuinely believed that arbitration might in fact end their intractable and miserable war. Their many exchanges, which extended over more than two years and consisted of notable travel, were no mere perfunctory exercises. On the contrary, they bespoke a meaningful commitment to making a success of the process. Pope Martin V might have failed, but that was not because the parties were proceeding in bad faith, lacked sincerity, or took the exercise lightly.

Second, one must recall that Pope Martin viewed arbitration – especially successful arbitration – as a device likely to enhance his own status and security. Remember that his own hold on the papal office was, at least initially, not all that firm. The English threat to convoke a Council when Martin withheld his approval of the Treaty would have struck home. For more than seventy years, European powers had freely transferred their loyalties among competing claimants to the papal throne. Supporting one or another rival pope became a matter not of religious conviction but of royal expediency or statecraft.

There was no assurance that the crowned heads of Europe would not revert to a practice to which they had long grown accustomed and from which they drew significant advantages. Indeed, political manipulation remained a real and present danger for much of Martin's pontificate.[127] Martin's success was thus neither automatic nor foreordained. The European scene could have just as easily relapsed into a state of endemic schism. Many expected just such an outcome. That Martin V placed his hope and faith in arbitration as a means of enhancing his own authority should not therefore be overlooked.

Third, the objection might be made that diplomacy of this sort should not count as an alternative form of dispute resolution since we ordinarily think of alternative dispute resolution as a substitute for the judicial process, and

127 See, for instance, Oakley, *Conciliarist Tradition*, *supra*, pp. 43–44; and H.S. Offler, Book Review [reviewing Walter Brandmüller, *Das Konzil von Pavia-Siena, 1423–1424*], *Journal of Theological Studies* 20 (1969), pp. 685, 686–687.

England and France were not suing each other, but in fact waging war. The response to this objection is straightforward and consists of two parts.

First, there is the judicial aspect and its relationship to medieval concepts of just war. The two phenomena were tightly connected in the medieval mind. In contrast to Carl von Clausewitz, who saw war as politics through other means,[128] the medieval mind viewed war as an extension of the judicial process. Both the judicial process and war were premised on the principle that rights that were violated needed to be vindicated and restored. Let us look first at the judicial process. Hostiensis (ca. 1200–1271), among the greatest of the decretalists, defined the *actio* – the cause of action by which litigants sought redress – as "a certain formula for asserting or prosecuting in the judicial process that which is one's own."[129] Bernard of Parma, the author of the *Ordinary Gloss* to Pope Gregory IX's *Liber Extra*, the principal collection of papal decretals in the thirteenth century, was even more explicit: *actio*, Bernard declared, was the "right to seek justice."[130]

The just war was defined in precisely the same terms, but involved, however, not the commencement of a lawsuit but a process of self-help through military action.[131] The canonist Gratian made this much clear in his *Decretum* (ca. 1140), when he quoted with approval a text of Isidore of Seville. Isidore taught that a just war required authorization from a magistrate. And the magistrate in turn needed proof that the war was to be fought either for the return of goods taken by an enemy or for the repulsion of an invading force.[132] Frederick Russell has thus written that "Gratian's conflation of war and justice ... emphasised the similarity between a judicial process and just war."[133]

But – and this is the second part of the objection – the violent vindication of rights carried its own obvious disadvantages – ruined lives, plundered landscapes, devastation, famine, death, and disease. Diplomatic intervention, and arbitration by disinterested parties, stood as an inviting substitute to the

---

128 Thomas Waldman, "Politics and War: Clausewitz's Paradoxical Equation," *Parameters* 40 (2010), pp. 1–13.

129 Hostiensis, *Summa*, Bk. II, *De libelli oblatione*, sec. 3 ("Est autem actio quedam formula agendi prosequendique in iudicio quod sibi debetur"). *Id.*

130 Bernard of Parma, *Glossa Ordinaria*, X.2.1.6, v. *actio intentetur* ("actio enim est ius prosequendi in iudicio quod sibi debetur").

131 Charles J. Reid, Jr., "The Rights of Self-Defence and Justified Warfare in the Writings of the Twelfth- and Thirteenth-Century Canonists," in Kenneth Pennington and Melodie Harris Eichbauer, eds., *Law as Profession and Practice: Essays in Honor of James A. Brundage* (Burlington, VT, 2011), pp. 73, 80–88.

132 C. 23, q. 2, c. 1; cf., C. 23, q. 2, d.p.c 2 (Cum ergo iustum bellum sit, quod ex edicto geritur, vel quo iniuriae ulciscuntur ...).

133 Frederick H. Russell, *The Just War in the Middle Ages* (Cambridge, UK, 1975), pp. 62–63.

forceful vindication of rights that was war. Seen in these terms, diplomacy and negotiation should plainly count as a form of alternative dispute resolution.

So, yes, Martin v failed. And, yes, his failure teaches us the important lesson that alternative dispute resolution requires a willingness on the part of all sides to a controversy to surrender something of value. The English, had they been a little less grasping when negotiating the Treaty of Troyes, might have achieved some genuinely lasting gains. Their greed resulted in the blowing up of the Treaty and, over the course of the next thirty years, their final defeat and expulsion from most of France. Hubris leads to nemesis the ancient Greeks might have said. But had the English been more willing to compromise, had they been willing to accept a more balanced version of the Treaty of Troyes, had they looked at the world the way Martin v evidently did, the political landscape of Europe might be different to this day.

No, we should not lay the failure of the Treaty of Troyes at Martin v's door. On the contrary, we should rightly account Martin v's efforts as an early and important landmark in the history of papal efforts to resolve situations of international conflict. For sure, Martin might have been motivated by the political precariousness of his own position, but in utilizing the tools of diplomacy he opened the door for future popes to become peace-makers.

2.6 *Medieval Arbitration in Context*

It must not be thought that the arbitration of disputes in the Middle Ages was a rare or abnormal occurrence. The case of Martin v's intervention in the Hundred Years War was chosen for its epic scale and dramatic qualities. It stands as an example of arbitration's use at the highest level of European politics.

But properly contextualized, these failed negotiations serve merely as a particularly prominent example of a recurring phenomenon – reliance on arbitration to resolve disputes in the Middle Ages. There is now a rich historiography, half a century long, on this topic. In an important article, written in 1970, Fredric Cheyette explored dispute settlement in eleventh- and twelfth-century France.[134] Law courts applying general and objective normative principles had not yet come into widespread use, but disputes were nevertheless being resolved.

Who was it, Cheyette asked, who had disputes that needed resolving? The disputants tended to come from the knightly class, from society's notables, those who had resources that might be infringed or unfairly agglomerated.[135]

134 Fredric L. Cheyette, "Suum Cuique Tribuere," *French Historical Studies* 6 (1970), pp. 287–299.

135 *Id.*, pp. 290–291.

And when these leading social figures claimed something that wasn't theirs, or perceived their interests violated by some interloper, they turned not to professional judges or courts, but to arbitrators, chosen more or less from the same elements of society as themselves, who might hear the matter, assess its pros and cons, and bring the parties to accept an outcome that at least did not involve violent self-help.[136] The value system that upheld this system was one involving honor, shame, and the necessity of keeping face. And thus a process was put in place ensuring that both sides could at least preserve the verisimilitude of a favorable outcome.[137]

Cheyette's study launched a number of similar inquiries examining the practice of alternative dispute resolution throughout the length and breadth of the medieval period. In 1978, historian Stephen D. White tested Cheyette's hypothesis as it applied to the region of western France – territory that had been excluded from Cheyette's examination.[138] Utilizing the extensive records kept by the Abbey of Marmoutier, White determined that even in the eleventh century there were courts that took evidence and tried, with varying success, to apply generally-applicable norms.[139] But more often, the courts and the other proto-institutions that heard such matters were interested not in the zero-sum game of judging winners and losers, but in arranging compromises that resulted in the fostering of lasting peace between the contesting parties.[140] Alternative dispute resolution, in other words, was preferred to the judicial process, both because judicially-imposed remedies were difficult to enforce and because negotiated compromise had the effect of establishing boundaries that the contending parties were likely to respect.[141]

Peace, however, was not always possible between the parties. Hatred and anger, particularly where the dispute involved not an argument over property rights, but crimes of passion and violence – murder, mayhem – sometimes overwhelmed informal mechanisms for keeping the peace. This, at least, is the thesis of William Ian Miller's investigation of informal dispute resolution

136 *Id.*, pp. 291–293.

137 *Id.*, pp. 291–292 ("The practice of giving everyone something was ... so prevalent that it is impossible to reconstruct any objective rules of decision. ... The norm [the arbitrators] applied was that both parties should be satisfied").

138 Stephen D. White, "Pactum ... Legem Vincit, et Amor Judicium: The Settlement of Disputes By Compromise in Western France," *American Journal of Legal History* 22 (1978), pp. 281–308.

139 *Id.*, pp. 285–293.

140 *Id.*, p. 300.

141 See, for example, Patrick Geary, *Living with the Dead in the Middle Ages* (Ithaca, NY, 1994), pp. 145–159 (describing the often inconclusive negotiations that were employed to resolve endemic feudal conflict in the absence of effective state or judicial authority).

in early medieval Iceland. At least where the grievance involved the violent death of close kin, Miller found a consistent tension between, on the one hand, the principles of vengeance and blood-feud and, on the other, a desire to use the principles of informal dispute resolution to reestablish amicable relations among the disputants.[142]

English law, too, recognized that there was real tension between private vengeance and the peaceful accommodation of conflict and that revenge sometimes carried the day.[143] Still, the social pressures favoring the non-violent, informal, and face-saving resolution of controversies remained substantial, as Richard Keyser shows in a study investigating the practical application of the maxim "agreement supersedes law, and love judgment" in Anglo-Norman England.[144] And, as Edward Powell has demonstrated, long after a formal system of courts came into being, deep into the fifteenth century, English disputants frequently preferred amicable, non-judicial alternative forms of peace-making.[145]

Indeed, the medieval English legal mind constructed a whole system of informal dispute resolution that sought to settle conflicts among cities, towns, universities, guilds, and other social, political, and cultural institutions.[146] Nor were the English alone. "In Germanic law, all administration of justice was strongly mixed with arbitral elements."[147] "In Italy, arbitral agreements and tribunals were already operating between public authorities in the eleventh and, to a greater extent, the twelfth centuries."[148] In late medieval Castile, where maritime disputes were common, a system of arbitration was created, "parallel" to the judicial process "which usually required that both parties recognize the fairness and finality of the arbitration."[149]

---

142 William Ian Miller, "Avoiding Legal Judgment: The Submission of Disputes to Arbitration in Medieval Iceland," *American Journal of Legal History* 28 (1984), pp. 95, 133.

143 Paul R. Hyams, *Rancor and Reconciliation in Medieval England* (Ithaca, NY, 2003), pp. 137–145.

144 Richard L. Keyser, "Agreement Supersedes Law, and Love Judgment: Legal Flexibility and Amicable Settlement in Anglo-Norman England," *Law and History Review* 30 (2012), pp. 37–88.

145 Edward Powell, "Settlement of Disputes by Arbitration in Fifteenth-Century England," *Law and History* 2 (1984), pp. 21–43.

146 See generally, Derek Roebuck, *Mediation and Arbitration in the Middle Ages: England 1154–1558* (Oxford, 2013).

147 Wilhelm G. Grewe, *The Epochs of International Law*, Michael Byers, tr. (Berlin, 2013), p. 96.

148 *Id.*

149 Eduardo Aznar Vallejo and Roberto J. González Zalacain, "Maritime Conflicts and Their Resolution in Late Medieval Castile," in Louis Sicking and Alain Wijffels, eds., *Conflict Management in the Mediterranean and the Atlantic, 1000–1800: Actors, Institutions, and Strategies of Dispute Settlement* (Leiden, 2020), pp. 109, 120.

Kings and other political leaders also made routine use of face-to-face negotiation to settle disputes amongst themselves – including wars – and sometimes submitted their quarrels to the arbitration of third parties. Thus Jenny Benham discusses the case of King Sancho VI of Navarre and King Alfonso VIII of Castile, who agreed to have their territorial dispute submitted to the arbitration of King Henry II of England.[150] Similarly, Jan Hendrik Verzijl identifies other notable negotiated resolutions, such as the decision in the years 1271–1276 by the Kings of Bohemia and Hungary to "entrust[] the settlement of their boundary dispute to Charles of Anjou, King of Naples."[151]

Canon law, also, made ample and extensive provisions for arbitration. The early decretalist, Tancred, in his *Ordo iudiciarius*, made reference to arbiters and arbitration. Arbiters, he asserted, were selected by the parties.[152] But Tancred also feared that arbitration might prove ineffective because the parties might prove unwilling to respect the results, and thus he required those submitting to arbitration pledge security in advance to ensure the enforcement of arbitral decrees.[153]

The *Liber Extra* included a title bearing the name "De Arbitris" ("On Arbiters"), which established a number of ground rules for the non-judicial settlement of disputes.[154] Peaceful resolution of controversies, Pope Alexander III wrote, is to be encouraged.[155] When selecting a collegial panel of arbiters, parties were instructed to choose an odd and not an even number to avoid impasses.[156] Arbiters might hear a challenge against an allegedly biased judge.[157] Remarkably, where local rules permitted, a woman might serve as arbiter.[158] A broad range of cases might be settled, but certain topics were off-limits, such as marriage,[159] crime,[160] or access to the sacraments.[161] These

150 Jenny Benham, *Peacemaking in the Middle Ages: Principles and Practice* (Manchester, UK, 2011), p. 187.

151 J.H.W. Verzijl, *International Law in Historical Perspective*, Part VIII, *Inter-State Disputes and Their Settlement* (Leiden, 1976), p. 210.

152 Tancred, *Ordo iudiciarius*, sec. *De arbitris*, in Friedrich Christian Bergmann, *Libri de Iudiciorum Ordine* (Aalen, 1965), p. 103.

153 *Id.*

154 X. 1.43.

155 X. 3.16.1 (Alexander III).

156 X.1.43.1.

157 X.1.29.39 (Gregory IX).

158 X.1.43.4 (Innocent IV).

159 X.1.41.9 (Gregory IX).

160 *Id.*

161 X. 1.43.2 (Alexander III).

questions were apparently too central to good Church order to leave to informal, often non-ecclesiastical settlement processes.

The canon lawyer William Durandus (ca. 1237–1296) included a discussion of arbitration in his treatise on judicial procedure. Where arbitration was concerned, Durandus insisted, one must distinguish between two offices – that of *arbiter* and that of *arbitrator*.[162] The arbiter is selected by the parties,[163] but is obligated to follow strict rules of law (*debet iuris ordinem servare*).[164] The arbitrator, on the other hand, aimed at a friendly settlement between the parties and did not need to observe strict procedural norms.[165] For Durandus, the arbitrator was practically synonymous with the *amicabilis compositor* – literally, a friendly mediator, someone whose role was to employ standards of fairness and equity to resolve disputes peacefully.[166] A layman might serve as an arbiter (or arbitrator), having been delegated proper authority from a judge.[167] Durandus followed the *Liber Extra* in stating that the subject matter of arbitration included most civil disputes, but excluded questions of criminal law or marriage.[168]

These categories, furthermore, were not entirely new in the middle ages. The *Digest* of Justinian also contained provisions related to arbitration, from which the medieval authors borrowed. *Compromissum* – a negotiated settlement – the Roman jurist Paulus wrote, had the effect of concluding litigation.[169] The praetor, Ulpian indicated, may not compel parties to settle their disagreement through arbitration. Such a choice must be freely made by the parties. But once the parties have submitted a matter to arbiters, the praetor had an obligation to ensure both the fairness and the success of the process.[170] Still, even at this stage, the praetor could not direct an outcome. Thus arbiters must not be subjected to interference, and might even choose, in a particular case, to withhold judgment altogether.[171] Free persons could serve as arbiters, but so also might freedmen.[172]

162 William Durandus, *Speculum Iudiciale*, 1.1., *Arbiter quid sit*, secs. 1 and 3.
163 *Id.*, sec. 1.
164 *Id.*, sec. 2.
165 *Id.*, sec. 3.
166 *Id.* Cf., Augustine Thompson, *Revival Preachers and Politics in Thirteenth Century Italy* (Eugene, OR, 2010) (reprint of 1992 edition), pp. 164–165 (translating *amicabilis compositor* as "friendly reconciler").
167 *Id.*, 1.1., *Arbiter quis possit esse*, sec. 5.
168 *Id.*, *Compromitti super quibus et a quibus possit*, sec. 1.
169 *Digest* 4.8.1 (Paulus).
170 *Digest* 4.8.3.1 (Ulpian).
171 *Digest*, 4.8.19, pr. (Paulus).
172 *Digest* 4.8.7 (Ulpian).

The office of arbitrator (alternatively, the *amicabilis compositor*), however, did not appear in the *Digest*. This office was more or less the creation of medieval lawyers. Reinhard Zimmermann has shown how these jurists essentially constructed this role from disparate snippets of Roman law of seemingly tangential relevance.[173] This is a point made even more forcefully by Andrew Godfrey: "It is clear ... that whatever the significance of the arbiter at Roman law, the concept was heavily developed through its association with ecclesiastical courts and the jurisdiction of the bishop from late antiquity."[174]

The intricacies of arbitration, and the enforcement of particular arbitration decrees, also drew the attention of some of the leading legal minds of the later medieval period. Thus Dante Fedele in his *Medieval Foundations of International Law*, discusses several arbitration cases in which the Roman lawyer Baldus de Ubaldis (ca. 1327–1400) became deeply enmeshed.[175] These included major cases such as the Parliament of Paris's attempt to settle a dispute "between the count of Savoy and the marquis of Saluzzo,"[176] and the enforcement of the Peace of Genoa (1392) between warring confederations of Italian city-states.[177]

The ability to arbitrate, conciliate, and arrive at the peaceful resolution of challenging disputes could even enhance one's reputation for sanctity and lead to canonization. That is the interesting story that Bryan Gibson tells about "Erwan Helouri, also known as Yvo Héloury, later St. Yves."[178] St. Yves (1253–1303) is known as the patron saint of lawyers, but his skill did not lie in sharp adversarial practice, but in "an ability to mediate between or assist people in intractable situations."[179] Indeed, St. Yves' modern biographer sees in him someone who might be described as an "advocate of what we would now call human rights and restorative justice."[180]

There were, furthermore, particular institutions within medieval society that seemed specially to favor alternatives to the judicial process. One might

173 Reinhard Zimmermann, *The Law of Obligations: Roman Foundations of the Civilian Tradition* (Oxford, UK, 1996), pp. 528–529. Cf., *Novella* 86.2 (legislation of Justinian directing the archbishop to hear cases and direct litigants to "friendly settlement" (*amicabilem conventum*) wherever possible).

174 Andrew M. Godfrey, *Civil Justice in Renaissance Scotland: The Origins of a Central Court* (Leiden, 2009), p. 367.

175 Dante Fedele, *The Medieval Foundations of International Law: Baldus de Ubaldis (1327–1400), Doctrine and Practice of the Ius Gentium* (Leiden, 2021), pp. 531–541.

176 *Id.*, p. 536.

177 *Id.*, p. 539.

178 Bryan Gibson, *Law, Justice, and Mediation: The Legend of St. Yves* (Hook, UK, 2008), p. 19.

179 *Id.*, p. 16.

180 *Id.*, p. 15.

thus single out monasteries. Thus we read in Giles Constable that "[i]n 1114 a layman who had several tithe disputes with the monks of Aniane agreed ... to submit one to the judgment of the local *boni homines* [good men], another to the parishioners, and the third to the bishop and his canons."[181] English monasteries made use of similar tools, although some cases did involve litigation and even required the king's involvement.[182] Disputes among monasteries in Scandinavia sometimes led to the appointment of arbitrators from the concerned religious houses, whose general preference was for "some sort of balanced outcome."[183] The great monastery at Monte Cassino had disputes with its neighbors that were settled by arbitration recommended and ratified respectively by Popes Callixtus II[184] and by Alexander III.[185]

Monasteries in Tuscany also employed arbitration, although Peter Coss indicates that this was sometimes accompanied by violence.[186] And sometimes violent skirmishing between monasteries – as documented in late eleventh century France – gave rise to mediated settlements.[187] What emerges from a survey of historical accounts is a picture of well-established medieval institutions – monasteries – that sought to use arbitration as a principal tool – although, for sure, not the only tool – to mitigate conflict. Why? One can speculate that monasteries might have been particularly motivated to use non-judicial forms of dispute resolution because of the unique characteristics of medieval monasticism. Monasteries were, after all, large landed estates that farmed, and tilled, and pastured, and needed good relations with their neighbors for their continuing success and prosperity. They were firmly planted within their communities, it was better for all concerned that long-term relations remained amicable, and that required the gifts of negotiation and compromise.

This body of materials, and this set of sensibilities continued well into the early modern period. One might consult the work of the Jesuit canonist Francis Xavier Schmalzgrueber (1663–1735) both as evidence of canon law's continuing

181 Giles Constable, *Monastic Tithes: From Their Origins to the Twelfth Century* (Cambridge, UK, 1964), p. 124.

182 Kevin L. Shirley, *The Secular Jurisdiction of Monasteries in Anglo-Norman and Angevin England* (Woodbridge, UK, 2004), p. 27.

183 Kim Esmark, "Disputing Property in Zealand: The Records of the Sorø Donation Book," in Kim Esmark, et al., eds., *Disputing Strategies in Medieval Scandinavia* (Leiden, 2013), pp. 181, 200.

184 Herbert Bloch, *Monte Cassino in the Middle Ages* (Rome, 1986), vol. I, p. 476.

185 *Id.*, vol. II, p. 1104.

186 Peter Coss, *The Aristocracy in England and Tuscany, 1000–1250* (Oxford, UK, 2020), p. 200.

187 Bruce C. Brasington, *Order in the Court: Medieval Procedural Treatises in Translation* (Leiden, 2016), pp. 23–24.

commitment to the peaceful resolution of disputes and for the extensive legal apparatus that was built to sustain and support the arbitral process.

What was the difference between an arbiter and a judge, Schmalzgrueber asked?[188] A judge may assert jurisdiction even over the unwilling, came the answer, while ordinarily an arbiter became involved only with the assent of the parties[189] (though the prince or the pope might compel even the unwilling to arbitration).[190] Who may submit a matter to arbitration? Those who enjoyed the "free administration of their own property" (*rerum suarum liberam administrationem habent*).[191] Who may serve as arbiters? Persons of any dignity or station, provided that they are not forbidden by law.[192] And who was forbidden by law? Minors, the insane, deaf-mutes, and the excommunicated came the reply.[193]

May a layperson serve as an arbiter in an ecclesiastical matter? Conditionally, yes, provided that they serve jointly with clerics and have received the specific approval of their ecclesiastical superior.[194] Expressly following Durandus, Schmalzgrueber distinguished between arbiters and arbitrators.[195] May a woman serve as an arbiter? Ordinarily no, except where by custom, right, or privilege a woman enjoyed jurisdiction.[196] On the other hand, it was clear (*clarum est*) that a woman might act as an arbitrator, since the process was "extra-judicial" (*actu extrajudiciali*) and implicated not the judicial but rather the amicable settlement of disputes (*amicabiliter potest componere*).[197]

An arbiter should ordinarily render his decision in writing, and where parties were absent, ensure that it was properly delivered.[198] Was the decision of an arbiter properly called a *sententia*, that is, a judgment? This was a matter of some dispute, Schmalzgrueber conceded, but because an arbiter had the power definitively to conclude disputes, he believed that this was appropriate.[199] And so Schmalzgrueber continued on like this for pages, addressing every conceivable issue that might arise concerning this alternative form of dispute

---

188 Franciscus Schmalzgrueber, *Jus Ecclesiasticum Universum Brevi Methodo ad Discentium* (Rome, 1844), vol. II, p. 445.
189 *Id.*
190 *Id.*, p. 451.
191 *Id.*, p. 448.
192 *Id.*, p. 452.
193 *Id.*
194 *Id.*, p. 453.
195 *Id.*, p. 447.
196 *Id.*, p. 452.
197 *Id.*, p. 453.
198 *Id.*, p. 458.
199 *Id.*, vol. IV, p. 413.

resolution. He was, in other words, system-building, erecting a comprehensive body of law and doctrine capable of answering most common and even many esoteric questions that occur when parties elect to forego the judicial process.

James Whitman has described the Roman and canon law of the Middle Ages "as a law of peace" precisely because of its commitment to arriving at friendly outcomes.[200] This seems to be an accurate observation. Yes, the law made provision for contentious trials, and, yes, trials were often heated and intense. But a non-judicial, negotiated outcome was frequently the preferred result. Medieval arbitration was about preserving the dignity of all the parties to a controversy; it was about the wise use of face-saving techniques; it was about the avoidance of zero-sum results, in which a party with nothing to lose resorts to self-help. At a grand scale, this was what Pope Martin V was attempting to accomplish in his endeavors to negotiate an end to the Hundred Years War. Even though he failed, we have used Martin's efforts to open a window onto this larger world. And this panorama that we have uncovered forms the background to the chapter that follows, beginning with Pope Leo XIII's successful negotiation of the Caroline Islands dispute between Germany and Spain.

Part 3: Modern Papal Diplomacy: Pope Leo XIII to Pope Francis

3.1 *Pope Pius IX and the Collapse of the Papal State*

We should now move forward in time by four centuries, to the election of Vincenzo Gioacchino Luigi Pecci as Pope Leo XIII. Like Martin V, Leo became Pope at a turning point in ecclesiastical history. Like Martin, there were questions whether Leo would ever achieve acceptance or enjoy legitimacy. And like Martin, Leo utilized papal arbitration of international controversies as one tool among many in a campaign to ensure that the papacy remained a relevant player on the world stage after suffering what most at the time deemed to be a catastrophic, if not fatal, loss – the violent termination of papal jurisdiction over what had been known for more than a millennium as the Papal State.

We might begin with a description of the Papal State. The deep historical origins of the Papal State can be traced to the sixth century, as the Roman Church began to exercise both secular and spiritual authority in the power vacuum that followed the collapse of Roman political authority in the Latin West.[201]

200 James Q. Whitman, *The Legacy of Roman Law in the German Romantic Era: Historical Vision and Legal Change* (Princeton, NJ, 1990), p. 6.

201 See, for instance, George E. Democopoulos, *Gregory the Great: Ascetic, Pastor, and First Man of Rome* (South Bend, IN, 2015), pp. 102–107.

The popes in the seventh century enjoyed relative autonomy over Rome and a patch of surrounding territory.[202] By the eighth century, however, the Popes of Rome felt their independence threatened from two directions – first from the Byzantine Emperor, which was represented on the Italian peninsula by the Exarchate of Ravenna; and, second, from the Lombards, who had settled in Northern Italy, establishing a Kingdom that had grown in power over the early and middle eighth century. Indeed, the Lombards conquered Ravenna in 751, thereby extinguishing the Exarchate and had begun to wage a campaign of military aggression against the papacy itself.[203]

Apprehensive of these threats, Pope Stephen II (reigned 752–757) negotiated an understanding with the Frankish King Pepin. The two men met in 754,[204] and the result, after some twists and turns, was the promulgation of the so-called "Donation of Pepin," which consisted of a pledge of defense against Lombard incursion; and a conferral to the Pope of certain lands in central and northern Italy.[205] In so acting, Pepin was repaying a debt – Stephen's immediate predecessor Pope Zachary had connived in Pepin's successful coup against the last of the Merovingian kings;[206] and, simultaneously, Pepin received the legitimacy that came from a privileged and prestigious ally – a revived papacy whose perceived sanctity might shelter him from further internal menace.[207]

This geographic unit came under the direct governance of the popes and remained the core of the Papal State for hundreds of years, well into the nineteenth century. In 1846, the year Giovanni Maria Mastai Ferretti was elected Pope Pius IX, the Papal State consisted of a swathe of central Italy that stretched from Rome eastward to the Adriatic coast, and north to include cities like Ferrara, Bologna, and Ravenna. This was "a territory which covered more than 41,000 square kilometers … with a population exceeding three million."[208] As

202 Peter Llewellyn, "The Popes and the Constitution in the Eighth Century," *English Historical Review* 101 (1986), pp. 42, 48–51; and John W. O'Malley, *A History of the Popes* (Lanham, MD, 2010), pp. 54–56.

203 Jan Hallenbeck, "Pavia and Rome: The Lombard Monarchy and the Papacy in the Eighth Century," *Transactions of the American Philosophical Society* 72 (1982), pp. 1, 59–69.

204 Thomas F.X. Noble, *The Republic of St. Peter: The Birth of the Papal State* (Philadelphia, 1984), pp. 80–81.

205 Timothy H. Maschke, *Called to Be Holy in the World: An Introduction to Christian History* (Eugene, OR, 2016), p. 105.

206 John W. O'Malley, *A History of the Popes: From Peter to the Present* (Lanham, MD, 2010), p. 58.

207 Colin Jones, *The Cambridge Illustrated History of France* (Cambridge, UK, 1994), p. 61.

208 Kevin T. Keating, *Papal Teaching in the Age of Infallibility, 1870 to the Present: A Critical Evalution With Historical Illustrations* (Eugene, OR, 2018), pp. 13–14.

head of state, the Pope exercised the power of command over the military,[209] the police, and the judiciary, and was empowered to sign the execution warrants of condemned prisoners.[210] And this was irrespective whether the papal subjects were Catholic, Protestant, or Jewish, religious believers, atheists, or skeptics.[211]

Let us return to that year 1846. The predicament that Leo XIII faced upon his election as pope was entirely due to Pius IX' election in 1846 and with the turbulent relations he experienced with political forces opposed to continued papal rule. The situation had been much exacerbated by Pius's predecessor, Gregory XVI. Gregory had been a reactionary's reactionary, who forbade even the introduction of railroads into the papal state.[212]

When Pius IX – often simply known as Pio Nono – was elected, there were hopes that he might be a liberal and reformer.[213] And for the first two years of his pontificate, it seemed that he was precisely that. He appointed Pellegrino Rossi – a layman, a serious scholar, and a one-time professor of constitutional law at the Sorbonne in France[214] – to serve essentially as his prime minister.[215] He expressed support for "freedom of association and of the press."[216] "He granted a general amnesty for political prisoners, repealed laws that barred Jews from certain professions," introduced "gas lighting in the streets,"[217] and even invited contractors to bid on the construction of the papal state's first railway.[218]

---

209 The Pope "had at his disposal 13,000 troops to protect his territory." *Id.*, p. 14.

210 Who would be executed by guillotine. Terry Gross, "Why Pius IX Might Be the 'Most Important Pope' in Modern Church History," *NPR*, April 24, 2018 (interview with papal historian David Kertzer).

211 Upon his election in 1846, Pius IX proposed to relax restrictions on the Jewish ghettoes of the papal states, but following his restoration in 1850, he "instituted many strongly anti-Semitic measures." Joe Holland, *Catholic Social Teaching: The Popes Confront the Industrial Age, 1740–1958* (Mahwah, NJ, 2003), p. 56.

212 Albert Schram, *Railways and the Formation of the Italian State in the Nineteenth Century* (Cambridge, UK, 1997), p. 102.

213 Owen Chadwick, *The Popes and European Revolution* (Oxford, UK, 1981), p. 565.

214 Daniel Halberstam, "Federalism: Theory, Practice, Law," in Michael Rosenfeld and András Sajó, eds., *Oxford Handbook of Comparative Constitutional Law* (Oxford, UK, 2012), pp. 576, 582; Walter Rech, "International Law as a Political Language, 1600–1859," in Giulio Bartolini, ed., *A History of International Law in Italy* (Oxford, UK, 2020), pp. 48, 72.

215 Owen Chadwick, *A History of the Popes, 1830–1914* (Oxford, UK, 1998), pp. 80–82.

216 Timothy C. Behr, "The Nineteenth-Century Historical and Intellectual Context of Catholic Social Teaching," in Gerard V. Bradley and E. Christian Brugger, eds., *Catholic Social Teaching: A Volume of Scholarly Essays* (Cambridge, UK, 2019), pp. 34, 41.

217 Dennis Castillo, *Papal Diplomacy From 1914 to 1989: The Seventy-Five Years War* (Lanham, MD, 2019), p. 8.

218 Schram, *Railways*, *supra*, p. 102.

Two years later, however, Rossi was assassinated in an urban uprising in the City of Rome – one of the many civic revolts that ripped through Europe in the tumultuous year of 1848.[219] The Roman street almost immediately welcomed news of the murder of the Pope's Secretary in throngs and songs.[220] Pius quickly lost control of the situation and was driven from the City of Rome itself.[221] He was forced to relocate to Gaeta, in the vicinity of Naples,[222] while a revolutionary government – the Republic of Rome – was established in the City by early 1849.[223] French and Austrian allies of the Pope eventually retook the City,[224] but not before encountering unexpectedly ferocious fighting, led by, among others Giuseppi Garibaldi, a Ligurian veteran of numerous Latin American wars,[225] now returned home and ready to fight for a unified Italy.[226]

Once securely back in Rome and restored in the papal palace in the year 1850, Pius IX dramatically changed directions. Effectively replacing the murdered Rossi, Pius IX named the reactionary Giacomo Antonelli as Secretary of State.[227] This appointment reflected a larger transformation as Pius IX turned away from an incremental liberalism and became a reactionary on matters both of politics and religion. One might note the politics first. He came to wield power in harsh, irresponsible, and destructive ways. Nothing perhaps typified his abuse of the temporal power like the papally-authorized kidnaping of Edgardo Mortara, in June of 1858.[228] Young Edgardo – he was only six years old – was a Jewish child secretly baptized by a Christian housekeeper.[229]

---

219 David Alvarez, *The Pope's Soldiers: A Military History of the Modern Vatican* (Lawrence, KS, 2011), p. 63.

220 Jonathan Sperber, *The European Revolutions, 1848–1851*, 2d ed. (Cambridge, UK, 1994), p. 238.

221 Garrett Green, "Modernity," in Gareth Jones, ed., *The Blackwell Companion to Modern Theology* (Malden, MA, 2004) pp. 162, 176.

222 Michael Rapport, *Nineteenth-Century Europe* (New York, 2005), p. 151.

223 David Ragazzoni and Nadia Urbinati, "Theories of Representative Government and Parliamentarism in Italy From the 1840s to the 1920s," in Pasi Ihalainen, et al., eds., *Parliament and Parliamentarism: A Comparative History of a European Concept* (New York, 2016), pp. 243, 247–248.

224 Derek Beals and Eugenio F. Biagini, *The Risorgimento and the Unification of Italy*, 2d ed. (London, 2013) (original edition, 1971), pp. 94–97; and David I. Kertzer, "The Lost Cause: Failed French Ultimata and the Restoration of Papal Rule in Rome in 1849," *Journal of Modern Italian Studies* 22 (2017), pp. 555–570.

225 Alfred Scirocco, *Garibaldi, Citizen of the World: A Biography* (Princeton, NJ, 2007), pp. 27–124.

226 Lucy Riall, *Garibaldi* (New Haven, CT, 2007), pp. 81–93.

227 Frank J. Coppa, *The Modern Papacy Since 1789* (London, 1998), p. 95.

228 Stephen Lubet, "Judicial Kidnaping, Then and Now: The Case of Edgardo Mortara," *Northwestern University Law Review* 93 (1998/1999), pp. 961, 961.

229 David Kertzer, *The Kidnapping of Edgardo Mortara* (New York, 1997), pp. 4–6.

His removal from the home of his parents was justified on the grounds that a baptized Christian child could not be raised by non-Christians.[230]

When an international outcry ensued, Pius IX hardened his position, choosing to raise Edgardo in the Vatican, "under [his] personal supervision."[231] "The universal outrage provoked by Pio Nono's determination to raise Mortara as a Catholic and to keep him away from his Jewish parents undermined the diplomatic position of the Holy See."[232] The kidnaping by Catholic authorities of two other Jewish children in the 1860s weakened the Catholic position even further and contributed materially to the political catastrophe that awaited the papacy in 1870.[233]

Pius IX's reactionary politics was matched equally by a theological retreat into a nostalgia that was traditionalist, utopian, and quite detached from reality. In December, 1864, Pius IX published his *Syllabus of Errors*,[234] a document that condemned a host of alleged erroneous propositions and doctrines. Pius censured those who refused to acknowledge that Catholicism should be the one, the only, and the formal state religion of all nations.[235] He denounced advocates for the freedom of the individual's religious conscience.[236] He dismissed the possibility that Protestantism might be accepted as a legitimate form of Christian faith.[237] He renounced the suggestion that the "Roman Pontiff can, and ought to, reconcile himself and come to terms with progress, liberalism, and modern civilization."[238]

---

230 *Id.*, pp. 147–161. In a frankly horrifying article, Romanus Cessario, the Adam Cardinal Maida Professor of Theology at Ave Maria University, attempts to justify Pius IX's actions. See Romanus Cessario, "Non Possumus," *First Things*, February, 2018.

231 Micah Schwartzman and Jocelyn Wilson, "The Unreasonableness of Catholic Integralism," *San Diego Law Review* 56 (2019), pp. 1039, 1040.

232 Frank J. Coppa, "Pio Nono and the Jews: From 'Reform' to 'Reaction,' 1846–1878," *Catholic Historical Review* 89 (2003), pp. 671, 687–688.

233 *Id.*, p. 688.

234 One historian has summarized the impact of the *Syllabus* on Catholic believers of the time: "[F]or most Catholics ... the *Syllabus* produced disorientation and dismay. The pope, it seemed, hoped for a return to the Middle Ages." David I. Kertzer, *Prisoner of the Vatican: The Popes, the Kings, and Garibaldi's Rebels in the Struggle to Rule Modern Italy* (Boston, 2004), p. 23.

235 *Syllabus of Errors*, no. 77.

236 *Id.*, no. 15 (rejecting the proposition that "Every man is free to embrace and profess that religion which, guided by the light of reason, he shall consider true").

237 *Id.*, no. 18 (repudiating the assertion that "Protestantism is nothing more than another form of the same true Christian religion, in which form it is given to please God equally as in the Catholic Church").

238 *Id.*, no. 80.

If the *Syllabus of Errors* was a retreat to a romanticized past that had never really existed, six years later the First Vatican Council similarly veered in the direction of theological utopianism with its decree *Pastor Aeternus*. This text embraced the proposal – which had been rejected by the medieval popes as inconsistent with sovereignty[239] – that papal decrees pronounced *ex cathedra* should be considered the infallible teaching of the Catholic Church and so binding for all time.[240]

This dreamscape – for such was the unreality of the moment – came to a thundering denouement two months later. The First Vatican Council adopted *Pastor Aeternus* on July 18, 1870.[241] That September, an Italian army, determined to unify the entire Italian peninsula under secular rule, captured the City of Rome.[242] Pius IX, who had refused favorable and face-saving terms of surrender,[243] retreated to the Vatican and pronounced himself a prisoner.[244] He thereafter steadfastly refused to venture forth from behind the Vatican's walls, and died there in in February, 1878.[245]

3.1.1 The Election of Pope Leo XIII

Gioacchino Pecci, the future Pope Leo XIII, was born to Count Ludovico Pecci, a member of the lesser nobility, in the town of Carpineto, some thirty-five miles outside Rome, in March, 1810.[246] Justin McCarthy (1830–1912), a well-known Irish journalist, parliamentarian, and liberal Catholic of the era,[247] wrote a fulsome, richly embroidered account of Leo XIII's life, first published

239 See generally Brian Tierney, *Origins of Papal Infallibility, 1150–1350: A Study on the Concepts of Infallibility, Sovereignty and Tradition in the Middle Ages* (Leiden, 1972). See also Gaines Post, who favorably reviewed Tierney's book and described the dilemma Tierney addressed: "If the prince or pope was not limited by the laws of his predecessors, how could any decree of the monarch be considered infallible and thus bind forever all succeeding emperors or popes?" Gaines Post, "Book Review," *Speculum* 49 (1974), pp. 762, 762.

240 *Pastor Aeternus* (1870), chapter 4.

241 Klaus Schatz, *Papal Primacy: From Its Origins to the Present* (Collegeville, MN, 1996), p. 162.

242 Giulio Bartolini, *A History of International Law in Italy* (Oxford, UK, 2020), p. 311.

243 *Id.*; O.J. Wright, *Great Britain and the Unifying of Italy: A Special Relationship?* (London, 2019), p. 193.

244 John R. Morss, "The International Legal Status of the Vatican/Holy See Complex," *European Journal of International Law* 26 (2016), pp. 927, 939.

245 John F. Pollard, *Money and the Rise of the Modern Papacy: Financing the Vatican, 1850–1950* (Cambridge, UK, 2005), p. 21; Robin Updike, "'Prisoner of the Vatican:' A Pope's Last Stand and the Birth of the New Italy," *The Seattle Times*, January 9, 2005.

246 Justin Corfield, "Leo XIII (1810–1903)," in Kenneth E. Hendrickson, *The Encyclopedia of the Industrial Revolution in World History*, (Lanham, MD, 2015), p. 539.

247 See Liam Harte, *The Literature of the Irish in Britain: Autobiography and Memoir, 1725–2001* (New York, 2009), pp. 54–59.

in 1896, and in an expanded second edition in 1899, which, discounting for its hagiographic qualities, still provides us with useful information.[248] The young Pecci, McCarthy tells us, was sent away to study at the Jesuit College in Viterbo at the age of eight.[249] Six years later, he "entered the schools of the Roman College, then restored to the Jesuits."[250] He was a leading student: "[H]e took the highest honours his teachers could bestow in philosophy, in mathematical science, and in chemistry. ... He wrote Latin, prose and poetry, at the age of twelve, and to science he turned with the avidity and the success of another Pascal."[251]

Pecci was plainly talented. He was also destined for the priesthood. In 1832, he was admitted to study at the Pontifical Academy of Noble Ecclesiastics, "the school for papal diplomats."[252] Ordained a priest two days before Christmas in 1837,[253] by his early thirties, in the year 1843, he was already entrusted with a delicate diplomatic assignment – nuncio to the Catholic nation of Belgium, then in the process of undergoing contentious liberalization.[254] The assignment called for a delicate balancing act, and the young Pecci struggled in the role.[255] After a few years, he was removed from the position and given an appointment as Archbishop of Perugia in 1846, at the still very young age of thirty-six.[256]

Pecci, however, overcame this early adversity and excelled in his new assignment. Again, Justin McCarthy might be quoted: "[Pecci] established colleges, schools, hospitals and all manner of charitable associations. He had a soul for art and artistic decoration and he contrived to add new beauties to the picturesqueness of one of the most picturesque of Italian cities."[257] He became a cardinal in 1853, while a youthful forty-three, and served in Perugia until shortly

248 Justin McCarthy, *Pope Leo XIII*, 2d ed. (New York, 1899).

249 *Id.*, p. 26.

250 *Id.*

251 *Id.*, p. 27.

252 Timothy G. McCarthy, *The Catholic Tradition: The Church in the Twentieth Century*, 2d ed. (Eugene, OR, 2012), p. 4; and Edmond Hugues de Ragnau, *The Vatican: The Center of Government in the Catholic World* (New York, 1913), p. 359.

253 McCarthy, *Pope Leo XIII*, *supra*, p. 27.

254 Vincent Viaene, *Belgium and the Holy See From Gregory XVI to Pius IX (1831–1859): Catholic Revival, Society and Politics in Nineteenth-Century Europe* (Leuven, 2001), pp. 391–404.

255 *Id.*, pp. 391–400; Oskar Köhler, "The World Plan of Leo XIII: Goals and Methods," Margit Resch, tr., in Hubert Jedin and John Dolan, eds., *History of the Church*, vol. IX, *The Church in the Industrial Age* (London, 1981), pp. 3, 7–8.

256 Russell Hittinger, "Pope Leo XIII (1810–1893)," in John Witte, Jr., and Frank S. Alexander, eds., *The Teachings of Modern Roman Catholicism on Law, Politics, and Human Nature* (New York, 2007), pp. 39, 41.

257 McCarthy, *Pope Leo XIII*, *supra*, p. 35.

before his election as Pope.[258] Politically shrewd, Pecci succeed in striking a balance – presenting himself as sufficiently conservative to win Pope Pius IX's favor, while yet revealing "an openness to modern civilization."[259] In 1877, a year before his death, Pius made Pecci *camerlengo*, papal chamberlain, among whose duties is the certification of the old pope's death.[260]

By tradition, the papal *camerlengo* ought not to be elected as the old pope's successor. The *camerlengo's* association with the old regime and his prominent role in the interim government following the death of the old pope will naturally cause many cardinals to want to chart a new course.[261] Pecci's election as pope represented an exception to this customary rule.[262] Yes, Pecci had connections to Pius IX, but he had also won the trust of liberals.[263] If Pius IX had run the Church aground, it was hoped that Leo might yet rescue it from those dangerous shoals.

3.2 *The Church in Crisis: Leo's Response*

In fact, the Church seemed to contemporaries to be in the midst of some very perilous waters. Indeed, to many, including many devout ecclesiastics, the papacy appeared to have been definitively shattered. What was the papacy without territory to govern? A modern international lawyer has posed the question sharply and well: "The Catholic Church had found itself in the precarious position of no longer being considered a sovereign equal among European states."[264] And if it was not a sovereign that controlled territory and disposed of its resources, then what was it? The twentieth-century Irish statesman and legal historian Daniel Binchy[265] captured the predicament well when he wrote that with the fall of Rome to the *Risorgimento* and the death of Pope

258 Hittinger, "Pope Leo XIII," *supra*, p. 41.

259 Owen F. Cummings, *Popes, Councils, and Theology: From Pope Pius IX to Pope Francis* (Eugene, OR, 2021), p. 59.

260 Michael P. Riccards, *Faith and Leadership: The Papacy and the Roman Catholic Church* (Lanham, MD, 2012), p. 297.

261 Francis A. Burkle-Young, *Papal Elections: In the Age of Transition, 1878–1922* (Lanham, MD, 2000), p. 56.

262 *Id.*, pp. 58–68.

263 Andrea Ciampani, "Rethinking the Origins of the Catholic Party in Liberal Italy (The *Unione Romana* (1877–1887)," in Jan de Maeyer and Vincent Viaene, eds., *World Views and Worldly Wisdom: Religion, Ideology, and Politics, 1750–2000* (Leuven, 2016), pp. 105, 108–110.

264 Leonard Francis Taylor, *Catholic Cosmopolitanism and Human Rights* (Cambridge, UK, 2020), p. 172.

265 Maurice Manning, "The Lives of Daniel Binchy: Irish Scholar, Diplomat, Public Intellectual," *The Irish Times*, June 18, 2016.

Pius IX, the Catholic Church "as a force in international politics seemed fated to disappear."[266]

Yet nothing of the sort happened. Gioacchino Pecci, elected Pope on the third ballot, only thirteen days after the death of his predecessor, was determined to restore the status and prestige of the Holy See. His efforts were audacious, comprehensive, focused, and consumed the entire length of his quarter-century long pontificate.[267]

If the papacy no longer possessed the territory that the legal understanding of sovereignty required, still, Leo reasoned, it might remain relevant, indeed, it might continue to exert real force, by becoming the voice of conscience to the Christian world. This aspect of Leo's program was especially evident in his handling of the so-called "social question."[268] Europe in the latter nineteenth century was both the focal point of the industrial revolution and a seething hotbed of revolutionary ferment. This unrest, grounded in the legitimate grievances of a dispossessed and impoverished laboring underclass, manifested itself in radical politics.[269]

Pope Leo XIII responded to this economic crisis with his famous encyclical *Rerum Novarum* (1891). He rejected the Communist call for a collectivist economy,[270] and defended the right of private property.[271] Property, Leo urged, arose from the human need for survival; its prudent management, best entrusted to individuals, not the state, ensured continued access to the necessities of life.[272] But private property was not an absolute or unqualified good. Rather, from this natural right, obligations also flowed. The owners of capital must regard their workers with dignity,[273] and must provide wages sufficient to support a family.[274] Labor unions, furthermore, must be permitted, encouraged, and, indeed, "should become more numerous."[275] Leo's endorsement has

266 Daniel Binchy, "The Papacy in a Changing World," *Studies: An Irish Quarterly Review* 26 (1937), pp. 641, 641.

267 Vincent Viaene, "'A Pope's Dilemma:' Temporal Power and Moral Authority in the History of the Modern Vatican," in Maeyer and Viaene, eds., *World Views and Worldly Wisdom*, *supra*, pp. 245, 253–255.

268 John A. Ryan and R.A. McGowan, *A Catechism of the Social Question* (New York, 1921), pp. 5–7.

269 Martin Malia, *History's Locomotives: Revolutions and the Making of the Modern World* (New Haven, CT, 2006), pp. 240–252.

270 *Rerum Novarum*, nos. 4–5.

271 *Id.*, nos. 6–9.

272 *Id.*

273 *Id.*, no. 20.

274 *Id.*, nos. 45–46.

275 *Id.*, no. 49.

ever since served as a kind of charter for the Catholic labor movement, both in Europe[276] and in the United States.[277]

Leo's encyclical immediately gained the respect of his contemporaries, even in the non-Catholic and the secular worlds. As one historian has put it, Leo was the "first [pope] in modern times to set the teachings of his church within a theoretical framework that was coherent and rigorous when judged by the best standards of its age."[278] *Rerum Novarum* also became the foundation-stone of most subsequent Catholic theories of social reform and social justice.[279] Leo's ambition to remake the papacy into the world's conscience was bearing its first fruits.

But just as important as was Leo's intervention in the economic sphere, was his commitment to restoring the Holy See as a significant actor in international affairs. And thus there occurred an onrush of diplomatic initiatives. In Germany, Leo succeeded in resolving on favorable terms Otto von Bismarck's *Kulturkampf* – the Iron Chancellor's campaign to subject the Catholic Church to the dictates of the German state.[280] He improved relations with Russia through a series of contacts with Czar Alexander III and his court so amicably that it led one modern historian to write of the "close collaboration" that was thereby achieved.[281] Leo attained some diplomatic victories with the United Kingdom,[282] although he ultimately lost his nerve when he published *Apostolicae*

276 Paul Misner, *Catholic Labor Movements in Europe: Social Thought and Action, 1914–1965* (Washington, DC, 2015), p. 9.

277 Thomas Massaro, "The Social Question in the Papacy of Leo XIII," in James Corkery and Thomas Worcester, eds., *The Papacy Since 1500: From Italian Prince to Universal Pastor* (Cambridge, UK, 2010), pp. 143, 159.

278 A.M.C. Waterman, "The Intellectual Context of 'Rerum Novarum,'" *Review of Social Economy* 49 (1991), pp. 465, 476.

279 Craig R. Prentiss, *Debating God's Economy: Social Justice in America on the Eve of Vatican II* (University Park, PA, 2008), p. 17; and J. Bryan Hehir, "From Leo XIII to John Paul II: The Evolution of Catholic Social Thought," *Commonweal*, May 3, 1991, pp. 281–282.

280 James E. Ward, "Leo XIII: The Diplomat Pope," *Review of Politics* 28 (1966), pp. 47, 56–57; cf., James E. Ward, "Leo XIII and Bismarck: The Kaiser's Secret Vatican Visit of 1888," *Review of Politics* 24 (1962), pp. 392–414 (exploring the many-layered visit of the newly-inaugurated German Kaiser Wilhelm II to the Vatican).

281 Emilio Cassese, "The Russian Secret Mission in the Vatican Between 1887 and 1906: Historical Dynamics and New European Alliances," in Antonello Biagini and Giovanna Motta, eds., *Empires and Nations From the Eighteenth to the Twentieth Century* (Newcastle-Upon-Tyne, UK, 2014), vol. 1, pp. 96, 101.

282 As for example when he negotiated on the matter of the appointment of bishops on the Island of Malta during the United Kingdom's governance of that Island. See Dennis Angelo Castillo, *The Santa Marija Convoy: Faith and Endurance in Wartime Malta, 1940–1942* (Lanham, MD, 2012), pp. 38–39. These negotiations led to the ratification in 1889 of a concordat – of decidedly limited scope – to govern relations between the Holy See and

Curae (1896), denying the validity of Anglican Orders.[283] Leo even had cordial relations with American President Theodore Roosevelt, who described him as "'a broad-minded man, with a genuine knowledge of foreign affairs, and of the needs of the time.'"[284]

While there are many dimensions to Leo's multi-faceted campaign to restore the Holy See as a serious participant in international affairs, in what follows we shall concentrate on only one aspect of this effort: Leo's use of papal arbitration to resolve disputes of the utmost gravity between states and thereby establish the Holy See as an impartial, fair-minded judge of international conduct.

3.3 *Spain, Germany, and the Caroline Islands*

The Caroline Islands are an elongated archipelago of coral atolls and small islands in the South Pacific – jurisdiction over which is now split between the Federated States of Micronesia and the island-nation of Palau.[285] What follows is an origins story – first, how it happened that the Caroline Islands came under the domination of European colonizers. And, second, how it happened that Pope Leo XIII was responsible for facilitating this outcome by using the tools of alternative dispute resolution.

This island chain is appreciated today for its immense biological and human diversity. Located slightly to the north of the Equator, the Caroline Islands stretch nearly 3,000 kilometers from East to West.[286] It is thought that the Caroline Islands were settled about two thousand years ago, "when immigrants from the south arrived on the western mountainous islands."[287] Radiocarbon dating provides corroborating evidence for this dating,[288] bearing in mind that

---

the United Kingdom. See Stella Fletcher, *The Popes and Britain: A History of Rule, Rupture and Reconciliation* (London, 2017), p. 153.

283 Bruce N. Kaye, *Frozen Institutions: Questions For the Church After Christendom* (Eugene, OR, 2022), pp. 45–47; and Brian Douglas, *A Companion to Anglican Eucharistic Theology*, vol. 1, *The Reformation to the Nineteenth Century* (Leiden, 2012), pp. 584–585.

284 William R. Nester, *Theodore Roosevelt and the Art of American Power: An American For All Time* (Lanham, MD, 2019), p. 239 (quoting Theodore Roosevelt).

285 C.D. Bay-Hansen, *Power Geopolitics in the Pacific Age: East Asia, the United Nations, the United States and Micronesia at the Edge of the 21st Century, 1991–2001* (Portland, OR, 2011), p. 180.

286 Paul Rainbird, *The Archaeology of Micronesia* (Cambridge, UK, 2004), p. 134.

287 James R. Hein, "Caroline Islands," in Rosemary Gillespie and David Clague, eds., *Encyclopedia of Islands* (Berkeley, CA, 2009), pp. 148, 148.

288 Maureece J. Levin, et al., "A Partial Chronological Sequence of Human Habitation For Pingelap Atoll (Pohnpei State, Federated States of Micronesia)," *Radiocarbon* 61 (2019), pp. 765, 766, 771.

migration occurred in stages and by different groups of persons.[289] The archaeological record suggests furthermore that while some islands were only sporadically inhabited, there are also in other locations the remains of stone walls and evidence of sustained and sophisticated construction.[290] The original culture was matrilineal,[291] made wide use of breadfruit as a staple crop,[292] and produced accomplished seafarers.[293]

Portuguese and Spanish adventurers arrived in the vicinity of the Caroline Islands in the sixteenth century. The Portuguese sea captain Diogo da Rocha, having become lost, made land in the Islands as early as 1525, and remained there for four months.[294] Spanish explorers arrived a few years later,[295] as did the English,[296] although the visits were few and casual for much of the sixteenth and seventeenth centuries.[297] Spain dispatched some missionaries to the Caroline Islands in the early eighteenth century, although the martyrdom of one their number largely put an end to this effort.[298] Only in the nineteenth century, did rival European powers begin to settle and exploit the peoples and resources of these islands.[299] By the early nineteenth century, whaling vessels from the United States and other nations were putting into the

289 Patrick Vinton Kirch, *On the Road of the Winds: An Archaeological History of the Pacific Islands Before European Contact*, rev. and expanded (Berkeley, CA, 2017), pp. 151–154.

290 Rainbird, *Archaeology*, *supra*, pp. 167–177.

291 Per Hage, "Was Proto-Oceanic Society Matrilineal?" *Journal of the Polynesian Society* 107 (1998), pp. 365–379; David Hanlon, "The 'Sea of Little Lands:' Examining Micronesia's Place in Our 'Sea of Islands,'" *The Contemporary Pacific* 21 (2009), pp. 91, 97; and Barbara Glowczewski, *Indigenising Anthropology With Guattari and Deleuze* (Edinburgh, 2020), p. 126, note 19.

292 Glenn Peterson, "Micronesia's Breadfruit Revolution and the Evolution of a Culture Area," *Archaeology in Oceania* 41 (2006), pp. 82–92.

293 Ward H. Goodenough, "Navigation in the Western Carolines: A Traditional Science," in Sandra Harding, ed., *The Postcolonial Science and Technology Studies Reader* (Durham, NC, 2011), pp. 159–174; and Mike T. Carson, *Archaeology of Pacific Oceania: Inhabiting a Sea of Islands* (London, 2018), pp. 229–243.

294 William A. Lessa, "An Evaluation of Early Descriptions of Carolinian Culture," *Ethnohistory* 9 (1962), pp. 313, 314–315.

295 Francis X. Hezel, "The Beginnings of Foreign Contact With Truk," *Journal of Pacific History* 8 (1973), pp. 51, 52.

296 William A. Lessa, "Drake in the South Seas," in Norman J.W. Thrower, ed., *Sir Francis Drake and the Famous Voyage, 1577–1580: Essays Commemorating the Quadricentennial of Drake's Circumnavigation of the Earth* (Berkeley, CA, 1984), pp. 60, 63.

297 Francis X. Hezel, "Early European Contact With the Western Carolines, 1525–1750," *Journal of Pacific History* 7 (1972), pp. 26–44.

298 Christophe Descantes, "The Martyrdom of Father Juan Cantova on Ulithi Atoll: The Hegemonic Struggle Between Spanish Colonialism and a Micronesian Island Polity," *Missionalia* 32 (2004), pp. 394–418.

299 Gonzaga Puas, *The Federated States of Micronesia's Engagement With the Outside World: Control, Self-Preservation and Continuity* (Canberra, Australia, 2021), p. 85.

Caroline Islands,[300] and in the 1880s the governments of Spain and Germany both concluded that the Caroline Islands should become a part of their overseas empires.[301]

The latter nineteenth century saw the last manic outpouring of European colonial ambition, as the nations of the Continent, having subjugated and exploited much of the world, set their sights on the remote South Pacific. The Spanish Crown had long regarded the Caroline Islands as its possession – it claimed the Islands by right of discovery, ignoring Diogo da Rocha's earlier arrival,[302] and it had named the Archipelago after King Carlos II.[303] Still, Spain was content for centuries to do little in furtherance of its claims.[304] The Germans, newcomers to the South Pacific, were prepared to prosecute their case more vigorously. They had sprinkled a few commercial outposts and coaling stations among the atolls, and proclaimed that the Caroline Islands were theirs, not by right of discovery, but by right of colonization.[305]

The two nations made a choreographed display of their opposing claims. Otto von Bismarck, the German Chancellor, "announced his intention of annexing the Carolines" in August, 1885.[306] "Spain immediately dispatched two warships, the *San Quentin* and the *Manila*, to take possession of the islands. Germany responded by ordering its naval cruiser *Iltis* to raise the flag over any islands not previously claimed by its rival."[307] There followed an unseemly scramble among competing vessels to raise their respective national colors on as many tiny islands and inlets as they could find.[308]

300 *Civil Affairs Handbook, East Caroline Islands* (Washington, DC, 1944) (United States, Office of Chief of Naval Operations), p. 18; Martin Zelenietz and David Kravitz, "Absorption, Trade and Warfare: Beachcombers on Ponape, 1830–1854," *Ethnohistory* 21 (1974), pp. 223, 228; and Laurence M. Carucci, Book Review (reviewing Francis X. Hezel, *The First Taint of Civilization: A History of the Western Caroline and Marshall Islands in Pre-Colonial Days*), *American Anthropologist* 87 (1985), pp. 428, 429.

301 Francis X. Hezel, *The First Taint of Civilization: A History of the Western Caroline and Marshall Islands in Pre-Colonial Days* (Honolulu, HI, 1983), pp. 306–313.

302 James Brown Scott, *The Spanish Origin of International Law: Francisco de Vitoria and His Law of Nations* (Oxford, UK, 1932), p. 124, note c.

303 David Hanlon, *Upon a Stone Altar: A History of the Island of Pohnpei to 1890* (Honolulu, HI, 1988), p. 31.

304 "But from the seventeenth century, maps of the Pacific showed the Caroline Islands as Spanish territory." James S. Olson, ed., *Historical Dictionary of European Imperialism* (New York, 1991), pp. 116, 117.

305 Francis X. Hezel, *Strangers in Their Own Land: A Century of Colonial Rule in the Caroline and Marshall Islands* (Honolulu, HI, 1995), p. 7.

306 *Id.*

307 *Id.*, pp. 7–8.

308 *Id.*, p. 8.

What motivated the decision-makers of these two nations? Probably a combination of national prestige – this was the age of colonialism after all, and nations staked their status and their sacred honor on their foreign holdings[309] – as well as internal political imperatives,[310] and dimly-conceived commercial and military interests.[311] Nonetheless, the struggle was very real, even if the contending vessels must have exuded a comic-opera-like appearance. And rather than risk a war, Bismarck proposed that the dispute, which was heating up, should be turned over to a neutral party, Pope Leo XIII, for resolution.[312]

3.4 *Pope Leo XIII Mediates the Caroline Islands Dispute*

Did Pope Leo XIII agree to hear the case as an arbiter or as a mediator? That was a question that contemporary commentators took quite seriously. The international lawyer Louis Selosse, writing in 1886, a year after Pope Leo passed judgment on the Caroline Islands dispute, described Leo's self-conception of his role in terms that have continuing relevance to canonistic theories of mediation. Selosse wrote (and I translate): "His Holiness Leo XIII was chosen, not as an arbiter, but as a mediator. The difference between the two roles is significant. The arbiter resembles a judge who searches, above all, for the right; the mediator, without neglecting the question of justice, looks to reconcile the parties."[313]

As we analyze Leo's decision, we shall see this distinction figure prominently. For Leo, rendering judgment was not about playing a zero-sum game. He took seriously the claims of both Spain and Germany, and sought to ensure that each side received at least a portion of the relief that they were seeking.

Leo commenced his judgment by siding with Spain's claim that its discovery of the Islands possessed substantial weight for the resolution of the question of sovereignty.[314] The right of discovery was the prevailing means of acquiring

---

309 Herman Joseph Hiery, *Fa'a Siamani: Germany in Micronesia, New Guinea and Samoa 1884–1914* (Wiesbaden, 2020), pp. 6–7.

310 Hartmut Pogge von Strandmann, "Domestic Origins of Germany's Colonial Expansion Under Bismarck," *Past and Present* 42 (1969), pp. 140, 144.

311 Kees van Dijk, *Pacific Strife* (Amsterdam, 2015), pp. 99–100.

312 Charles Stephenson, *Germany's Asia-Pacific Empire: Colonialism and Naval Policy, 1885–1914* (Woodbridge, UK, 2009), p. 6.

313 I am translating the following passage: "S.S. Léon a été choisi, non comme arbitre, mais comme médiateur. La différence entre les deux rôles est notable. L'arbitre ressemble au juge qui cherche avant tout où est le droit; le médiateur, sans négliger la question de justice, cherche à concilier les parties." Louis Selosse, *L'affaire des Carolines: Étude de droit internationale* (Paris, 1886), pp. 57–58.

314 "Proposal of His Holiness, Leo XIII, in the Question of the Caroline Archipelago and the Palaos," reprinted in *Principles for Peace: Selections From Papal Documents, Leo XIII to Pius XII* (Washington, DC, 1943), p. 23.

sovereignty in the sixteenth century, at the time Spanish ships first made contact with the Caroline Islands, and this mattered a great deal.

But the law of discovery was a matter of weight, and was not in itself wholly determinative of the outcome. What mattered nearly as much in Leo XIII's estimation was the solicitude Spain demonstrated towards the native peoples. "[W]e cannot mistake the beneficent course of Spain in regard to these islanders."[315] Spain acted "for the benefit of the natives."[316] Spain's conduct was compassionate, benign, and always kept the good of the natives in view. This much was a "constant tradition and conviction."[317] Leo piled up the superlatives, perhaps as a diplomatic device to cushion the concessions he was poised to make to the Germans.

Of course, Leo's praise of Spanish "conscientiousness" can and should be criticized. The "benefits" Spain allegedly conferred on the inhabitants of the Caroline Islands were precisely the sorts of actions that colonial powers routinely did: challenge and subvert long-standing-native culture and customs in order to substitute one's own value system in a domineering act of coercion and, ultimately, subjugation. Spain was using the standard tools in the colonizer's handbook to exploit and erase indigenous lands and people. Leo, however, did not see cultural obliteration as a cause for concern. Indeed, given his own value system, which remained steadfastly, uncritically Eurocentric, he deemed it praiseworthy and unproblematic. We can and should find his practical endorsement of colonialism an untenable position,[318] but we should nevertheless, for the sake of analysis, try to see the world through Leo's eyes.

And if we do that, we can understand the balance Leo was attempting to strike between Spanish and German interests. Having spoken effusively of the Spanish commitment to the Caroline Islands, Leo indicated that the Germans also had rights that required respect since it had attained "effectual occupation" of the territory.[319] For that reason, Leo permitted Germany to maintain "liberty of commerce, of navigation, and of fishery within the islands."[320] Germany was also to be allowed to "establish[] a naval and a coaling station" in the archipelago, and was given the same rights as "Spanish subjects" to found and cultivate "agricultural establishments."[321]

---

315 *Id.*, p. 24.

316 *Id.*

317 *Id.*

318 Charles Keith, *Catholic Vietnam: A Church From Empire to Nation* (Berkeley, CA, 2012) p. 91 (noting that nineteenth-century attitudes about missionizing "did not yet reflect the moral critique of colonial rule that came from [the] Vatican after World War I").

319 "Proposal of His Holiness," *supra*, p. 24.

320 *Id.*

321 *Id.*, pp. 24–25.

Again, what we are witnessing is the careful work of someone who considered his role that of mediation. He wanted to ensure that each side came away from the process with at least some of what they sought. He thereby also hoped that both nations would regard the Papacy as a fair-minded and responsible actor on the world stage, thus elevating the Holy See in the eyes of the global community.

In a subsequent allocution to the College of Cardinals, Leo situated his decision firmly within the rules of international law.[322] If one attended to the law, Leo explained, one would note the convergence of two different sets of principles. On the one hand, Spain discovered the islands, as attested in the works of the earliest geographers. Not only that, Spain sent missionaries – veritable apostles – to the Islands, seeking to convert the native peoples. Indeed, Pope Clement XI – Leo's illustrious predecessor – had commended the King of Spain for these activities as early as 1706.[323] Taking an historically grounded view of international law – namely that the law in effect at the time of discovery should govern the disposition of the case – Leo declared that Spanish sovereignty must be given recognition.[324]

But the Germans were also able to point to "more recent facts" that strengthened their position under the "law of nations."[325] The Germans exercised the legitimate right to occupy "empty territory" (*in terras vacuas*).[326] The Spaniards had not made use of the land. The Germans had.[327] Furthermore, other nations – such as Great Britain – never recognized the Spanish claim over the Carolines.[328] (That these lands were not empty, but occupied by ancestral peoples with a long history, was simply erased from view, given the colonialist commitments of nineteenth-century international law).

Still, nineteenth-century international law was Leo's tool for resolving the dispute at hand, and thus he indicated, given Spain and Germany's competing claims, that he had to settle the matter by reference to equity (*aequitatem*). Each nation had legitimate rights and interests (*iurium et commodorum*)

---

322 "Allocution *Etsi Res* to the College of Cardinals," in *Principles of Peace*, *supra*, pp. 33–35. Latin text found at *Acta Sedis Sanctae* 18 (1886), pp. 309–311.

323 *Etsi Res*, *supra*, p. 33.

324 *Id.*, p. 34.

325 I am here paraphrasing the Latin text ("idque, si recentia quaedam facta animadvertantur, ratum iure gentium videri"). ASS 18, p. 310.

326 *Id.*

327 *Id.* Pope Leo's vocabulary, it must be noted, rendered the native inhabitants of the Islands invisible.

328 *Id.*

that required protection. And so Leo fashioned a compromise that sought to attain the "greatest peace" (*concordiae maximae*).[329] Indeed, Leo attested that "concord" – *concordia* – the "public good" – *rerum publicarum* – and finally "justice" and "religion" (*iustitia religioque*) all favored the balancing of interests he had struck.[330]

Leo was also being obviously political in deciding as he did. He said as much to the College of Cardinals, when he wrote that "Providence willed that two illustrious nations should do homage to the supreme authority in the Church by asking it to fulfill an office so much in keeping with its nature."[331] In a thank-you note sent to Otto von Bismarck, the Pope struck the same theme, expressing his gratitude to the Chancellor for permitting the Holy See to once again exercise its power to moderate international disputes.[332]

Thus Leo had achieved one of the principal objectives of his papacy. After a period of uncertainty and doubt, the Papacy had reestablished its relevance on the world stage. Writing in 1937, the historian Carl Conrad Eckhardt declared: "The historic position of the papacy as a temporal authority was given recognition when in 1885 Germany and Spain selected Leo XIII as arbiter in a dispute concerning ownership of the Caroline Islands."[333] James Brown Scott, the international lawyer, said much the same: "This is a most important case of the modern world, as it involved the interests of great nations."[334] The loss of the Papal State did not mean the final destruction of the Papacy as an institution with international significance after all.

Spain, however, did not long enjoy its status as sovereign of the Caroline Islands. Spain attempted to establish an administrative presence on the Islands, but proved to be "[b]adly overextended."[335] A more muscular Germany thus soon edged Spain out of the picture, and found itself by 1899 as both the *de facto* and *de jure* ruler of the territory.[336]

---

329 *Id.*

330 *Id.*, p. 311.

331 *Etsi Res*, in *Principles*, *supra*, p. 35.

332 Leo XIII, "Letter *Cum de Carolinis Insulis* to Prince Bismarck of Germany," in *Principles*, *supra*, pp. 31–32.

333 Carl Conrad Eckhardt, *The Papacy and World Affairs: As Reflected in the Secularization of Politics* (Eugene, OR, 2016) (reprint of 1937 edition), p. 237.

334 Scott, *Spanish Origin*, *supra*, p. 124, note c.

335 David Hanlon, *Making Micronesia: A Political Biography of Tosiwo Nakayama* (Honolulu, 2014), p. 31.

336 John Bassett Moore, ed., *A Digest of International Law* (Washington, DC, 1906), vol. V, p. 863.

Pope Leo, on the other hand, continued to exert himself on the world stage. In part, his efforts were motivated by the expanding missionary activity of the Catholic Church, especially in Africa.[337] Thus he condemned the slave trade. "Slavery," he wrote, "opposes religion and human dignity."[338] Slavery was a "gloomy plague" that should be abolished.[339] In furtherance of this goal, he lent important strategic and practical support to campaigns to eradicate, at long last, the enslavement of human beings,[340] dispatching Cardinal Charles Lavigerie, Archbishop of Carthage and Algiers in North Africa, on a European speaking tour to stir the public to action.[341]

Indeed, one modern writer noted that "[beginning in] 1888, Cardinal Charles Lavigerie, with the sanction of the Pope, had sought to lead a new crusade against the African slave trades not just in his native France but throughout Europe."[342] Lavigerie's "campaign culminated in an international conference in 1889" in Brussels, to which numerous European nations and the United States sent delegates, and which produced "the first comprehensive multilateral treaty directed specifically against the slave trade."[343]

So Leo XIII found yet one more avenue by which to enhance the Holy See's stature on the international stage. Still, despite his clear-sightedness on the slavery question, Leo could not free himself from the colonialist paradigm within which he moved and breathed. This much was evident when in 1890 and 1891 he mediated the dispute between Portugal and Belgium on the proper

---

337 V.Y. Mudimbe, *The Idea of Africa* (Bloomington, IN, 1994), p. 106.

338 Leo XIII, *Catholicae Ecclesiae*, no. 2 (1890). Two years earlier, Leo wrote to congratulate the nation of Brazil on its abolition of slavery, seeing its establishment as "wholly opposed to that which was originally ordained by God and by nature." Leo XIII, *In Plurimis* (1880), no. 3.

339 Leo XIII, *Catholicae Ecclesiae*, *supra*, no. 2.

340 McCarthy, *Pope Leo XIII*, *supra*, pp. 142–149.

341 Eugene Schuyler, "The African Slave-Trade: American Interest in Its Suppression," *The Anti-Slavery Reporter* 9 (January, 1889), pp. 38–39.

342 Richard Huzzey, *Freedom Burning: Anti-Slavery and Empire in Victorian Britain* (Ithaca, NY, 2012), p. 162; cf., Amalia Ribi Forclaz, *Humanitarian Imperialism: The Politics of Anti-Slavery Activism, 1880–1940* (Oxford, 2015), pp. 17–23; and Daniel Laqua, "The Tensions of Internationalism: Transnational Anti-Slavery in the 1880s and 1890s," *International History Review* 33 (2011), pp. 705–726 (both works elaborating further on Catholic efforts, stimulated by Pope Leo XIII and Cardinal Lavigerie, to combat the slave trade).

343 Seymour Drescher, "From Consensus to Consensus: Slavery in International Law," in Jean Allain, ed., *The Legal Understanding of Slavery: From the Historical to the Contemporary* (Oxford, UK, 2012), pp. 85, 98.

boundary of the Congo Free State.[344] In the middle 1890s, furthermore, Leo was drawn into the protracted struggle to establish a boundary between Haiti and the Dominican Republic (called Santo Domingo in the sources),[345] although he proved unable to mediate this disagreement to a satisfactory conclusion.[346]

3.5 *The Theory Behind Leo's Mediation*

Leo was not content merely to act. He also desired to give his actions firm grounding in the ecclesiastical tradition. Thus in his encyclical *Diuturnum* (1881), Leo laid out the theological principles that justified the papal mediation of international disputes. Leo began with a reflection on the origins of the power of governance. He rejected the propositions of certain unnamed philosophers – he seems to have had Jean Jacques Rousseau principally in mind[347] – who saw governmental power as derived from a cession of rights by individuals to the community, which then acts in the name of the people.[348] No, Leo countered, governmental power had its source from God, a point he believed could be demonstrated both by an appeal to Scripture and to human reason.[349]

Happily, Leo went on, the European powers seemed to recognize the truth of this assertion.[350] Rulers and subjects alike have come to appreciate that the exercise of political power must therefore conform to Christian principles.[351] This did not mean that states were directly subject to papal authority. Civil states were a part of the divine plan and enjoyed an appropriate autonomy within the larger social order,[352] provided that they served always the interests

344 John Tracy Ellis, "Catholic Church and Peace Efforts," *Notre Dame Lawyer* 9 (1934), pp. 173, 207.

345 A. Poujol, "Haití el arbitraje de sus fronteras," *Revista Nacional* 28 (Argentina, 1899), pp. 169–180; and A. Poujol, *Le Différend entre Haïti et Saint Domingue au sujet de leurs frontières nationales* (Paris, 1900).

346 Jakob Zollmann, "Interstate Mediation and Arbitration: Concepts, Cases, and Actors of Third Party Dispute Resolution (Seventeenth to Nineteenth Century)," in Karl Härter, et al., eds., *On Mediation: Historical, Legal, Anthropological, and International Perspectives* (New York, 2020), pp. 153, 165; and J.H.W. Verzijl, *International Law in Historical Perspective* (Leiden, 1976), p. 269.

347 Edward F. Murphy, *St. Thomas' Political Doctrine and Democracy* (Ph.D. dissertation, Catholic University of America) (Washington, DC, 1921), p. 7, note 80.

348 *Diuturnum* (1881), nos. 5 and 12.

349 *Id.*, nos. 8–9.

350 *Id.*, no. 21.

351 *Id.*, nos. 21–22.

352 Thomas J. Bushlack, *Politics for a Pilgrim Church: A Thomistic Theory of Civic Virtue* (Grand Rapids, MI, 2015), p. 54 ("For ... Leo the state has an ontological status rather than a purely contractual or contingent status").

of the common good.[353] But where states sought guidance, particularly in their relations with one another, the Holy See stood ready to help as interlocutor and good shepherd.[354]

In his correspondence with the rulers of nations, Leo expressed his more concrete expectations that the Holy See should become a judge to which states might entrust their bitterest disagreements in hope of resolution. In a letter in February, 1899, to the Russian Secretary for Foreign Affairs, Mikhail Nikolayevich Mouraviev, Leo had his Secretary of State, Mariano Cardinal Rampolla, propose that the forthcoming Hague Convention on Peace (1899) should make affirmative provision for the papal negotiation of international conflict.[355] And in May of that year, Leo wrote directly to Queen Wilhelmina of the Netherlands, declaring that the papacy "has been invested with the highest possible mission, that of being a mediator of peace."[356] Czar Nicholas II, who was one of the principal organizers of the Hague Convention, invited Leo to the event, but in the end objections by the nation of Italy made attendance impossible.[357]

As a ruler who had effectively lost temporal power, Leo conceived that the papacy was uniquely equipped to be a neutral mediator for at least three reasons. First, the Holy See territorially and politically lacked a stake in the outcome. Leo, in other words, turned the papacy's perceived weakness into a strength. No longer was the papacy open to the criticism that it was acting in bad faith because of its own potential conflicts of interest. It was a neutral among the nations of the world. Second, the Holy See claimed to be the authentic interpreter of the natural law, which gave it privileged access to a transcendent body of norms by which to settle disputes.[358] Thus he rejected "the right of the stronger" to govern in favor of discernible, transcendent principles of justice.[359] Third, alone among the nations, Leo believed, the Holy See

---

353 *Diuturnum*, no. 16.

354 *Id.* no. 22. Cf., Gary J. Adler, *Secularism, Catholicism, and the Future of Public Life: A Dialogue with Ambassador Douglas W. Kmiec* (Oxford, UK, 2015), pp. 103–104, and note 258 (further developing these points).

355 "Second Diplomatic Note of Cardinal Rampolla, Secretary of State, to Count Mouraviev, Secretary of Foreign Affairs of Russia," in *Principles, supra*, p. 95.

356 Leo XIII, "Letter, *Nous ne Pouvons*, to Queen Wilhelmina of the Netherlands" (May 29, 1899), in *Principles, supra*, p. 99.

357 David Alvarez, "The Holy See and the First Hague Peace Conference (1899)," *Archivum Historiae Pontificiae* 26 (1988), pp. 431–438.

358 Indeed, the Holy See continues to claim this status. See Gerald Coleman, "Discerning the Meaning of *Humanae Vitae*," *Theological Studies* 79 (2018), pp. 864, 867–868.

359 Heinz-Gerhard Justenhoven, "Peace Through a Public Global Authority in Papal Teaching from Leo XIII to John XXIII," in Heinz-Gerhard Justenhoven and James Turner, eds.,

possessed the moral suasion not only to settle disputes, but also to win over the recalcitrant and thereby secure willing compliance.

What to make of Leo's efforts? On the one hand, he was still operating within a traditional frame of reference. He wished to restore the Holy See to something of the prestige and power that his predecessor had so recklessly squandered. He was thus prepared to utilize any available tool to keep the Holy See politically and diplomatically relevant. But it is significant that he chose the mediation of international disputes as a vehicle for that particular ambition.

One can justly criticize aspects of Leo's program. His preoccupation with rebuilding the Vatican's depleted reputation inextricably entangled him with the worst aspects of the colonial order. His opposition to slavery was laudable. But it was simply wrong for the Pope – or any religious leader – to recognize and grant legitimacy to enterprises like King Leopold II of Belgium's unjust and inhumane pillaging of the Congo Free State. As early as 1890, the African-American journalist and Christian minister George Washington Williams used the expression "crimes against humanity" to describe King Leopold's indecent management of the Congo.[360] These charges were published widely "in many American and European newspapers"[361] and surely would have been known to Leo XIII's Secretariat of State, at least in their general outlines. Joseph Conrad's *Heart of Darkness* was published between 1899 and 1902, and made plain to a European readership the wickedness of Leopold's policy of exploitation.[362] It can be safely said that a well-informed Vatican was not entirely in the dark about the Belgian monarch's character or his depredations.

Even bearing in mind these criticisms, it can also be said that Leo's mediation of the Caroline Islands dispute has had an enduring significance for the history of international law. It was an important articulation of the

Rethinking the State in the Age of Globalisation: Catholic Thought and Contemporary Political Theory (New Brunswick, NJ, 2003), pp. 167, 172. Cf., Ignacio de la Rasilla, *In the Shadow of Vitoria: A History of International Law in Spain* (1770–1953 (Leiden, 2018) p. 81 (on Leo's encouragement of natural law as a cornerstone of international law).

360 Adam Hochschild, *King Leopold's Ghost: A Story of Greed, Terror and Heroism in Colonial Africa* (New York, 2019), p. 102 (Williams as African-American); p. 103 (information that he was a Christian minister); and pp. 111–112 ("crimes against humanity").

361 Mahmood Mamdani, "Beyond Nuremberg: The Historical Significance of the Post-Apartheid Transition in South Africa," in Karen Engle, et al., eds., *Human Rights Agenda* (Cambridge, UK, 2016), pp. 329, 356, note 17.

362 Maya Jasanoff, "How *Heart of Darkness* Revealed the Horror of Congo's Rubber Trade," *Literary Hub*, December 7, 2017; and Maya Jasanoff, "With Conrad on the Congo River," *New York Times*, August 18, 2017.

historically-grounded "possessory doctrine" of sovereign title.[363] It endorsed the principle of "inter-temporality" – the teaching that international disputes should be resolved in accord with the state of the law at the time the claims first came into being.[364] It recognized as well that sovereign power might be conditioned on its effective exercise and on the justified interests of other parties.[365] His ideas have continuing relevance for the contemporary development of international norms.[366]

Again, one might cite the always enthusiastic, sometimes extravagant Justin McCarthy. "Statesmanship and philanthropy are combined" in Pope Leo, he wrote.[367] "[H]e made it his task to maintain peace among his neighbours."[368] For sure, Leo was a creature of his time, and for sure, he committed errors and misjudgments, even when seen on his own terms. But he played a bad hand well, and made the Catholic Church relevant on the world stage, when it was in peril of losing its standing.

3.6 *Papal Peacemaking since Pope Leo XIII*

3.6.1 Pope Benedict XV

Pope Leo XIII died in July, 1903 and was succeeded by Giuseppe Melchiorre Sarto, who was one of ten children born into a poor, working-class family in Venetia.[369] When Sarto, who took the name of Pius X, died a little more than eleven years later, in August, 1914, he was succeeded by Giacomo Paolo Battista della Chiesa who was elected Pope in September, 1914, and assumed the name of Benedict XV. Benedict was a trained lawyer who had degrees in both civil and canon law.[370] Like Leo XIII, Benedict studied at the Pontifical Academy of Noble Ecclesiastics, where he early came to the attention of Leo's Secretary of State, Cardinal Rampolla.[371] If Leo's pontificate was preoccupied with the quest to restore the Holy See's relevance, Benedict's tenure as pope – he died

363 Marta Lorente, "Historical Titles v. Effective Occupation: Spanish Jurists on the Caroline Islands Affair (1885)," *Journal of the History of International Law* 20 (2018), pp. 303, 305.

364 Eirik Bjorge, *The Evolutionary Interpretation of Treaties* (Oxford, UK, 2014), pp. 142–149.

365 Matthew M. Ricciardi, "Title to the Aouzou Strip: A Legal and Historical Analysis," *Yale Journal of International Law* 17 (1992), pp. 301, 392–393, note 562.

366 Andreas Follesdal, "The Principle of Subsidiarity as a Constitutional Principle in International Law," *Global Constitutionalism* 2 (2013), pp. 37, 46–47.

367 McCarthy, *Pope Leo XIII, supra*, p. 266.

368 *Id.*, p. 267.

369 Frances Alice Forbes, *Life of Pius X* (New York, 1918), pp. 1–12.

370 Walter H. Peters, *The Life of Benedict XV* (Milwaukee, WI, 1959), pp. 11, 16.

371 *Id.*, p. 16.

in January, 1922, of pneumonia – was dominated by the First World War, which had broken out shortly before his election, and by its aftermath.

Pope Benedict consistently urged the belligerents to rely on the good offices of the Holy See to settle their dispute and end the carnage of the War.[372] He wanted peace to prevail and appreciated that the belligerents needed to accommodate one another's interests in order to make that happen. In a letter that subsequently received wide newspaper coverage, Benedict denounced the War as "the 'suicide of civilized Europe.'"[373] On All Saints Day, November 1, 1914, Benedict published his first encyclical letter. Entitled *Ad Beatissimi Apostolorum*, its focus was the War. Anticipating the doom that was to come, Benedict wrote: "On every side the dread phantom of war holds sway; there is scarce room for another thought in the minds of men. The combatants are the greatest and wealthiest nations of the earth; what wonder, then, if, well provided with the most awful weapons modern military science has devised, they strive to destroy one another with refinements of horror."[374]

In the summer of 1917, shortly after America's entry into the War, Benedict circulated a Peace Note to the belligerents.[375] The Czar had already fallen, though the Bolsheviks would not seize power until the following fall. Benedict feared that worse yet was to come.[376] Benedict understood that peace demanded meaningful, even sacrificial compromise. Benedict therefore proposed that each belligerent should surrender real things of value. There was to be "[r]eciprocal renunciation of war indemnities" by all sides.[377] All sides, furthermore, should be required to "evacuat[e] ... all occupied territories."[378] And the parties were to submit their grievances to "[i]nternational arbitration."[379]

The proposal failed. The British opposed it because they were looking forward to the possibility of victory and with it the attainment of global

372 Patrick J. Houlihan, "Pope Benedict xv and the Forgotten Campaign to End World War I," *America*, August 3, 2017; Terry Philpot, "World War I's Pope Benedict xv and the Pursuit of Peace," *National Catholic Reporter*, July 19, 2014.

373 Agnes de Dreuzy, *The Holy See and the Emergence of the Modern Middle East: Benedict xv's Diplomacy in Greater Syria (1914–1922)* (Washington, DC, 2016), p. 81 and note 40 (quoting Benedict xv).

374 Benedict xv, *Ad Beatissimi Apostolorum* (1914), no. 3.

375 John F. Pollard, *Benedict xv: The Unknown Pope and the Pursuit of Peace* (New York, 1999), pp. 123–128.

376 *Id.*, p. 123.

377 *Id.*, p. 126.

378 *Id.*

379 *Id.*

"economic supremacy."[380] The French were stung by the suggestion that they should surrender claims for reparations. They had suffered greatly and believed the Germans should be made to pay. French public opinion thus denounced the Pope as *"le Pape Boche."*[381] But the Americans proved to be the real obstacle to peace. And at least one historian puts the responsibility directly on the shoulders of the American President, Woodrow Wilson. The Americans had now joined the War, they meant to win it, and "the Calvinist president of the United States" saw the chance to "set[] himself up as a new moral authority in the world."[382] Wilsonian arrogance, in other words, slammed the door on Benedict's peace plan.

Benedict, however, still sought opportunities to be constructive. Excluded from participation in the Versailles peace conference,[383] in December, 1918, he published another encyclical, *Quod iam diu*, which aimed to define the terms of the peace. He expectantly prayed: "Soon the delegates of the various nations will meet in solemn congress to give the world a just and lasting peace."[384] He asked that all Catholics, everywhere, not only pray for the success of the conference, but actually work to implement whatever final decisions were agreed to.[385] At the conclusion of the conference, Benedict issued still another encyclical, *Pacem, Dei Munus Pulcherrimum* ("Peace, the Most Beautiful Gift of God"), urging the nations of the world to adopt the League of Nations[386] and pledging the Church to aid in the humanitarian reconstruction of Europe.[387]

In all of this, Pope Benedict XV was zealous and committed to the cause of peace. Indeed, he had internalized lessons he must have absorbed from Pope Leo XIII and from Cardinal Rampolla, whose protégé he had been.[388] The papacy was not merely relevant when it acts to guide warring nations to peace, it was performing a meritorious service.

---

380 *Id.*, p. 133.

381 John F. Pollard, "Papal Diplomacy and the Great War," *New Blackfriars* 96 (2015), pp. 147, 155. *Boche* was a French slur for German soldiers, meaning, roughly "wooden head," or "blockhead." See Alice L. Conklin, et al., *France and Its Empire Since 1870*, 2d ed. (Oxford, 2015), p. 132.

382 Pollard, "Papal Diplomacy," *supra*, p. 155.

383 Philpot, "World War I's Pope Benedict," *supra*; and Houlihan, "Pope Benedict XV," *supra*.

384 Benedict XV, *Quod iam diu* (1918) no. 1.

385 *Id.*, no. 2.

386 Benedict XV, *Pacem, Dei Munus Pulcherrimum* (1920), no. 17.

387 *Id.*, no. 18. Cf., Robert John Araujo, "The Holy See: International Person and Sovereign," *Ave Maria International Law Journal* 1 (2011), pp. 1, 16–17 (further evaluating Benedict XV's contributions to international diplomacy).

388 Gary Lease, "Vatican Foreign Policy and the Origins of Modernism," in Darrell Jodock, ed., *Catholicism Contending with Modernity: Roman Catholic Modernism and Anti-Modernism in Historical Context* (Cambridge, UK, 2000), pp. 31, 43.

3.6.2 St. John Paul II

In recent times, perhaps few popes have been as active in the cause of peace and diplomacy than Pope St. John Paul II and Pope Francis. We shall discuss each in turn.

In the course of his twenty-seven year long pontificate, John Paul II involved himself in a number of major diplomatic endeavors, although I shall discuss only two of these. The first of these was his successful mediation of the Beagle Channel dispute between the nations of Chile and Argentina, near the beginning of his pontificate. The second was his unsuccessful effort to prevent the United States from launching its ill-fated war on Iraq in 2003.

3.6.2.1 *The Beagle Channel*

The Beagle Channel is one among the network of passages that allow vessels to traverse Cape Horn between the Atlantic and Pacific Oceans. Chile and Argentina had long-standing, conflicting claims to the Channel which they sought to settle in protracted discussions throughout the 1970s.[389] But near the end of the decade negotiations had ceased and it appeared as if the two sides might be at the brink of war.[390]

"Faced with the tense situation, on 22 December 1978, Pope John Paul II offered mediation through his special envoy Cardinal Antonio Samoré and both sides accepted the offer."[391] On January 8, 1979, Chile and Argentina signed the Act of Montevideo, promising a peaceful resolution of the dispute and pledging to abide by the papally-negotiated settlement.[392] In a message to the two nations, John Paul II declared his intention to rely on "the requirements of justice, fairness, and prudence" to guide his decision-making.[393] A negotiating team headed by Cardinal Samoré began to work with the two sides by early 1980.[394]

The process was neither smooth nor swift. Argentina's involvement in the Falklands War caused negotiations to cease at least temporarily;[395] Cardinal

389 James L. Garrett, "The Beagle Channel Dispute: Confrontation and Negotiation in the Southern Cone," *Journal of Interamerican Studies and World Affairs* 27 (1985), pp. 81, 86–97.

390 Michael A. Morris, *The Strait of Magellan* (Dordrecht, the Netherlands, 1989), pp. 81–82.

391 Yoshifumi Tanaka, *The Peaceful Settlement of International Disputes* (Cambridge, UK, 2018), p. 124.

392 Matthew C. Mirow, "International Law and Religion in Latin America: The Beagle Channel Dispute," *Suffolk Transnational Law Review* 28 (2004), pp. 1, 12–13.

393 "Message of His Holiness John Paul II to the Presidents of Argentina and Chile," December 12, 1978.

394 Thomas Princen, "International Mediation: The View From the Vatican," *Negotiation Journal* 3 (1987), pp. 347, 348.

395 Daniel K. Gibran, *The Falklands War: Britain Versus the Past in the South Atlantic* (Jefferson, NC, 2008), p. 66.

Samoré died in 1983;[396] but eventually, discussions resumed, and an agreement was announced by the two nations in October, 1984.[397] Following the formal ratification of a treaty of friendship between the two nations, a signing ceremony occurred at the Vatican.[398] In a speech to the diplomatic corps accredited to the Holy See, John Paul II commended the two nations, speaking of their "iron will" to achieve peace, and also suggesting that the Holy See stood ready to resolve other seemingly insoluble conflicts.[399] He proposed that the keys to attaining such results must include "reciprocity, solidarity, and the effective collaboration which is the fruit of the other two."[400]

3.6.2.2 *St. John Paul II and the American War on Iraq*

It is probably safe to say that the decision by the United States to go to war against the nation of Iraq was made more or less as the result of the successful terrorist attacks of September 11, 2001. The collapse of the twin towers of New York City's World Trade Center, and the destruction of a substantial part of the Pentagon left many Americans not only traumatized but in a mood to settle, for good, what was perceived to be a festering hostility to America in many quarters of the Middle East.[401] The nation was ready for war,[402] and the dream in many policy circles was to bring to heel any number of Middle Eastern nations.[403]

Iraq, however, was singled out as the most immediate, and the most attractive prize, because the United States had fought a war against that nation once

396 Henry Kamm, "Cardinal Samoré Vatican Mediator," *New York Times*, February 3, 1983.

397 Lisa Lindsley, "The Beagle Channel Settlement: Vatican Mediation Resolves a Century-Old Dispute," *Journal of Church and State* 29 (1987), pp. 435, 447–448; Lydia Chavez, "Argentina and Chile in Accord on Beagle Channel," *New York Times*, October 5, 1984.

398 Samuel Koo, "Argentina and Chile Sign Treaty on Beagle Channel," *Associated Press*, May 2, 1985.

399 "Address of His Holiness John Paul II to the Diplomatic Corps Accredited to the Holy See," January 12, 1985, no. 2.

400 *Id.*, no. 3.

401 Jonathan Freedland, "Turning Towards Iraq," *The Guardian*, November 20, 2001; Anne Applebaum "The New New World Order: America and the Neo Geopolitics," *Hoover Institution*, December 15, 2001, hoover.org/sites/default/files/uploads/documents/0817939024_1.pdf ("Like the Cold War, the War on Terrorism appeases the idealism of Americans: we are, after all, fighting to rid the world of an evil"). *Id.*, p. 9.

402 In the words of Hans Blix, United Nations arms controller: "The United States was like a giant gorilla wounded by a small arrow from a pygmy. It was a humiliation. They needed to strike back at someone, and the Taliban in Afghanistan were not enough." Pelle Axelsson, "Hans Blix: The Search For Weapons of Mass Destruction," *Global Policy*, March 17, 2023, globalpolicyjournal.com/blog/17/03/2023/hans-blix-search-weapons-mass-destruction.

403 Joe Conason, "'Seven Countries in Five Years:' Wesley Clark's New Memoir Casts More Light on the Bush Administration's Secret Strategies for Regime Change in Iran and Elsewhere," *Salon*, October 12, 2007; Glenn Greenwald, "Wes Clark and the Neocon Dream," *Salon*, November 26, 2011.

before, at the head of an international coalition in 1991. In August, 1990, the President of Iraq, Saddam Hussein, had made the decision to invade and annex the neighboring nation of Kuwait.[404] The United States, acting to enforce a United Nations Security Council Resolution calling for the removal of Iraqi forces from Kuwait,[405] expelled the Iraqi army and restored Kuwaiti sovereignty.[406] More controversially, Saddam Hussein was allowed to remain President of Iraq, although the nation was made to bear the weight of crushing economic sanctions that killed tens of thousands and stunted the lives of hundreds of thousands more.[407]

In the months following the September 11, 2001, attacks, stories circulated that Saddam Hussein might have had a role to play in the attacks,[408] and if he did not, then at the very least he was operating a large and active program for the manufacture of weapons of mass destruction. This impression was fed by strategically-published reports in outlets like *The New York Times*,[409] although in hindsight these stories were seen as weakly documented and poorly researched.[410] Highly-placed spokespersons of the United States government – most notably, Secretary of State Colin Powell at the United Nations – sought to make the case that Saddam Hussein was a clear and present danger to his

404 Efraim Karsh and Inari Rautsi, "Why Saddam Hussein Invaded Kuwait," *Global Politics and Strategy* 33 (1991), pp. 18–30.

405 United Nations Security Council Resolution no. 678 (November 29, 1990) S_RES_678(1990) =EN.pdf.

406 William C. Martel, *Victory In War: Foundations of Modern Strategy*, rev. and expanded ed. (Cambridge, UK, 2011), pp. 235–236.

407 Usha Natarajan, "Accounting for the Absence of the Rule of Law: History, Culture, and Causality," in Jeremy Farrall and Hilary Charlesworth, eds., *Strengthening the Rule of Law Through the U.N. Security Council* (London, 2016), pp. 43, 51 ("Iraq has been 'in a class by itself' as the recipient of 'the longest, most comprehensive, and most severe multilateral sanctions regime ever imposed.'"). *Id.*, p. 51 (quoting David Cortright and George Lopez, *The Sanctions Decade: Assessing U.N. Strategies in the 1990s* (Boulder, CO, 2000), p. 8). *Id.* Cf., Beate Bull and Arne Tostensen, "Bolstering Human Rights by Means of 'Smart' Sanctions?" in Hugo Stokke and Arne Tostensen, eds., *Human Rights in Development Yearbook 1999/2000: The Millennium Edition* (The Hague, 2001), pp. 83, 100–104 (documenting the vast number of deaths caused by sanctions).

408 Bruce C. Riedel, "9/11 and Iraq: The Making of a Tragedy," *Brookings Institution*, September 17, 2021, brookings.edu/blg/order-from-chaos/2021/09/17/9-11-and-iraq-the-making-of-a-tragedy/.

409 Matthew Evangelista and Judith Reppy, "Much Ado About Democracy: Some Skeptical Observations on Democracies and War," in Matthew Evangelista, et al., eds., *Democracy and Security: Preferences, Norms, and Policy-Making* (London, 2008), pp. 167, 180.

410 Jesse Kornbluth, "Judith Miller Carried Water for the USA's Worst Debacle Since Vietnam," *Observer*, April 8, 2015, observer.com/2015/04/judith-miller-carried-water-for-the-usas-worst-debacle-since-vietnam/; Erik Wemple, "A Journalist's Defense of Her Flawed Reporting," *Washington Post*, April 12, 2015.

neighbors and the larger world.[411] In the end, these spokespersons were unconvincing. The United Nations Chief Arms Inspector, Hans Blix, was unable to document the presence of weapons of mass destruction in Iraq,[412] and the United Nations Security Council chose not to lend its support to an American invasion of Iraq.[413]

Faced with considerable international opposition, President George W. Bush decided that he would organize what came to be called "the coalition of the willing," to participate in the invasion of Iraq.[414] In fact, this coalition – which was unimpressive in its numbers[415] – assembled in the face of surging international opposition to the proposed invasion. Millions of persons marched in protest around the world, seeking to avert war and bring about instead the peaceful resolution of the dispute.[416]

Among the international leaders voicing strong opposition to the war was the future Saint, Pope John Paul II. In his homily for Christmas Eve, 2002, the Pope spoke of the birth of Jesus as "a sign of peace for those suffering from conflicts of every kind."[417] The Pope had dropped a hint, and the next day,

---

411 Glenn Kessler and Colum Lynch, "Powell Lays Out Case Against Iraq; Evidence Shows Hussein Foiled Inspections, Secretary Tells U.N.," *Washington Post*, February 6, 2003; cf., Joe Conason, "The Case for War Has Not Been Made," *Salon*, February 5, 2003.

412 Maggie Farley, "Showdown With Iraq: Inspection Report Firms Up Council's Opposition to War," *Los Angeles Times*, February 15, 2003; Deborah Jerome-Cohen, "A Case for Iraq Inspections," *Newark Star-Ledger*, February 16, 2003.

413 Shelley Emling, "U.N. Split on Iraq War: France, Russia, China Say Facts Don't Support Call for Military Action," *Atlanta Journal Constitution*, February 15, 2003. Indeed, United Nations Secretary General Kofi Annan described the War as a violation of international law. Ewan MacAskill and Julian Borger, "Iraq War was Illegal and Breached U.N. Charter, Says Annan," *The Guardian*, September 15, 2004.

414 Steven R. Brydon, *American Propaganda From the Spanish-American War to Iraq* (Lanham, MD, 2022), p. 222.

415 Ivo H. Daalder, "The Coalition That Isn't," *Brookings Institution*, March 24, 2003, brookings.edu/opinions/the-coalition-that-isnt/.

416 See, for example, Lynette Clemetson, "Protest Groups Using Updated Tactics to Spread Antiwar Message," *New York Times*, January 15, 2003; Lynette Clemetson, "Thousands Converge in Capital to Protest Plans for War," *New York Times*, January 19, 2003; Marlise Simons, "In the Street, Across Europe, a Weekend of Antiwar Rallies," *New York Times*, January 20, 2003; Cara Mia DiMassa and Erika Hayasaki, "Tens of Thousands March in Opposition to War in Iraq," *Los Angeles Times*, February 16, 2003; "At Least 200,000 Protest in Australia," *Los Angeles Times*, February 17, 2003; "Across Europe, Millions Protest a War in Iraq," *Washington Post*, March 15, 2003; Evelyn Nieves, "Worldwide, Civil Disobedience; Protesters Speak and Act Out Against War," *Washington Post*, March 21, 2003; Evelyn Nieves, "From Sea to Sea, Rallies For, Against the War; One of the Largest Shows of Civil Disobedience Since Vietnam War Results in About 420 Arrests," *Washington Post*, March 22, 2003.

417 John Paul II, Homily of the Holy Father, Midnight Mass, Christmas, 24 December, 2002, no. 4.

in his Christmas message to the world, he was more direct in expressing his wishes.[418] He prayed that God might "put an end once and for all to the senseless spiral of blind violence, and in the Middle East, ... extinguish the ominous smouldering of a conflict which, with the joint efforts of all, can be avoided."[419] It was not lost on observers that the Pope hoped that a Middle Eastern war might be averted.[420]

These statements, however, were merely the prelude to a major diplomatic initiative in the first months of 2003 to prevent, if at all possible, a war between the United States and Iraq. The pontiff's push for peace began with his New Year's message, delivered January 1, 2003.[421] It took the form of an extended reflection on Pope John XXIII's encyclical *Pacem in Terris*, issued forty years before. *Pacem in Terris* – literally, "Peace on Earth" – was a daring encyclical, a prophetic message, delivered by a terminally ill Pope St. John XXIII, to a world shaken by the close call that was the Cuban Missile Crisis.[422]

John XXIII spoke about peace as something more than merely the absence of violence or war. Peace was a state of substantively just relations prevailing among all persons. Peace, as John XXIII understood it, required that human rights and human dignity be respected both by governments and by private interests.[423] And it further demanded that geopolitical disputes be settled not be force of arms but by negotiation and compromise.[424] Peace-making was the point of the encyclical, and that required "a mutual assessment of the arguments and feelings on both sides, a mature and objective investigation of the situation, and an equitable reconciliation of opposing views."[425]

John Paul II now wished to expand upon this text in light of the rising threat of Middle Eastern conflict. His predecessor, the Pope explained, had understood the common good to embrace not only nations but the entire

418 Beth Schuster, "World Has Edgy Little Christmas," *Los Angeles Times* December 26, 2002.

419 Urbi et Orbi Message of His Holiness Pope John Paul II, December 25, 2002, no. 4.

420 "Pope Urges End to War and 'Spiral of Violence,'" *Daily Telegraph*, December 26, 2002; Frances D'Emilio, "Pope Deplores 'Senseless Spiral of Blind Violence:' Thousands Hear Pontiff's Plea for Peace," *Calgary Herald*, December 26, 2002.

421 Pacem in Terris: A Permanent Commitment. Message of his Holiness Pope John Paul II, for the Celebration of the World Day of Peace, January 1, 2003.

422 Drew Christiansen, "A Vision of Peace: How the Prophetic 'Pacem in Terris' Helped Change the World," *America*, March 27, 2013.

423 John XXIII, *Pacem in Terris*. See, for instance, no. 40 (workers should not "be subjected to arbitrary treatment"); no. 51 ("Women are gaining an increasing awareness of their natural dignity"); no. 54 ("The attainment of the common good is the sole reason for the existence of civil authorities").

424 *Id.*, nos. 92–93.

425 *Id.*, no. 93.

world.[426] And if that were the case, John Paul II went on, then international law and the United Nations both required reinvigoration. Human rights and an Augustinian conception of political order seemed like natural premises upon which to build.[427] And the matter was urgent. The Middle East had reached explosive temperatures, and he challenged "those in positions of responsibility [to] undergo a veritable revolution in the way they use power."[428] War, the Holy Father explained two weeks later, to the diplomatic corps posted to the Holy See, "is always a defeat for humanity."[429] If war must be fought, it is only "as the very last option and in accordance with very strict conditions."[430]

Having made his premises and preconditions clear, John Paul II next embarked on a course that would have been familiar to his predecessor Martin V. He engaged in intense, personal diplomacy with those who had the power of choosing war. On February 14, John Paul II met with Tariq Aziz, the Iraqi Foreign Minister, urging him to cooperate with the United Nations.[431] Four days later, on February 18, the Pope met with Kofi Annan, the Secretary General of the United Nations, and jointly they emphasized "the 'essential role of the United Nations at the present hour.'"[432] A few days later, on February 22, John Paul II met with Tony Blair, the British Prime Minister, in a meeting that was expected to be difficult.[433] Acting in apparent coordination with the Pope, the future Cardinal Wilton D. Gregory, then serving as President of the United States Conference of Catholic Bishops, issued a statement calling upon the United States government to "hear and heed the persistent pleas of Pope John Paul II."[434]

And, again, much like Martin V, John Paul II turned also to trusted cardinals to carry his message to the capital cities of the potential belligerents. To Saddam Hussein, John Paul II sent Cardinal Roger Etchegaray (1922–2019), a veteran and respected French Church leader. He had been General Secretary of

426 John Paul II, "Pacem in Terris: A Permanent Commitment," *supra*, no. 5.

427 *Id.*, no. 6.

428 *Id.*, no. 7.

429 Address of His Holiness John Paul II to the Diplomatic Corps, January 13, 2003, no. 4.

430 *Id.*

431 Victor L. Simpson, "Iraqi Official Gets an Audience with Pope, Hears Plea; the Pontiff Urged Deputy Prime Minister Tariq Aziz's Government to Comply With U.N. Demands," *Philadelphia Inquirer*, February 15, 2003.

432 "Pope Meets With Annan; Blair to Visit Next; Pontiff and the British Leader Are at Odds on the Issue of a Potential U.S.-Led War on Iraq," *Los Angeles Times*, February 19, 2003.

433 Stephen Bates, "Blair to Have Private Audience with Pope," *The Guardian*, February 19, 2003; Paddy Agnew, "Blair Set for Tough Talks with Pope," *The Irish Times*, February 22, 2003.

434 "Statement on Iraq from Bishop Gregory, February 26, 2003," United States Conference of Catholic Bishops, usccb.org/resources/statement-iraq-bishop-gregory-february-26-2003.

the French Episcopal Conference in the 1970s,[435] and special papal representative to Rwanda in the wake of that nation's genocide,[436] and to East Timor, during the period of that nation's transition to independence.[437] Cardinal Etchegaray later reported that he met with Saddam Hussein for ninety minutes and told the media that "'I am convinced that Saddam Hussein wants to avoid war.'"[438]

And to the United States, John Paul II sent Cardinal Pio Laghi (1922–2009). Laghi was a veteran diplomat. In the middle and latter 1970s, he had been the papal nuncio to Argentina,[439] and served as Apostolic Delegate and Pro-Nuncio to the United States for most of the 1980s.[440] Laghi was politically gifted. One author has noted: "His friends included Golda Meir, Mother Theresa, and George H.W. Bush."[441] His personal connections with the Bush family would come to play a role in his diplomatic outreach. In the 1990s, finally, he returned to Rome, serving at the Congregation for Catholic Education.[442] At points in the 1990s, he was considered *papabile* but was nearly 83 at the conclave following John Paul II's papacy, and was simply too advanced in years for serious consideration.[443]

John Paul II had written a personal letter to George W. Bush which he entrusted to Cardinal Laghi. The letter's contents have now been declassified, and they reveal little. John Paul II beseeched President Bush to listen to the words that Cardinal Laghi was to speak. The letter's message was, the Holy Father wrote, "'what lies in the depth of my heart for the good of all people.'"[444] The outreach to the President, in other words, was personal, friend to friend.[445] Cardinal Laghi and President Bush were asked to have a conversation about

---

435 Lucian N. Leustean, *The Ecumenical Movement and the Making of the European Community* (Oxford, UK, 2014), p. 108.

436 Philippe Denis, *The Genocide Against the Tutsi, and the Rwandan Churches: Between Grief and Denial* (Woodbridge, UK, 2022), p. 91.

437 John D'Arcy May, *"The Heaviest Blow:" The Catholic Church and the East Timor Issue* (Münster, 2004), p. 195.

438 "Vatican Backs Efforts to Prevent Iraq War, Disarm Saddam," *America*, March 3, 2003.

439 Jeffrey Klaiber, *The Church, Dictatorships, and Democracy in Latin America* (Eugene, OR) (reprint of 1998 edition), p. 14.

440 John L. Allen, Jr., "Vatican Diplomat, Pio Laghi, Dead at 86," *National Catholic Reporter*, January 12, 2009.

441 Luis Rosales and Danile Olivera, *Francis, a Pope for Our Time: The Definitive Biography* (Boca Raton, FL, 2013), p. 52.

442 "U.S. Papal Nuncio Gets Vatican Post," *Los Angeles Times*, April 14, 1990.

443 Peter Hebblethwaite, *Pope John Paul II and the Church* (Kansas City, MO, 1995), pp. 226–227.

444 Paul Moses, "Vatican Diplomacy and the Iraq War: Unheeded Warnings," *Commonweal*, January 13, 2020 (quoting Pope John Paul II).

445 Johanna Newman, "Pope's Emissary Meets With Bush, Calls War 'Unjust,'" *Los Angeles Times*, March 6, 2003.

peace. Their exchange was not meant to be memorialized in writing. It was, in other words, diplomatic, in all of the many nuances of that term. Beyond this simple insight, we are left to speculate.

Why such urgency on behalf of peace? We know from John Paul II's own writings that he viewed war with horror. His perspective was deeply colored by his own experience in wartime Poland, and his revulsion at war comes through clearly in a reflection he wrote on the occasion of the fiftieth anniversary of the commencement of World War II.[446] The war was a "murderous madness" which ought never to be repeated.[447]

In furtherance of his commitment to peace, the Italian jurist Ugo Colombo Sacco thus noted that John Paul II deliberately narrowed the grounds of just-war theory.[448] As Colombo Sacco read John Paul II, it became clear that "the supremacy of peace has to be pursued as a very precious good, if not the most precious good for mankind."[449] Wars of defense alone were permitted, and then only "as a last resort that requires the previous exhaustion of all diplomatic means available."[450]

Why this narrowing of the tradition? In addition to the youthful Karol Wojtyla's first-hand experience of war, Heinz-Gerhard Justenhoven adds a second deeply personal factor: the final peaceful resolution of the Cold War, in the years 1989 to 1991, taught John Paul II that concerted non-violent action not only prevented a potential nuclear holocaust between the superpowers, but brought about a just conclusion to what seemed like an insane and intractable stand-off.[451] If patient waiting, and persistent, but peaceful insistence on mutual respect and rights, succeeded not only in preventing nuclear war but achieving justice, then such a course seemed compelling now.

In the end, of course, we know that the war was not averted. We know also that no weapons of mass destruction were ever found in Iraq.[452] The War's very

---

446 Message of His Holiness John Paul II on the Occasion of the Fiftieth Anniversary of the Beginning of the Second World War (1989), no. 4 ("I personally witnessed this distressing reality").

447 *Id.*, no. 5.

448 Ugo Colombo Sacco, *John Paul II and World Politics: Twenty Years of Search for a New Approach, 1978–1998* (Leuven, 1999), pp. 47–50.

449 *Id.*, p. 47.

450 *Id.*

451 Heinz-Gerhard Justenhoven, "The Peace Ethics of Pope John Paul II," *University of St. Thomas Law Journal* 3 (2005), pp. 110, 120.

452 J.D. Maddox, "The Day I Realized I Would Never Find Weapons of Mass Destruction in Iraq," *New York Times*, January 29, 2020; Nomaan Merchant, "Iraq WMD Failures Shadow US Intelligence 20 Years Later," *AP*, March 23, 2023, apnews.com/article/iraq-war-wmds-us-intelligence-f9e21ac59d3a0470d9bfcc83544d706e.

premise and pretext were unsound. And we know, finally, that the Iraq War proved immensely costly.

Brown University maintains a website called "The Costs of War Project," which has done substantial scholarship on the grave human and economic toll of American Middle Eastern wars, particularly the War in Iraq. One can find on that website articles such as the one by David Vine and a group of co-authors which notes that "[b]y 2007, more than 4.7 million [Iraqis] were living in displacement as [internally displaced persons] and refugees or asylum seekers outside the country."[453] Or the article by Neta Crawford that estimates the ultimate financial cost of the Iraqi intervention to amount to over two and a half trillion dollars by 2050, when factoring in "the costs of future U.S. veterans medical and disability care."[454] Or, finally, the article by Stephanie Savell that takes account of the destruction of Iraqi infrastructure by the inevitable grinding of the gears of war – of "[h]ospitals, clinics, and medical supplies, water and sanitation systems, electricity, roads and traffic signals, infrastructure for farming and shipping goods, and much more" – to conclude that the indirect death toll may number in the millions.[455]

St. John Paul II had the foresight and the wisdom to fear precisely this sort of outcome and, furthermore, the gift of imagining an alternative world where none of this death and destruction need have occurred. Would that he had been heeded!

3.6.3 Pope Francis

3.6.3.1 *Personalistic Peacemaking*

Pope Francis, finally, has also engaged in fruitful acts of diplomacy. In his address to the United Nations' General Assembly, in September, 2015, Francis encouraged the world's representatives to make use of "the uncontested rule of law and tireless recourse to negotiation, mediation, and arbitration" to resolve conflict.[456] In conflict zones throughout the world, Francis declared,

453 David Vine, et al., "Creating Refugees: Displacement Caused by the United States' Post-9/11 Wars," Watson Institute International and Public Affairs, Brown University, September 21, 2020, p. 14.

454 Neta C. Crawford, "Blood and Treasure: United States Budgetary Costs and Human Costs of 20 Years of War in Iraq and Syria, 2003–2023," Watson Institute International and Public Affairs, Brown University, March 15, 2023, p. 1.

455 Stephanie Savell, "How Death Outlives War: The Reverberating Impact of the Post-9/11 Wars on Human Health," Watson Institute International and Public Affairs, Brown University, May 15, 2023.

456 "Address of His Holiness Pope Francis to the General Assembly of the United Nations," September 25, 2015, http://holyseemission.org/contents/statement/56054736193b87.20279259.php.

"real human beings [must] take precedence over partisan interests, however legitimate the latter may be."[457] In other venues, Pope Francis has stressed that central to peacemaking is "solidarity" with the "marginalized" and the vulnerable.[458] His vision of peacemaking, in other words, is personalistic in its focus, recognizing, of course, the necessity of dealing diplomatically with nation-states, but never losing sight that peace must begin with bringing aid and comfort to the victims of violence.

3.6.3.2 *Early Commitment to South Sudan*

Personalism – a commitment to always remember that it is innocent individuals who bear the brunt of state violence – has guided Pope Francis through a long series of diplomatic involvements across the world.[459] But if a commitment to the protection of vulnerable persons has been a steady guidepost for Pope Francis, it is also true that he has engaged in more classic forms of diplomatic activity. Thus, for instance, he helped to negotiate a thaw in the relations between the United States and Cuba in the latter stages of Barack Obama's presidency,[460] and was among the moral voices calling for a non-violent resolution to the American stand-off with the nation of Syria in 2013.[461] But let us focus on one initiative in particular, and that is Pope Francis' efforts to resolve the civil war that gripped the nation of South Sudan from 2013 to 2020 and that continues to simmer at reduced levels of violence even to the time of writing.

Geographically, South Sudan is situated on the African Continent, barely north of the Equator. "Roughly the same size as France and a little smaller than Texas ... South Sudan's climate is tropical, with high humidity and significant rainfall."[462] Politically, South Sudan is the world's newest nation-state, having gained its independence from Sudan in 2011.[463] Independence was hard-won.

---

457 *Id.*

458 "Urbi et Orbi Message of Pope Francis," December 25, 2022.

459 Thomas J. Massaro, "The First Jesuit Pope: The Contribution of His Jesuit Charism to His Political Views," in Alynna J. Lyon, et al., eds., *Pope Francis as a Global Actor: Where Politics and Theology Meet* (New York, 2018), pp. 41, 52; John L. Allen, Jr., "Resilient Pope Presides Over a Decidedly Multilateral Holy Week," *Crux*, April 10, 2023, cruxnow.com /vatican/2023/04/resilient-pope-presides-over-a-decidedly-multilateral-holy-week.

460 John Hooper, "Pope Francis and the Vatican Played Key Roles in U.S.-Cuba Thaw, Leaders Reveal," *The Guardian*, December 17, 2014; Dan Roberts and Rory Carroll, "Obama and Raúl Castro Thank Pope for Breakthrough in U.S.-Cuba Relations," *The Guardian*, December 17, 2014.

461 Charles J. Reid, Jr., "'War Begets War, Violence Begets Violence,'" *Huffington Post* September 4, 2013; Charles J. Reid, Jr., "The Modern Papacy and War," *Huffington Post*, April 13, 2015.

462 Sophie and Max Lovell-Hoare, *South Sudan: The Bradt Travel Guide* (Guilford, CT, 2013), p. 3.

463 Jeffrey Gettleman, "Newest Nation Is Full of Hope and Problems," *New York Times*, July 8, 2011; Jeffrey Gettleman, "Struggle Over, Independent South Sudan Rejoices," *New York Times*, July 10, 2011; and Matt Flegenheimer, "Pride Is Tinged With Sadness as a Nation Is Born," *New York Times*, July 13, 2011.

It was finally acknowledged through democratic means – being approved by referendum.[464]

This political solution, however, came at the end of a long period of bloodshed that stretched back into the nineteenth century and continued intermittently into the early twenty-first.[465] This outcome reflected long-standing cultural and religious differences between a predominantly Islamic north and a southern region whose predominant religious commitments are either indigenous or Christian.[466] Catholics make up the largest portion of those who are Christian.[467]

Almost immediately after gaining independence, however, South Sudan fell into factionalism, civil war, and strife, driven by a mix of tribalism, religion, and the raw desire for plunder.[468] The president of South Sudan, Salva Kiir, was a member of the Dinka tribe, while his principal rivals belonged to the Nuer, and these differences contributed to the fighting.[469] A number of pitched battles were waged,[470] but fighting also took the form of spreading, metastasizing civil strife that by 2018 had left an estimated 383,000 dead.[471]

Urged on by the religious leaders of South Sudan and other regions,[472] Pope Francis committed the resources of the Holy See to ending this conflict. The story of this Papal odyssey is less one of a single, smashing success than slow, persistent, patient perseverance that has extended over nearly the entire

464 Darin E.W. Johnson, "Revolution, Peace, and Justice in Sudan," *University of Pennsylvania Journal of International Law* 43 (2021), pp. 187, 225.

465 Douglas H. Johnson, *The Root Causes of Sudan's Civil Wars: Old Wars and New Wars*, expanded 3d ed. (Woodbridge, UK, 2016), pp. 4–7; Randolph Martin, "Sudan's Perfect War," *Foreign Affairs* 81 (March/April, 2002), pp. 111, 120–121; and Carolyn Fluehr-Lobban, "Protracted Civil War in the Sudan – Its Future as a Multi-Religious, Multi-Ethnic State," *Fletcher Forum of World Affairs* 16 (1992), pp. 67–80.

466 William Narteh Gblerkpor and Kodzo Gavua, "South Sudan, Republic of," in Toyin Falola and Daniel Jean-Jacques, eds., *Africa: An Encyclopedia of Culture and Society* (Santa Barbara, 2016), vol. III, pp. 1128, 1132.

467 Jacqueline Wilson, *The Religious Landscape in South Sudan: Challenges and Opportunities for Engagement* (Washington, DC, 2019) (United States Institute of Peace), p. 5.

468 Jason K. Stearns, "Rebels Without a Cause: The New Face of African Warfare," *Foreign Affairs* 101 (2022), pp. 143, 149–150; Alex de Waal, "When Kleptocracy Becomes Insolvent: Brute Causes of the Civil War in South Sudan," *African Affairs* 113 (2014), pp. 347–369.

469 Reem Omer, "South Sudan: From Independence to a Detrimental Civil War," *Harvard International Review* 37 (2016), pp. 11–12.

470 See, for example, Jacey Fortin and Josh Kron, "New Wave of Violence Ripples Across South Sudan's Capital," *New York Times*, July 11, 2016; Jacey Fortin and Josh Kron, "Factional Fighting Breaks Out in South Sudan's Capital," *New York Times*, July 9, 2016.

471 Megan Specia, "383,000 Estimated Death Toll in South Sudan's War," *New York Times*, September 27, 2018.

472 "Editorial: Saving South Sudan," *America*, February 3, 2014; "South Sudan at Crossroads Say Its Bishops," *Caritas*, February 4, 2014; Chris Herlinger, "Crisis Grips a Fragile New South Sudan," *National Catholic Reporter*, February 25, 2014.

length of Francis's pontificate. And while his efforts have not yielded an unambiguous triumph for diplomacy, one might be permitted cautious optimism that they may yet improve the situation.

Elected Pope in March, 2013, by the end of that year, South Sudan was already a focus of Francis's concern. In his very first Christmas message to the world, in December, 2013, Pope Francis prayed that God might "[f]oster social harmony in South Sudan, where current tensions have already caused too many victims and are threatening peaceful coexistence in that young state."[473] He followed this prayer of solidarity with a diplomatic initiative in early 2014.[474] In January of that year, the Apostolic Nuncio for South Sudan – essentially, the Holy See's ambassador – conveyed the message that South Sudanese "political leaders" must "resolve their differences through dialogue."[475] In February, 2014, Francis met at the Vatican with a leader of South Sudan's ruling party,[476] and in March he dispatched a leading African Church leader – Peter Cardinal Turkson – to mediate peace efforts.[477] At Easter, 2014, the Pope prayed again for South Sudan,[478] while strategically-timed news stories highlighted the necessity of urgent action.[479]

Pope Francis continued his involvement in 2015. In September of that year he met with Archbishop Paulino Lukudo Loro, of Juba, the South Sudanese capital.[480] Two months later, in November, Pope Francis met with Salva Kiir, the South Sudanese president, in Entebbe, in Uganda, on a papal trip to that nation.[481] The Pope kept up these efforts the following year, meeting with the

---

473 "Urbi et Orbi Message of Pope Francis," December 25, 2013.

474 "Address of His Holiness Pope Francis to the Members of the Diplomatic Corps Accredited to the Holy See," January 13, 2014 ("recall[ing] in particular the establishment of diplomatic relations with South Sudan").

475 "Pope Calls For Peace in South Sudan," *Catholic Radio Network*, January 21, 2014, catholicradionetwork.org/2014/01/21/pope-calls-for-peace-in-south-sudan/.

476 "Pope Calls for Peaceful End to S. Sudan Conflict," *Sudan Tribune*, February 11, 2014.

477 "Cardinal Turkson Brings Pope's Good Wishes to South Sudan," *Catholic Radio Network*, March 18, 2014, catholicradionetwork.org/2014/03/18/cardinal-turkson-brings-popes-good-wishes-to-south-sudan/.

478 "Urbi et Orbi Message of Pope Francis," April 20, 2014 ("we beg for an end to … the acts of violence in South Sudan").

479 Paul Jeffrey, "Bishop: South Sudan Has Become 'the Place Where God Weeps,'" *National Catholic Reporter*, April 23, 2014; Adelaide Mena, "Churches Critical to Development of South Sudan," *National Catholic Reporter*, March 6, 2014.

480 "The Archbishop of Juba Will Inform Pope Francis on the Situation in his Country," *agenzia fides* (Information Service of the Pontifical Mission Societies), fides.org/en/news/38397-AFRICA_SOUTH_SUDAN_The_Archbishop_of_Juba_will_inform_Pope_Francis_on_the_situ-ation_in_his_country.

481 Harriet Sherwood and Alon Mwesigwa, "Pope Francis Uses Mass in Uganda to Preach Reconciliation and Peace," *The Guardian*, November 28, 2015; "Pope Francis Receives Rousing Welcome In Uganda," *Nation* (Kenya), November 28, 2015.

bishops of South Sudan in January, 2016,[482] and once again sending Cardinal Turkson to that troubled country.[483] In October, a breakthrough seemed imminent, when Pope Francis accepted an invitation to visit South Sudan.[484] Alas, no breakthrough occurred, and the visit had to be postponed.[485]

But even if a papal visit had to be deferred, Pope Francis renewed yet again in 2017 and in 2018 his long journey for peace in South Sudan. He forwarded financial assistance,[486] he hosted meetings at the Vatican,[487] and he established a Vatican consulate in South Sudan.[488]

3.6.3.3 *Vatican Negotiations, 2019*

In April, 2019, Pope Francis brought Salva Kiir to the Vatican, together with his principal rival, Riek Machar, leader of the Nuer tribe, and the nation's new vice-president designate. The purpose was a spiritual retreat.[489] CNN reported what occurred at its conclusion: "Pope Francis has broken with papal protocol by kneeling to kiss the feet of South Sudan leaders at the Vatican."[490] President Kiir was especially shocked. Responding to the Pope's gesture, he said, "'It was

---

482 Peter Kenney, "Pope Francis Meets Sudan Bishops as UN Documents Atrocities in the South," *ecunews.com*, ecumenicalnews.com/article/pope-francis-meets-sudan-bishops-as-un-documents-atrocities-in-the-south/37685.htm; "Pope Francis Blesses South Sudan and Sudan, Says Bishop Loku," *Catholic Radio Network*, January 26, 2016, catholicradionetwork.org/2016/01/26/pope-francis-blesses-south-sudan-and-sudan-says-bishop-loku/.

483 "Pope's Envoy in South Sudan in Pursuit of Peace-Building," *Vatican Radio*, July 21, 2016, www.archivioradiovaticana.va/storico/2016/07/21/popes_envoy_in_south_sudan_in_pursuit_of_peace-building_/en-1245851; Tito Justin, "Vatican Envoy Urges South Sudan Peace," *Voice of America*, July 19, 2016, www.voaafrica.com/a/vatican-envoy-urges-south-sudan-peace/3426134.html.

484 Inés San Martin, "Top Christians in South Sudan Urge Pope To Visit to Foster Peace," *Crux*, October 29, 2016; "Pope Francis Accepts Church Leaders' Invitation to Visit South Sudan," *Reuters*, October 27, 2016.

485 Lorna Donlon, "South Sudan Visit With Pope Francis 'Not Cancelled' But Postponed Until It Can Best Effect Peace, Says Welby," *The Tablet*, June 1, 2017.

486 Ismail Akwei, "Pope Francis Donates Over $500,000 to South Sudan After Failed Visit," *Africanews*, June 22, 2017, africanews.com/2017/06/22/pope-francis-donates-over-500k-to-south-sudan-after-failed-visit//.

487 Junno Arocho Esteves, "War and Greed: Rome Events Shed Light on Conflict in South Sudan, Congo," *National Catholic Reporter*, November 21, 2017.

488 "Juba Welcomes Establishment of Vatican Consulate in South Sudan," *Catholic Radio Network*, June 12, 2018, catholicradionetwork.org/2018/06/12/juba-welcomes-establishment-of-vatican-consulate-in-south-sudan/.

489 Giada Aquilino, "Spiritual Retreat With South Sudan Leaders in Vatican: Time to Choose Life," *Vatican News*, April 11, 2019, vaticannews.va/en/vatican-city/news/2019-04/spiritual-retreat-south-sudan-leaders-vatican-choose-life.html.

490 Delia Gallagher and Emily Dixon, "Pope Francis Kisses Feet of Once-Rival Sudan Leaders," *CNN*, April 12, 2019.

a blessing and can be a curse if we play games with the lives of our people.'"[491] Andrea Tornielli, of the Vatican Dicastery for Communication, writing in the *Vatican News*, connected the Pope's gesture to the Pope's philosophy of peacemaking, which requires "reciprocal forgiveness."[492]

Was the Pope wise was to make this self-effacing gesture? Was it the right thing to do? Salva Kiir and Riek Machar are hardened men. In February, 2018, more than a year before Pope Francis knelt to kiss their feet, a report of the United Nations Commission on Human Rights identified and condemned numerous war crimes by military commanders and the troops under their command, and concluded that there was a "grave lack of accountability for gross human rights violations and serious violations of international law perpetrated by all parties."[493] Subsequent efforts to bring the perpetrators to justice have been abandoned,[494] and in 2022, fresh rounds of accusations were made against the South Sudanese leadership.[495]

In judging the Pope's actions, however, reference should be had to the principles he has established for peacemaking. He wished to avoid taking sides and he desired to alleviate misery on the ground. A successful peace, on this understanding, was to be measured in terms of lives not only saved but made secure against the scourges of war. With this goal in mind, Francis has continued to exert leadership in trying to broker a lasting peace in that troubled nation.[496] For sure, a critic might say that the Pope is being "played;" that conditions have not been made better; that human suffering is being prolonged; and that the

---

491 Paul Samusano, "Salva Kiir: 'I Trembled When the Pope Kissed Our Feet,'" *Vatican News*, May 16, 2019, vaticannews.va/en/africa/news/2019-05/salva-kiir-i-trembled-when-the-pope-kissed-our-feet.html. Kiir is described in a BBC profile as "[a] committed Christian" who "regularly speaks at the Roman Catholic cathedral in Juba." "Salva Kiir: South Sudan's President in a Cowboy Hat," *BBC News*, June 21, 2018.

492 Andrea Tornielli, "The Gesture of the Servant of the Servants of God," *Vatican News*, April 12, 2019, www.vaticannews.va/en/pope/news/2019-04/pope-francis-kisses-feet-leader-south-sudan-retreat-vatican.html.

493 Report of the Commission on Human Rights in South Sudan, United Nations General Assembly, February 23, 2018, A/HRC/37/71, p. 15.

494 Robbie Gramer, "U.S. Quietly Gives Up on South Sudan War Crimes Court," *Foreign Policy*, July 20, 2021.

495 "Statement by Yasmin Sooka, Chair of the Commission on Human Rights in South Sudan, to the Human Rights Council," March 18, 2022, ohchr.org/en/statement-yasmin-sooka-chair-commission-human-rights-south-sudan-human-rights.

496 At Christmas, 2019, Pope Francis and two other world religious figures, Justin Welby, Archbishop of Canterbury and head of the Anglican Church, and John Chalmers, a leader in the Church of Scotland, issued a joint statement urging the South Sudanese leadership "to maintain a pledge to form a coalition government." "Pope Francis' Christmas Day Message: Hope in the Darkness," *Washington Post*, December 25, 2019.

guilty remain unpunished. But the retort comes back: What is the alternative? Surrender to the forces of darkness and despair? Even Pope Francis, however, has conceded that the conflict continues on the ground.[497]

3.6.3.4 *Papal Pilgrimage, February, 2023*

Still, with an abundance of hope, Pope Francis journeyed to South Sudan at beginning of February, 2023.[498] It was an expedition, the Pope surely knew, that carried diplomatic and even some personal risk. Strife, tension, and violence still percolated.[499] In December, 2022, a Human Rights Watch report indicated that even though the new national unity government had succeeded in keeping the peace in many places, "wartime abuses are raging unabated in some states."[500] Reuters added that killings were ongoing, and that the numbers of internally displaced persons remained an ongoing humanitarian calamity.[501] Hunger similarly continued to be an acute and growing crisis.[502] The political atmosphere remained troubled as well. Thus in the midst of this ongoing disintegration, President Salva Kiir had a group of journalists detained for broadcasting unflattering images of himself.[503]

---

497 Linda Bordoni and Nathan Morley, "Pope Francis Prays For Peace in South Sudan," *Vatican News*, December 11, 2022, vaticannews.va/en/pope/news/2022-12/pope-francis-appeal-prayers-peace;south-sudan.html.

498 Thus in his annual address to the diplomatic corps accredited to the Holy See, Pope Francis stated that his hope "for peace" and his willingness to "contribute to the process of national reconciliation." *Address of His Holiness Pope Francis to Members of the Diplomatic Corps Accredited to the Holy See*, January 9, 2023.

499 "Violence in South Sudan's Upper Nile Displaces 9,000 – U.N. Delegate," *Reuters*, December 7, 2022, reuters.com/world/africa/violence-south-sudans-upper-nile-displaces-9000-un-agencies-2022-12-07/; Deng Machol, "Explosion of Violence in South Sudan Threatens Peace Pact," *A.P. News*, July 18, 2022, apnews.com/article/pope-francis-africa-sudan-violence-race-and-ethnicity-da3703b03b97e053f912dcbfda9b1718.

500 Nyagoah Tut Pur, "Has South Sudan's Conflict Really Ended? Accountability for Conflict Related Abuses Key," *Human Rights Watch*, December 14, 2022, hrw.org.news/2022/12/14/has-south-sudans-conflict-really-ended.

501 "South Sudan Violence Has Killed 166 Civilians, Displaced Over 20,000 – U.N.," *Reuters*, December 14, 2022, reuters.com/world/africa/south-sudan-violence-has-killed-166-civilians-displaced-over-20000-un-2022-12-14/.

502 "People Eating Leaves to Survive in South Sudan as Aid Fails to Keep Pace with Spiralling Hunger Crisis – Oxfam," *Oxfam International*, December 1, 2022, oxfam.org/en/press-releases/people-eating-leaves-survive-south-sudan-aid-fails-keep-pace-spiralling-hunger; "Hunger and Malnutrition Being Driven by Climate Crisis and Conflict in South Sudan," *Unicef*, November 3, 2022, unicef/org/press-releases/hunger-and-malnutrition-being-driven-climate-crisis-and-conflict-south-sudan.

503 George Wright, "South Sudan: Journalists Held Over Film of President Appearing to Wet Himself," *BBC*, January 7, 2023, bbc.com/news/world-africa-64198312; Dipo Faloyin,

What in such a context, might a religious leader accomplish? In fact, Pope Francis had put a good deal of planning into his pilgrimage to South Sudan and had invited as traveling companions Justin Welby, the Archbishop of Canterbury, and Dr. Iain Greenshields, Moderator of the General Assembly of the Church of Scotland.[504] A well-sourced story in the *Vatican News*, published on the eve of the papal visit, acknowledged that there was still "much violence at a local level" and "'a very serious crisis going on,'" but asserted that even in the face of these ongoing emergencies, the intention was to bring hope to the suffering and the promise that harmony, reconciliation, and progress might triumph in the end.[505] Certainly, long suffering South Sudanese looked to the papal visit as a source of encouragement.[506] An Anglican archbishop working with Archbishop Welby added: "'This is a pilgrimage of peace. … Now is the moment of conversion.'"[507] Even so, news reports had it that 27 persons were killed in civil strife during the week of the Pope's visit.[508]

The ongoing violence surely heightened the gravity of the papal message. The Pope accentuated, forcefully and publicly, to the nation's political leadership the need to keep the peace.[509] At a speech at the presidential palace, with Salva Kiir and Riek Machar in attendance, the Pope declared: "'Leave the time of war behind and let a time of peace dawn.'"[510] The speech he delivered was rich in both history and hope. He recalled the praise the ancient Greek historian Herodotus heaped on the civilization of the Nile River, and summoned

"6 Journalists Arrested Over Video of South Sudan President 'Urinating on Himself,'" *Vice*, January 11, 2023, vice.com/en/article/dy7bp7/salva-kiir-south-sudan-journalists-arrested.

504 Lisa Zengarini, "Abp. Welby Asks for Prayers Ahead of Ecumenical Pilgrimate to South Sudan," *Vatican News*, January 30, 2023, vaticannews.va/en/church/news/2023-01-welby-asks-for-prayers-for-south-sudan-ahead-of-ecumenical-visit.html.

505 Joseph Tulloch and John Baptist Tumusiime, "'Great Sense of Hope' Ahead of Pope's Visit to South Sudan," *Vatican News*, January 28, 2023, vaticannews.va/en/pope/news/2023-01/pope-francis-solidarity-south-sudan-father-jim-greene-interview.html (quoting Fr. Jim Greene, Executive Director of Solidarity with South Sudan).

506 Tonny Onyulo, "'He Is the Only Hope We Have,' Say Refugees in South Sudan About Pope's Visit," *Detroit Catholic*, January 30, 2023.

507 Christopher White, "Pope Francis' Plea for Trip to Congo and South Sudan: No More Bloodshed," *National Catholic Reporter*, January 30, 2023 (quoting Archbishop Ian Ernest).

508 Nicole Winfield and Deng Machol, "Pope Heads to South Sudan to Urge Peace as Fighting Kills 27," *The Independent*, February 3, 2023.

509 Declan Walsh, et al., "In South Sudan, Pope Recounts Troubles of Young, Fractured Nation," *The New York Times*, February 4, 2023.

510 Christopher White, "Pope, Archbishop of Canterbury Beg For Peace in Historic Joint Visit to South Sudan," *National Catholic Reporter*, February 3, 2023.

his audience once again to aspire to those lofty heights.[511] He reminded South Sudan's leaders of their 2019 meeting at the Vatican, and chastised them: "No more bloodshed, no more conflicts, no more violence and mutual recriminations about who is responsible for it, no more leaving your people athirst for peace."[512] To the people of South Sudan, he held out hope for political reform: "The growth of a sound democracy is essential to the life of a Republic."[513] And in his message to the clergy, the Pope called for self-sacrificing courage.[514]

The Pope also met with refugees displaced by the violence. It has been estimated that at least one-third of the nation has been forced to flee their homes, either because of violence or because of natural catastrophe.[515] But Francis plainly wished to move beyond the abstractions that numbers and demographics represent. Thus, before speaking, Francis listened to a group of children describe their plight and then heard from human-rights representatives.[516] Addressing the refugees, he acknowledged the enormity of the crisis. "A country with the greatest enduring refugee crisis on the continent: at least four million children of this land are displaced; food insecurity and malnutrition affect two-thirds of the population."[517]

Still, the Pope wished to leave his audience with a sense of optimism, even in spite of the present bleakness: "I see you with empty hands but hearts full of faith. You bear the burden of a painful past, yet you never stop dreaming of a better future. In our meeting today, we would like to give wings to your hope."[518] He pledged his own continuing commitment and solidarity with the nation: "'I am here with you, and I suffer for you and with you.'"[519]

---

511 Pope Francis, "Meeting With Authorities, Civil Society and the Diplomatic Corps, Address of His Holiness," February 3, 2023, www.vatican.va/content/francesco/en/speeches/2023/february/documents/20230203-autorita-sudsudan.html.

512 *Id.*

513 *Id.*

514 Deborah Castellano Lubov, "Pope to South Sudan's Clergy: We Need Courageous Souls Ready to Die for Africa," *Vatican News*, February 4, 2023, vaticannews.va/en/pope/news/2023-02/pope-francis-departs-the-democratic-republic-of-congo11.html.

515 Chico Harlan and Katharine Houreld, "'Pope Francis Tells Leaders of Troubled South Sudan: 'Enough!'" *Washington Post*, February 3, 2023.

516 Lisa Zengarini, "Pope to Displaced South Sudanese: Be Seeds of Hope and Rebirth," *Vatican News*, February 4, 2023, vaticannews.va/en/pope/news/2023-2/pope-to-south-sudanese-idps-be-seeds-of-hope-for-peace.html.

517 Address of His Holiness (Pope Francis) (Meeting With Internally Displaced Persons), February 4, 2023.

518 *Id.*

519 Jason Horowitz and Declan Walsh, "Hopes For Peace in South Sudan Are Pinned on a Papal Visit," *The New York Times*, February 4, 2023, p. A11.

Pope Francis also made it an emphasis to address the women of South Sudan.[520] Horrific accounts of sexual violence have been documented in South Sudan,[521] and once again Francis wished to instill hope.[522] Speaking to the general public, the Pope declared: "Please, protect, respect, appreciate, and honor every woman, every girl, young woman, mother, and grandmother. … Otherwise there will be no future."[523] This much, the Pope reminded his listeners, was the obligation of "every South Sudanese citizen."[524] Archbishop Welby and Reverend Greenshields made sure to reinforce the message.[525]

The purpose of the journey, Pope Francis reiterated, was reconciliation.[526] It was the reason the papal trip featured the ecumenical presence of other religious leaders.[527] "'Even if our hearts bleed for the wrongs we have suffered, let us refuse, once and for all, to repay evil with evil,'" Francis declared at the final Mass he offered in South Sudan.[528] Elsewhere he said, summoning the political leadership to their responsibilities: "They [the people] need fathers, not overlords. They need steady steps towards development, not constant collapses."[529] In an ecumenical prayer, the pope pleaded for "a peace that integrates diversity and promotes unity in plurality."[530] In his airplane press conference on the way back to Rome, the Pope addressed the problem of tribalism: "There needs

520 Nicole Winfield and Deng Machol, "Pope Encourages South Sudanese, Will Raise the Plight of Women," *The Independent*, February 4, 2023.

521 Commission on Human Rights in South Sudan "Conflict-Related Sexual Violence Against Women and Girls in South Sudan," Human Rights Council, United Nations, March 21, 2022, ohchr.org/sites/default/files/2022-03/A_HRC_49_CRP_4.pdf.

522 Philip Pulella, "Protect, Advance Women For a Better South Sudan, Pope Says," *Reuters*, February 4, 2023, reuters.com/world/africa/protect-advance-women-better-south-sudan-pope-says-2023-02-04.

523 Winfield and Machol, "Pope Encourages South Sudanese," *supra*.

524 Elise Ann Allen, "Church Encourages Women in South Sudan to Break Through Cultural Barriers," *Crux*, February 6, 2023, cruxnow.com/pope-in-south-sudan-congo/2023/02/church-encourages-women-in-south-sudan-to-break-through-cultural-barriers.

525 Linda Bordoni, "Ecumenical Leaders to South Sudan's Rulers: Peace Is In Your Hands," *Vatican News*, February 3, 2023, vaticannews.va/en/church/news/2023-02/ecumenical-pilgrimage-peace-south-sudan-pope-welby-greenshields.html.

526 Christopher White, "Francis Urges Divided South Sudan Christians to Reject Tribalism, Embrace Nonviolence," *National Catholic Reporter*, February 4, 2023.

527 John Baptist Tumusiime, "Pope Francis Concludes Ecumenical Visit to South Sudan," *Vatican News*, February 6, 2023, vaticannews.va/en/africa/news/2023-02/pope-francis-concludes-ecumenical-visit-to-south-sudan.html.

528 Nicole Winfield and Deng Machol, "Pope Makes Final Bid for Peace, Forgiveness in South Sudan," *The Independent*, February 5, 2023.

529 Oliver Browning, "Pope Francis Meets With People Displaced by Conflict in South Sudan," *The Independent*, February 4, 2023.

530 Pope Francis, "Ecumenical Prayer," February 4, 2023, www.vatican.va/content/francesco/en/speeches/2023/february/documents/20230204-preghieraecumenica-sudsudan.html.

to be dialogue between the different tribes."[531] Unity, harmony, rapprochement, cooperation, consensus – these were the papal goals, and they could be summarized in that single elusive word, "peace."

Several days after returning to Rome, Francis reflected at a general audience on what he thought his mission accomplished: "together with dignity, all together, and with mutual respect, together in the name of Christ, our hope, to go forward. Do not exploit; go forth together."[532]

One is struck at how different Pope Francis' diplomacy is from that of his predecessors. Leo XIII had been asked by heads of state to resolve their disputes. Benedict XV, in contrast, responded to the global crisis of the First World War, but did so primarily by appealing to heads of state. John Paul II's diplomacy, in contrast, bears resemblances both to Leo's negotiated settlement of a dispute between nations, but also resembles Benedict XV's repeated appeals to the combatants to end the fratricide of World War I. Still, John Paul's diplomacy took on a traditional form. He dealt with fully-recognized sovereigns and their duly authorized representatives.

Pope Francis, in contrast at least to Leo XIII and John Paul II, took the initiative to resolve a crisis of seemingly interminable, intractable violence in a tribal state that had only recently gained its independence through a prolonged and violent civil war. The situation thus called for an unconventional response. What stands out about Francis' attempt at peace-making has been its comprehensiveness, its tenacity, and its inventiveness. The Pope clearly has an end in mind, and that is a nation living in unity and peace, with sufficient stability to feed itself, and ensure its basic needs, and enough transparency and respect for norms to shield and shelter the operation of at least minimal standards of democracy. Francis must know that these goals will not come easily. Indeed, he is surely aware that they are unlikely to be accomplished during his pontificate. So the goal must also be to set South Sudan on a hopeful trajectory towards a better, more untroubled future. It is, in other words, alternative dispute resolution as process – determined, indefatigable, invincible process.

531 Pope Francis, "In-Flight Press Conference," February 5, 2023, www.vatican.va/content/francesco/en/speeches/2023/february/documents/20230205-voloritorno-sudsudan.html.

532 Pope Francis, "General Audience," February 8, 2023, www.vatican.va/content/francesco/en/audiences/2023/documents/20230208-udienza-generale.html.

Part 4: Alternative Dispute Resolution and the 1917 Code of Canon Law

4.1 *Codification and the Spirit of Nineteenth-Century European Law*

We shall now shift our focus away from the Holy See as global mediator. We turn next to the use of arbitration and mediation as a means of resolving litigation between private parties under the Code of Canon Law that was in effect from 1917 to 1983.

A brief word of explanation is in order at this point because it is not at all intuitive that the law of the Catholic Church should have been reduced to codification.

To comprehend why the Catholic Church codified its law it is necessary to begin with an understanding of the historical movements that drove the larger codification movement that swept so much of the world – not only in Europe, but even in parts of the United States.[533] The first was simply the temper of the times. Codification began in France at the end of the eighteenth century in the aftermath of a Revolution that sought to ground the legal order not in revealed texts or in traditional precepts, but in "the general will" of the people and "the common good" of society.[534]

French law had been local, provincial, particular, historically contingent, honeycombed with special privileges and immunities.[535] To those not trained in the legal profession, it had become indecipherable, if not irrational. There should be a better reason for a rule than that it was handed down in a royal grant or some local concession. There was thus a felt imperative to create a body of law that "should be clear"[536] and "complete in its field."[537] The Enlightenment had discredited the old legal order, but simultaneously promised to bring illumination to a dusk-enshrouded world.[538] That was the case as much with law as with politics or philosophy.[539]

---

533 Wienczyslaw Wagner, "Codification of Law in Europe and the Codification Movement in the Middle of the Nineteenth Century in the United States," *Saint Louis University Law Journal* 2 (1953), pp. 335, 340–346.

534 Tamar Herzog, *A Short History of European Law: The Last Two and a Half Millennia* (Cambridge, MA, 2018), p. 185 ("general will" and "common good"); and pp. 208–211 (the creation of the French Code).

535 Rodolfo Batiza, "Origins of Modern Codification of the Civil Law: The French Experience and Its Implications for Louisiana," *Tulane Law Review* 56 (1981/1982), pp. 477, 482–483.

536 André Tunc, "Grand Outlines of the Code Napoleon," *Tulane Law Review* 29 (1954/1955), pp. 431, 434.

537 *Id.*, p. 435.

538 Angelo Piero Sereni, "The Code and the Case Law," in Bernard Schwartz, ed., *The Code Napoleon and the Common-Law World* (New York, 1956), pp. 55, 57.

539 Rodolfo Batiza, "The French Revolution and Codification: Comment on the Enlightenment, the French Revolution, and the Napoleonic Code," *Valparaiso Law Review* 18 (1984),

Codification was the method devised to bring clarity from confusion.[540] It was intended as the application of reason to law.[541] It aimed to reduce the law to discernible, universally understood, readily applicable propositions, principles, and norms.[542] By codification, furthermore, was not meant the collection and collating of statutes, still less the assembling or digesting of cases. A codified body of law was meant to present "a rational and unifying logic."[543] The codifiers' task was thus to translate diffuse sources into the crystalline purity of reasoned, normative declarations "at the level of general principles or rules."[544]

An example of this process at work is the Civil Code's definition of "ownership" as "the right to use, enjoy, and dispose of property fully and freely, subject to the limits and conditions for doing so determined by law."[545] Compare this definition to the way American lawyers, when asked to define ownership, tend to mumble on about bundles of sticks, and the differences between the systems becomes clear.

The codification movement was also connected with the nationalism of the nineteenth century. "The ideal of a cohesive nation state was implicit in the scope of a civil code."[546] Over the course of the nineteenth century, most of the nation-states of Europe adopted civil codes, modeled in general outlines on the French original, but adapted to suit local needs.[547] And so the nations of Europe, one after another, codified their national laws. Napoleon himself speeded the process. Thus Napoleon "applied French codes in territories under French occupation, such as northern Italy, Belgium, the Netherlands, Luxembourg, Monaco, and several German polities."[548]

---

pp. 675–682; and Gunther A. Weiss, "The Enchantment of Codification in the Common-Law World," *Yale Journal of International Law* 25 (2000), pp. 435, 451–453.

540 Charles Sumner Lobingier, "Napoleon and His Code," *Harvard Law Review* 32 (1918/1919), pp. 114, 117–134.

541 Weiss, "Enchantment," *supra*, p. 452; H. Patrick Glenn, "The Grounding of Codification," *U.C. Davis Law Review* 31 (1998), pp. 765, 766, and note 4.

542 Lobingier, *supra*, p. 131.

543 Alain A. Levasseur, "Portalis and Pound: A Debate on 'Codification,'" *Louisiana Law Review* 81 (2021), pp. 1113, 1116.

544 Pierre Legrand, 'Strange Power of Words: Codification Situated," *Tulane European and Civil Law Forum* 9 (1994), pp. 1, 31.

545 I am here quoting the Quebec Civil Code, Article 947, which closely tracks the French Code Civil. See Alain A. Levasseur, "The Boundary of Property Rights: La Notion de Biens," *American Journal of Comparative Law* 54 (2006), pp. 145, 146, note 6.

546 Stephen Jacobson, "Law and Nationalism in Nineteenth-Century Europe: The Case of Catalonia in Historical Perspective," *Law and History Review* 20 (2002), pp. 307, 312.

547 Roscoe Pound, "The French Civil Code and the Spirit of Nineteenth Century Law," *Boston University Law Review* 35 (1955), pp. 77, 77.

548 Herzog, *Short History*, *supra*, p. 211.

Other states, outside of Napoleon's immediate orbit, also adopted codes of their own.[549] Thus it became the case "above and beyond what Napoleon himself aspired to achieve, that as the nineteenth century advanced, many members of elite groups around the globe came to view the French codes, most particularly the Civil Code, as useful instruments."[550] Finally, in 1900, Germany, much of whose legal academy had resisted codification for most of the nineteenth century,[551] adopted the *Bürgerliches Gesetzbuch*, its own codification of the civil law, making the circle complete as it were.[552]

Standing behind the codification movement was not only a commitment to Enlightenment ideals, and to the primacy of the nation-state, but finally also to the jurisprudential school of thought known as legal positivism. Rooted in the proposition that law consisted of the dictates of the sovereign power to the exclusion of all other sources,[553] legal positivism stood ready to give further justification to codification and to ensure that its assumptions be seen as self-evidently correct.[554]

Codification has, in recent times, been justly criticized. Its pretense to universal reason, critics contend, in reality cloaks political choices that are otherwise controversial. Thus Pierre Legrand has written that "a political agenda in favor of the universalization of law through codification may find that it can only achieve its goal by resorting to the effective denial of sites of contestation within itself."[555]

And if we were examining codification from the standpoint of speculative jurisprudence, or even from the perspective of the reform of the canon law, this would be a point well worth pursuing. But these are not our concerns. Rather,

549 Such as in Austria in 1811. Gert Brüggemeyer, "Constitutionalisation of Private Law: the German Perspective," in Tom Barkhuysen and Siewert Lindenbergh, eds., *Constitutionalisation of Private Law* (Leiden, 2006), pp. 59, 60.

550 Herzog, *Short History*, *supra*, p. 211.

551 H. Patrick Glenn, *The Cosmopolitan State* (Oxford, UK, 2013), p. 66.

552 Reinhard Zimmermann, "The German Civil Code and the Development of Private Law in Germany," *Oxford Comparative Law Forum* 1 (2006), at oulf.ac.uk.

553 Gerald J. Postema, "The British Tradition of Legal Positivism," in Torben Spaak and Patricia Mindus, eds., *The Cambridge Companion to Legal Positivism* (Cambridge, UK, 2021), pp. 176, 189–196.

554 René David and John E.C. Brierly, *Major Legal Systems in the World Today: An Introduction to the Comparative Study of Law*, 2d ed. (New York, 1978), pp. 62–63; and Guido Comparato, *Nationalism and Private Law In Europe* (Oxford, UK, 2014), pp. 71–74. Cf., Boaventura de Sousa Santos, *Toward a New Legal Common Sense: Law, Globalization, and Emancipation*, 3d ed. (Cambridge, UK, 2020), p. 101 (making the point that positivistic accounts of codified law as complete and exclusive statements of the law often failed in practice). *Id.*

555 Pierre Legrand, "Codification and the Politics of Exclusion: A Challenge for Comparativists," *U.C. Davis Law Review* 31 (1998), pp. 799, 800.

our focus is to resolve a paradox: how did it happen that the Catholic Church codified its law? Especially because so much about the Catholic Church and its canon law suggests that it should never have done so.

4.2 *The Codification Movement and the Canon Law*

4.2.1 The Paradox Stated

Thus history confronts us with an incongruity. It ought to be that the canon law of the Catholic Church should have been highly resistant to the codification movement. Canon law, after all, is the unfolding of tradition. It is the product not of reason alone, but the amalgam of reason and revelation (to be sure, accreted with some very particular and mundane rules). It is the flashing insights of popes and councils in a conversation spanning the ages. Codification was, in contrast, the product of a skeptical, secularizing commitment to Enlightenment principles. It was given impetus, after all, by that religious skeptic, Napoleon Bonaparte. That should have been enough, one would think, to taint, at least for Catholics, the whole idea of codification.

And, certainly, the nineteenth-century popes viewed themselves as implacable foes of Enlightenment – with its reason unaided by Revelation, and its commitment to a thorough-going secularism. One might consider Pope Gregory XVI (reigned 1831 to 1846) and his Encyclical *Mirari Vos*, published in 1832. About *Mirari Vos*, Fr. Charles Curran has written that it "well illustrates the Catholic Church's *intransigent* opposition to Enlightenment ideas."[556] One need only look at Gregory's language for confirmation of Fr. Curran's reading of the Encyclical. Concerning the Enlightenment, Pope Gregory wrote: "Depravity exults; science is impudent; liberty, dissolute. The holiness of the sacred is despised."[557]

If the nineteenth-century popes were enemies of the Enlightenment, it is also the case that Catholic jurisprudence, then and now, rejects the kind of legal positivism that informed the codification movement. Thus the International Theological Commission has written: "Under the pretext that every claim to possess an objective and universal truth would be the source of intolerance and violence ... a juridic positivism is espoused, which renounces any reference to an objective ontological criterion of what is just. In this perspective, the final horizon of law and the moral norm is the law in force, which is considered to be

556 Charles E. Curran, "Churches and Human Rights: From Hostility/Reluctance to Acceptability," in Charles E. Curran, ed., *Change in Official Catholic Moral Teachings* (New York, 2003), pp. 38, 39 (emphasis in original).

557 *Mirari Vos*, no. 5.

just by definition since it is the will of the legislator."[558] On the Catholic understanding of law, therefore, it is impossible for a code to capture the wholeness of the law, for the law stands over, above, and apart from the legislator and the legislative will. On the historical record, the codification movement drew inspiration from secularizing, rationalist tendencies current in nineteenth-century Europe. Why then? How then? Did the Catholic Church codify its law?

4.2.2 Codification Comes to the Catholic Church

To account for the triumph of the codification movement within the Catholic Church, plainly, recourse must be had not to philosophy, but to the contingencies of historical circumstance. One might begin with the First Vatican Council, convoked by Pope Pius IX. That Council did more than adopt the doctrine of papal infallibility. There was in the air of the Council a felt need for law reform. James Coriden has well captured the mood of the day.[559] Throughout early modernity, from the sixteenth century to the middle of the nineteenth, the Vatican had continued to publish a steady stream of laws but gave scant regard to their organization. "They were not systematically arranged; often they were listed in chronological order ... The canons had grown into a large thicket in which living and dead branches intertwined."[560]

This tangled mess of texts and sources required organization. And codification seemed like the best means of bringing order from chaos, since this was what was occurring in the nations of Europe. Bishops attending the First Vatican Council took a very practical view of matters. They needed to know the law. They thus insisted that an organized distillation of the law be produced – a text, like the French *Code Civil*, that could be comprehensible alike to expert canonists and to lonely pastors in the field.[561]

Paradoxically, this urgent desire to codify the canon law was lent further strength by the simmering nationalism of the latter nineteenth century. The characteristics of the nation-state, after all, included a particular people,

558 International Theological Commission, "In Search of a Universal Ethic: A New Look at the Natural Law" (2009), no. 7, *vatican/va/roman_cura/congregations/cfaith/cti_documents/rc_con_cfaith_doc20090520_legge_naturale_enhtml#4.3_From_natural_law_to_the_norm_of_natural_justice*.

559 James A. Coriden, *An Introduction to Canon Law*, rev. ed. (London, 2004), pp. 26–27.

560 *Id.*, p. 27.

561 Maurice van Stiphout, "On the Roles of the State and Canon Law in the Nineteenth and Early Twentieth Centuries," in Martin Schermeier, et al., eds., *De rebus divinis et humanis: Essays In Honour of Jan Hallebeek* (Göttingen, 2019), pp. 427, 439.

bound together by custom, culture, and a shared spirit, and governed by a single sovereign through its duly promulgated law.[562]

Canon lawyers looked at the Catholic Church through a similar lens. As early as the end of the sixteenth century, Catholic writers had been claiming that the Catholic Church shared the essential characteristics of the nation-state.[563] Thus Cardinal Robert Bellarmine (1542–1621) proposed that the Church should be understood as a nation. Like the nation, it was a *societas perfecta* ("perfect society") that contained within itself all of the attributes of a properly sovereign state – people, customs, culture, spirit, law, jurisdiction, enforcement – albeit, principally directed at supernatural ends.[564]

The latter nineteenth-century Catholic world was exceptionally well-prepared to receive this sort of teaching. In his history of Catholicism since the French Revolution, John McGreevy has detailed the ways in which the Church constructed its own universe of being, separate and apart from, but yet cognate with, developments in the nation-state.[565] As one reviewer has thus summarized McGreevy's findings, the Church throughout this age was busy "erecting ... a rigidly ordered parallel world set against unruly civil society."[566] "Autonomy," another commentator has noted, "is clearly the key notion."[567] "The idea is that both the Church and the State, each in its own order, are perfect societies."[568]

This model of Church as parallel nation-state became the backbone of a proposed constitution for the Church – to be known as *Supremi Pastoris* – that was debated at the First Vatican Council but had not yet been adopted

562 Frank Polzenhagen and René Dirven, "Rationalist or Romantic Model in Globalisation?" in Gite Kristiansen and René Dirven, eds., *Cognitive Sociolinguistics: Language Variation, Cultural Models, and Social Systems* (Berlin, 2008), pp. 237, 245.

563 Wim Decock, "Neo-Thomism, Law, and Society: A Prolegomenon to Further Study," in Wim Decock et al., eds., *Neo-Thomism in Action: Law and Society Reshaped by Neo-Scholastic Philosophy, 1880–1960* (Leiden, 2021), pp. 7, 18.

564 Ormond Rush, "Roman Catholic Ecclesiology From the Council of Trent to Vatican II and Beyond," in Paul Avis, ed., *The Oxford Handbook of Ecclesiology* (Oxford, UK, 2018), pp. 263, 266–267; Ormond Rush, *The Vision of Vatican II: Its Fundamental Principles* (Collegeville, MN, 2019), p. 82.

565 John T. McGreevy, *Catholicism: A Global History From the French Revolution to Pope Francis* (New York, 2022), pp. 85–89 and 104–106.

566 Paul Elie, "The Reinvention of the Catholic Church," *The Atlantic*, December 11, 2022 (January/February 2023 issue), theatlantic.com/magazine/archive/2023/01/catholic-church-changes-roe-v-wade-pope-francis/672235/.

567 Hildegard Warnink, "The Roman Catholic Church and Autonomy," in Hildegard Warnink, ed., *Legal Position of Churches and Church Autonomy* (Leuven, 2001), pp. 251, 253.

568 *Id.*

by the time Rome fell to the *Risorgimento*.[569] This vision of Church captured the imagination of a generation of Catholics who had come to look upon the papacy, battered and bruised though it was, as a font of justice and a guide to right action in the world.[570] It was only natural, therefore, for canonists imbued in this mode of thought to perceive codification as the appropriate expression of Church law, since the Church was like other nation-states, at least in the sense of being self-governing and self-sufficient, possessed of the attributes of sovereignty and international status, and an authoritative preceptor for human affairs.[571]

4.2.3 The Task and Accomplishment of Cardinal Pietro Gasparri

Adjourned in haste, the First Vatican Council did not take concrete action on the codification of canon law. But in 1904, in the *motu proprio Arduum sane munus*, Pope St. Pius X decreed that there should be produced and published an updated and comprehensive volume of law – "lucidly organized" (*lucido ordine digestae*) – and "adapted for the use of our own day" (*ad nostrorum temporum conditionem propius aptatis*).[572] Modernized, in other words, to fit the temper of the times. And that meant codified.[573] The express language of *Arduum sane munus*, furthermore, specified that this task should be entrusted to Pietro Cardinal Gasparri (1852–1934), papal lawyer and diplomat, who should preside over a commission formed for this assignment.[574]

Gasparri's nomination, then, leads us to the final impelling circumstance that drove the codification process – and that is the personality of Cardinal Gasparri, who combined in the same individual a keen legal imagination, profound diplomatic skill, and an inexhaustible capacity for hard work.[575] Indeed, Gasparri's career almost perfectly bridged the worlds of the academy and the statesman. He was the author of three path-breaking treatises – *De*

---

569 Patrick Granfield, "The Church as *Societas Perfecta* in the Schemata of Vatican I," *Church History* 48 (1979), pp. 431–446.

570 Peter Raedts, "The Church as Nation State: A New Look at Ultramontane Catholicism (1850–1900)," *Dutch Review of Church History* 84 (2004), pp. 476, 485.

571 René Metz, "Pouvoir, centralisation, et droit: La codification du droit de l'Église catholique au début du XXe siècle," *Archives de sciences sociales des religions* 26 (1981), pp. 49, 55.

572 Pius X, *Arduum sane munus*, *Acta Sanctae Sedis* 36 (1904), pp. 549, 551.

573 Libero Gerosa, *Canon Law* (New York, 2002), p. 52; and James E. Risk, "*Arduum Sane Munus*: A Retrospective," *Theological Studies* 5 (1944), pp. 184–197.

574 John T. Noonan, Jr., *Power to Dissolve: Lawyers and Marriages in the Courts of the Roman Curia* (Cambridge, MA, 1972), p. 164.

575 Alberto Lupano, "Pietro Gasparri (1852–1934)," in Orazio Condarelli and Rafael Domingo, eds., *Law and the Christian Tradition in Italy: The Legacy of the Great Jurists* (London, 2021), pp. 348–361.

Matrimonio ("On Marriage");[576] *De Sacra Ordinatione* ("On Holy Orders");[577] and *De Sanctissima Eucharistia* ("On the Most Holy Eucharist").[578]

He was also Pope Benedict XV's Secretary of State during and after the First World War. Indeed, he worked closely with Benedict in crafting his peace proposal of the summer of 1917.[579] At a time when the military draft was leading to civil unrest in the United States,[580] Gasparri and Benedict asserted that the belligerent nations of World War I should abolish conscription.[581] He continued on as Secretary of State under Pope Pius XI and was responsible for negotiating the Lateran Treaty with Benito Mussolini,[582] by which the Italian government recognized the sovereignty of the Holy See and its status at international law.[583]

It was this very busy man who was also principally responsible for producing the first codification of canon law.[584] Stephan Kuttner has described his method of proceeding. Working with a body of consultants, Gasparri divided

576 Pietro Gasparri, *Tractatus canonicus de matrimonio* (Paris, 1904).

577 Pietro Gasparri, *Tractatus canonicus de sacra ordinatione* (Paris, 1893/1894).

578 Pietro Gasparri, *Tractatus canonicus de sanctissima Eucharistia* (Paris, 1897).

579 David Alvarez, *Spies at the Vatican: Espionage and Intrigue From Napoleon to the Holocaust* (Topeka, KS, 2002), pp. 110–111.

580 See, for instance, Scott H. Bennett and Charles F. Howlett, *Antiwar Dissent and Peace Activism in World War I America: A Documentary Reader* (Lincoln, NE, 2014), pp. 186–233; Jeanette Keith, *Rich Man's War, Poor Man's Fight: Race, Class, and Power in the Rural South During the First World War* (Chapel Hill, NC, 2004), pp. 173–204; J. Blake Perkins, *Hillbilly Hellraisers: Federal Power and Populist Defiance in the Ozarks* (Urbana, IL, 2017), pp. 67–96.

581 Blandine Chelini-Pont, "Papal Thought on Europe and the European Union in the Twentieth Century," in Lucian N. Leustean and John T.S. Madely, eds., *Religion, Politics, and Law in the European Union* (New York, 2010), pp. 125, 127; "Pope in New Note to Ban Conscription; Gasparri Decries Wilson Peace Plan; Allies Scoff at Berlin Professions," *New York Times*, September 23, 1917. Gasparri's and Benedict's opposition to conscription found a receptive audience in some Catholic enclaves. Thus Daniel Mannix (1864–1963), the redoubtable Archbishop of Melbourne spoke out repeatedly and harshly against conscription in Australia. See Madeleine Chiam, *International Law in Public Debate* (Cambridge, UK, 2021), pp. 162–163; Douglas E. Delaney, *The Imperial Army Project: Britain and the Land Forces of the Dominions and India, 1902–1945* (Oxford, 2018), p. 121.

582 Kurt Martens, "The Position of the Holy See and Vatican City State in International Relations," *University of Detroit Mercy Law Review* 83 (2006), pp. 729, 740–742; and John F. Pollard, *The Vatican and Italian Fascism, 1929–1932: A Study in Conflict* (Cambridge, UK, 1985), pp. 42–50.

583 Cedric Ryngaert, "The Legal Status of the Holy See," *Göttingen Journal of International Law* 3 (2011), pp. 829, 833–834; James A. Coriden, "Diplomatic Recognition of the Holy See," *Jurist* 48 (1988), pp. 483, 485; Lester Harris, "Recognition of the Holy See," *Dickinson Law Review* 55 (1950), pp. 235, 240.

584 John A. Alesandro, "One Hundred Years Since the 1917 Code of Canon Law," *Studia Canonica* 51 (2017), pp. 357, 367–370.

this assembly "into two groups or commissions."[585] "'Each commission was composed roughly of ten members.'"[586] They would meet at different times on different days, and this arrangement permitted Gasparri to preside at all of their meetings.[587] In collaboration with his consultants, and a larger congregation of cardinals, Gasparri also developed the organizational framework for the new code.[588]

It took Gasparri thirteen years from the date of his appointment to complete his task. By the Apostolic Constitution *Providentissima Mater Ecclesia*, on May 27, 1917, the lawyer-Pope Benedict XV promulgated the new Code of Canon Law, to take effect the following Pentecost Sunday, May 19, 1918.[589]

4.3 *The Promulgation of the 1917 Code of Canon Law*

Several prefatory documents were included with the Code of Canon Law when it finally went into effect in the spring of 1918. Two are of particular relevance. The first text, entitled simply *Praefatio*, connected the Code to the Church's long legal history. It began by noting that the Church had an ancient legal tradition that could be traced as early as the Council of Nicaea (325 CE), and that was continuous throughout the middle ages and early modern period. Gratian, the medieval popes, and such important early modern figures as Pope Benedict XIV (reigned 1740–1758) received prominent mention. Codification was something new. But Cardinal Gasparri, in authoring this text, wanted to make it seem as if it was simply a natural outgrowth of a living tradition that adapts itself seamlessly from age to age.[590]

Following the preface, there appeared Benedict XV's decree, *Providentissima Mater Ecclesiae*. Its language and ecclesiology were confrontational – of a piece with the *societas perfecta* thinking that had so dominated at the First Vatican Council. In vindication of its freedom, the Church, through its Popes and its Ecumenical Councils, had continued to exercise its proper and primordial right to legislate (*ius ferendarum legum proprium ac nativum*).[591] The exercise of this right, Benedict further informed readers, provided marvelous benefits not only to believers but to public welfare and civilization.[592] He duly

585 Stephan Kuttner, "The Code of Canon Law in Historical Perspective," *Jurist* 28 (1968), pp. 129, 135.

586 *Id.* (Quoting Gasparri).

587 *Id.*

588 *Id.*, p. 134.

589 John A. Abbo, "The Revision of the Code," *Jurist* 20 (1960), pp. 371, 371.

590 "Praefatio," in *Codex Iuris Canonici* (Westminster, MD, 1961), pp. xxi–xliii.

591 Benedict XV, *Providentissima Mater Ecclesia*, in *Codex Iuris Canonici*, *supra*, p. xlv.

592 *Id* ("rei publicae utilitatem civilemque cultum mirifice provexit").

acknowledged St. Pius X's role in establishing the commission that produced the Code.[593] He then "decreed and commanded" that the Code "have the force of law for the universal Church," and that it be preserved and safe-guarded with all vigilance.[594]

It is impossible not to read his pronouncement in the light of then-prevailing jurisprudence about sovereignty and law-giving. And that jurisprudence was positivistic in tone and temper.[595] To be sure, the Church remained the guardian and the guarantor of the natural law, and it continued to be bound by the precepts of Scripture and Tradition. But henceforward the Pope would also be known as the supreme legislator or law-giver with respect to the canon law.[596] Among canonists, this expression has in fact become a kind of short-hand. In classroom usage, in casual discussions about the law, canonists routinely speak of the "law-giver" when they have in mind the pope. A *societas perfecta* model of Church, it seems, required an unambiguously supreme law-giver and that source of law would become the Holy See.[597]

4.4 *The 1917 Code of Canon Law: A Descriptive Summary*

The 1917 Code itself consisted of five books. Book One is entitled "General Norms," and it defined the basic principles of law that should govern the Church. We learn there such basic principles as: laws should ordinarily be prospective, not retrospective in effect;[598] laws which impose a penalty or restrict rights should be strictly construed;[599] and "custom is the best interpreter of law."[600] This is the sort of stuff of Book One.

Book Two is entitled *De Personis* – "On Persons." It consisted of 639 canons, and was predominantly concerned with establishing the rules governing clerical or religious life. Only its final forty-four canons, cc. 682–725, entitled *De Laicis* addressed the laity. The laity, we discover in the opening canon, had the right to receive from clerics spiritual goods, most especially those needed

593 *Id.*, p. xlvi.

594 *Id.*, pp. xlviii ("vim legis posthac habere pro universa Ecclesia decernimus, iubemus, …").

595 See, for example, John Westlake, *International Law*, Part 1, *Peace* (Cambridge, UK, 1904), p. 6 (taking a rigorously positivistic view of the international order).

596 Monica-Elena Herghelegiu, *Reservatio Papalis: A Study on the Application of a Legal Prescription According to the 1983 Code of Canon Law* (Berlin, 2008), p. 66.

597 Perhaps it is not accidental that this period also witnessed the dramatic expansion of papal power over the dissolution of marriages "in favor of the faith." See Noonan, *Power to Dissolve*, pp. 368–378.

598 C. 10 (1917 Code).

599 C. 19 (1917 Code).

600 C. 29 (1917 Code).

for salvation.[601] Most of the canons that followed, however, were not focused on spelling out in any detail what these spiritual goods might be, but, rather, established the ground rules for the founding and governance of lay associations of the faithful.

Book Three, *De Rebus*, "On Things," contained 826 canons, and covered a great deal more than what we might associate with ownership or possession. Thus we find canons on the sacraments, such as marriage,[602] Holy Orders,[603] baptism,[604] and all of the others. The logic was that these are spiritual goods, as necessary to life as the material, tangible objects that we commonly group under a heading like "Things." Similarly, we find in Book Three canons on the teaching authority of the Church.[605] Only the final fifty-six canons address "The Temporal Goods of the Church."[606]

Book Four, *De Processibus*, "On Procedure," had 643 canons, and governed the judicial processes of the Church. Canon 1552, sec. 1, its first provision, began with a broad statement of jurisdictional competence: The Church, by right, possessed the authority to adjudicate matters in its ecclesiastical tribunals.[607] Canon 1552 went on in section 2 to declare that in appropriate circumstances Church tribunals might hear causes pertaining to private matters[608] or to crimes.[609] Subsequent canons defined such matters as who may be a judge,[610] who may take testimony,[611] the use of advocates,[612] and the right to appeal an adverse judgment.[613]

Book Five, finally, treated issues associated with criminal wrong-doing and contained 220 canons. Questions covered included the nature of criminal wrong-doing,[614] criminal states of mind, including aggravating and mitigating

601 C. 682 (1917 Code).
602 Cc. 1012–1143 (1917 Code).
603 Cc. 948–1011 (1917 Code).
604 Cc. 737–779 (1917 Code).
605 Cc. 1322–1408 (1917 Code).
606 Cc. 1495–1551 (1917 Code).
607 C. 1552 (1917 Code). ("Nomine iudicii ecclesiastici intelligitur controversiae in re de qua Ecclesia ius habet cognoscendi, coram tribunali ecclesiastico, legitima disceptatio et definitio."
608 C. 1552 sec. 2.1 (1917 Code) ("personarum physicarum vel moralium iura persequenda aut vindicanda, vel earundem personarum, facta iurdicia declaranda; et tunc iudicium est contentiosum").
609 C. 1552, sec. 2.2 (1917 Code).
610 Cc. 1574–1575 (1917 Code).
611 Cc. 1580–1584 (1917 Code).
612 Cc. 1655–1666 (1917 Code).
613 C. 1594 (1917 Code).
614 Cc. 2195–2198 (1917 Code).

circumstances,[615] types and kinds of punishment,[616] followed by types and kinds of offenses.[617]

4.5 *The Canons on Alternative Dispute Resolution*

It should be evident that the canons on procedures anticipated that the greatest part of an ecclesiastical tribunal's docket should be filled with contentious trials. Most of the discrete provisions of Book Four, *De Processibus*, envisioned an adversary process.

Deep within the interstices of Book Four, however, one finds Section II, Title XVIII, which was entitled *De modis evitandi iudicium contentiosum* – literally, "On the Means of Avoiding Contentious Judgment." Title XVIII was further subdivided into two chapters, the first of which was entitled *De Transactione* ("On Settlement"), and which consisted of four canons;[618] and the second of which was entitled *De compromisso in arbitros* ("On Compromise by Arbitrators"), and which similarly contained four canons.[619] We shall begin with *De Transactione*, "On Settlements."

4.6 De transactione (*"On Settlements"*) (*Canons 1925–1928*)

Law is language.[620] We should begin with that simple truism. The norms that the canon law prescribed for the Catholic Church were encased in a legal Latin that was both highly technical and very old. When the law-giver articulated particular rules in 1917, the language that was used was both deliberately chosen and came with a deep history. If we really wish to understand the norms governing alternative dispute resolution, then we must attend both to this deep history and the technical precision with which it was used. And if we do that, we shall learn that the law-giver carefully selected words and phrases that expressed a strong preference that disputes be settled, where possible, by non-contentious means.

Let us first focus on the word *transactio*. The Benedictine canonist Charles Augustine (1872–1943), translated this term as "compromise," and went on to state: "A compromise may be defined as the surrender of a supposed legal claim

615 Cc. 2199–2211 (1917 Code).
616 Cc. 2214–2313 (1917 Code).
617 Cc. 2314–2414 (1917 Code).
618 Cc. 1925–1928 (1917 Code).
619 Cc. 1929–1932 (1917 Code).
620 Harold J. Berman, *Law and Language: Effective Symbols of Community*, John Witte, Jr. ed. (Cambridge, UK, 2013), pp. 69–71.

by peaceful settlement and for a consideration."[621] His source for this definition was not canonical, but an American treatise on contract law,[622] Edward Avery Harriman's *The Law of Contracts*.[623]

Felix Capello (1879–1962), an Italian Jesuit canonist who taught at the Gregorian University in Rome for thirty-nine years,[624] and who wrote in Latin, offered the following: "Understood broadly, *transactio* is any kind of disposition or agreement by which a matter is settled between certain parties, whether to avoid or conclude litigation, or for other reasons."[625] Like Augustine, Capello considered settlements to be a kind of contract.[626]

I shall now examine in greater depth the canons that govern the creation and enforcement of settlements (*transactiones*). The most important of the four canons was *c.*1925, and that shall be a major focus of much of what follows. We might begin by reproducing first the Latin text of *c.*1925, followed by my own close English paraphrase.

*C.*1925, sec. 1: "Cum valde optandum, sit ut lites inter fideles evitentur, iudex exhortationes adhibeat, ut cum aliqua contentiosa controversia quae privatum eorum bonum respiciat, ei proponitur iudicii forma dirimenda, per transactionem, si qua concordiae spes affulgeat, lis componatur."[627]

*C.*1925, sec. 1: "Since it is a strong preference that litigation among the faithful be avoided, the judge is obliged to exhort the parties, where they are contending over some litigable controversy that bears on their private benefit, to abandon the judicial process and settle through mutual agreement their litigation where there is hope of peaceful resolution."

It is one thing to translate a text. But something more to understand it. And for appropriate understanding, it is just as important – especially when we are considering a legal text – to come to an appreciation of the word choices made by the legislator, in the legislator's own language. Hence, I would like to single out several key expressions from this text for closer inspection.

---

621 P. Charles Augustine, *A Commentary on the New Code of Canon Law*, 2d ed. (St. Louis, MO, 1923), vol. VII, p. 352.

622 *Id.*, p. 352, note 1.

623 Edward Avery Harriman, *The Law of Contracts*, 2d ed., rev. and enlarged (Boston, 1901), p. 59.

624 "March 25th: Servant of God (SG), Felix Maria Capello, S.J.," jesuit.org.sg/mar-felix-maria-capello-sj/.

625 "Sensu *lato*, transactio est quaelibet negotii compositio, seu pactio qua negotium inter certas personas componitur, sive ad litem vitandum aut finiendum, sive ob alias causas." Felix M. Capello, *Summa Iuris Canonici in Usum Scholarum* (Rome, 1940), vol. III, p. 248 (emphasis in original).

626 *Id.*

627 *C.*1925, sec. 1 (1917 Code).

4.6.1 *Valde optandum*

We should begin with the expression *valde optandum*, which I have translated as "strong preference." The *Oxford Latin Dictionary* defines the word "valde" as "vigorously," "powerfully," "with a powerful voice, or sound."[628] It is often used as an intensifier. Consider the following passage from Cicero: "*quicquid valde utile sit, id fieri honestum etiamsi antea non videretur.*"[629] Cicero is making a moral argument: "whatever is really, truly useful" may prove to be morally praiseworthy, even if this was not previously apparent. Cicero's choice of *valde* intensifies the claim – which I have chosen to intensify by my use of the expression, "really, truly." Still, there is an aspect of politeness to *valde*, in contrast with imperious insistence.[630] Its rhetorical style is that of warm, inviting encouragement.

Now what of *optandum*? Grammatically, it is a gerundive of obligation. It conveys a sense of "necessity."[631] *Optandum* is derived from the verb *opto, optare*, which means "to desire," "pray for."[632] We find an example of its use in Pliny the Younger's *Panegyricus*, his speech in praise of the Emperor Trajan. Pliny writes: "*maxime optandum, ut ea pro quibus aguntur principi gratiae multa sint.*"[633] "It is always most desirable that we have much gratitude for our prince."

Armed with this knowledge, we can penetrate more deeply the mind of the legislator. Yes, Book Four, the Book on Procedures, is filled with the regulatory detail required to ensure a fair trial. But what the legislator wants – really, truly desires – is the non-judicial settlement of contested matters.

4.6.2 *Contentiosa controversia*

I have translated this phrase as "litigable controversy." The adjective *contentiosa* is simply enough defined. One might consult the treatise of Arthur Vermeersch (1858–1936) and Joseph Creusen (1880–1960) as evidence of its usage.[634] There were, Vermeersch and Creusen asserted, two types of judicial proceeding at canon law: *contentiosum et criminale*, "contentious and criminal."[635] Tracking

628 P.G.W. Glare, ed., *Oxford Latin Dictionary* (Oxford, UK, 1982), p. 2005.

629 Cicero, *De Officiis*, Bk. III, 103.

630 Jon Hall, *Politeness and Politics in Cicero's Letters* (Oxford, UK, 2009), p. 201.

631 Henryk Hoffmann, *Latin In Modern Fiction: Who Says It's a Dead Language?* (Wilmington, DE, 2021), p. 85.

632 Glare, ed., *Oxford, supra*, p. 1260.

633 Pliny, *Panegyricus*, 25.1.

634 Arthur Vermeersch and Joseph Creusen, *Epitome Iuris Canonici cum Commentariis* (Rome, 1928).

635 *Id.*, vol. II, p. 2.

closely *c.*1552, the two authors went on to define the contentious lawsuit as involving all litigation that sought to challenge, claim, or declare legal rights.[636] A modern American lawyer would thus be on safe ground to conclude that the when the law-giver used *contentiosa* in connection with the extra-judicial settlement of disputes, he meant it to embrace every type of civil litigation.

The noun *controversia*, however, deserves closer, more sustained attention. The expression has its roots in Greek philosophical training, which demanded that aspiring practitioners learn to "speak[] for and against each side" of a case.[637] Cicero adapted this technique to his own purposes, using it to rhetorical advantage in both moral and legal argument.[638]

An especially important figure in the development of the meaning of this term of art is Seneca the Elder (ca. 54 BCE–ca. 39 CE). Who was Seneca? He was first a man of the provinces – "The Seneca family lived in Corduba … [in] southern Spain."[639] He spent portions of his young adulthood in Rome, but was in Spain between the years 8 BCE and 1 CE, where he enjoyed the births of his three sons. He was back in Rome for good by the year 5 CE.[640] His life, in other words, paralleled neatly the rise of the Roman oratorical and legal practices that would so deeply shape juristic Latin across the millennia.

He is also the author of the *Controversiae*, ten books of declamations, drawn from Roman courtroom practice. In his preface to Book I, Seneca offered his understanding of what the word *controversia* meant.[641] They were, Seneca averred, what Cicero called "*causae*" – exercises, yes, but of a specialized sort that implicated great questions of law and politics.[642] Seneca assembled his *Controversiae* to instruct his young sons in Roman forensics.[643] Seneca was not the only compiler of *controversiae*, though he was the first whose work

636 *Id.*, p. 3. Cf., c. 1552, sec. 2.1 (1917 Code) ("personarum physicarum, vel moralium iura persequenda aut vindicanda, vel earundem personarum facta iuridica declaranda").

637 Michael Mendelson, "*De Oratore* and the Development of *Controversia*," in Richard O. Brooks, ed., *Cicero and Modern Law* (New York, 2016), pp. 123, 128 (reprinted from Michael Mandelson, ed., *Many Sides: A Protagorean Approach to the Theory, Practice, and Pedagogy of Argument* (Dordrecht, the Netherlands, 2010), pp. 135–172, 269–270, 276–277. Cf., Michael Mendelson, "Everything Must Be Argued: Rhetorical Theory and Pedagogical Practice in Cicero's *De Oratore*," *Journal of Education* 179 (1997), pp. 15, 20 ("[Cicero] will claim that the ability to speak on either side of any topic is the mark of 'the one and only true and perfect orator,'" (quoting *De Oratore*, 3.21.80).

638 Lex Paulson, *Cicero and the People's Will: Philosophy and Power at the End of the Roman Republic* (Cambridge, UK, 2023), p. 39.

639 Miriam Griffin, "The Elder Seneca and Spain," *Journal of Roman Studies* 62 (1972), pp. 1, 4.

640 Lewis A. Sussman, *The Elder Seneca* (Leiden, 1978), pp. 22–23.

641 Seneca the Elder, *Controversiae*, Bk. I, pr., 12.

642 *Id.*

643 *Id.*, Bk. I, pr. 6.

survived. Exercises of this sort, furthermore, served valuable educational purposes throughout the Roman period,[644] even if they did not always realistically reflect legal practice.[645]

But if the word *controversia* carried a pedagogical connotation, it also sometimes simply signified legal disputes. We see this usage occur with some frequency in the *Lesser Declamations*, often (but probably mistakenly) attributed to Quintilian and dating probably to the second century CE.[646] We find there cases posing questions like the following: Was the heir – whose body could not be found – dead, or abducted?[647] This raises a *controversia* as to law and facts. A father mistakenly accused an innocent man of the rape of his daughter, and the accused was put to death. The father's trial poses a *controversia* – a controverted question – at law.[648] Or we encounter reminders about the complexity of legal practice: Thus, it is possible to compare laws, the author admonishes, but we must bear in mind that their application depends on the *controversia* before the court.[649] Adolf Berger thus defines *controversia* used in this sense: "A general term for a legal controversy between private individuals, a dispute before a court."[650]

The word *controversia* continued to convey this wide range of meanings throughout the medieval period.[651] And in the early modern period, we confront volumes like Lüder Mencke, *Gymnasium polemicum juris complectens plures quam* DCXX *selectas controversias juris naturalis et gentium, Juris Publici Romano-Germanic, juris civilis, feudalis, et canonici* ("The Polemical Handbook of Law Containing More Than 620 *Controversiae* Between Natural Law and the Law of Nations, and Roman Public and Germanic Law, and the Civil, Feudal,

644 Stanley Bonner, *Education in Ancient Rome: From the Elder Cato to the Younger Pliny* (New York, 2012) (reprint of 1977 edition), pp. 309–327.

645 But as Emanuele Berti notes, the fictitious character of some of the legal scenarios represented in the *controversiae* did not make them less valuable for educational purposes. Emanuele Berti, "Law in Declamation: The *Status Legales* in Senecan *Controversiae*," in Eugenio Amato, et al., eds., *Law and Ethics in Greek and Roman Declamation* (Berlin, 2015), pp. 7, 31–32.

646 D.R.B. Shackleton-Bailey, "Introduction," [*Quintilian*]*: The Lesser Declamations* (Cambridge, MA, 2006) (Loeb Classical Library), vol. I, p. 1.

647 *Id.*, vol. II, p. 432–433 (Declamation 388, 11).

648 *Id.*, vol. I, pp. 216–217 (Declamation 270, 2).

649 *Id.*, vol. I, pp. 252–253 (Declamation 274, 1).

650 Adolf Berger, *Encyclopedic Dictionary of Roman Law* (Philadelphia, 1953), p. 415.

651 See, for example, John O. Ward, *Classical Rhetoric in the Middle Ages: The Medieval Rhetors and Their Art 400–1300, with Manuscript Survey to 1500 CE* (Leiden, 2019), p. 205, note 393; Samuel E. Thorne, "The Assize *Utrum* and Canon Law in England," *Columbia Law Review* 33 (1933), pp. 428, 432, note 18.

and Canon Law");[652] or Adam Joseph Greneck, *Theses sive Controversiae Juridicae ex Selectissimis Juris Universi tum Publici, tum Canonici, tum Privati* ("Juridic Theses or Controversies Selected from Universal, Public, Canonical, or Private Law");[653] or Samuel Johann Horack, *Controversiae canonico-morales de restitutione et poenitentia* ("Canonical-moral Controversies About Restitution and Penance").[654]

Based on this history of usage, we should ascribe to *controversiae* a broad significance. They were disagreements, disputes, conflicts, quarrels, debates. They were open questions, colored in shades of gray. Which norms applied? And why? Which litigant had the superior claim? And why? *Controversiae* were doubtful matters, and the law-giver plainly did not favor a zero-sum game when such cases came before the judge.

The law-giver could have chosen the narrower, more technically precise term of art, *actio*. This was a term rooted in Roman law and was used continuously throughout the middle ages. Hostiensis described the *actio* as "a certain formula for acting or proceeding to judgment."[655] We saw in Part 2 *actio* described as "the right to seek justice." The medieval lawyers, furthermore, were not merely copying their sources from ancient originals, but in fact fertile and inventive in their development of *actiones* unknown to Roman law.[656] Nor was *actio* merely some medieval antique. It was a term familiar as well to the many commentators who elucidated and elaborated on the meaning of the 1917 Code.[657] We can therefore conclude that the law-giver consciously chose to employ the more expansive term. And the law-giver further signaled that *controversiae* should be resolved, wherever possible, by negotiated compromise. Furthermore, it is also clear that the legislator wished to utilize the broadest possible definition of what constituted an open question susceptible to negotiated settlement.

---

652 Lüder Mencke, *Gymnasium polemicum juris complectens plures quam DCXX selectas controversias juris naturalis et gentium, Juris Publici Romano-Germanici, juris civilis, et canonici* (Leipzig, 1689).

653 Adam Joseph Greneck, *Theses sive Controversiae Juridicae ex Selectissimis Juris Universi tum Publici, tum Canonici, tum Privati* (Vienna, 1718).

654 Samuel Johann Horack, *Controversiae canonico-morales de restitutitone et poenitentia* (Olmütz, Czech Republic, 1737).

655 Hostiensis, *Summa*, Bk. II, *De libelli oblatione*, sec. 3 (*actio quaedam formula agendi prosequendi in iudicio*). *Id.*

656 Harold J. Berman, *Law and Revolution: The Formation of the Western Legal Tradition* (Cambridge, MA, 1983), p. 241.

657 See, for example, Guido Cocchi, *Commentarium in Codicem Iuris Canonici ad Usum Scholarum* Guido Cocchi (Turin, 1930), vol. IV, *De Processibus*, pp. 148–175.

4.6.3 *Inter fideles*

Canon 1925 further specified that it was litigation "among the faithful" (*inter fideles*) that must be avoided. Once again, we see a noun – *fideles* – selected for its extreme breadth. If we want to appreciate the expansiveness of this word-choice, we should attend again to the structure of Book Two, *De Personis* ("On Persons"). The whole point and purpose of Book Two was to differentiate among various types and grades of persons. It was all about structure, hierarchy, and function. Book II began with the "baptized," "who are duly enrolled in the Church of Christ, with all the rights and duties of Christians."[658] Among the baptized, there were minors,[659] who were further subdivided among male[660] and female minors,[661] and those who were above or below the age of seven.[662] Then there were those who have attained the age of majority.[663] There were, furthermore, not only physical persons, but corporate persons, which might include everything from parishes, to seminaries, to local dioceses.[664]

There was also the sharpest distinction of all, and that was between the clerical and the lay states. Clerics were "those who have been freed for divine ministry."[665] Among clerics, furthermore, one can identify many hierarchical grades.[666] There were "bishops, priests, and [other] ministers."[667] Jurisdictionally, furthermore, there was "the supreme pontiff," the "subordinate episcopate," and all of the other grades and types of clerics who have been instituted by the Church.[668] Clerics alone enjoyed the powers of Holy Orders and jurisdiction.[669] "All of the faithful" (*omnes fideles*), finally, owed to clerics the reverence due to their different grades and duties, and should they cause any "real injury" to a cleric (*realem iniuriam*) they were guilty of the crime of sacrilege.[670]

658 C. 87 (1917 Code) ("Baptismate homo constituitur in Ecclesia Christi persona cum omnibus christianorum iuribus et officiis").
659 C. 88, sec. 1 (1917 Code).
660 C. 88, sec. 2 (1917 Code).
661 *Id.*
662 C. 88, sec. 3 (1917 Code).
663 C. 89 (1917 Code).
664 C. 99 (1917 Code).
665 C. 108, sec. 1 (1917 Code) ("Qui divinis ministeriis, per primam ... mancipati sunt, clerici dicuntur").
666 C. 108, sec. 2 (1917 Code) ("Non sunt omnes in eodem gradu, sed inter eos sacra hierarchia est in qua alii aliis subordinantur") ("Nor are all of the same grade, but among them, there is a sacred hierarchy, in which some are subordinated to others").
667 C. 108, sec. 3 (1917 Code).
668 *Id.*
669 C. 118 (1917 Code).
670 C. 119 (1917 Code).

In all of this, notice what was not a feature. Except for occasional asides, such as the obligation binding on all faithful Catholics to show deference to clerics, there was no over-arching treatment of the *fideles* – "the faithful." Yes, as noted, the law did speak of "the laity," but even this category was largely undeveloped. The law on persons was fairly obsessed with drawing distinctions. It was concerned with exploring and explaining what made one class of persons different from another. But Book Two was notably deficient in identifying what united all Catholic believers under the law.

That was what makes canon 1925, sec. 1's use of the phrase "among the faithful" so special. The use of the noun *fideles* was deliberately all-embracing. It was all-encompassing. It stood in sharp contrast with the many narrow distinctions made among the different types and grades of persons found elsewhere in the Code. *Fideles* included clerics, bishops, the baptized, deacons, archdeacons, and *monsignori*. It included as well Catholic corporations and institutions like religious orders, schools, or hospitals. And, of course, the laity. Of whatever rank and status, the faithful were encouraged to settle their disputes peacefully. This was really and truly the preference of the law-giver in as many cases as possible. And the law-giver had entrusted the responsibility to ensure the amicable settlement of disputes to the judge. So who was the judge, according to the law?

4.6.4 The Role of the Judge in Canon 1925

The Latin reads: *iudex exhortationes adhibeat* – "the judge is obliged to exhort the parties." We should next consider what is meant by the word *iudex* in the 1917 Code of Canon Law, and to do so, we should once again return to history.

4.6.4.1 Iudex (*The Judge*)

Gratian's *Decretum* is a good place to start a discussion of the ecclesiastical judge. In the first place Gratian premised his understanding of the good judge on the ideal qualities of the law. The law is made to restrain the wicked and to keep the innocent safe;[671] the law, furthermore, must be "honest, just, capable of being followed, and in accord with nature and the customs of the homeland, suitable to time and place, necessary, useful, and clear."[672] The judge, Gratian concluded, should adjudicate according to these laws, and not feel free to depart from them.[673] Minimally, Gratian thought, a judge should not

671 D. 4, c. 1.

672 D. 4, c. 2 ("Erit autem lex honesta, iusta, possibilis, secundum naturam, secundum consuetudinem patriae, loco temporique conveniens, necessaria, utilis manifesta quoque …").

673 D. 4, d.p.c. 2.

be insane, or a woman, or a *servus* (of servile status), since he thought none of these categories of persons capable of judging.[674] A judge should not use power tyrannically,[675] but should rather serve the cause of mercy and justice.[676]

The papal legislation of the middle ages added further refinement to Gratian's rather cursory description of a judge's suitability and comportment. A judge was called *iudex* because he spoke the law to the people, and because he abided in justice.[677] Judges should be *discretos*, Pope Alexander III wrote – "distinguished" – and rule according to the norms of law.[678] Honorius III instructed judges to pay attention to evidence, of course, but also to "have God always before their eyes" (*Deum habentes prae oculis*).[679]

Judges, the popes were well aware, might be susceptible to improper influence. Hence, the popes insisted that judges be sensitive to conflicts of interest, and avoid adjudicating cases that involved either their own status and wealth,[680] or that of family members.[681] A judge, Durandus added in his *Speculum Iudiciale*, was either the Ordinary – that is, either, at the apex of the hierarchy, the pope, or at least the bishop of a particular territory – or the bishop's representative (termed the *officialis*) to whom a general grant of judicial power had been given.[682]

James Brundage describes a gradual professionalization of the office of judge over the course of the high and later middle ages. He notes that one witnessed in the thirteenth century, local Church councils – Tours in France, Buda in Hungary – require judges to have received advanced training in canon law.[683] Mid-thirteenth-century popes, like Innocent IV, came to rely on "trained lawyers to handle specialized cases" that litigants brought to Rome for resolution.[684] By the time one arrives in the fifteenth century, credentialization had become a meaningful phenomenon. Thus one finds Pope Martin V mandating that "no one should be appointed as an auditor of the Rota unless

674 C. 3, q. 7, d.p.c. 1.
675 C. 15, q. 7, c. 1.
676 D. 45, c. 10.
677 X. 5.40.10 (St. Gregory the Great).
678 X. 4.14.1.
679 X. 2.19.13.
680 X. 1.29.17 (Alexander III).
681 X. 2.6.4 (Innocent III).
682 Durandus, *Speculum Iudiciale*, 1.1., *De Officio Ordinarii*, sec. 2.
683 James A. Brundage, *The Medieval Origins of the Legal Profession: Canonists, Civilians, and Courts* (Chicago, 2008), p. 375, note 13.
684 James A. Brundage, "The Learned Judge: The Development of an Ideal," *University of St. Thomas Law Journal* 1 (2003), pp. 434, 440.

he was a well-known doctor of law of unblemished reputation who had taught for at least three years since receiving the doctorate."[685]

Late nineteenth- and early twentieth-century canonistic commentary reviewed and synthesized this body of material. Thus Sebastiano Sanguineti (1829–1893) wrote that a judge had to be "suitable" (*idoneus*). Negatively, he must not be insane, or too young, or a heretic, or excommunicated; and affirmatively, he had to possess the requisite training, judgment, and training "to fulfill the requirements of the office" (*ad proprium munus adimplendum*).[686] Mariano De Luca, meanwhile, stressed the high level of professionalism he expected to see in a judge. A judge must administer justice without favoritism, must resolve cases without notable delay, and must render judgment in accord with the allegations and proofs asserted at trial.[687] *Scientia* – "knowledge" – Michel Bargilliat (1853–1926) finally stressed the importance of legal training to the office of judge. The judge must be learned not only in the law but "in all things that pertain to the law" (*omnia adjuncta juris*).[688]

Our discussion of the judge has thus far been conducted in isolation from a larger matrix of theological ideas. But we should now situate the judicial function within the *societas perfecta* ecclesiology that dominated canonistic thinking at the end of the nineteenth century. For that purpose, we might turn to the work of Septimio Vecchiotti (1810–1880), who was a friend of Cardinal Pecci and had served in a variety of diplomatic posts on behalf of Pope Pius IX.[689]

Writing in 1875, Vecchiotti located the judicial function firmly within the ecclesiology of Vatican I.[690] The Church, Vecchiotti asserted, was founded by Christ as an unequal society, in which some held ordinary power, and others did not; and in which some were empowered to rule, while others were subjected to the governance of their superiors.[691] The Church, furthermore, was

685 Brundage, *Medieval Origins, supra*, pp. 376–377.

686 Sebastiano Sanguineti, *Iuris Ecclesiastici Institutiones in Usum Praelectionum*, 4th ed. (Rome, 1901), p. 442.

687 Mariano De Luca, *De Iudiciis Ecclesiasticis Civilibus Compendium Iuxta Ordinem Decretalium*, 2d ed. (Rome, 1902), p. 77.

688 Michel Bargilliat, *Praelectiones Juris Canonici*, 3d ed. (Paris, 1915), vol. II, p. 380.

689 Carlo Tomassini, "Vecchiotti, Settimio Maria, serviglianese vescovo, nunzio apostolico, docente," luoghifermani.it/?p=4960 (2015).

690 Septimio Vecchiotti, *Institutiones canonicae: ad usum seminariorum accommodatae* (Turin, 1875), pp. 194–215.

691 *Id.*, p. 194. Cf., Martin Madar, p. 13 *The Church of God and Its Human Face: The Contribution of Joseph A. Komonchak to Ecclesiology* (Eugene, OR, 2019) ("One of the central affirmations of *societas perfecta* ecclesiology was that the church is an unequal and hierarchical society"). *Id.*

entirely distinct from civil society, and minimally dependent upon it.[692] Civil power had as its purpose the provision of material advantages to its members and the preservation of civic peace;[693] the Church, on the other hand, looked to spiritual ends and eternal life, but in the fulfillment of its responsibilities, it also made use of earthly means and instruments.[694]

There were, in other words, two distinct powers within the same civil society, the ecclesiastical and the human.[695] But within its proper competence, the Church retained legislative, coercive, and judicial power.[696] And the judge, by virtue of his share in the judicial authority, possessed the power of commanding and forbidding (*iubendi vel vetandi*), and of coercing and punishing (*coërceri et puniri*).[697] The canon-law judge, in other words, was a close analogue to his civil-law counterpart. And this is what we should expect in a thought-world that conceived of the Church as something simultaneously separate from and parallel to the secular world.

Armed with this historical background, we should turn next to the 1917 Code's discussion of the office of judge. Every diocese must have at least one judge, formally known as the *officialis*,[698] although the Code anticipated that in the usual case more judges would need to be appointed. These additional judges were known as "synodal judges," and exercised judicial power delegated to them by the bishop.[699] They must be priests of proven rectitude and expert in canon law.[700] Judges' preeminent responsibility, of course, was to hear cases and resolve them in accord with the norms of the law.[701]

But what of the judge's role in the non-judicial settlement of controversies?

4.6.4.2 Exhortationes adhibeat

I have translated this passage as stating that the judge "is obliged to exhort the parties." The *Oxford Latin Dictionary* defines *exhortatio* as "[t]he action of admonishing or encouraging, exhortation."[702] But while the word means

692 Vecchiotti, *Institutiones*, *supra*, p. 194 ("eamque [Ecclesia] a civili societate omnino distinctam esse, ab eaque minime dependentem"). *Id.*

693 *Id.*, p. 199.

694 *Id.*

695 *Id.*

696 *Id.*, pp. 207–215.

697 *Id.*, p. 214.

698 C. 1573, sec. 1 (1917 Code) (although in the case of especially small dioceses, the bishop might exercise the judicial power directly). *Id.*

699 C. 1574, sec. 1 (1917 Code).

700 *Id.*

701 C. 1578 (1917 Code).

702 Glare, ed., *Oxford*, *supra*, p. 642.

encouragement, it does not mean "mandate." This much becomes clear when we look at some classical usages. Quintilian urged his young orators-in-training to learn philosophy as a necessary adjunct to their trade, but he was quick to reassure his students that this word of advice (*exhortatio*) did not mean that they therefore must become philosophers.[703] Boethius' *Consolation of Philosophy* was an imagined dialogue between the imprisoned philosopher and a personified Philosophy who had given him encouragement (*exhortatio*) in his moment of most urgent need.[704] Boethius was reassured by these teachings, but was not in any way commanded. We can conclude that *exhortationes* was chosen deliberately as a kind of restraint on judicial power. The judge was limited in the steps he might take. He might encourage, induce, cajole, but he must not command parties to settle their disputes amicably.

But the obligation on the judge to steer litigants to settlement remained absolute. That is the meaning of the verb *adhibeat* (*adhibeo*, *adhibere*) which I have rendered as "obliged." The verb's primary meanings include "to hold out" as well as "to apply, attach (fetters) to; to apply."[705] It is the giving of oneself fully. When St. Augustine wanted to describe the total commitment of the sinner to seek forgiveness, he wrote: "ipse sibi adhibeat paenitendo" ("[The sinner] must surrender totally to penance").[706]

There was, however, an element of clericalism to the system envisioned in canon 1925. This much comes through clearly in canon 1925, sec. 3, which advised judges against involving themselves personally in directing litigants towards the settlement of disputes, at least in the average run of cases. Such involvement, the law-giver wrote, was not consistent with "the dignity of one who judges" (*dignitati iudicantis*).[707] Best to entrust this responsibility to a subordinate, like one of the synodal judges.[708]

Why? The judge is clearly conceived of as someone of exalted status. In a Church that was a society of unequals, as Vecchiotti put it, the judge must be careful in the ways in which he interacted with litigants. Unless, one supposes, one of the litigants was a person of some importance, it would seem a tarnishing of judicial dignity to get too personally involved. Litigants might see the

703 Quintilian, *Institutio Oratoria* 12.2.6 (= Donald A. Russell, ed. and tr., *Quintilian: The Orator's Education* (Cambridge, MA, 2001) (Loeb Classical Library), vol. v, pp. 222–223.

704 Boethius, *Consolatio Philosophiae* v.1.3 (=S.J. Tester, tr., *Consolation of Philosophy* (Cambridge, MA, 1973) (Loeb Classical Library), pp. 384–385.

705 Glare, *Oxford*, *supra*, p. 40.

706 St. Augustine, *Questionum in Heptateuchum Libri Septem*, Bk. IV (Quaest. Numerorum), quaestio 25, line 587.

707 C.1925, sec. 3 (1917 Code).

708 *Id.*

judge in the fullness of his humanity, as someone with passions and partialities and imperfections. And this might offend against the majesty of the law and call into question its neutrality. Indeed, it might even unbalance the hierarchy that must prevail between litigant and court. This interpretation of canon 1925, sec. 3, is given support in the commentary of Matteo Conte a Coronata (1889–1961), who wrote that it was always easy – too easy – for a judge who directly involved himself in settlement negotiations to reveal his preferences, and if that were to happen then the appearance of impartiality would be lost and the cause of justice thereby thwarted.[709]

4.6.4.3 Quae privatum eorum bonum respiciat

Finally, what of that phrase *quae privatum eorum bonum*, which I have translated as "bears on their private benefit?" Like much of the rest of *c.*1925, sec. 1, the expression "private benefit" must be understood expansively. Thus the canonist Guido Cocchi explained that it embraced any sort of real or personal right.[710]

But why, one might ask, in a parallel society, oriented to spiritual ends, should the law concern itself at all with the resolution of disputed claims over rights to material goods? Why shouldn't the distribution of material goods be left to secular society? The answer to these questions might be found in a theology that continued, despite all of the disruptions of the latter nineteenth century, to emphasize the communal, common-good relations of believers. Thomas Aquinas had written, in the thirteenth century, of a common good that featured "a just division of property and resources" among the members of the Christian community.[711] This much remained the teaching of theologians like Francisco Suarez in the sixteenth century,[712] Alphonsus de Liguori in the eighteenth,[713] and it informed the thinking of canonists in the nineteenth and twentieth centuries.[714] When disputes arose over whether rights of property had been violated, and when and how to make victims of wrong-doing

709 Matteo Conte a Coronata, *Institutiones Iuris Canonici ad Usum Utriusque Cleri et Scholarum* (Rome, 1941), vol. III, p. 366.

710 Cocchi, *Commentarium, supra*, vol. IV, *De Processibus*, p. 417.

711 Charles J. Reid, Jr., "Thomas Aquinas (1225–1274)," in Orazio Condarelli and Rafael Domingo, eds., *Law and the Christian Tradition In Italy: The Legacy of the Great Jurists* (London, 2021), pp. 98, 109.

712 Paul Pace, "Francisco Suárez and Justice: A Common Good Perspective," *Gregorianum* 93 (2012), pp. 497, 502–525.

713 Alphonsus de Liguori, *Guide For Confessors* (Morrisville, NC, 2018), pp. 41–42.

714 Charles E. Curran, *The Origins of Moral Theology in the United States: Three Different Approaches* (Washington, DC, 1997), pp. 99–100.

whole, it seemed like second nature to the canonists to offer at least the possibility of peaceful resolution of disputes.

4.6.5 The Teachings of the Commentators

In common with other contemporary systems of law that have their roots in the Romanist legal order of the Middle Ages, canon law has always placed a premium on the teachings of professors and others learned in the law. With that in mind, we should turn to some of the notable commentaries on canon 1925 in order to grasp their understanding of how the system was supposed to work. What questions did they deem to be important? What solutions did they propose? We might begin with the important work of two Jesuit professors of Law, Franz Xavier Wernz (1842–1914) and Pietro Vidal (1867–1938).[715]

Wernz and Vidal posed the question, can a settlement arrived at freely by the parties through negotiation violate the requirements of the just price? *Laesio enormis* was the term of art associated with the just price. Literally translated, the expression meant "great injury" and had its origins in legislation by Diocletian subsequently reproduced in Justinian's *Codex*.[716] As early as the *Codex*, it was recognized that great injury occurred where the price at which something (real estate, goods, or other articles of commerce) was sold at less than half its market value.[717] This was a teaching endorsed and further developed by the medieval Romanists, canonists, and scholastics.[718]

Wernz and Vidal were agreed; a sale might be invalidated should the sales price be less than one-half of market value.[719] But did the same rule apply to the settlement of claims arrived at by negotiation? There were canonists who maintained, by analogy to the just price, that such settlements were invalid for that reason alone. On the other hand, Wernz and Vidal noted, if a settlement occurred in an ecclesiastical court, and was sworn to by the parties, the solemnity of the oath supported settlements that were *laesio … enormissima* – truly enormous discounts of as much as two-thirds.[720] And if this was the case, then Wernz and Vidal reasoned, they stood with those canonists who "altogether

---

715 Franz Xavier Wernz and Pietro Vidal, *Jus Canonicum* (Rome, 1927), vol. VI (*De Processibus*).

716 Codex 4.44.2; and Codex 4.44.8. Cf., Alan Watson, "The Hidden Origins of Enorm Lesion," *Journal of Legal History* 2 (1981), pp. 186–193 (exploring the history of these texts).

717 Watson, *supra*, "Enorm Lesion," p. 189.

718 John W. Baldwin, "The Medieval Theories of the Just Price: Romanists, Canonists, and Theologians in the Twelfth and Thirteenth Centuries," *Transactions of the American Philosophical Society* 49 (1959), pp. 22–27 and 35–46.

719 Wernz and Vidal, *supra*, p. 621.

720 *Id.*

denied" (*omnino negabant*) the right to rescind a settlement simply because it was for a sum less than half the market value of the object of the agreement.[721]

It is possible to see, standing behind this conclusion, a robust concept of personal freedom. Wernz and Vidal were absolutely insistent that settlement negotiations be free – *transactio tamen **libere** fiat necesse est* – "the settlement must be *free*," the two canonists wrote, italicizing the word *libere*.[722] It is for this reason, they asserted, that judges must never compel parties to enter negotiations.[723] To be sure, Wernz and Vidal were no libertarians. They were not opposed to the just price. And if they had been asked, it is likely they would have defended just-price theory on the protections it afforded vulnerable participants in the marketplace. But where a freely-negotiated settlement was at issue, they were well-prepared to tolerate a wide range of outcomes.

The Benedictine canonist Ulrich Beste (1885–1976) explored the outer limits of the subject-matter susceptible to arbitration. He considered the issue not in terms of categories of substantive law, but in terms of the character of the controversy that came before the bench. There were, he said, three elements that had to be satisfied for a valid settlement under canon 1925. First, the parties agreeing to the settlement had to have the capacity to contract.[724] Why? Because the settlement amounted to a contract between the parties, and capacity therefore had to be a prerequisite. Second, the outcome of the case actually had to be uncertain.[725] Otherwise, the canonical requirement that there actually be a "controversy" (*controversia*) remained unsatisfied. Finally, the settlement had to be the result of a mutual surrender of rights, and could not be a mere gratuity granted by one party to the other.[726] Beste left to the reader's power of inference to identify the underlying substantive legal issues. For Beste, the obligation of the peaceful resolution of contentious matters was quite vast indeed.

Finally, there is the Franciscan canonist Stanislaus Woywod (1880–1941). Woywod was German-born, but he came to the United States at a young age and he wrote for an American audience. During his time in the United States, he taught at St. Bonaventure College (now University) in New York State, and at several Franciscan houses of study.[727] He served as the "first

721 *Id.*

722 *Id.*, p. 618.

723 *Id.*, pp. 618–619.

724 Udalricus Beste, *Introductio in Codicem* (Naples, 1956), p. 903.

725 *Id.* Or, as Beste put it, *res incerta vel controversia* ("a matter uncertain and controverted").

726 *Id.*

727 B.C. Gerhardt, "Woywod, Stanislaus," *Encyclopedia.com*; and "Stanislaus Woywod, O.F.M.," *Franciscan Friars of Holy Name Province*, "Deceased Friars," hnp.org/about-us-/our-friars/deceased-friars/stanislaus-woywod/.

superior of Holy Name College, his province's theological house of studies in Washington, D.C."[728]

In his introduction to canon 1925, sec. 1, Woywod wrote: "As it is highly desirable that litigation be avoided among the faithful, the judge shall admonish the parties between whom some civil controversy about their own private affairs has arisen and which they have taken to court to have it settled by judicial trial, to come to a compromise if there appears to be some hope of a friendly settlement."[729] Although Woywod did not refer to Scripture at this point in his commentary, he clearly had in mind Paul's admonition to his Corinthian followers not to take each other to court.[730] Canon 1925, on Woywod's reading, served not only the private good of the parties, but the good of the entire Church. The Church is the Body of Christ, and litigation both wounds that Body and is a cause for scandal for those outside the fold.

Woywod went on to reinforce his point by quoting extensively from the New York Practice Act, which spelled out in detail the obligations of the civil-law judge to seek the non-judicial resolution of litigation.[731] He wished to impress on an American readership that the obligation to seek the peaceful, non-judicial resolution of disputes was not unique to canon law, but common to many legal orders. Did he mean also to suggest that lay Catholic judges might profitably consult the canon law to inform their consciences when encouraging litigants to settle? Woywod was sufficiently inter-disciplinary that the thought likely crossed his mind.

4.6.6 How Canon 1925 Might Have Worked

Canon 1925 was not the only provision of the 1983 Code governing the non-judicial settlement of disputes. Canon 1926 specified that the civil law of the place in which the settlement was initiated (*in quo transactio initur*) should govern, unless that law conflicted with divine or ecclesiastical law.[732] This provision corresponded neatly with canon 1925, by providing firm guidance on choice of law. Suppose a controversy involving some substantial private matter – say, a tort that has inter-state effect, or a contract to be performed in multiple locations. Canon 1926 eliminated ambiguity over whose law applied. Presumably, it was the civil law prevailing in the diocese in which the settlement was begun. Why begun? Because, again, in a transaction that spanned

728 B.C. Gerhardt, "Woywod, Stanislaus," *New Catholic Encyclopedia*, vol. 14 (2003), p. 860.

729 Stanislaus Woywod, *A Practical Commentary on the Code of Canon Law* (New York, 1925), vol. II, p. 321.

730 1 *Corinthians* 6: 1–9.

731 Woywod, *Practical Commentary*, *supra*, pp. 321–322.

732 C.1926 (1917 Code).

multiple jurisdictions, one was given unambiguous directions on place, time, and priority of law.[733] Choice of law is a field that was then – and remains today – fraught with the fear of uncertainty, and the legislator meant to relieve that anxiety by providing fixed and sure guidance.

Canon 1927, in turn, restricted the subject-matter susceptible to settlement. Disputes over the validity of marriage, or over criminal culpability[734] could not validly be subject to settlement.[735] Canon 1928, sec. 2, finally, indicated that ordinarily the parties to a settlement were expected to bear their own expenses.[736]

How might this system have worked in practice? In posing this question, it should be said that there is little evidence that it was widely used to settle disputes among the laity, though, certainly, matters were likely different where disputes involved ecclesiastical institutions and persons. A series of hypothetical scenarios might illustrate its range of applicability. But in developing these scenarios, I should add, I brought to bear a deliberately American perspective. In the United States, even in the early and middle part of the twentieth century, it was always open to even Catholic litigants to sue ecclesiastical institutions in the civil courts. And so my first two hypothetical situations pose problems involving litigation brought by laypersons against Church institutions or personnel. The European context, as I develop below, would have been different.

Suppose a parishioner, Ms. Adams, a member of St. Zygmunt Gorazdowski Parish, slipped, fell, and fractured her hip in the Parish's parking lot because the Parish had failed to remove ice and snow from its surface. Ms. Adams has a claim against the Parish. But she is also a serious Catholic, and so she – personally or through her lawyer – first contacted the diocese. May the chief judge of the diocese – the *officialis* – encourage Ms. Adams to settle her dispute with the Parish non-judicially, under the terms of canon 1925? It would seem that not only might the *officialis* do so, he was affirmatively admonished to urge Ms. Adams to use the means of alternative dispute resolution to settle the matter.

Or consider Fr. Herbert, who composes popular church music. He learned that the lay music director of St. Guthlac's Parish has been using his music

733 In essence, canon 1927 "canonized" the civil law, that is, made it a part of canon law for purposes of resolving the dispute. The 1917 Code (as well as the 1983 Code) canonized large bodies of civil law for the purpose of managing its affairs. Thus canon 1529 (1917 Code) "canonized" and made part of the canon law the civil law of contracts in which particular churches are located. Canons 1519–1520 (1917 Code) spoke in similar terms about the civil law of property. Cf., Thomas Owen Martin, "The Present Status of Canon Law," *Ohio State Law Journal* 20 (1959), pp. 388, 404–411 (further discussing the ecclesiastical practice of "canonizing" portions of the civil law).

734 A prescient fear of plea bargaining?

735 C.1927, sec. 1 (1917 Code).

736 C.1928, sec. 2 (1917 Code).

without the proper permissions. He has the right to bring a suit for copyright infringement. But would Fr. Herbert? Should Fr. Herbert have recourse to the civil courts? No, once again, such a dispute would seem to be best handled through the mechanism for amicable settlement provided by canon 1925. To be sure, these are not exactly the private parties contemplated by the canon. But these are nevertheless cases that arise under the civil law, not under the canon law, and this at least opens the door to reliance on canon 1925.

The two hypothetical scenarios I have provided each involve at least one ecclesiastical litigant and they each posed complications. The settlement involving Ms. Adams at least theoretically implicated parish resources, even though the cost of the settlement would likely be borne by the parish's insurer. Still, even in such a case, a settlement involving ecclesiastical funds was permitted under canon 1927, sec. 2, provided the norms governing the alienation of ecclesiastical property were observed.[737] But now suppose that Fr. Herbert did not want a cash settlement for copyright infringement. Suppose instead he just sought to have the music director at St. Guthlac's stop using his music. There is nothing in the canon that would prevent the two sides from agreeing to what would amount to a kind of consent decree – the music director will cease his infringement, and Fr. Herbert will drop his claim.

But now suppose a wholly private dispute between two Catholic lay persons. Jack and Howard own adjoining parcels of land on the shore of some northern Minnesota lake. Jack built a fishing lodge which Howard has concluded interferes with his right to the quiet enjoyment of his property. He has the right to bring suit in civil court. But Howard, like Jack is a serious Catholic. And so before filing suit, the two prospective litigants sought the advice of the diocesan *officialis*, who encouraged them to settle their dispute amicably and non-judicially. They chose to take this course and asked the *officialis* to moderate their dispute. The *officialis* responded favorably, heard each party out, and suggested an outcome that seemed fair to all involved. This was how canon 1925 was supposed to work.

At least, this is how canon 1925 would have likely functioned in the United States. In the European context, however, the relationship between the Catholic Church was – and often is still – governed by concordats. What is meant by the term "concordat"? It is a legal document functionally comparable to a treaty,[738]

737 C.1927, sec. 2.

738 Roland Minnerath, "The Position of the Catholic Church Regarding Concordats From a Doctrinal and Pragmatic Perspective," *Catholic University Law Review* 47 (1998), pp. 467, 467–468.

which creates an "international obligation."[739] Concordats recognize an official role for the Church within the State. By their terms, ecclesiastical officials exercised competence that had real civil effect. Similarly, state officials may be required to know and apply ecclesiastical norms in what might – to American eyes – seem like a wholly secular proceeding. Thus canon law and the laws of particular nation-states interacted in ways that were simultaneously interdependent and cooperative. A judge in such a state might find herself, in other words, in a context in which the Code of Canon Law obligated her to some application of the law not as a religious believer but as an officer of the state.

A review of some of these concordats illustrates the ways in which Church and State intersected. According to the Concordat Between the Holy See and Spain, August 27, 1953, the Church was recognized as a "perfect society" (*sociedad perfecta*).[740] Spain recognized the right of the Church to acquire property,[741] to establish parishes and other ecclesiastical institutions,[742] and, in some circumstances to receive subventions from the State for their operation.[743] The Catholic Church and the Spanish government, furthermore, agreed to a dense set of rules governing the intersection of ecclesiastical and secular courts.[744] In 1933, the Church entered into the Dollfuss Concordat with the Republic of Austria,[745] which authorized "state financial aid to the Church,"[746] and placed "marriages between Catholics once more under the jurisdiction of ecclesiastical courts."[747] The Concordat Between the Holy See and the Dominican Republic, June 16, 1954, recognized the right of the Church to own property[748] and to be exempt from certain forms of tax.[749] The Dominican Government

---

739 Finn Seyersted, "Jurisdiction Over Organs and Officials of States, the Holy See, and Intergovernmental Organisations," *International and Comparative Law Quarterly* 14 (1965), pp. 31, 46.

740 Concordat Between the Holy See and Spain, August 27, 1953, Art. I.2.

741 *Id.*, Art. IV.1.

742 *Id.*, Art. XI.1.

743 *Id.*

744 *Id.*, Art. XVI. 1–3.

745 Engelbert Dollfuss (1892–1934) was the Chancellor of Austria. An ally of Benito Mussolini, Dollfuss was nevertheless murdered by Nazi sympathizers in 1934. See Christian Goeschel, *Mussolini and Hitler: The Forging of the Fascist Alliance* (New Haven, CT, 2018), pp. 55–56.

746 John F. Pollard, *The Papacy in the Age of Totalitarianism, 1914–1958* (Oxford, UK, 2014), p. 254.

747 William M. Johnston, *The Austrian Mind: An Intellectual and Social History, 1848–1938* (Berkeley, CA, 1972), p. 57.

748 Concordat Between the Holy See and the Dominican Republic, June 16, 1954, Art. XXIII.1–3.

749 *Id.*, Art. XIV.1–3.

further obligated itself to provide support for impoverished parishes,[750] as well as schools and nursing homes,[751] and agreed to recognize as holidays a number of Catholic feastdays.[752]

There is no need to go on. The point is simply this: the canons governing the non-judicial settlement of disputes must necessarily operate differently in nations in which the relationship of Church and State was subjected to detailed, treaty-based regulation.

4.6.7 Why Canon 1925? Resolving a Paradox

Canon 1925 presents us with a paradox. The law-giver clearly lavished time and attention on this canon. And it was the subject of careful and searching analysis by several generations of canonists. But this leaves us with the question, "why?" After all, as already noted, there is little evidence that the canon was widely used.

Five reasons suggest themselves for the treatment law-givers and commentators accorded the non-judicial settlement of disputes. The first reason might be called "aspirational." Jurisprudence teaches us that all law contains some aspirational quality. One sees this feature prominently in the large body of transnational human-rights law that has emerged in recent decades.[753] We are aspirational when we ask, through the language of human rights, for the cessation of war and violence and the prosecution of war criminals, or when we seek to ensure that the starving be fed, and the homeless housed. Yes, we certainly want these norms to be more than aspirational.[754] We really do want to see the prosecution of the guilty and the protection of the vulnerable. But we are always at least aspirational in what we hope the law can accomplish.

And thus there is a sense in which canon 1925 was aspirational. Christians should live in harmony with one another. They really ought to avoid the law-courts and settle their differences amicably and respectfully amongst themselves. They should be quick to repair injury. Seen in this light, canon 1925 was a summons to this higher, aspirational way of life.

---

750 *Id.*, Art. VII.2.

751 *Id.*, Art. XIX. 1.

752 *Id.*, Art. XVIII.

753 Thus it has been written: "Human rights are a form of aspirational law by means of which humans establish goals for themselves concerning the kinds of speicies they are committed to becoming ... and the kinds of societies they are committed to creating." Philip Harvey, "Aspirational Law," *Buffalo Law Review* 52 (2004), pp. 701, 723.

754 Emmanuel K. Nartey, *Accountability and Corporate Human Rights Violations in Tort and International Law* (Newcastle-upon-Tyne, 2021), p. 88.

Second, there is the theological element. On the prevailing ecclesiology of the day, the Church was a perfect society, whose members might live in the world but not be of the world. Christians suing Christians in secular courts of law, on this view, was a failure. The Church had built a parallel structure to the courts and had done so because *it was in its nature to do so*. Canon 1925 thus stood as a theological invitation to Christians everywhere to employ the very practical tools of negotiation and compromise to resolve their disagreements. Courts of law are blunt, zero-sum mechanisms that frequently leave all participants worse off. The nurturing Church knows its sheep and will shepherd them to peaceful verdant pastures.

Third is the political dimension. One would be naive to think that there was not a political aspect to canon 1925. Yes, Church and State were parallel societies, self-sufficient and independent, but they were also in competition with one another. And in this rivalry, Pope Leo XIII left no doubt about where one's loyalty should lie: "As to which should be preferred no one ought to balance for an instant. It is a high crime indeed to withdraw allegiance from God in order to please men, an act of consummate wickedness to break the laws of Jesus Christ, in order to yield obedience to earthly rulers."[755] Canon 1925 had been included in the Code very much in the spirit of Leo's admonition. While the state is a natural institution and provided definite benefits to humankind, if we can, we should choose to arrange our affairs in accord with a higher law.

Taken in tandem, the theological and political dimensions return us to Vecchiotti on the function of judicial power within the canon law. Ecclesiastical judicial power was a practical instantiation of the Church as *societas perfecta*, and a superior means of resolving disputes. Really, who wouldn't want to use such a valuable resource?

Fourth is the historical. Arbitration, mediation, the negotiated settlement of disputes had all been a part of the Church's tradition for centuries, as Parts 2 and 3 have outlined. And so Cardinal Gasparri and the Popes he served – Pius X, Benedict XV – chose to retain its legal form. Was this simply inertia, the dead hand of an accumulated past, nothing more than legislative stagnation? Or was there a genuine hope that by inserting into the Code a set of statutes governing the settlement of disputes, and by expressing a strong preference for their use, that a revival of an ancient and revered institution might thereby be stimulated? My own guess is that the legislator hoped to reinvigorate the old practice and to give it a renewal on life.

Fifth and last is the practical dimension. It must have been anticipated that there would be at least an occasional need to resolve disputes through

755 Leo XIII, *Sapientiae Christianae* (1890), no. 7.

negotiation and compromise. And undoubtedly, the canons were occasionally used, and their spirit must have guided the arbitration of disputes between or among ecclesiastical institutions. Therefore a legal structure would be constructed to facilitate that foreseeable possibility. The result was canons 1925 to 1928 of the 1917 Code.

4.7 De compromisso in arbitros (*"On Compromise through Arbitration"*) (*Canons 1929–1932*)

Canons 1925 to 1928 aimed to create a legal structure that facilitated a negotiated end to legal disputes. It was a system, plainly, that would be driven by the interaction of the parties themselves. The judge might urge and prompt, nudge and hint, but there was no provision for the judicial supervision of the process. The parties and their legal representatives retained the freedom to make use of the system and were the ones responsible for making the process work. The law allowed the two sides substantial room for maneuver. The parties themselves might sit down, face-to-face, and craft a settlement, or their attorneys might take the lead. They might employ trained ecclesiastics to guide them to a settlement of their dispute, but the spirit of the canons was kept even if they utilized purely secular resources. In the end, however, the success or failure of the process depended on the willingness of the parties to drop their most intransigent demands and settle their differences amicably.

Canons 1929 to 1932, however, contemplated a different process, one that involved not only the supervision of the process but even the imposition of a settlement where the parties failed to reach agreement. These four canons, in other words, created a system that envisioned arbiters (and arbitrators, we shall discover that the medieval distinction between these offices retained its vitality) taking testimony, reviewing evidence, resolving thorny questions of law, and finally arriving at a binding outcome.

4.7.1 Canon 1929: Structure and Function

Once again, we should begin with the language of the canons. And once again, we should commence with the canon that brought the system into being. And that was canon 1929.

Let us start with the Latin of canon 1929: "Ad evitandas iudiciales contentiones, partes possunt quoque inire conventionem, qua controversia commitatur iudicio unius vel plurium qui ad normam iuris quaestionem dirimant, vel de bono et aequo negotium pertractent et transigant; illi *arbitri*, isti *arbitratores*, proprio nomine appellantur."

And now my English paraphrase of the text: "In order to avoid litigation, parties are empowered to enter a pact by which their case is submitted to judgment by one or more persons who may hear and resolve the matter either by the norms of law or by principles of equity [*de bono et aequo*]. The former [i.e., those who judge according to the norms of law] are known as arbiters; the latter [i.e., those who rely on equity], are known as arbitrators."

We should note some contrasts with canon 1925. Canon 1925 was addressed principally to the judge. It imposed an affirmative duty on the judge to recommend to litigants the advantages of a peaceful settlement of their disputes. Derivatively, it imposed an obligation on the entire Catholic faithful (*inter fideles*) to seek the cordial accommodation of their claims wherever that was possible.

Canon 1929, on the other hand, was directed at the litigants and prescribed for them a more formal process of alternative dispute resolution. The canon spoke about *partes possunt* – which I have translated as "the parties are empowered." The parties, in other words, might agree to submit their cause to arbitration (*inire conventionem*) even in the absence of encouragement from the judge.

And if the parties did opt to follow the norms of canon 1929, then certain consequences followed. First, the outcome of the arbitration was binding upon the parties. That is the clear meaning of the phrase *commitatur iudicio* – "committed to judgment" – and the verb *dirimant* – to "impose judgment on" or "to settle."[756] "Judgments" and "impositions," after all, carry a mandatory and not a discretionary force.

And, second, the parties had to make a choice: Did they want to have their cases decided by an *arbiter* or an *arbitrator*? Actually, as we recall from our discussion of Durandus and other sources we reviewed in Part 2, this was a meaningful choice. Much depended on the characterization of the person (or persons) selected to rule on the case.

Finally, Felix Cappello noticed that canons 1925 and 1929 had different objectives. The objective of canon 1925 was to attain a *transactio* between the contending parties; the purpose of canon 1929, however, was to achieve a *compromissum*.[757] The *transactio*, Cappello noted, was a *conventio*, a kind of agreement reached by the parties themselves, through whatever process seemed best adapted to the situation;[758] the *compromissum*, however, was a judgment imposed on the parties, and hence its processes bore a close resemblance to a judicial proceeding.[759]

---

756 Glare, ed., *Oxford*, *supra*, p. 548.
757 Cappello, *Summa*, *supra*, vol. III, p. 251.
758 *Id.*
759 *Id.* ("Quare hoc institutum magis iudicio accedit").

4.7.2 *Arbiter vel Arbitrator?*

The textbook by Vermeersch and Creusen explored these two offices with some degree of depth. They noted that the distinction between arbiters and arbitrators was known in the medieval law[760] – a fact that we have already noted. Under the 1917 law, the two canonists continued, an arbiter is understood as a person designated by private agreement to resolve a controversy according to the norms either of the canon or the civil law, and then impose a judgment on the parties.[761] An arbitrator, Vermeersch and Creusen added, was like an arbiter in many respects, but was not obliged to follow the norms of law. Rather, the arbitrator might resolve the case according to *de aequo et bono*, a richly textured phrase which we shall discuss in greater depth in the next section. But insofar as Vermeersch and Creusen were concerned, the arbitrator who judged by reference to *de aequo et bono* substituted his prudential judgment (*pro prudente*) for the strict norms of law, and decided the matter according to his best understanding of justice and mercy.[762]

Vermeersch and Creusen also spoke to the required qualifications of arbiters and arbitrators. Regarding arbiters, they indicated that there were certain classes of persons who were disqualified from service by reason of natural law. This category included the under-aged, the insane, and the chronically alcoholic.[763] Others might be excluded by reason of ecclesiastical law. Laypersons, for instance, were disqualified from hearing cases involving ecclesiastical goods. Similarly, the excommunicated and the infamous were excluded.[764]

Vermeersch and Creusen, remarkably perhaps, took a more expansive view of who might serve as arbitrators. The same natural-law prohibitions applied, but the ecclesiastical law restrictions did not.[765] In other words, although they did not say this expressly, even those suffering under excommunication or otherwise considered infamous were able, at least by implication, to serve as an

760 Vermeersch and Creusen, *Epitome*, *supra*, vol. III, p. 111.

761 *Id.*

762 *Id.*

763 *Id.*, p. 112.

764 *Id.* The canon law recognized two forms of infamy, *infamia iuris* ("infamy of law") and *infamia facti* ("infamy in fact"). Infamy of law was a penalty that was attached to certain crimes at canon law. Frank J. Rodimer, *Canonical Effects of Infamy In Fact: A Historical Synopsis and a Commentary* (Washington, DC, 1954), p. 37. Infamy in fact "is rather the natural reaction of good and prudent men to the misconduct of their fellow man. It is in the broad sense of the word a penalty of the natural order whereby a delinquent loses the respect of his fellows." *Id.* Vermeersch and Creusen did not distinguish between these two categories in their commentary.

765 *Id.* ("A munere *arbitratoris* nemo solo ecclesiastico excluditur").

arbitrator, at least where the matter concerned a private dispute between laypersons over purely secular goods.

Felix Cappello, on the other hand, parted company with Vermeersch and Creusen on who might serve as an arbiter or arbitrator. Vermeersch and Creusen had emphasized the minimal requirements for the office, while granting enormous latitude to the parties. Cappello stressed instead that the arbiter must be "good" and "skilled" and prepared to resolve the case according to the norms of law;[766] the same admonition, he added, pertained to the arbitrator, except that the arbitrator must be experienced in matters related to *ex bono et aequo*.[767]

Stanislaus Woywod called particular attention to the "quasi-judicial power" exercised by arbiters. They were authorized "to summon the parties, examine witnesses, and in general proceed in the manner in which the judge of a court proceeds."[768] Just as he had with canon 1925, Woywod once again drew a comparison to the civil law, using the New York Practice Act as a model. Civil litigants in New York may use arbitration to settle some dispute and turn to the civil courts to have the judgment confirmed.[769] Canon law operated on the same set of principles.[770]

More theoretically inclined than Woywod, Wernz and Vidal explained how arbiters came to have such power. To be sure, they stated, arbiters (and arbitrators) lacked jurisdiction, and were, according to the canon law private persons to whom jurisdiction cannot be granted; nevertheless, their powers were equivalent to those of judges-delegate (*ad instar potestatis iudicum delegatorum*). They had that power simply because the efficient operation of the system of arbitration demanded it.[771]

At the risk of being anachronistic, one might draw a comparison between arbiters under canon 1929 and the process of contemporary commercial arbitration. An arbiter operating under the rules established by the American Arbitration Association, in hearing a commercial case, can take testimony, review evidence, examine documents, and in rendering a final decision makes reference to statutes, case law, and relevant doctrines of law.[772] This kind of process, pretty

766 *Id.*, p. 252.
767 *Id.*
768 Woywod, *Practical Commentary*, *supra*, vol. II, p. 323.
769 *Id.*, p. 324.
770 *Id.*, pp. 323–324.
771 Wernz and Vidal, *supra*, vol. VI, p. 633.
772 See *Commercial Arbitration Rules and Mediation Procedures: Including Procedures For Large, Complex Commercial Disputes* (American Arbitration Association), adr.org/commercial.

clearly, was what the law-maker contemplated in decreeing that arbiters should judge *ad normam iuris* – "according to the rule of law."

But what of arbitrators? How were they supposed to proceed? To answer that question, we should take a more extended look at what was meant by *de bono et aequo*.

4.7.3 *De bono et aequo*

Let us explore this word choice, *de bono et aequo*. Gasparri did not randomly select this turn of phrase for its sonority and Latinity, but because of its deep, two-thousand-year-old history. Superficially, literally, the expression might be translated as "the good and the fair," or "the good and the just." And while such a translation would not be wrong, a lesson in history strengthens and deepens its meaning. So it is to that history that we should attend.

The phrase *de bono et aequo* has its history in a distinction nearly as old as Roman law itself, and that is the question, should cases be decided in accord with the strict letter of the law? Or should they be decided in accord with more flexible standards of fairness, justice, or mercy?

Some of our earliest examples of the contrast between law and equity can be found in Seneca's *Controversiae*. To be sure, many of the problems he mooted had an unreal quality to them, but the very extremeness of their facts helps to elucidate how the Romans of Seneca's age understood especially the flexibility and fairness that judging according to the principles of equity required. One might consider a couple of Seneca's examples:

Suppose a husband and wife who were intensely in love and who swore an oath that should either one die, the other one would commit suicide.[773] Suppose further that the wife had vowed to obey her father in all things. The husband departed on a trip and subsequently sent the deliberately false message that he had died. Before learning the truth, the wife jumped from a cliff, but survived. Her father then demanded that she divorce her husband and told her that if she failed to so, he would disinherit her. Despite all of this, she wished to remain with her husband. Might she be relieved of the oath she took to her father?[774] Seneca noted that the *controversia* was entirely concerned with *aequitas*, "equity," and that questions of equity were resolved not by recourse to strict rules but by *tractatio* – which in context meant the reflective weighing and balancing of principles.[775] And in the body of the *controversia*, we find

773 Seneca, *Controversiae*, Bk. II, *Cont.* 2, 1.

774 *Id.*

775 *Id.*, Bk. II, *Cont.* 2, 5. Cf., Glare, ed., *Oxford, supra*, p. 1954 (defining *tractatio* as "the handling of a case, theme, etc., especially the treatment of matters of morality, justification, etc., as opposed to questions of law").

precisely that, as a group of jurists ponder the relative weight and merits of truth, loyalty, oath-taking, and the pathology of entangled human relationships.

Or there was the case of the married couple living under a tyrant's rule. The husband plotted to kill the tyrant. Aware of the plot, the tyrant tortured the wife, rendering her barren, but she remained silent. The husband later killed the tyrant and divorced his wife on account of barrenness. She brought an action against him for ingratitude (*ingrati actio*).[776] Seneca recalled the argument. A suit for ingratitude, he reported it being said, was a matter of both law and equity – the suit was an *actio* and must be brought at law, but one could not measure gratitude except through an understanding of the totality of the circumstances and a developed sense of fairness and that demanded equitable deliberation (*in aequitatis tractationem*).[777]

Sensitivity to person, to place, to time, to circumstance, these were some of the elements that comprised the Roman concept of equity. The wisdom to discern subtle differences, the capacity to distinguish between good will and depravity, a proficient talent for interpreting human behavior and human relationships – these were the skills needed by those who pondered how to reach the equitable solution.

The word pairing *bono et aequo* emerged in this early period of classical history and came to be employed in contexts that emphasized the application of equitable principles instead of the strictness of the law. One sees the expression occurring as early as Terence's play *Adelphoi*.[778] Sometime later, Sallust used the term to describe the justice meted out to an assassin in the employ of the Numidian king Jugurtha.[779] Livy similarly used the term in describing the punishment of assassins.[780] In these latter two examples, at least, the expression was utilized to capture the sense of immediate and rough justice that awaited those who violated good order in abrupt and profound ways.

When we come to the *Rhetorica ad Herennium*, once attributed to Cicero but now recognized as the product of an unknown author, working sometime in the years 86 to 82 BCE,[781] we see *de bono et aequo* being used in ways that approximated our understanding of equitable principles. *Bono et aequo* now represented a concept of justice that stood apart from the written law, but without which the law would seem unduly harsh, or lifeless, or unfair. Thus the author of the *Rhetorica* declared, where a text was ambiguous, it was good

776 *Id.*, Bk. II *cont.* 5, pr.
777 *Id.*, *cont.* 5, 17.
778 Terence, *Adelphoi*, line 987.
779 Sallust, *Bellum Jugurthinum*, 35.7.
780 Livy, *Ab Urbe Condita*, Bk. 42,41.
781 Harry Caplan, "Introduction," in [*Cicero*]: *Rhetorica ad Herennium*, Harry Caplan, tr. (Cambridge, MA, 1954) (Loeb Classical Library), pp. vii, xxvi.

to seek clarity by asking whether one's interpretation corresponded with "the fair and the good" (*ex aequo et bono*).[782] At another place in the *Rhetorica*, we find *aequo et bono* being described as a constituent part of the law, in its widest signification.[783] The author of the *Rhetorica* claimed in yet another place that *Ius* – by which was meant the entire legal order – was premised upon the "fair and the good" (*ex aequo et bono*), and was thus naturally inclined in the direction of truth and the common good.[784]

Cicero made generous use of the expression in his *Pro Caecina* when he denounced his adversary for hiding behind technicalities of meaning when it was plain that justice was on the other side.[785] Seneca the Younger, a century later, in his *De Clementia*, his essay "On Mercy," wrote that Mercy in judgment was free, nor was it bound to some narrow verbal formula (*sub formula*), but it adjudicated in accord with the good and the fair (*ex bono et aequo*).[786] The second-century CE biographer Suetonius recalled that the Emperor Claudius decided cases on the basis of equity (*ex bono et aequo*).[787] The verbal significance of *de bono et aequo* had now become firmly fixed. Four centuries later, we find the Gallic bishop Sidonius Apollinaris (ca. 430–ca. 481/490 CE), using the term when instructing his correspondent, the Breton military leader Riothamus, to judge a case he had sent him fairly.[788]

Thus it is no surprise to see the jurists, whose work forms the backbone of Justinian's *Digest*, employ this expression. For the Roman lawyer Celsus, the entire law was the practical implementation of equity. Thus law itself was "the art of the good and the just" (*ius est ars boni et aequi*).[789] And if the whole of the law was to be permeated with goodness and justice, then it was no surprise to see adverbial clauses like *de bono et aequo* reproduced in the *Digest*, as when Celsus went on to speak of the duty to satisfy one's contractual obligations.[790] The term was similarly used to signify the necessity of moving beyond sterile

---

782 *Rhetorica ad Herennium*, Bk. II, 11 (= Loeb Classical Library, p. 86).

783 *Id.*, Bk. II, 13 (= Loeb Classical Library, p. 90).

784 *Id.* (= Loeb Classical Library, p. 94).

785 Cicero, *Pro Caecina*, 66 (using, in rapid succession, *aequum et bonum*; *boni et aequi*; and *ex aequo et bono*).

786 Seneca the Younger, *De Clementia*, II.7.3 (= Seneca, *Moral Essays*, John W. Basore, tr. (Cambridge, MA, 1928) (Loeb Classical Library), vol I, p. 444).

787 Suetonius, *Lives of the Twelve Caesars*, Bk. V (Claudius), 14 (= *Suetonius*, J.C. Rolfe, tr. (Cambridge, MA, rev. 1997) (Loeb Classical Library) vol. II, p. 26.

788 Sidonius, *Letters*, Bk. III.9 (to Riothamus) (= *Sidonius, Letters III–IX*, W.B. Anderson, tr. (Cambridge, MA, 1965) (Loeb Classical Library) p. 36.

789 *Digest*, 1.1 (Ulpian) (The excerpt is from Ulpian; but Ulpian attributes the expression to Celsus).

790 *Digest* 45.1.91.3 (Paulus) (Again, the excerpt is from Paulus, but Paulus attributes the expression to Celsus).

formalism.[791] *De bono et aequo* was thus used to demand the attainment of just results, even if one had to step outside the constricted world of *actiones* and *replicationes* to reach that lofty goal. And so the phrase was used in this manner throughout the *Digest*.[792] This much was noted by the nineteenth-century jurist John George Phillimore (1808–1865).[793]

This tradition, this commitment to substantive fairness even at the expense of particular provisions of the statutes transferred easily to the medieval jurists. One thus finds in the *Brachylogus*, once dated to 1110, now more likely dateable to 1160,[794] the admonition that "when equity appears to contradict written law, we judge according to equity."[795] The Roman lawyers Azo (ca. 1150–1225) and Accursius (1182–1263) believed that there were two forms of equity – the *aequitas civilis*, the spirit, the teaching, and the innate, embedded rightfulness of the positive, enacted law of the realm – and the *aequitas naturalis*, the overarching sense of fair play and substantive justice that permeated the cosmos even in the absence of the written law.[796] This idea, furthermore, was repeated with much the same meaning in the medieval commentaries on the law merchant.[797]

Turning to the medieval canonical tradition, Peter Landau informs us that Gratian only rarely made reference to equitable principles.[798] Still, there is one passage in Gratian's *Decretum* that well captures the meaning of *de bono et aequo*. In *Causa* 32, *quaestio* 6,[799] Gratian referenced the woman caught in adultery as told in the Gospel of John.[800] The accusers brought forth the

791 W.W. Buckland, *Equity in Roman Law* (London, 1911), pp. 11–14.

792 See, for example, *Digest* 9.4.30 (Gaius) (rights of absentees protected on basis of equity (*ex bono et aequo*)); *Digest* 21.1.18 (Gaius) (*ex bono et aequo* used as a practical synonym for "reasonableness"); *Digest* 28.3.17 (Papinian) (paternal intent prevails when interpreting a will, and not the technicalities of legal form, *ex bono et aequo*); *Digest* 47.10.11.1 (Ulpian) (the action for defamation, the *actio iniuriarum*, is premised on equitable considerations, *ex bono et aequo*).

793 John George Phillimore, *Principles and Maxims of Jurisprudence* (Union, NJ, 2001) (reprint of 1856 edition), p. 268.

794 See Brasington, *Order in the Court*, supra, pp. 125–126, note 79.

795 Eduard Böcking, ed., *Corpus Legum sive Brachylogus Iuris Civilis* (Berlin, 1829), p. 156 ("sin vero aequitas iuri scripto contraria videatur, secundum ipsam iudicandum est").

796 Renato Beneduzi, *Equity in the Civil Law Tradition* (Cham, Switzerland, 2021), p. 85.

797 Charles Donahue, Jr., "Equity in the Courts of Merchants," *Tijdschrift voor Rechtsgeschiedenis* 72 (2004), pp. 1, 22; and Charles Donahue, Jr., "Medieval and Early Modern *Lex Mercatoria*: An Attempt at the *Probatio Diabolica*," *Chicago Journal of International Law* 5 (2004), pp. 21, 34.

798 Peter Landau, "*Aequitas* in the *Corpus Iuris Canonici*," *Syracuse Journal of International and Comparative Law* 20 (1994), pp. 95, 98.

799 C. 36, q. 6, pr.

800 John 8: 1–11.

woman, pronouncing to Jesus that she had been caught in the very act.[801] Jesus knelt down and began to write in the sand while, one-by-one, the accusers drifted away.[802] Finally, there was no one left to lodge an accusation, and Jesus informed the woman that he would not judge her.[803] For Gratian, this was a "judgment in equity" "(*equitatis sententiam*)."[804] It stood above the law, went beyond the law, examined the heart, and rendered a merciful verdict.

Gratian attracted commentators, the greatest of whom was probably Huguccio (fl. 1187). Regarding Huguccio's treatment of equity, Charles Lefebvre, medieval scholar and Dean of the Roman Rota (1976–1978), wrote that he "places clear emphasis on equity's character of indulgence. Doubtless, he occasionally assimilates equity to law, but he insists that natural equity 'moves to justice and mercy' (*justitiam et pietatem suadet*)."[805]

Another half-century after Huguccio, the canonist Hostiensis further explored the scope and significance of equity. For Hostiensis, equity was part of the order of the universe itself, since it had its source in the natural law (*aequitas a iure naturali descendens*).[806] While Gratian drew the connection between equity and divine mercy, Hostiensis incorporated mercy within his definition of equity (*iustitiae dulcore misericordiae temperata*).[807] It necessarily followed for Hostiensis that equity "prevails over the *ius strictum* [the law's strictness] and the *rigor canonicus* [canonical firmness]."[808] Indeed, "Hostiensis considered equity a reasonable way to render justice."[809]

Now let us return to that choice of words found in canon 1929, *de bono et aequo*. Concentrated within this compact phrase we have identified two millennia's worth of jurisprudence that sought to balance flexibility grounded in fairness with the strict and impersonal application of legal norms. And of course the law-giver knew that it was impossible to construct a legal order that favored one side of this equation to the exclusion of the other. Every legal order must have some mechanism for balancing these two indispensable but very distinct legal values.

---

801 John 8: 4.
802 John 8: 9.
803 John 8: 10–11.
804 C. 36, q. 6, pr.
805 Charles Lefebvre, "Natural Equity and Canonical Equity: Note," *Natural Law Forum* 8 (1963), pp. 122, 128 (citations omitted).
806 Beneduzi, *Equity*, *supra*, p. 80 and note 165 ("justice tempered with the sweetness of mercy").
807 *Id.*, p. 80, note 169.
808 *Id.*, p. 80.
809 Antonio Padoa-Schioppa, *A History of Law in Europe: From the Early Middle Ages to the Twentieth Century* (Cambridge, UK, 2007), p. 208.

Thus canon 1929 afforded litigants a choice. They could seek a judgment from an arbiter in accord with the norms of law (*ad normam iuris*). Or they might select a less formal process that relied upon canonical equity (*de bono et aequo*). The one process was formal, precise, strict. It was intended to arrive at an unimpeachably correct and exact outcome. The other made use of more elastic categories of right and wrong, in order to come to a resolution that was substantively just and pleasing to all. No zero-sum games.

The remainder of the Code's treatment of arbiters and arbitrators was unremarkable. Canon 1930 indicated that the rules governing choice of law in canon 1926 also governed arbitrations.[810] Canon 1931 prohibited lay arbiters from hearing cases involving clerics.[811] And canon 1932, finally, instructed those who wished neither to negotiate a settlement or employ arbitration to be prepared to litigate their dispute in accord with the law's procedural norms.[812]

4.8 *Significance of Alternative Dispute Resolution in the 1917 Code of Canon Law*

We can identify a number of significant points from our discussion of alternative dispute resolution under the 1917 Code of Canon Law. First, non-judicial resolution of disputes was an important value for the law-giver. We gain a sense of just how important it was from the language the law-giver used: *valde optandum*. "A really strong preference." Yes," the law-giver can be read as saying, "I have given you a large body of carefully-drafted procedural norms for the conduct of a contentious trial, but first, you really, truly must try to settle your dispute amicably and outside of the courtroom."

Second, the negotiation of settlements and the arbitration of disputes were confined to questions of private law. To be sure, within this category, every imaginable dispute might be subject to non-judicial resolution. The hypothetical scenarios I posed represent only a tiny sampling of the kinds of cases that judges might urge to settlement.

But, third, arbitration and mediation did not extend to administrative matters entrusted to the discretionary judgment of ecclesiastical officials. The discretion of Church officials, it was thought, must be free. An appeal of an abuse of discretion might always be taken appealed to Rome, but such a step was rare.[813] More often, such decisions were non-reviewable. And they

810 Canon 1930 (1917 Code).

811 Canon 1931 (1917 Code).

812 Canon 1932 (1917 Code).

813 In 1917, the norms for such an appeal would have been found in two sources. First, the Apostolic Constitution *Sapienti Consilio*, promulgated by Pope Pius X in 1908, which delineated the competences of the particular Roman congregations; and, second, in the

were certainly not reviewable by judges whose offices depended upon the power vested in bishops or other ordinaries. On the top-down ecclesiology of the post-Vatican-One Church, furthermore, the non-reviewable character of such decisions made imminent good sense. The Church was a hierarchy of unequals, in which those filling high positions commanded, and those playing lesser roles assented.

Fourth, we also learned about the powers that judges did and did not possess. Judges, at least some of the canonists insisted, must be genuinely learned, gifted in legal reasoning and wise in human affairs. In instructing judges to encourage the settlement of disputes, the law-giver wanted them to act as much pastorally as judicially. The good pastor wants peace, concord, and the repair of differences within the flock. The judge wants an outcome that will result in justice but yet not leave the parties embittered or hostile. Still, the judge had to tread carefully. The judge must encourage. But the judge must never insist. That would threaten the freedom of the parties to choose the course they deem best suited for themselves.

Fifth, and finally, the parties were empowered. They might choose to resolve their dispute in a number of ways. As canon 1925 proposed, they could negotiate an outcome between themselves, at the prompting of the judge. But they might also select arbiters who were directed to rule in accord with the norms of law. Such arbiters acted in a quasi-judicial manner, and so could summon witnesses, take testimony, and make all relevant decisions regarding facts and law necessary for the proper disposition of the case. Alternatively, the parties might also elect to use arbitrators, who were permitted to use flexible procedural norms and rely on equitable principles (*de bono et aequo*) in order to reach a substantively just decision.

Part 5: The Second Vatican Council, Due Process, and the Extra-judicial Review of Administrative Acts

5.1 *The Breakup of the Old Political Order and the Coming of the New*

The great twentieth-century engine of ecclesial transformation was the Second Vatican Council, which met between 1962 and 1965. One major reason the Council seemed necessary was the virtual disappearance of the old political

norms of the Apostolic Signatura. See John C. Meszaros, "Procedures of Administrative Recourse," *Jurist* 46 (1986), pp. 107, 109–111; and Ignacio Gordon, "Normae Speciales Supremi Tribunalis Signaturae Apostolicae: Editio Aucta Introductione, fontibus et notis," *Periodica* 59 (1970), pp. 75–166.

order and its replacement by something new. The First Vatican Council had assembled during the apex of an era of high monarchism. The Catholic Habsburg dynasty controlled much of central Europe from its capital in Vienna. In 1870, the Emperor Franz Joseph was forty years old, in the prime of his political ascendancy, and he governed with the kind of vigilant patriarchalism that thrilled his supporters and antagonized his foes.[814]

In England, the indomitable Queen Victoria presided with an unweathered granite-like firmness over a colonial empire upon which it was observed, with only slight exaggeration, the sun never set. India, Australia, Canada,[815] parts of Africa, were all enfolded within this Empire, bound by ties of greater or lesser strength. The entire edifice was built upon a foundation of blood and sand – a colonial order that brutally repressed and even slaughtered indigenous peoples for the benefit of enriching Anglo-Saxon settlers and the home country.[816] Still, to the late nineteenth-century observer the whole facade must have seemed impermeable to time itself.[817]

The Netherlands was governed by a monarchy that had, in mid-century, introduced some democratic reforms.[818] King Leopold II, on the other hand, the ruler of neighboring Belgium, governed autocratically and strip-mined his

814 Karen Owens, *Franz Joseph and Elisabeth: The Last Great Monarchs of Austria-Hungary* (Jefferson, NC, 2014), p. 132 ("The central government in the mind of Franz Joseph was to serve the populace as a protectorate").

815 Under the British North America Act, 30 & 31 Vict. c. 3 (1867), Canada was established as a Dominion, whose Parliament remained subject to the Crown and whose foreign policy remained tethered to Great Britain.

816 Randeep Ramesh, "India's Secret History: 'A Holocaust, One Where Millions Disappeared,'" *The Guardian*, August 24, 2007; Dinyar Patel, "Viewpoint: How British Let One Million Indians Die in Famine," *BBC News*, June 11, 2016, bbc.com/news/world-asia-india-36339524; Lorena Allam and Nick Evershed, "The Killing Times: The Massacres of Aboriginal People Australia Must Confront," *The Guardian* March 3, 2019; Asafa Jalata, "The Impacts of English Colonial Terrorism and Genocide on Indigenous/Black Australians," *Sage Open*, vol. 3, no. 3 (July–September, 2013); John Harris, "Hiding the Bodies: The Myth of the Humane Colonisation of Aboriginal Australia," *Aboriginal History* 27 (2003), pp. 79–104; Michelle Gordon, *British Colonial Violence in Perak, Sierra Leone, and the Sudan* (Ph.D. Dissertation, Royal Holloway, University of London, 2017); Nigel Jones, "Britain's Bloody History in Sudan," *The Spectator*, April 25, 2023.

817 See, for instance, Barbara Caine, "'My Vast Empire and All Its Many Peoples:' Queen Victoria's Imperial Family," in Sarah Carter and Maria Nugent, eds., *Mistress of Everything: Queen Victoria in Indigenous Worlds* (Manchester, UK, 2016), pp. 125–143. Among Queen Victoria's titles was "Empress of India." See Miles Taylor, *Empress: Queen Victoria and India* (New Haven, CT, 2018), p. 1.

818 Many of these reforms were adopted in the wake of the turmoil of 1848 and included such steps as the granting of religious tolerance to Catholics. See Gerlof D. Homan, "Catholic Emancipation in the Netherlands," *Catholic Historical Review* 52 (1966), pp. 201–211.

colonies of resources ruthlessly.[819] In Russia, there governed Czar Alexander II,[820] who was not as autocratic as his father, Czar Nicholas I.[821] Victor Emmanuel had become the king of a rapidly unifying Italian peninsula in 1861.[822] The Spanish had recently overthrown their reigning monarch, Queen Isabella, in 1868,[823] but in 1870, the Cortes invited Amadeo, Duke of Aosta, to succeed to the throne.[824]

In Germany, momentum was rapidly building for unification, a process carefully shepherded by Chancellor Otto von Bismarck on behalf of Prussian King Wilhelm I.[825] This goal was at long last accomplished in the final months of 1870, when a number of German states, following the victorious Franco-Prussian War, voted to join Prussia in a confederated Germany.[826] In January, 1871, Wilhelm was proclaimed Emperor of a new and united German nation.[827]

Politically, France stood as the outlier to this pan-European consolidation of monarchy, as the failed Empire of Napoleon III, defeated in the Franco-Prussian War, yielded to the Third Republic in the year 1870. The Third Republic

---

819 Adam Hochschild, *Lessons from a Dark Time and Other Essays* (Berkeley, CA, 2018), pp. 94–105.

820 On the one hand, Alexander II emancipated the Russian serfs. See Victor Leontovitsch, *The History of Liberalism in Russia* (Pittsburgh, PA, 2012), pp. 107–114; on the other hand, he abrogated the Polish constitution and incorporated that nation directly into Russia. Malte Ralf, *Imperial Russian Rule in the Kingdom of Poland, 1864–1915* (Pittsburgh, PA, 2021), pp. 29–57.

821 Czar Nicholas I governed as the "Autocrat" of Russia – meaning that he was the apex of all power in the Russian Empire, over Church as well as State. Richard S. Wortman, *Scenarios of Power: Myth and Ceremony in Russian Monarchy From Peter the Great to the Abdication of Nicholas II* (Princeton, NJ, 2006), p. 133; and Anna Aydinyan, *Formalists Against Imperialism: The Death of Vazir-Mukhtar and Russian Orientalism* (Toronto, 2022), pp. 109–111.

822 Bruno Aguilera-Barchet, *A History of Western Public Law: Between Nation and State* (Cham, Switzerland, 2015), p. 522.

823 James A. Baer, *Anarchist Immigrants in Spain and Argentina* (Urbana, IL, 2015), p. 18.

824 C.J. Bartlett, "After Palmerston: Britain and the Iberian Peninsula, 1865–1876," *English Historical Review* 109 (1994), pp. 74, 80.

825 Otto Pfanze, "Bismarck and German Nationalism," *American Historical Review* 60 (1955), pp. 548, 550–558.

826 Nicholas Sambanis, et al., "Nation-Building Through War," *American Political Science Review* 109 (2015), pp. 279, 285–291; and Roberto Vivarelli, "1870 in European History and Historiography," *Journal of Modern History* 53 (1981), pp. 167–188.

827 David M. Edelstein, *Over the Horizon: Time, Uncertainty, and the Rise of Great Powers* (Ithaca, NY, 2017), p. 42; and Stefan Berger, "Building the Nation Among Visions of German Empire," in Stefan Berger and Alexei Miller, eds., *Nationalizing Empires* (Budapest, 2015), pp. 247, 251 ("1871 was in many respects not the end point of a long process of nation formation but the beginning of a remarkably successful and rapid process of nation building under the umbrella of empire").

aimed to govern by secular ideals, to be sure, and it tested French Catholicism, but it was also the case that by 1875, "seven Frenchwomen in every thousand were nuns."[828] At the level of popular devotion, France in the latter nineteenth century was still the country of St. Bernadette,[829] St. Thérèse of Lisieux,[830] and the burgeoning cults of John Vianney, beatified 1908 and canonized 1925;[831] and of Joan of Arc, beatified in 1908, and canonized in 1920.[832]

This was a world, in other words, in which monarchy, at least in most places, was perceived as the natural, ordained and self-evidently correct form of government. This was a world, seen from an elite perspective, that was comfortably hierarchical, and seemingly secure against all foes. This was a world in which a kind of peaceful, sort of nostalgic popular devotion flourished, even after, even in spite of all of the turmoil of the early nineteenth century. This was the world of *Pastor Aeternus*, the First Vatican Council's decree on papal infallibility, and it was a world in which *Supremi Pastoris* – the First Vatican Council's ecclesiastical constitution – seemed like a logical and reasonable extension of the prevailing political order.

It was a political order, we know now, that was being radically undermined in the last decades of the nineteenth century, by oppressive economic forces that in turn begat violent revolutionary resistance. By the early 1900s, the global community had observed revolutionary events coursing throughout the Old World – an uprising in Łodż, in Poland, in 1905;[833] an insurrection against

828 Roger Magraw, *France 1800–1914: A Social History* (New York, 2014) (reprint of 2002 edition) p. 166.

829 Lourdes, the site where Bernadette experienced her visions of the Virgin Mary, "was institutionalized as a pilgrimage site in the 1870s." Kim Timby, *3D and Animated Lenticular Photography: Between Utopia and Entertainment* (Berlin, 2015), p. 201.

830 Felicity Leng, *Smiles of God: The Flowers of Saint Thérèse of Lisieux* (London, 2003), p. 140.

831 George William Rutler, *The Curé D'Ars Today: St. John Vianney* (San Francisco, 1988), pp. 21–35.

832 Nadia Margolis, "The 'Joan Phenomenon' and the French Right," in Bonnie Wheeler and Charles T. Wood, eds., *Fresh Verdicts on Joan of Arc* (New York, 1996), pp. 265, 269. Nor was France alone in its popular devotion or its Catholic social vitality. In Italy, one saw the ministry of St. Don Bosco (1815–1888), who founded the Salesian religious order and who served particularly the dislocated and estranged urban youth of the industrial revolution (see, for example, Francis-Vincent Anthony, et al., "Impact of Religion on Socioeconomic Rights: An Empirical Study of Italian Students' Attitude," in Hans-Georg Ziebartz, ed., *International Empirical Studies on Religion and Socioeconomic Human Rights* (Cham, Switzerland, 2020), pp. 63, 66.

833 Andreas R. Hofmann, "Reweaving the Urban Fabric: Multiethnicity and Occupation in Łodż, 1914–1918," in Marcus Funck and Roger Chickering, eds., *Endangered Cities: Military Power and Urban Societies in the Eras of the World Wars* (Leiden, 2004), pp. 81, 83.

the Russian Czar, also in 1905;[834] and the rebellion of the Young Turks in the Ottoman Empire, in 1908.[835] Tremors, harbingers, anticipations of the earthquake that was to come with the hecatomb of World War I.

By the end of World War I, Austria had become a Republic, Hungary had gained its independence, and the Habsburg Empire was no more, its last reigning monarch, the beatified Charles I, exiled finally to Madeira after failed attempts to reclaim the throne.[836] The German Empire, so majestically proclaimed in 1871, was also swept away, the chaos of 1918 eventually evolving into the tragic and short-lived Weimar Republic.[837] And, of course, Czar Nicholas II and his family, murdered by the Bolsheviks,[838] who consolidated control over Russia and its Empire beginning in November, 1918.[839]

World War II left even more unimaginable wreckage in its train. The killing was immense, unparalleled. Millions died in the First World War. Millions more in the Second. And there were the genocides, such as the Turkish brutal mistreatment of the Armenians,[840] and the mass starvation in Ukraine, the result of Soviet policy.[841] And, finally, the unspeakable atrocity of the Holocaust, the willful and wicked destruction of six million Jews in Europe.

---

834 Abraham Ascher, "Introduction," in Jonathan D. Smele and Anthony Heywood, eds., *The Russian Revolution of 1905: Centenary Perspectives* (New York, 2005), pp. 1–12; and Joshua Rubenstein, *Leon Trotsky: A Revolutionary's Life* (New Haven, CT, 2011), pp. 25–54.

835 Erik Jan Zürcher, "The Young Turk Revolution: Comparisons and Connections," *Middle Eastern Studies* 55 (2019), pp. 481–498 and Nader Sohrabi, "Global Waves, Local Actors: What the Young Turks Knew About Other Revolutions and Why It Mattered," *Comparative Studies in Society and History* 44 (2002), pp. 45–79.

836 Marc Stegherr, "'Kings by the Grace of the People are No Grace for the People:' The Post-World-War-One Order and Its Conservative Critics," in Ioan Bolovan and Oana Mihaela Tămaş, eds., *World War I and the Birth of a New World Order: The End of an Era* (Newcastle-upon-Tyne, 2020), pp. 256, 257.

837 Peter C. Caldwell, "The Weimar Constitution," in Nadine Rossol and Benjamin Ziemann, eds., *The Oxford Handbook of the Weimar Republic* (Oxford, UK, 2022), pp. 119–140.

838 "The Czar's Death," *New York Times*, August 1, 1918; and S. Frederick Starr, "You Can't Murder History," *New York Times Book Review*, July 19, 1992.

839 Laura Engelstein, *Russia in Flames: War, Revolution, Civil War, 1914–1921* (Oxford, UK, 2018), pp. 630–632; Sabine Dullin, "L'entre-voisins en période de transition étatique (1917–1924): La frontiére épaisse des bocheviks à l'Est de l'Europe," *Annales, Histoire, Sciences Sociales* 69 (2014), pp. 383–414.

840 Ronald Grigor Suny, *"They Can Live in the Desert But Nowhere Else:" A History of the Armenian Genocide* (Princeton, NJ, 2015), pp. 281–327; Vahakn N. Dadrian, "The Armenian Genocide as a Dual Problem of National and International Law," *University of St. Thomas Journal of Law and Public Policy* 4 (2010), pp. 60–82; and Mark L. Movsesian, "Elusive Equality: The Armenian Genocide and the Failure of Ottoman Legal Reform," *University of St. Thomas Journal of Law and Public Policy* 4 (2010), pp. 1–17.

841 Oleh Wolowyna, "A Demographic Framework for the 1932–1934 Famine in the Soviet Union," *Journal of Genocide Research* 23 (2021), pp. 501–526.

The old Empires had vanished. The British Empire, mortally wounded in the First World War, essentially liquidated its final holdings in the 1940s and 1950s. India gained its independence, as did Britain's African colonies. The Japanese Empire, too, was gone. The French fought – and lost – colonial wars in Indochina and Algeria.

Monarchy had not entirely disappeared. But it was hollowed out. Yes, there were still kings and queens in a few European nations – the United Kingdom, the Netherlands, Belgium, Luxembourg, Norway, Sweden – but these were constitutional monarchies, with royal families serving largely vestigial, ceremonial roles. Hardly the stuff of Wilhelm I, or Queen Victoria, or the Russian Czars. Replacing those old monarchs on the world stage were, in many but not all instances, constitutional democracies that recognized and reinforced the rights of citizen-members of the body politic, who were deemed at law to participate equally in society. These new forms of government had their blemishes, they over-promised, and, too often, under-delivered. But they were radically different, politically and constitutionally, from what had gone before.

Was it possible, in these changed conditions, to maintain a backward-looking, nostalgic ecclesiology that modeled itself upon absolutist doctrines of government, that loudly proclaimed the fundamental and radical inequality of its members, and that largely pretended that the cataclysms of the twentieth century had not altered the landscape irretrievably? Questions such as these circulated in the post-World-War-II Catholic environment.

5.2 *The Theological Transformation of the Twentieth Century*

If the fundamentally transformed geopolitical terrain was one factor contributing to the felt necessity to reimagine the Church's structure and place in the world, a second contributing ingredient was the incubation and growth of new ways of doing theology that had emerged over the course of the twentieth century.

One might begin with a precocious band of French theologians who posed important questions in the years just before and after 1900. Members of this intellectual circle included Louis Duchesne (1843–1922). Duchesne, was among the first Catholic Church historians to recognize and apply modern methods of historical criticism to ancient texts[842] and he produced a series of path-breaking studies in early ecclesiastical history. He was elected to the French Academy in 1910.[843] Marie-Joseph Lagrange (1855–1938) taught Church

842 Ward De Pril, "Modernism and the Problematic Relation Between History and Theology: The Search for a Compromise by Louvain Historians and Theologians (1870–1910)," *Church History and Religious Culture* 91 (2011), pp. 377, 380–382.

843 See, for instance, *Early History of the Christian Church: From Its Foundation to the End of the Fifth Century*, Claude Jenkins, tr., 3 volumes (London, 1909–1924); Louis Duchesne, *The Churches Separated From Rome*, Arnold Harris Mathew, tr. (London, 1907); and Louis

History and Scripture, founded the École biblique in Jerusalem,[844] and published a number of works on the Scriptures.[845] Finally, there was Alfred Loisy (1857–1940), who examined the origins of the earliest Church and Scripture, and raised unsettling questions about the composition of the Pentateuch and the reliability of *Genesis* as historical text.[846]

Each of these scholars, in their own distinctive ways, had begun to use historical and critical methods current in the latter nineteenth century to ask discomforting questions about the sources of Christian – and in particular, Catholic – history. And controversy soon descended upon them. Pope Pius X had grown suspicious of modern methods of theological inquiry, and in 1907 he issued the encyclical known as *Pascendi Dominici Gregis*.[847] Thus was born the so-called Modernist Controversy. The enemies, Pius gravely warned, were inside the Church. They "lie hid ... in her very bosom and heart."[848] "Modernists," Pius continued, "place the foundation of religious philosophy in that doctrine which is usually called *Agnosticism*."[849] These thinkers were "guided by the theory that faith must be subject to science," and they aimed at nothing less than "to introduce a new theology" to replace the truths of Catholic doctrine.[850] Modernism, the Pope concluded, was "the synthesis of all heresies."[851]

Duchesne, *Christian Worship, Its Origin and Evolution: A Study of the Latin Liturgy Up to Charlemagne*, M.L. McClure, tr. (London, 1903). Cf., "Louis Duchesne," *Catholic Historical Review* 8 (1922), pp. 214–216 (providing further biographical details); and Massimo Faggioli, *John XXIII: The Medicine of Mercy* (Collegeville, MN, 2014), pp. 32–33 (on the influence Louis Duchesne had on the young Angelo Roncalli's intellectual formation).

844 Owen F. Cummings, *Popes, Councils, and Theology: From Pope Pius IX to Pope Francis* (Eugene, OR, 2021), pp. 67–68.

845 Karim Schelkens, et al., *Aggiornamento? Catholicism From Gregory XVI to Benedict XVI* (Leiden, 2013), p. 81. Cf., Marie-Joseph Lagrange, *La méthode historique: La critique biblique et l'Église* (Paris, 1904); Marie-Joseph Lagrange, *Le judaisme avant Jésus-Christ* (Paris, 1931); and *Évangeli selon saint Jean* (Paris, 1936) (a representative bibliography).

846 See, for example, Francesco Turvasi, *The Condemnation of Alfred Loisy and the Historical Method* (Rome, 1979), p. 162 (on the condemnation of Loisy's rejection of Mosaic authorship of the Pentateuch); and Sonya Shetty Cronin, *Raymond Brown, 'The Jews,' and the Gospel of John: From Apologia to Apology* (London, 2015), 16 (on Loisy's rejection of the early chapters of *Genesis* as historical). Loisy's views were criticized by Pope Leo XIII as early as the 1890s. See Harvey Hill, "Leo XIII, Loisy, and the 'Broad School:' An Early Round of the Modernist Crisis," *Catholic Historical Review* 89 (2003), pp. 39, 47–51. Cf., Alfred Loisy, *L'Évangile et L'Église* (Paris, 1904); and Alfred Loisy, *Les Évangiles synoptiques* (Paris, 1907) (prominent examples of Loisy's scholarship).

847 Pius X, *Pascendi Dominici Gregis* (1907).

848 *Id.*, no. 2.

849 *Id.*, no. 6 (emphasis in original).

850 *Id.*, no. 18.

851 *Id.*, no. 39.

In retrospect, it is fine to write about the diffuseness of Pius' definitions and the amorphousness of his terms. "The Modernist appears now as philosopher, then as apologist, elsewhere as historian or critic, other times as reformer or as theologian."[852] Pius X was chasing phantoms, and he thought they were everywhere. We are tempted therefore to minimize the threat he posed to sophisticated academic inquiry. But in the moment, Pius' ambition to capture by a single label vast fields of scholarship had the effect of chilling independence of thought. And his denunciation echoed and reverberated. By the very capaciousness of his condemnation, he cast a shadow over theological innovation that would persist for decades. "[T]hinking," one historian has written, "became a dangerous act."[853]

Duchesne, Lagrange, and Loisy, all were at least temporarily tarnished by the label of "Modernist." Duchesne's historical account of early Christianity was placed on the Index of Forbidden Books.[854] Lagrange was formally cautioned and even ceased to pursue more speculative lines of inquiry.[855] Hardest hit, and the hardest to hit back, was Loisy. Excommunicated by Pius X, he published an autobiography – known in English as *My Duel With the Vatican* – and continued his research in the French secular academy.[856]

Still, although inquiry might have been dampened, it was not altogether deterred. The Modernist crisis was a fever, and the fever eventually broke. Scholarship, even highly innovative scholarship, continued. A rising generation of scholars began to ask, and to answer, yet more foundational questions about the life and meaning of the Church in the world.

Marie-Dominique Chenu (1895–1990) rejected as sterile the neo-scholasticism that dominated the Catholic academy in favor of a historically-situated Thomism that "relocated Aquinas back in the cultural, historical, and intellectual world of the thirteenth century."[857] His ambition was the "theological renewal" of the Church itself.[858] Henri de Lubac (1896–1991) sought the

852 C.J.T. Talar, "'The Synthesis of All Heresies' – 100 Years On," *Theological Studies* 68 (2007), pp. 491, 493.

853 Anthony M. Maher, *The Forgotten Jesuit of Catholic Modernism: George Tyrell's Prophetic Theology* (Minneapolis, MN, 2018), p. 17.

854 Karim Schelkens, "Papal Leadership in the First Half of the Twentieth Century: Resistance and Renewal," in Richard R. Gaillardetz, ed., *The Cambridge Companion to Vatican II* (Cambridge, UK, 2020), pp. 41, 43.

855 "Our Founder, Father Marie-Joseph Lagrange, O.P.," *École biblique et archéologie française de Jérusalem*, ebaf.edu/ecole-biblique/father-marie-joseph-lagrange-op/.

856 See generally, Alfred Loisy, *My Duel With the Vatican: The Autobiography of a Catholic Modernist*, Richard Wilson Boynton, tr. (New York, 1924).

857 Brian J. Shanley, *The Thomist Tradition* (Dordrecht, 2002), p. 7.

858 Christophe F. Potworowski, *Contemplation and Incarnation: The Theology of Marie-Dominque Chenu* (Montreal, QB, 2001), p. 226.

revitalization of the study of Scripture in the Church,[859] and much else besides. He wanted to know the relationship of the natural to the supernatural,[860] and to explain the Church in terms that moved beyond the old *societas perfecta* ecclesiology of the First Vatican Council.[861]

A little younger than Chenu and de Lubac, and protégés or students of the older men were Yves Congar (1904–1995) and Edward Schillebeeckx (1914–2009), both of whom were Belgian, not French. Like Chenu and de Lubac, Congar was interested in historical retrieval and renewal. He wrote learnedly of the medieval papacy.[862] He urged, on the basis of historical argument, the reconciliation of Eastern and Western Churches,[863] and found value in sincere dialogue with Protestant Christians.[864] Instead of a rigid hierarchy of unequals, Congar proposed an ecclesiology that integrated laity and clergy in a single unifying vision of Church.[865] Like the others, Schillebeeckx questioned neo-scholasticism,[866] and promoted instead the practice of a deeply-lived faith in Jesus Christ.[867] He published important works on eschatology,[868] the sacraments,[869] and the relationship of the human person and divinity.[870]

---

859 Kevin L. Hughes, "The Spiritual Interpretation of Scripture," in Jordan Hillebert, ed., *T & T Companion to Henri de Lubac* (London, 2017), pp. 205–224.

860 Jacob W. Wood, *To Stir a Restless Heart: Thomas Aquinas and Henri de Lubac on Nature, Grace, and the Desire for God* (Washington, DC, 2019), pp. 22–28.

861 Hans Boersma, *Nouvelle Théologie and Sacramental Ontology: A Return to Mystery* (Oxford, UK, 2009), pp. 244–269.

862 Terence L. Nichols, *That All May Be One: Hierarchy and Participation in the Church* (Collegeville, MN, 1997), p. 148; Avery Dulles, *The Catholicity of the Church* (Oxford, UK, 1985), p. 128, note 1.

863 Elizabeth Teresa Groppe, *Yves Congar's Theology of the Holy Spirit* (Oxford, UK, 2004), pp. 75–76.

864 Paul D. Murray, "Expanding Catholicity Through Ecumenicity in the Work of Yves Congar: *Ressourcement*, Receptive Ecumenism, and Catholic Reform," *International Journal of Systematic Theology* 13 (2011), pp. 272–302.

865 Isaac Kizhakkeparampil, *The Invocation of the Holy Spirit as Constitutive of the Sacraments According to Cardinal Yves Congar* (Rome, 1995), pp. 54–55.

866 Erik Borgman, "Retrieving God's Contemporary Presence: The Future of Edward Schillebeeckx's Theology of Culture," in Lieven Boeve, et al., eds., *Edward Schillebeeckx and Contemporary Theology* (London, 2010), pp. 235, 247; Jürgen Mettepenningen, *Nouvelle Théologie – New Theology: Inheritor of Modernism, Precursor of Vatican II* (London, 2010), p. 125.

867 See, for instance, Edward Schillebeeckx, *Jesus: An Experiment in Christology*, Hubert Hoskins, tr. (New York, 1979); and Edward Schillebeeckx, *Christ, the Sacrament of the Encounter With God* (New York, 1963).

868 Edward Schillebeeckx, *The Problem of Eschatology*, Boniface A. Willems, tr. (New York, 1969).

869 Edward Schillebeeckx, *The Sacraments in General: A New Perspective*, Boniface A. Willems, tr. (New York, 1968); Edward Schillebeeckx, *Sacramental Reconciliation* (New York, 1971).

870 Edward Schillebeeckx, *Man as Man and Believer*, Boniface A. Willems, tr. (New York, 1967); Edward Schillebeeckx, *A Personal God?*, Bastian van Iersel, tr. (New York, 1973); Edward Schillebeeckx, *God Among Us: The Gospel Proclaimed* (New York, 1983).

All four scholars encountered problems with ecclesiastical authority during their careers. Chenu had a book placed on the Index,[871] and he also lost his professorship at Le Saulchoir, the Dominican house of study in Belgium (Chenu would later receive other academic appointments).[872] Henri de Lubac was similarly ordered to stop teaching for most of the 1950s and "his books were removed from Jesuit libraries."[873] Yves Congar was forced to undergo a period of exile in the 1950s, after being removed from his position in Paris.[874] Schillebeeckx was investigated by the Congregation for the Doctrine of Faith in the 1970s and 1980s.[875]

It is also true that all four were eventually rehabilitated. Chenu, Congar, and de Lubac all played active advisory roles as so-called *periti* ("experts") at the Second Vatican Council.[876] Congar and de Lubac served at the express invitation of Pope John XXIII.[877] At the Council, Schillebeeckx "attended as a theological advisor to the Dutch Bishops ... in particular ... Bernard Jan Cardinal Alfrink, Archbishop of Utrecht."[878] Late in life, Congar and de Lubac would be made cardinals.[879]

There was also an American theologian, whose career tracked closely with these other writers, John Courtney Murray (1904–1967). Murray remains famous for his work on the relationship of Church and State,[880] but his writings,

871 Fergus Kerr, "Chenu's Little Book," *New Blackfriars* 66 (1985), pp. 108–112.

872 Janette Gray, "Marie-Dominique Chenu and Le Saulchoir: A Stream of Catholic Renewal," in Gabriel Flynn and Paul D. Murray, eds., *Ressourcement: A Movement For Renewal in Twentieth-Century Catholic Theology* (Oxford, UK, 2012) pp. 205, 209.

873 Joseph T. Lienhard, "'Faith of Our Fathers:' The Fathers of the Church and Vatican II," in Kevin McMahon, ed., *Divine Promise and Human Freedom in Contemporary Catholic Thought* (Lanham, MD, 2015), pp. 1, 4.

874 Paul J. Philibert, "Yves Congar: Theologian, Ecumenist, and Visionary," *U.S. Catholic Historian* 17 (1999), pp. 116, 118.

875 Ted Schoof, ed., *The Schillebeeckx Case*, Matthew J. O'Connell, tr. (Ramsey, NJ, 1984).

876 Patricia Plovanich, "Chenu, Marie-Dominique (1895–1990)," in Orlando Espín and James B. Nickhoff, eds., *An Introductory Dctionary of Theology and Religious Studies* (Collegeville, MN, 2007), p. 228; Thomas F. O'Meara, "Dominican and Jesuit Theologians at an Ecumenical Council: Yves Congar and Karl Rahner," *Journal of Jesuit Studies* 7 (2020), pp. 459–471; and Robin Darling Young, "A Soldier of the Great War: Henri de Lubac and the Patristic Sources for a Premodern Theology," in James L. Heft, ed., *After Vatican II: Trajectories and Hermeneutics* (Grand Rapids, MI, 2012), pp. 134, 137.

877 Andrew Dean Swafford, *Nature and Grace: A New Approach to Thomistic Ressourcement* (Eugene, OR, 2014), p. 60.

878 Kevin P. Considine, *Salvation For the Sinned-Against: Han and Schillebeeckx in Intercultural Dialogue* (Eugene, OR, 2015), p. 36.

879 Robert McClory, "Why Yves Congar is Relevant Today," *National Catholic Reporter*, June 6, 2013; "Cardinal de Lubac, 95, of France, An Architect of Church's Renewal," *The New York Times*, September 5, 1991.

880 John Courtney Murray, *We Hold These Truths: Catholic Reflections on the American Proposition* (Lanham, MD, 2005) (reprint of 1960 edition); and John T. Noonan, Jr., *The*

like those of Chenu, Congar, de Lubac, and Schillebeeckx, ranged widely across periods and disciplines.[881] He was subjected to censorship for a while in the 1950s,[882] but he was restored to good graces as a *peritus* at the Second Vatican Council.[883] As we shall see, he also played a strategic role in the Canon Law Society of America.

This group of thinkers came to be known, pejoratively at first, then more affirmingly, as the *Nouvelle Théologie*.[884] They were the "new theologians," and they aimed at the renewal of the Church through a recovery of an accurate historical record. They understood the reality of historical change, they apprehended that historical scholarship was not about the excavation of proof-texts with which to brow-beat one's opponents, and they sought to see the past with fresh eyes.[885] In their quest, they were joined by other like-minded writers and scholars. Hans Küng (1928–2021) examined that old medieval movement, the Conciliarists, to find inspiration for restructuring the contemporary Church along more participatory lines.[886] Brian Tierney (1922–2019) similarly mined the writings of the twelfth- and thirteenth-century canon lawyers to prove that the conciliarist ideal had a deep – and quite orthodox – history within the Church's own juristic tradition.[887]

Collectively, these new theologians had rejected the old *societas perfecta* ecclesiology. According to the newcomers, the Church might be seen as a *communio* – a "communion" of believers, or it might be understood as a "mystical body" – an idea that had been given a qualified endorsement in

---

Lustre of Our Country: The American Experience of Religious Freedom (Berkeley, CA, 1998), pp. 330–348.

881 See, for example, the essays collected in J. Leon Hooper, ed., *Bridging the Sacred and the Secular: Selected Writings of John Courtney Murray* (Washington, DC, 1994).

882 Susanna De Stradis, "Not Quite Silenced: Understanding the Censoring of John Courtney Murray," *Commonweal*, December 9, 2021.

883 Thomas W. O'Brien, *John Courtney Murray in a Cold War Context* (Lanham, MD, 2004), p. 100.

884 Barry Hudock, *Struggle, Condemnation, Vindication: John Courtney Murray's Journey Toward Vatican II* (Collegeville, MN, 2015), p. 72.

885 Gabriel Flynn, "*Resourcement* and Theologies of Communion," in Lewis Ayres and Medi Ann Volpe, eds., *The Oxford Handbook of Catholic Theology* (Oxford, UK, 2016), pp. 683–700.

886 Christopher Ruddy, "Yves Congar and Hans Küng at Vatican II: Differing Paths of Church Reform," *Ecclesiology* 10 (2014), pp. 159, 170–185; and Massimo Faggioli, *A Council For the Global Church: Receiving Vatican II in History* (Minneapolis, MN, 2015), pp. 86–91.

887 Brian Tierney, *Foundations of the Conciliar Theory: The Contributions of the Medieval Canonists From Gratian to the Great Schism*, enlarged new edition (Leiden, 1997) (originally published by Cambridge University Press, 1955).

Pope Pius XII's encyclical *Mystici Corporis* in 1943.[888] But a society that was radically and fundamentally unequal? That was defined jurisdictionally by measured and graduated powers to compel and the corresponding obligation to obey? And that was clericalist to its core? Such an ecclesiology was no longer credible. An avenue was thereby being opened to imagine the Church's ecclesiology in terms very different from that of the nineteenth century. The ground was being prepared for something that was new and exciting and different.

5.3 *Vatican Council II and a Renewed and Updated Ecclesiology*

There was a triumphal quality to the opening ceremony of the Second Vatican Council. Pope John XXIII was carried into St. Peter's Basilica on the *sedia gestatoria* – the portable seated throne used to transport popes for centuries. The Holy Father wore the traditional triple tiara, crafted from silver and gold, heavily jeweled, surmounted by a cross. A procession of thousands of bishops, cardinals, and church dignitaries streamed into St. Peter's in ordered ranks. It made for timeless pageantry. By the Council's end, however, neither the *sedia gestatoria* or the triple tiara made much sense, and within a few years after the Council's close, both disappeared from use. Timeless speedily became outdated.

The Council altered the life of the Church in many respects, but what is of particular concern for our purposes are two documents, known as *Lumen Gentium*, the "Dogmatic Constitution on the Church," and *Christus Dominus*, the "Decree on the Pastoral Office of Bishops."

5.3.1 *Lumen Gentium*

Lumen Gentium was approved by the Second Vatican Council by an overwhelming vote in November, 1964. It is called a "Constitution," but it should not thereby be mistaken for a constitution in the American sense of that word. It does not allocate powers among different branches of government; it is not meant to prescribe legally binding obligations; nor does it guarantee rights in any juridic sense. It operates, rather, at the level of faith and first principles.

The text's near-unanimous approval masked some fundamental alterations between its first, tentative draft and its final form. The Theological Commission that had prepared the first draft entitled its opening chapter "The Nature of the Church Militant," and "was roundly criticized for being too juridical and clerical, dominated by a pyramidal view."[889] Council fathers further "complained

888 Pius XII, *Mystici Corporis* (1943).

889 Paul McPartlan, "The Church," in Ayres and Volpe, *Oxford Handbook*, *supra*, pp. 198, 208.

that it portrayed the laity too much as mere appendages of the hierarchy."[890] After some spirited debate, in place of this recapitulation of older views, the Council chose to define the Church as a "mystery" and as a "sacrament."

Walter Kasper, subsequently elevated to the rank of Cardinal, explained that the decision to employ the word "mystery" was intended to reject neo-scholastic ways of talking about the Church and substitute for it a transcendent understanding.[891] As such, Church-as-mystery is connected to realities that can only partially be understood in this world, such as "God's presence and [God's] salvific plans."[892] And as for sacrament, Cardinal Avery Dulles well-captured its meaning when he proposed that among its other understandings, the Church as sacrament should serve as "a *sign* or symbol, signifying the unity and communion willed by God."[893]

But even if the Church was understood as mystery and as sacrament, there were nonetheless aspects of it that could be defined, explained, and understood, and the body of *Lumen Gentium* was dedicated to their explication. It did so through beautiful and rich imagery and metaphor. The Church was "a sheepfold whose one and indispensable door is Christ."[894] "The Church is a piece of land to be cultivated, the tillage of God."[895] The Church is "the house of God," and the "new Jerusalem," whose members are "living stones."[896] It is "the spotless spouse of the spotless Lamb."[897] The language was poetic, evocative, grounded in Scripture, and it made manifest "that the Church was not simply the product of its structure, its hierarchy, and its set of laws."[898] Plainly, we are moving in a different mental universe from the fixations with sovereignty, power, subjection, and hierarchical governance that so indelibly characterized the attitudes and assumptions of Pope Pius IX and the Council Fathers at Vatican I.

Beyond the poetry and the evident beauty, there was in *Lumen Gentium* a single dominant metaphor that controlled the others. And that was the

---

890 Richard P. McBrien, "The Church (*Lumen Gentium*)," in Michael A. Hayes and Liam Gearon, eds., *Contemporary Catholic Theology: A Reader* (New York, 1999), pp. 279, 280.

891 Maureen Sullivan, *The Road to Vatican II: Key Changes in Theology* (New York, 2007), p. 92.

892 Idara Otu, *Communion Ecclesiology and Social Transformation in African Catholicism: Between Vatican Council II and African Synod II* (Eugene, OR, 2020), p. 63.

893 Avery Dulles, "The Sacramental Ecclesiology of *Lumen Gentium*," *Gregorianum* 86 (2005), pp. 550, 553 (emphasis in original).

894 *Lumen Gentium*, no. 6.

895 *Id.*

896 *Id.*

897 *Id.*

898 Colleen McDannell, *The Spirit of Vatican II: A History of Catholic Reform in America* (New York, 2011), p. 91.

Church as the "People of God."[899] Who comprises this People of God? In 1917, the answer would have been straightforward: Baptized Catholics. Although Gasparri did not analogize Baptism quite this way, it would have been easy and appropriate to say that Baptism incorporated one into the Church in the same way that naturalization incorporated one as a citizen into the secular body politic. *Lumen Gentium*, however, made the answer both more ambiguous and more complicated. Just consider the way two scholars have recently described Vatican II's People of God as "those who share in the new covenant inaugurated by Christ's death and resurrection and which he celebrated with his disciples in the Last Supper."[900] Catholics? Yes, of course. But what of the Orthodox? What of more traditional Protestants, like Episcopalians? What of more enthusiastic, exuberant, free-form, non-hierarchical modern Christian movements?

The idea of the People of God is thus both expansive and elastic. Certainly, the People of God included Catholics. *Lumen Gentium* said as much when it declared that the most complete expression of the People of God was the Catholic Church.[901] But *Lumen Gentium* also "recognize[d]" the "many ways" in which the Church was "linked" to those baptized who belonged to other Christian communities.[902] And it even acknowledged the good relations the Church enjoyed with non-Christian communities and even the religiously skeptical and the atheistic.[903] To use a modern vocabulary, Vatican II's People of God was not defined over and against some radically dissimilar "Other," who could be caricatured as an enemy and an outsider. People of God as metaphor, rather, describes what amounts to a series of adaptable, adjustable concentric circles that operate not to exclude, but to include within its flexible boundaries a vast variety of different grades and degrees of relationship.

Baptism, furthermore, conferred on all Christian believers a fundamental equality and a sacral character: "The baptized … are consecrated as a spiritual house and a holy priesthood."[904] The People of God formed not only a holy priesthood, but "a royal priesthood."[905] And not priesthood only, the People of

899 *Lumen Gentium*, no. 9. Cf., Mark Oppenheimer, *Knocking on Heaven's Door: American Religion in the Age of Counterculture* (New Haven, CT, 2003), p. 66 (describing the People of God as "a new and conspicuous metaphor").

900 Darren Duerksen and William A. Dyrness, *Seeking Church: Emerging Witnesses to the Kingdom* (Downer's Grove, 2019), p. 113.

901 *Lumen Gentium*, nos. 8, 10–12.

902 *Id.*, no. 15.

903 *Id.*, no. 16.

904 *Id.*, no. 10.

905 *Id.*

God "share[] also in Christ's prophetic office."[906] The entire People of God were instituted as "disciples of Christ, persevering in prayer and praising God."[907] Thus the People of God have a "common identity," and a common calling to sanctify and make holy the world.[908]

Granted, even though *Lumen Gentium* declared that the People of God constituted a "common priesthood," it also acknowledged a "ministerial priesthood" which differed from other members of the People of God "in essence and not only in degree."[909] This essential difference qualified the ministerial priesthood for leadership: "The ministerial priest, by the sacred power he enjoys, teaches and rules the priestly people."[910] The ministers, furthermore, were to be subdivided into ranks – bishops, priests, and deacons.[911] Let us focus in particular on bishops, who were seen as successors of the Apostles and "joined" with the Pope into "one apostolic college."[912] The Council emphasized that the office of bishop was called into being for "the service of the community,"[913] and that role became a main theme of a second conciliar decree, *Christus Dominus*.

5.3.2 *Christus Dominus*

Promulgated in October, 1965, *Christus Dominus* had as its special subject the office of bishop. This document identified both the powers of the office of bishop and the purposes to which those powers should be put. Individual bishops, in their dioceses, possess "all the ordinary, proper, and immediate authority ... required for the exercise of their pastoral office."[914]

But the decree was not principally concerned with power relations.[915] Rather, its chief focus was the bishop's obligation to serve the needs of his flock. Within their dioceses, bishops were obligated to serve the needs of the people entrusted to them. "In exercising their office of father and pastor, bishops should stand in the midst of their people as those who serve."[916] They must "feed their sheep in the name of the Lord as their own."[917] They should teach

906 *Id.*, no. 12.
907 *Id.*, no. 10.
908 Jos Moons, *The Holy Spirit, the Church, and Pneumatological Renewal* (Leiden, 2022), p. 97.
909 *Lumen Gentium*, no. 10.
910 *Id.*
911 *Id.*, no. 20.
912 *Id.*, no. 22.
913 *Id.*, no. 20.
914 *Christus Dominus*, no. 8(a).
915 Matthew Levering, "Christus Dominus," in Matthew Lamb and Matthew Levering, eds., *The Reception of Vatican II* (Oxford, UK, 2017), pp. 147, 163.
916 *Christus Dominus*, no. 16.
917 *Id.*, no. 11.

and proclaim the Gospel,[918] and do so "in a manner adapted to the needs of the times."[919] They are also to "promote dialogue" with "human society" in a manner that reflects "humility and mildness."[920] They are required to reach out to the margins, to "migrants, exiles, and refugees."[921]

Still, bishops were expected to exercise a power of governance over their dioceses. They should ensure that the teaching office was properly carried out,[922] and that ecclesiastical property was not misused.[923] They may and should make use of the priests and deacons of their dioceses in the discharge of these responsibilities,[924] and they must always remember that they were connected to their clergy by "bonds of supernatural charity."[925] In everything that they do, finally, bishops must "be mindful of their obligation to give an example of holiness in charity, humility, and simplicity of life."[926]

For sure, in all of this, there were continuities with the way the office of bishop had been defined for centuries. The Council did not radically revise the office of bishop, but it did enlarge the range of episcopal responsibilities. Bishops were expected to devote themselves ever more fully to the needs of their flocks. They were to show themselves as pastors and shepherds, and not simply as rulers and administrators. And they were to relate, productively and cordially, not just with the Catholic community, but with the larger secular world.

5.3.3 The Felt Necessity for a New Code of Canon Law

If *Lumen Gentium* was not a "constitution" in the narrow, juridic sense of the word, it was nevertheless true that the decrees and documents of the Second Vatican Council were, in some meaningful way, "constitutional." This is a point that Massimo Faggioli makes in his history of the reception of the Council. On the subject of "religious freedom," and "ecumenical dialogue," and "liturgical reform," and in its condemnation of anti-Semitism, the Council

918 *Id.*, no. 12.
919 *Id.*, no. 13.
920 *Id.*, no. 14.
921 *Id.*, no. 18.
922 *Id.*, no. 12.
923 *Id.*
924 *Id.*, no. 15.
925 *Id.*, no. 28.
926 *Id.*, no. 15. Cf., Nancy Bauer, "The 1983 *Codex Iuris Canonici*: A Holiness Code?" in Kurt Martens, ed., *A Service Beyond All Recompense: Essays in Honor of Monsignor Thomas J. Green* (Washington, DC, 2018), pp. 61, 68.

was establishing fundamental governing principles for the future life of the Church.[927] And if the Council was "constitutional" in these extended and manifold ways, it was also "constitutional" in that it demanded a new body of canon law to govern a Church that was no longer organized along nineteenth-century *societas perfecta* lines.

It is a truism, probably even a cliché, to claim that law is a product of its time, and, as such, must be understood within the limitations and horizons of the world that produced it. And that was plainly true of the 1917 Code of Canon Law. A wide and distant gulf separated the model of Church that stood behind and animated the 1917 Code, and the model of Church proposed by the Second Vatican Council. The 1917 Code envisioned a Church that was ruled by a tightly integrated, top-down command structure, with the Pope as Vicar of Christ governing infallibly when the need arose. It was a Church made manifest in its juridic structure – secure, majestic, impregnable, invincible. It was also radically unequal, preoccupied with status and rank, and the 1917 Code concretized those features in its provisions.

Lumen Gentium and *Christus Dominus* redirected the Church's orientation. To be sure, the Pope remained the Vicar of Christ, and governed infallibly in at least some circumstances. Bishops were still described as the successors of the Apostles. But the roles they played had been reimagined. They were no longer princes of the Church, but servants of the People of God. Servants, to be sure, who still possessed the power of governance, but it was a power of governance that aimed always to meet the needs of the persons entrusted to their care.

And this meant that the 1917 Code was suddenly perceived as a radically, fundamentally out-of-date text. It simply could no longer function as the living law of the Catholic Church. John Alesandro captured the urgency of the moment well in his introduction to the Canon Law Society of America's *Commentary* on the new Code that was promulgated in 1983: "Probably more than any of the twenty other ecumenical councils, Vatican II required a whole set of laws for its proper administration."[928] The 1917 Code had become a relic unworthy of veneration. It had to be done away with, stored in a closet somewhere, out of sight, so that a new law, one dedicated to meeting the needs of the People of God, might arise in its place.

Hyperbole? Without a doubt. But Alesandro had a point. The 1917 Code had become out of date and out of step. This much was clear even to the Council

---

927 Massimo Faggioli, *A Council for the Global Church: Receiving Vatican II In History* (Minneapolis, MN, 2015), pp. 154–155.

928 John A. Alesandro, "General Introduction," in *The Code of Canon Law: A Text and Commentary* (New York, 1985), pp. 1, 5.

participants, even before the Council adjourned. Therefore, just a little more than two months before he died, Pope St. John XXIII appointed a commission for the revision of the law – the Pontificia Commissio Codicis Iuris Canonici Recognoscendo ("The Pontifical Commission for the Reform of the Canon Law").[929]

5.4 *Meanwhile, in America, a Sudden and Intense Interest in Due Process*

Recall from our discussion of canons 1925 and 1929 of the 1917 Code, that the use of the mechanisms of alternative dispute resolution were strictly limited to private disputes between litigants. Remember also that Pope Pius X had surrounded the appeal of administrative acts of Church officials with strict rules. These were the discretionary acts of ecclesiastical authority figures, and so could not be questioned by third parties. Someone who perceived himself or herself harmed, let's say by an arbitrary decision by a bishop, might, as noted in Part 4, appeal to the Signatura or to one of the Roman congregations. But that was to take the matter up the chain of command. It was, however, impossible for a third party, located outside of this chain of command, to review, let alone question, or recommend the reversal of an episcopal decision. No mere follower of Jesus would dare to tell one of the Apostles that he had done something wrong. And what you could not do to the Apostles, you could not do to their successors, the bishops.

It was precisely this premise that came to be radically, deeply challenged, particularly in the United States, and especially by the Canon Law Society of America, at the end of the 1960s. One does well, however, to begin not with the Canon Law Society's effort to use the tools of alternative dispute resolution to enforce accountability in the Church, but with the intellectual climate within which its members moved and breathed.

The end of the 1960s witnessed the emergence of an intense concern with the protection of the rights of the vulnerable. There was a great fear among elite lawyers and judges that the arbitrary actions of official power-brokers might harm those incapable of resistance. This was a period, in other words, when one discerns a laudable solicitude for social justice by those in a position to do something about it.

This intellectual climate helps to explain the remarkable United States Supreme Court decision of *Goldberg v. Kelly*,[930] viewed by no less an authority

929 *Id.* Cf., Richard G. Cunningham, "The Principles Guiding the Revision of the Code of Canon Law," *Jurist* 30 (1970), pp. 447–455 (examining the guiding principles adopted by the Commission for the reform of the law).

930 *Goldberg v. Kelly*, 397 U.S. 254 (1970).

than retired Supreme Court Justice Stephen Breyer as a "landmark decision" in the field of administrative procedure.[931] The plaintiffs in *Goldberg* were residents of New York City who had been receiving federal or state financial assistance, but who faced the termination of their benefits "without prior notice or hearing, thereby denying them due process of law."[932]

In the factual situation found in *Goldberg*, where the stakes were high – the plaintiffs' very subsistence was at issue – the Court held that the plaintiffs were constitutionally entitled to a prior hearing on the merits.[933] More generally, the Court declared as a matter of principle: "The opportunity to be heard must be tailored to the capacities and circumstances of those who are to be heard."[934] That administrative acts might be thoughtlessly or negligently harmful, and that due process required both the review and the remediation of those decisions, were the unspoken, unquestioned premises.

Notice, that the hearing the Supreme Court mandated did not involve questions of wrong-doing subject to civil remedy – breach of contract, say, or tortious intrusion on the rights of third persons – but a new set of concerns occasioned by the complexities of modern administrative decision-making. There were many pressure points where a heedless governmental agency might harm the rights of those dependent on its services, and those injured parties were now given the right to be heard. This much was the promise of *Goldberg v. Kelly*.

5.5 *A Constitution for the Church?*

Why does this sudden American attentiveness for the protection of the powerless from arbitrary governmental action matter so much to a discussion of alternative dispute resolution at canon law? It is significant because precisely the same debate over the necessity of protecting the rights of subordinates from arbitrary decision-making was occurring in canonistic circles, particularly in the United States. Like the thoughtless social-welfare agencies of New York City, bishops, or their staff, or their delegates, might blunder, they might harm those whom they were consecrated to serve, and where they did, it was believed that arbitration and conciliation provided appropriately-tailored remedies for abuse.

931 Stephen Breyer, et al., *Administrative Law and Regulatory Procedure: Problems, Text, and Cases*, 8th ed. (New York, 2017), p. 615.

932 *Goldberg, supra*, 397 U.S. at 257.

933 *Id.*, at 263–264.

934 *Id.*

Within the United States, the intellectual foundations for this awakening of canonistic interest in due process were laid at a symposium hosted in October, 1967, by the Canon Law Society of America and Fordham University on the subject of "A Constitution for the Church," the proceedings of which were published the following year.[935]

Bishop Alexander Carter (1909–2002) of the Ontario Diocese of Sault Ste. Marie and President of the Canadian Bishops' Conference, delivered the symposium's introductory remarks, and stated that he looked forward to the fostering of an orderly, law-based, and democratic Catholic Church. And he said that he was far from alone in his hopes. Permeating the contributions to the volume, he noted was "the wish to see the whole community involved in the law-making process."[936] "[D]ue process," Bishop Carter continued, was overdue, and should be "welcome to [those] who cherish[] freedom."[937] He had confidence in the good sense of believing Catholics and proclaimed that "[t]he *sensus fidelium* functions in the Church."[938]

Bishop Carter's introduction set the tone and the major key for the conference's participants. A number of contributors built the case that the Church should not only be conceived of constitutionally, but that it should be rights-based and that those rights required protection from arbitrary action coming from the top. Thus that most prolific scholar Fr. Andrew Greeley (1928–2013) argued, on the basis of St. John XXIII's *Pacem in Terris*' endorsement of the relationship of human dignity and human rights,[939] that the modern Church must be decisively collegial in governance.[940] Indeed, he claimed that in a highly-educated and complicated modern world, "collegial decision-making is no longer optional."[941] And, he added, there were corollaries that followed from the principle of collegiality. Persons might disagree and where they disagreed, fair-minded review by third parties must be made available.[942]

---

935 James A. Coriden, ed., *We the People of God: A Study of Constitutional Government For the Church* (Huntington, IN, 1968).

936 Alexander Carter, "Introduction," in *We the People, supra*, p. ix.

937 *Id.*, p. x.

938 *Id.*, p. xi.

939 *Pacem in Terris* (1963) ("But first We must speak of man's rights. Man has the right to live. He has the right to bodily integrity and to the means necessary for the proper development of life. ... Morever, man has a natural right to be respected. ... Human beings have also the rights to choose for themselves the kind of life which appeals to them"). *Id.*, nos. 11, 12, and 15.

940 Andrew Greeley, "A Social Organizational View of the Catholic Church," in *We the People, supra*, pp. 81, 84–85.

941 *Id.*, p. 86.

942 *Id.*, pp. 88–89.

Donald P. Warwick (1934–1997), Director of Comparative International Studies and Lecturer in Sociology at Harvard University,[943] took Fr. Greeley's arguments to their logical conclusion.[944] It was necessary, Warwick declared, for the success of the modern Church, to de-emphasize hierarchy and implement "a large scale decentralization of authority."[945] He stressed, furthermore, that a component of decentralization must be a type of law reform that opened the Church's practices to public scrutiny and made them transparent to the world.[946]

A paper by John Courtney Murray (1904–1967) was included with the other contributions. Murray had agreed to present a paper at the Symposium but died in the summer of 1967, before having an opportunity to compete his draft. A paper he had recently written for the Jesuit magazine *America* was therefore substituted, and fit very neatly with the themes of the conference.[947]

In that paper, Murray made it clear that he did not favor the radical decentralization of the Church.[948] Indeed, he had appreciative thoughts about ecclesiastical authority. Most particularly, it promotes unity, an essential characteristic of the Church.[949] But those who governed the Church must in turn recognize that it is "an interpersonal community."[950] The Church, after all, was the People of God, whose "basic condition ... is ... one of equality in dignity and freedom."[951] Nevertheless, it was also true, Murray went on, that since the Church was comprised of human beings, authority was subject to being abused.[952]

And abuse of authority was never more vividly manifested than when a believer was improperly corrected or punished.[953] Meticulously, step-by-step, Murray reasoned his way to a carefully articulated conclusion, and that was a summons to create institutional protections that shielded the individual from abusive superiors: "What comes to the fore today is the need that the

943 "Sociology Lecturer Warwick Dies at 63," *The Harvard Crimson*, December 11, 1997, thecrimson.com/article/1997/12/11/sociology-lecturer-warwick-dies-at-63/.

944 Donald P. Warwick, "Personal and Organizational Effectiveness in the Roman Catholic Church," in *We the People*, *supra*, pp. 91–110.

945 *Id.*, p. 97.

946 *Id.*, p. 100.

947 James A. Coriden, "Editor's Preface," in *We the People*, *supra*, pp. xiii, xvi.

948 John Courtney Murray, "Freedom, Authority, Community," in *We the People*, *supra*, pp. 145–157.

949 *Id.*, pp. 153–154.

950 *Id.*, p. 154.

951 *Id.*, p. 150.

952 *Id.*, pp. 154–155.

953 *Id.*, p. 155.

corrective or punitive function of authority should be performed under regard for what is called, in the common-law tradition, 'due process.' The demand for due process of law is an exigence of Christian dignity and freedom. It is to be satisfied as exactly in the Church as in civil society (one might indeed say, more exactly)."[954]

It was left finally to Brian Tierney, the medieval historian from Cornell University, to argue that these calls for democratic participation, mutual respect, and the preservation of rights, were entirely consonant with the tradition of the Church.[955] He harkened specifically back to the Conciliarist tradition that did so much to repair that seemingly irreparable breach in the Church, the Great Western Schism.[956] "Western constitutionalism," Tierney wrote, "is not something foreign to the tradition of the Catholic Church. If we chose to adopt constitutional forms in the structure of the modern Church we should not be borrowing from an alien system. Rather, we should be reclaiming a rich part of our own inheritance."[957]

The Symposium's participants did more than present papers. They also crafted a "Position Paper" that asserted that due process must be a part of Church renewal. They supported that Position Paper with a second document, entitled "Points from the Discussion," which identified some of the main themes of the papers presented and the debate that ensued.[958]

In those documents, one finds a deep questioning of the old methods of adversary process and a belief that at the heart of Church renewal there must be placed a commitment to reforming the methods of dispute resolution. Thus we find statements like: "Institutionalization can be a destructive, self-justifying force, but what the world needs now is the example of good institutions."[959] And good institutions must be grounded, in turn, on "effective procedures," which can "foster[]" "the love relationship between persons."[960]

To that end, it was insisted that alternative dispute resolution should be assigned a primary role in healing the lasting hurt that arises from strife-filled adversariness. As the Report put it: "There are many disputes which arise in the

954 *Id.*

955 Brian Tierney, "Roots of Western Constitutionalism in the Church's Own Tradition: The Significance of the Council of Constance," in *We the People, supra*, pp. 113–128.

956 *Id.*, pp. 119–125.

957 *Id.*, p. 127.

958 "Points From the Discussions", in *We the People, supra*, pp. 19–23. The document indicates that the "Points" are meant to keep a record of "a few of the moments or themes of the discussions," and were not intended as "expressions of consensus." *Id.*, p. 19.

959 *Id.*, p. 20.

960 *Id.*

Church wherein the parties do not want to go formally to court. To solve these disputes in a spirit of fairness and charity, there should be a system of boards of arbitration and mediation."[961] Arbitrators and conciliators, the Position Paper maintained, ought to include "clergy, religious, and laymen," and must aim to achieve "a common-sense equitable solution to the disputes brought before them."[962] "Law," the Symposium participants concurred, "is a means to achieve ends; it is an enabling instrument."[963] The law, they concluded, needed "to employ less formal norms, regulations, standards, understandings, administrative procedures, etc."[964]

The Position Paper left a vast number of questions unasked, let alone unanswered. What, precisely, qualified as a subject suitable for arbitration? Could parishioners seek to arbitrate the reassignment of a popular pastor? Could a teacher dismissed from a parochial school, say on the ground of religious dissent, argue that the principal or pastor was mistaken? Or, alternatively, that a diversity of religious viewpoints should be accommodated in a gesture towards ecumenism? Could a religious order running a controversial mission activity challenge the bishop's decision to shut it down? Could an independent arbitration panel that included laypersons really make decisions such as these? Under the old law, the possibility of even suggesting such a process would have seemed absurd. But now the Church was conceived as the People of God, and their pastors were called to service. Could the People of God really exercise some genuine oversight responsibility *vis à vis* their bishops, where it seemed that bishops were failing to render the services prescribed in *Lumen Gentium*?

The 1917 Code of Canon Law permitted conciliation on none of these topics. It was entirely concerned with the resolution of private disputes that had, for the most part, relatively little bearing on ecclesiastical matters. Those complaints were handled through hierarchical recourse, principally to the Signatura. But now the proposal for conciliation advanced by the Canon Law Society of America suggested that alternative forms of dispute resolution might become appropriate vehicles for something that had never before existed but that would come into being piecemeal, through an extended process of arbitration, conciliation, negotiation, and even litigation, and that was a living constitutional framework that relied heavily on precedent and procedure, overlaid on top of a highly traditional, heavily monarchical Catholic

961 "Position Paper: Towards Constitutional Development Within the Church," in *We the People*, *supra*, pp. 5, 13.

962 *Id.*

963 "Points from the Discussions," *We the People*, *supra*, p. 22.

964 *Id.*

Church.[965] Still, this was the age of *Goldberg v. Kelly*, when the twin promises of due process of law and reliance on conciliation, mediation, and other forms of dispute resolution to right historic (or even quite quotidian) wrongs were at their absolute apogee.

5.6 *Report of the ad hoc Committee on Due Process*

Remarkably, the American Catholic bishops found reason to view kindly the Canon Law Society's general recommendations. In their November, 1968, meeting, the National Conference of Catholic Bishops publicly acknowledged the need for a reform of the canon law, and invited Catholic groups to submit proposals, including specifically on the topic of the protection of rights within the Church.[966] In so acting, the American bishops were responding to a call of the 1967 World Synod of Bishops to explore the juridic means by which the rights of believers might be protected at Church law.[967] The Canon Law Society of America was among the groups that answered the bishops' call.

The Canon Law Society assembled a committee that included some of the leading Catholic legal and theological minds in the United States, both lay and clerical. There was Avery Dulles (1918–2008), who was then a professor at Woodstock College, which was a major Jesuit seminary. Fifty years old at the time of his appointment, Dulles had already distinguished himself by the publication of several major works of theology.[968] There was also William Bentley Ball (1916–1999), who was even then establishing himself as a zealous advocate on behalf of the cause of religious liberty.[969] Anthony Padovano (1934–present), was then a Catholic priest – he would subsequently leave the priesthood – and

965 The "Points for Discussion" made clear that these were the intentions of at least some of the Symposium participants: "We are not uncomfortable in proposing western constitutional forms as possible models for the Church's government ... because these forms are increasingly prevalent and acknowledged as successful in the world of today." *Id.*, p. 21.

966 Joseph L. Bernardin, "The NCCB on the Subject of Due Process," in *On Due Process* (National Conference of Catholic Bishops, 1970), p. 1.

967 Article 7 of the principles for the reform of Church law adopted by the 1967 World Synod of Bishops declared that a new Code of Canon Law must do more than proclaim a set of rights in the Church, but should provide actually effective means of vindicating those rights. The language of Article 7 is reproduced in Kurt Martens, "The Law That Never Was: The *Motu Proprio Administrativae Potestatis* on Administrative Procedures," *Jurist* 68 (2008), pp. 178, 181, note 6.

968 See for example, Avery Dulles, *Princeps Concordiae: Pico della Mirandola and the Scholastic Tradition* (Cambridge, MA, 1941); Avery Dulles, *A Testimonial to Grace* (New York, 1946); and Avery Dulles, *The Dimensions of the Church: A Postconciliar Reflection* (Westminster, MD, 1967).

969 Wolfgang Saxon, "William Ball Is Dead at 82; Defended Religious Rights," *New York Times*, January 18, 1999.

a very promising theologian.[970] John H. Mansfield (1928–2014) was a Professor of Law at Harvard University and a committed Catholic.[971] John T. Noonan, Jr. (1926–2017), Professor of Law at Boalt Hall at the University of California-Berkeley and a deeply-trained historian and moral philosopher, had completed two major studies of doctrinal change in the Catholic Church – on usury and on contraception.[972] He would later serve more than three decades as a federal appellate judge. There were other luminaries also on the Committee.[973] It was chaired by Fr. Robert T. Kennedy (1929–2019), a priest of the Archdiocese of New York, a graduate of Harvard Law School, and a holder of a J.U.D. from the Lateran University, who would become the President of the Canon Law Society in 1970 and serve for many years as Professor of Canon Law at the Catholic University of America.[974]

The Committee presented its report at the annual convention of the Canon Law Society of America, held in October, 1969, in Cleveland, Ohio.[975] The Report opened with a strong endorsement of the centrality of rights in Canon Law. "The adequate protection of human rights," the text proclaimed, "is a matter of concern to all men of good will; the adequate protection of specifically ecclesial rights and freedoms has become a matter of increasing concern to all members of the Church."[976]

A Preamble identified specific rights that required protection, such as "[t]he right and freedom to hear the Word of God;" "[t]he right to education, to

970 See, for example, Anthony Padovano, *Who Is Christ?* (Notre Dame, IN, 1967); and Anthony Padovano, *The Estranged God: Modern Man's Search for Belief* (New York, 1966).

971 See the remembrances collected in "In Memoriam: John H. Mansfield," *Harvard Law Review* 128 (2014), pp. 521–539.

972 See John T. Noonan, Jr., *The Scholastic Analysis of Usury* (Cambridge, MA, 1957); and John T. Noonan, Jr., *Contraception: A History of Its Treatment by the Catholic Theologians and Canonists* (Cambridge, MA, 1968).

973 Such as Georges Tavard (1922–2007), a French-born theologian who served as a *peritus* at the Second Vatican Council. See Eleanor Chute, "George H. Tavard, February 6, 1922–August 13, 2007: Respected Theology Professor at Mount Mercy College," *Pittsburgh Post-Gazette*, August 15, 2007; and William W. Bassett (1932–1922), who taught Canon Law at the Catholic University of America, and also served for many years on the Law Faculty of the University of San Francisco. "In Memory of William W. Bassett, Jr.," mooreandsnear.com/tribute/details/9059/William-Bassett-Jr/obituary.html.

974 Robert M. O'Grady, *The Boston Pilot* April 12, 2019, thebostonpilot.com/article.php?ID=184790. Cf., Brandon P. O'Brien, "'Our System:' Father Robert T. Kennedy, the American Legal Tradition, and the Development of Administrative Law in the Revision of the Code of Canon Law," *Jurist* 77 (2021), pp. 361–406 (providing further biographical detail).

975 "Report of the Ad Hoc Committee on Due Process to the Canon Law Society of America," *Canon Law Society of America Proceedings* 31 (1969), pp. 18–51.

976 *Id.*, p. 20.

freedom of inquiry, and to freedom of expression in the sacred sciences;" "[t]he right to free assembly and association in the Church;" and "such inviolable and universal rights of the human person as the right to the protection of one's reputation."[977] Crucially, the Report added: "[P]rocedurally, ... every individual [must] be accorded certain protections in administrative and judicial procedures."[978] "It is the noblest service of the law to afford effective safeguards for the protection of rights."[979]

But there was an immediate and obvious problem with the implementation of a human-rights agenda in the canon law, and that was the legal status of the bishop in canon law. In contrast to the American constitutional order, which features checks and balances among competing branches of government, the canon law envisioned a unity of power concentrated in the head. *Lumen Gentium* and *Christus Dominus* had defined the powers of bishop as including the offices of authoritatively sanctifying, teaching, and governing, a collection of responsibilities that has often gone by the shorthand statement that the bishop acts as "priest, prophet, and king."[980] To be sure, the decree on the laity, *Apostolicam Actuositatem*, had taught that laypersons shared in these threefold powers,[981] but in the end, even the Canon Law Society conceded that "the bishop has the fullness of governmental power – legislative, executive, and judicial."[982] And this concession raised the further question: How, as a matter of logic and law, could a bishop acting in his judicial capacity be expected to review without prejudice a decision that he had just made in his executive or administrative capacities?[983]

To this objection, the Canon Law Society offered four responses. First, they stole a glance at the uniqueness of the American system of government, with its three branches, each with the capacity to check the other. There was plenty of room within such a system for due process to flourish.[984]

But, the Report continued, there were many nations in the world that were not like the United States at all. But this did not mean that these other regimes and realms were despotisms lacking in procedural fairness. No, the Committee

977 *Id.*, p. 19.

978 *Id.*, p. 20.

979 *Id.*

980 See, for instance, Peter De Mey, "The Bishop's Participation in the Threefold *Munera*: Comparing the Appeal to the Pattern of the *Tria Munera* at Vatican II and in the Ecumenical Dialogues," *Jurist* 69 (2009), pp. 31–58.

981 Amanda C. Osheim, "The Christian Faithful," in Gaillardetz, ed., *Cambridge Companion*, *supra*, pp. 212, 225.

982 "Report," *supra*, p. 21.

983 *Id.*, p. 20.

984 *Id.*, p. 21.

asserted, procedural rights, "are relevant to all forms of government, even the most centralized."[985] Even in these states, due process was possible and often flourished. Regardless of the way in which "authority is distributed or not distributed," the elements of a fundamentally fair procedural safety net remain intact.[986] "The right to be heard in defense of one's rights ... is not limited to those who live in a government characterized by separation of powers."[987] The right to present evidence, the power to appeal an adverse decision, the capacity to bring to official attention the possibility that an administrative decision has unwittingly inflicted harm could be found in many systems of law.[988]

Second, the Report contended that it was already the case, even under the 1917 Code, that the bishop was bound to obey the forms of law when adjudicating disputes. The 1917 Code had created a dense network of procedural safeguards. There was a right of counsel under the old law, a right to admit evidence, a burden of proof that had to be satisfied, a right to appeal an adverse decision, and other protections that effectively foreclosed the possibility that a bishop might act arbitrarily when sitting in his judicial capacity.[989] A right to due process, on this reasoning, was not some radical, alien innovation, but simply built on protections already embedded within the law. Furthermore, they were not seen as constraints upon episcopal power.[990] Superiors in the Church were as obliged as anyone to preserve and protect the rights of those alleging they were harmed by official acts.

Third, the Society rejected the contention that a Church that advocated for human rights necessarily undermined the prerogatives and privileges of bishops. "The declaration and protection of fundamental rights," the Committee wrote, "by guaranteeing proper substantive and procedural safeguards is one of the most important exercises of governmental authority by the bishop."[991] By long ecclesiastical tradition, the bishop was the source of justice within his community.[992] A bishop from whom justice flowed should accordingly be zealous

985 *Id.*

986 *Id.*

987 *Id.*

988 *Id.*

989 *Id.*, pp. 21–22.

990 *Id.*, p. 22 ("All of these are in the nature of procedural limitations upon the bishop, and yet they have been thought to be consistent with the centralization of all governmental authority in the local bishop"). *Id.*

991 *Id.*

992 Claudia Rapp, *Holy Bishops in Late Antiquity: The Nature of Christian Leadership in an Age of Transition* (Berkeley, CA, 2005), pp. 242–252.

in upholding and respecting human rights. Hence: "[T]he bishop loses nothing by being required to respect them."[993]

Fourth, and finally, the Society called attention to the Second Vatican Council, which had articulated a strong case for human rights in the civil arena. The Council had praised and recommended such civil rights as the right to association, to self-development, to family, and a host of others.[994] The Council called upon the global community to respect all of these rights, and still others besides. It would amount to a contradiction in terms, the Committee attested, for the Church to celebrate, promote, and salute human rights in the secular world, while simultaneously depriving its most loyal followers of the same set of rights in the ecclesial realm.[995] And not only that. It would also be a betrayal of the spirit of Council: "That the Church must develop adequate institutions to keep pace with modern society is implicit in the whole program of aggiornamento, which inspired the Second Vatican Council."[996]

5.7 *Conciliation and Arbitration: The Canon Law Society's Proposals*

The Committee identified as its principal concern a desire to supervise the Church's administrative apparatus, which was, at the time of writing, undergoing "the fastest rate of growth."[997] Boards and commissions, parish councils, and "departments and agencies" were proliferating, at a rate that caused the Committee members to fear that discretion might be abused simply because the increased numbers multiplied the odds.[998] Thus the Report's authors indicated that their primary objective was "the resolution of conflicts involving the exercise of administrative authority in the Church."[999]

To that end, the Committee proposed three means for vindicating rights within the Church: "Conciliation;" "Arbitration;" and "Judicial Process." The order is significant. Conciliation must be the tool Christians should first turn to in any dispute. "It is not the litigious, but the poor in spirit who are called blessed by Jesus."[1000] Litigation, they wrote, should be disfavored for three reasons. First, such a step was discouraged by Scripture. Paul the Apostle had admonished his followers not to go to court, but to settle their differences with one another amicably, either between themselves or before the community of

993 "Report," *supra*, p. 22.
994 *Id.*, pp. 22–23.
995 *Id.*, p. 23.
996 *Id.*
997 *Id.*, p. 26.
998 *Id.*
999 *Id.*
1000 *Id.*

believers.[1001] Christians should naturally wish to implement in their lives the lessons of their sacred texts. Second, there was the practical reason. Litigating against an institution like the Catholic Church, with "its resources and ability to engage in protracted litigation," is not feasible for most private parties.[1002] Finally, third, most disputes in the secular world are not litigated but resolved "through a negotiated settlement."[1003] If Christians did not take seriously their own founding Scriptures, they should at least follow the model set by the world in the resolution of its disputes.

5.7.1 Conciliation

Thus the Society recommended conciliation as its first, most-preferred means of dispute resolution. Conciliation, with the goal of not just settling a dispute, but reconciling the contending parties, was seen as the form of dispute resolution most consistent with Christian teaching about love of enemies, forgiveness, and peacemaking.[1004]

Still, even conciliation was susceptible to toxic power dynamics. Thus there was always the danger that the process could become abusive of a weaker, more vulnerable party. For that reason, the Society proposed that conciliation must aim at becoming a dialogue of equals. Thus there should be an "opportunity of a face-to-face dialogue."[1005] The dialogue partners should set aside the defense of abstract principles (such as "the right of conscience," or "the rights of authority"), and focus on their immediate points of disagreement in a spirit of friendship and Christian love.[1006] The dialogue, furthermore, should be open, honest, and transparent, and hence there must be no concealment – of relevant evidence, of hidden agendas, or anything else.[1007] "Wounds should be healed quickly."[1008]

The creation of such a system, the Report stressed, should be seen merely as a practical application of canon 1925 of the 1917 Code. That provision in the law strongly encouraged private parties to settle their disputes amicably. And the logic of canon 1925 could easily be extended to the amicable conciliation of differences where some administrative action had caused harm.[1009] (The

1001 1 *Corinthians* 6: 1–8.
1002 "Report," *supra*, p. 27.
1003 *Id.*
1004 *Id.*, pp. 26–27.
1005 *Id.*, p. 27.
1006 *Id.*, p. 28.
1007 *Id.*
1008 *Id.*
1009 *Id.*, p. 27.

fact that the prior legal regime had effectively foreclosed this possibility was silently elided over).

To guide and effectuate the process of conciliation, it was proposed that each diocese should create "A Council of Conciliation," with a membership recruited from among the priests' senate and the faculty of local Catholic colleges.[1010] It would become the panelists' task to imbue the process of conciliation with professionalism, empathy, and fairness.[1011] To ensure that no one was taken advantage of, both sides could be assisted by "one or two advisors – theologians, lawyers, friends, or whomever he chooses."[1012]

Because the process was intended as reconciliation, the Council was without power to force a settlement on the parties, relying instead on voluntariness and good will.[1013] On the other hand, where the conciliators concluded that one or the other of the parties was not proceeding in good faith, the conciliators had the power to admonish them and even, in extenuating circumstances, to report them to the Ordinary (i.e., the bishop), or, where it was the bishop who was proving recalcitrant, to report the bishop to "the Chairman of the Bishops' Committee on Arbitration and Mediation."[1014]

5.7.2 Arbitration

"Hopefully," the Canon Law Society declared, "the vast majority of controversies will be settled through the Process for Conciliation."[1015] If healing was the objective, then healing was best accomplished through voluntary rapprochement, through a mutual willingness to compromise, finally, through a shared commitment to put the dispute in the past and look forward to a renewed relationship. But if conciliation was not possible in a given case, or if it proved inefficacious, or if one or the other of the parties rejected it, the Committee recommended as its second-best option the process of arbitration.

In language that echoed the 1917 Code's definition of the arbiter and the arbitration process, the Society wrote: "Arbitration is defined as the reference of a dispute, by voluntary agreement of the parties, to an impartial person or persons for determination on the basis of evidence and arguments presented by such parties who agree in advance to accept the decision of the arbitrator or arbitrators as binding."[1016]

1010 *Id.*, p. 31.
1011 *Id.*, p. 33.
1012 *Id.*
1013 *Id.*, p. 34.
1014 *Id.*
1015 *Id.*, p. 28.
1016 *Id.*

The Society underscored the formality of the arbitration process. It was not a negotiation aimed at the renewal of friendly relations. It involved, rather, at least some of the elements of a contentious trial.[1017] The Society further recommended that every diocese should establish, parallel with the Council of Conciliation, an "Office of Arbitration."[1018] As with the Council of Conciliation, appointments to the Office should be made both by the local bishop and by the priests' senate.[1019] The composition of the group, furthermore should include a cross-section of priests, religious, and laypersons.[1020]

Arbitrators[1021] were to "be selected for their impartiality and competence."[1022] They were instructed to develop a body of rules that guaranteed their professionalism and independence.[1023] There was an expectation that arbitrators would be very busy, and that arbitrators would usually proceed collegially, on panels consisting of at least three members.[1024] Thus dioceses were urged to nominate at least ten persons to serve as arbitrators "to insure an adequate choice of selection for the parties."[1025] The parties were expected to agree on the names of arbitrators to hear their case, but if they could not, then it belonged to the Chair of the Office of Arbitration to select those empowered to hear the matter.[1026]

A strong air of formality surrounded the procedures proposed for the arbitration process. Proceedings should be under oath.[1027] The parties might "be represented at hearings by counsel or other authorized representative."[1028] Evidence might be taken in person, by deposition, or by affidavit.[1029] It was hoped that the arbitrators could resolve the dispute by unanimous vote, but if they could not, then a decision by a majority should be considered binding.[1030]

1017 *Id.*, pp. 28–29.
1018 *Id.*, p. 35.
1019 *Id.*
1020 *Id.*, p. 36.
1021 Although the medieval canon law, and even the 1917 Code of Canon Law, distinguished between arbiters and arbitrators, the proposed alternative dispute resolution norms did not maintain that distinction. The Committee Report termed as "Arbitrators" those who, under the 1917 Code would have functioned as "arbiters." And it called "Conciliators" those who would have acted as "arbitrators" under the old law.
1022 *Id.*
1023 *Id.*
1024 *Id.*, p. 39.
1025 *Id.*, p. 36.
1026 *Id.*, p. 37.
1027 *Id.*, p. 38.
1028 *Id.*
1029 *Id.*
1030 *Id.*, p. 39.

The parties were expected, for the most part, to bear their own expenses, but the arbitrators might, in a particular instance, require one side to bear some or all of the other side's costs.[1031] In all of these rules, the Canon Law Society's recommendations resembled – at least in general outline – the proceedings of an American courtroom, or at least the commercial arbitration conducted under the auspices of the American Arbitration Association. Since arbitration was intended to reach a final judgment on the merits, the Committee further proposed the creation of a "Court of Arbitration" that should "function as a board of review" that was not to investigate the merits of the result but could "hear and render decisions" on procedural questions that the hearing panel had overlooked or misjudged.[1032]

As it did with its discussion of Conciliation, the Committee grounded its proposed system firmly on the 1917 Code. Thus the Report looked to canon 1929 of the old Code, when it asserted that "the proposals of this Society do not represent a radical innovation in the governmental life of the Church."[1033]

5.7.3 The Judicial Process

Finally, the Committee made clear that it did not wish to abolish the contentious trial, recognizing that despite its limitations, there were also positive features to the judicial process: "Judicial interpretation of law, judicial delineation of rights, increasingly more precise from case to case, and judicial precedent" were all aspects of the legal process that were worth retaining.[1034]

5.7.3.1 *Summary*

The Committee closed its report with a more general discussion of administrative power within the Church. Its recommendations on Conciliation and Arbitration were prompted, the Society wrote, by the very real prospect that administrative authority might be abused, either in particular instances or in a general run of cases. Just as a "School Board should state its basic policies in regard to hiring and firing teachers," or a "Building Commission should publish the guidelines that will govern its decisions on applications for construction," so Catholic dioceses should be open, articulate, and transparent in establishing policies to guide the exercise of administrative discretion.[1035] The Report's drafters were clear. They did not want to abolish discretion and saw

1031 *Id.*, pp. 40–41.
1032 *Id.*, p. 41.
1033 *Id.*, p. 29.
1034 *Id.*, p. 29.
1035 *Id.*, pp. 43–44.

real value in a continuing robust role for administrative discretion: "Discretion is indispensable for tailoring decisions to unique facts and circumstances in particular cases, and for creative solutions to new problems."[1036] What the Committee wanted was to cabin discretion, to contain it in such a way that it did not cause inadvertent hurt especially to the vulnerable. And so it was hoped that if Catholic dioceses took these steps, then the need to utilize the alternative dispute recommendations the Society had published should be lessened, or perhaps even be largely eliminated.[1037]

What stands out in this remarkable document is the degree to which the abuse of administrative power was feared. To be sure, the Church had only recently emerged from the 1950s, a time during which some of its most prominent theologians – Congar, de Lubac, Murray, – were censored or silenced. *Aggiornamento* was the great slogan of St. John XXIII. The word meant openness – to ideas, to persons, to the fresh air of new ways of thinking.[1038] Openness, novelty, the saying or doing of things previously unthought of, all involved a willingness to take risks. The creation of a new and robust set of procedural norms was seen as a safeguard, an assurance, finally even a talisman that effectively promised that we should not again return to those beforetimes, when loyal servants of the Church were punished for daring to think bold, new ideas.

The machinery that the Canon Law Society sought to install, moreover, was meant to work on previously forbidden ground. The 1917 Code contained detailed provisions for the mediation and arbitration of disputes, but those were disputes between private parties, haggling over private points of controversy. The mechanisms the Committee on Due Process sought to erect were directed at creating a review process by which a bishop, or his staff, or subordinates, who acted arbitrarily or capriciously, might be subject to correction. And that correction would come not from hierarchical superiors – say, from the Signatura or the Congregation of Bishops in Rome – but from mixed panels of laypersons, priests, and religious, staffing more or less permanent offices within the diocese. The proposal pledged a sea change, and depended on cooperative bishops. Authorize conciliators to find someone acting in bad faith, or even just carelessly, empower arbitrators to reach binding decisions, and one has effected nothing short of a revolutionary redistribution of power within the Church.

1036 *Id.*, p. 30.

1037 *Id.*, p. 44.

1038 Michael R. Candelaria, *Popular Religion and Liberation: The Dilemma of Liberation Theology* (Albany, NY, 1990), p. 42.

It was left to Thomas Gumbleton (1930–present), Auxiliary Bishop for the Archdiocese of Detroit, to offer both the theological and the practical justifications for the Committee's Report.[1039] For his theological foundation, Bishop Gumbleton looked first to a book that had just recently been published by Cardinal Leon-Joseph Suenens of Belgium, *Coresponsibility in the Church*.[1040] In that volume, Cardinal Suenens averred that Vatican II had subtly shifted the permissible ways in which to conceive of ecclesiastical hierarchy. Coresponsibility, Cardinal Suenens stated, must be seen as "the Central Idea of Vatican II."[1041]

Cardinal Suenens derived his understanding of coresponsibility from the core texts of the Council. Thus *Lumen Gentium* made it clear that baptism must be accounted a great sacrament because it is through baptism that "the People of God" ... "[becomes] a single reality."[1042] All members of the Church must therefore assume a responsibility for its success – bishops, priests, deacons, theologians, the laity. To be sure, Cardinal Suenens wrote, "the structure of the Church is hierarchical,"[1043] but within that hierarchy there is "a common priesthood" and "a common holiness" that must be recognized and cultivated, expanded and developed.[1044]

Bishop Gumbleton used Cardinal Suenens' theology of coresponsibility as a foundation to state a series of "conclusions" about its implications for due process.[1045] Thus Gumbleton asserted that bishops should feel an obligation to make "a patient effort at reconciliation prior to any kind of penalty inflicting procedure."[1046] He had become personally aware, in his brief time as auxiliary bishop, of the use of "excessive power" in the precipitous punishment of clerics and religious who were later found not to deserve it.[1047] Another conclusion Gumbleton drew was that due process must extend to every Christian. Again, he was aware of children expelled from parochial schools without justification or "due process."[1048] Schoolchildren as much as priests were entitled to have their rights respected.

1039 Thomas J. Gumbleton, "Due Process in the Church," in *Canon Law Society of America Proceedings*, 31 (1969), pp. 1–9.
1040 *Id.*, p. 3. Cf., Leon-Joseph Suenens, *Coresponsibility in the Church*, Francis Martin, tr. (New York, 1968).
1041 Suenens, *Coresponsibility*, *supra*, p. 29.
1042 *Id.*, p. 30.
1043 *Id.*, p. 191.
1044 *Id.*, p. 193.
1045 Gumbleton, "Due Process," *supra*, p. 4.
1046 *Id.*
1047 *Id.*, p. 7.
1048 *Id.*

Gumbleton was thus moved to state his final conclusion: A bishop should be "willing to settle disputes that arise, even those that involve himself, and impose penalties in the settlement of them, only after employing procedures of conciliation and mediation and fact-finding by individuals or boards whose objectivity and impartiality are beyond dispute."[1049] Bishops should recognize, finally, that they perform a truly great and authentically episcopal service when they defend and conserve "the rights of every member of the local Church."[1050] The spirit of *Goldberg v. Kelly* was alive and well.[1051]

5.8 Nihil obstat

The Canon Law Society's Report quickly won wide assent within the larger Catholic community. Thus in 1969, the *Catholic Lawyer*, published by St. John's University in New York, and which featured a cross-section of leading Catholic legal scholars on its Board of Advisors,[1052] reprinted the Report.[1053] Again in 1969, and also again in the *Catholic Lawyer*, the great Hungarian-American Jesuit canonist Ladislas Orsy (1921–present) wrote of "The Spirit of Common Law and the Reform of Canon Law."[1054] Fr. Orsy made the case that canon lawyers seeking to reform the system of Church law could benefit greatly from consulting the common-law tradition. Thus he asserted that the separation of powers one finds in common-law systems might help to restrain the abuses of authority that comes from the concentration of all power – executive, legislative, and judicial – in the hands of a single official.[1055] Another source of inspiration for Fr. Orsy was the requirement that the judge at common law be transparent, accountable, and independent. It mattered that judges in the common-law tradition had to explain their reasoning in opinions that could be

---

1049 *Id.*, p. 8.

1050 *Id.*

1051 The United States was not the only nation that created norms and mechanisms for handling administrative appeals. The West German Church, for instance, was similarly active. See, for instance, Paul Wesemann, "Fora Arbitrii Conciliationis et Tribunalia Administrativa in Germania," *Monitor Ecclesiasticus* 100 (1975), pp. 189–194; Paul Wesemann and Klaus Lüdicke, "De Organis Iustitiae Adminstrativae in Dioecesibus Reipublicae Foederalis Germaniae Statutis: Fora Arbitrii Conciliationis, Tribunalia Adminstrativa," *Periodica* 67 (1978), pp. 731–736.

1052 Such as William Bentley Ball, the Church-State lawyer; Vernon X. Miller, who had stepped down as the Dean of the Catholic University of America School of Law in 1968 but had continued to teach at that institution; and Fr. Robert F. Drinan, then a Professor of Law at Boston College, but who would be elected to the U.S. House of Representatives in 1970.

1053 "Due Process in Canon Law," *Catholic Lawyer* 15 (1969), pp. 278–307.

1054 Ladislas Orsy, "The Spirit of Common Law and the Reform of Canon Law," *Catholic Lawyer* 15 (1969), pp. 65–76.

1055 *Id.*, pp. 67–70.

critiqued by the larger legal community.[1056] If one could summarize Fr. Orsy's essay in two words, those words would be "Due Process."

The *Jurist*, meanwhile, the academic journal of the Department of Canon Law at the Catholic University of America, published as the lead article of its 1969 issue an essay entitled "Towards a Declaration of Christian Freedoms."[1057] Summarizing the findings of a second symposium sponsored by the Canon Law Society of America, this one on rights in the Church, the document declared that the time had come to reassert a central role for freedom within the Church and that this commitment in turn demanded a faithful devotion to rights and due process.[1058] "Rights without remedies are mere legal hoaxes," the authors jointly stated.[1059] And, the symposium participants went on, it was precisely for that reason that the Canon Law Society had produced its document on Due Process, with its detailed system of conciliation, arbitration, and formal review.[1060]

It was in this mood of excitement and expectancy that the National Conference of Catholic Bishops themselves republished the Canon Law Society Report under the title of *On Due Process*, recommending its experimental use in American dioceses.[1061] The Bishops then forwarded the document to the Holy See, seeking from the Vatican a decree of *nihil obstat*. When we speak of *nihil obstat*, reference must be had to the intricate system of censorship that existed under the 1917 Code, which still governed the Church in the 1970s.[1062] On one hand, the 1917 Code announced that the Church possessed both the right and the solemn duty to review any written book published by a Catholic author for possible doctrinal error and, should such error be detected, forbid its publication.[1063] On the other hand, where nothing objectionable was identified, the book might receive a decree of *nihil obstat*. This Latin term simply

1056 *Id.*, p. 69. Fr. Orsy made the final point that outside of marriage cases, which comprise "99.5 percent of the cases before the Sacred Roman Rota," the system of ecclesiastical courts had effectively ceased to function *Id.* There could be no justice, he plausibly insisted, where it was impossible to state a claim, or to bring a case, or, for that matter, to find a judge competent to hear the case.

1057 "Towards a Declaration of Christian Freedom," *Jurist* 29 (1969), pp. 1–9.

1058 *Id.*, p. 5–6.

1059 *Id.*, p. 6.

1060 *Id.*

1061 *On Due Process*, rev. ed. (Washington, DC, 1972), p. 3.

1062 Canons 1384–1405 (1917 Code).

1063 C. 1384, sec. 1 (1917 Code). The Church defended this practice on the ground that it was the "protectress of natural law and the guardian and interpreter of the divine law" (I am here translating Cocchi, *Commentarium*, *supra*, vol. III, p. 145 ("Ecclesia sit tutrix naturalis, custos et interpres Iuris divini ..."). *Id.*

meant "nothing objectionable," or, more literally, "there is nothing standing in the way."[1064] Such a decree was not a formal approval of the book's contents.[1065] It was, rather, a declaration that the publication did not offend Catholic doctrine and so served as a kind of warranty of safe use to a Catholic readership.[1066]

If, however, this was the formal understanding of what a *nihil obstat* meant, all of the participants knew that the stakes were higher where the document *On Due Process* was concerned. A *nihil obstat* was more than a mere authorization to publish. *On Due Process* was meant to alter the juridic landscape in some unprecedented ways. And a *nihil obstat* meant that the Holy See would not stand in the way.

In 1972, the Holy See responded to the request, under the name of Pope Paul VI himself.[1067] The approval was a conditional one. The Holy See was not prepared to go as far as the Canon Law Society wished. It insisted that neither arbitrators or conciliators possessed any "power to force the participants to adopt a solution."[1068] Effectively, this made the system voluntary. Bishops and other hierarchical superiors might submit to the jurisdiction of conciliators or arbitrators, and might even agree to abide by the outcome, but none of this could be compelled. Still, the arbitrator retained the power to "determine" whether the parties were "cooperating in good faith."[1069] The remedy for lack of good faith, however, was limited – notification of the Ordinary where a subordinate was concerned; or notification of "the Chairman of the Bishops' Committee on Arbitration and Mediation" where it was a bishop who demonstrated an absence of good faith.[1070] The affected person might need to explain himself or herself, but the law specified no further consequences.

Pope Paul VI's *nihil obstat*, furthermore, indicated in two places that it was granted only provisionally, "experimentally," in the language of the document.[1071] The Vatican also made clear that it was left to the discretion of the local bishop whether or not to implement a system of conciliation or arbitration in his diocese. "[T]he process for arbitration may be experimented with … to the

1064 James A. Coriden, "Nihil Obstat," in *Encyclopedia.com*, encyclopedia.com/religion/encyclopedias-almanacs-transcripts-and-maps/nihil-obstat.

1065 James A. O'Donohoe, "Administrative Aids to the Bishop," *Jurist* 20 (1960), pp. 13, 18.

1066 John A. Goodwine, "Problems Respecting the Censorship of Books," *Jurist* 10 (1950), pp. 152, 174.

1067 "Nihil Obstat for Due Process," *Jurist* 32 (1972), pp. 291–292.

1068 *Id.*, p. 291.

1069 *Id.*

1070 *Id.*

1071 *Id.*

extent that it seems wise to individual Ordinaries."[1072] Flexibility and voluntariness were thus made the touchstones of implementation. The local bishop thus had the freedom to determine whether and how seriously a review of alleged due process violations could be conducted by conciliators or arbitrators who, at least as conceived by the Canon Law Society, need not even be priests.

The issuance of the *nihil obstat* was a remarkable development. A range of cases involving allegations that administrative power had been abused by an ecclesiastical superior – the sorts of allegations that were simply non-reviewable at the local level under the 1917 Code – were now at least potentially subject to scrutiny, provided all of the interested parties consented. It was not what the Canon Law Society sought in making its report. But the document, even as modified by the Holy See, went further than anything before it. It was generally understood in the middle 1970s that administrative recourse under the prevailing law was "often impossible from a practical standpoint," and it was hoped that the provisional norms might therefore answer some large, unmet needs.[1073] Regrettably, however, this was also the high-water mark for due process and alternative dispute resolution in the canon law. The zenith. The apex. For the 1983 Code of Canon Law would hedge back on these procedural innovations in some important ways.

5.9 *The 1983 Code of Canon Law: Declaration of Rights*

On January 25, 1983, Pope John Paul II promulgated a new Code of Canon Law, intended to replace the 1917 version. The decree accompanying the Code's promulgation, known as *Sacrae Disciplinae Leges*, lacked the triumphalist claims of sovereign power found in Benedict XV's *Providentissma Mater Ecclesia*. John Paul II did not claim an abstract right to legislate, nor did he juxtapose his authority over and against that of the state. Rather, he chose to emphasize the practical and pastoral aspects of the new Code. It was the product of a years-long collaboration, and "it corresponds perfectly with the teaching and character of the Second Vatican Council."[1074] "[I]n a particular way," the Pope added, the new law corresponded to Vatican II's "ecclesiological teaching."[1075] Vatican II had made the People of God a primary focus, and the

1072 *Id.*

1073 Adam Maida, "Rights in the Church," in George J. Dyer, ed., *A Pastoral Guide to Canon Law* (Dublin, 1977), pp. 30, 41.

1074 John Paul II, Apostolic Constitution *Sacrae Disciplinae Leges*, in *Code of Canon Law: Latin-English Edition* (Washington, DC, 1983), p. xii.

1075 *Id.*, p. xiv.

Code was meant to give this conciliar vision a juridic framework, that nevertheless simultaneously preserved the Church's "hierarchical authority."[1076]

If the papal tone differed substantially from 1917, then so also did the substantive provisions of the new Code. Fundamentally, the new law had a different structure from its predecessor. It was divided into seven books, not five, and the books bore different titles and arranged the law in a highly dissimilar fashion. The heart of the 1983 Code, moreover, was Book II, entitled "The People of God." It is the longest of the books in the Code, consisting of 543 canons, somewhat less than a third of the entire Code's 1752 canons.

In keeping with the Second Vatican Council's endorsement of rights-talk,[1077] the new law provided a charter of rights and obligations pertaining to all of the Christian faithful. Canon 225, sec. 1, thus declared, in language reminiscent of *Lumen Gentium*, that all Christian faithful have, in virtue of their baptism, both the right and the duty to work individually or in groups for the effective spread of the Gospel throughout the world.[1078] All persons – including lay Christians – have the right and the obligation to acquire knowledge of Christian doctrine "adapted to their capacity and condition."[1079] This general right and duty entailed the further, more specific right, of all Catholics to pursue specialized training in "the sacred sciences ... in ecclesiastical universities or faculties."[1080] All parents, additionally, have both the right and the obligation to ensure the education of their children in the faith.[1081] And so forth.

It was, in other words, a declaration of rights much in keeping with the spirit of the Council and the Canon Law Society's aspirations, even if the final document was the result of compromise and still stood in need of vigorous implementation. But it was precisely in the implementation that questions occurred. It is a truism of the legal order – not merely canon law, but western legal systems generally – that there can be no right without a remedy.[1082]

1076 *Id.*, p. xv.

1077 See, for instance, J. Bryan Hehir, "The Modern Catholic Church and Human Rights: The Impact of the Second Vatican Council," in John Witte, Jr., and Frank Alexander, eds., *Christianity and Human Rights: An Introduction* (Cambridge, UK, 2010), pp. 113–134; and Jean Porter, "From Natural Rights to Human Rights: Or, Why Rights Talk Matters," *Journal of Law and Religion* 14 (1999/2000), pp. 77–90.

1078 Canon 225, sec. 1 (1983 Code).

1079 Canon 229, sec. 1 (1983 Code).

1080 Canon 229, sec. 2 (1983 Code).

1081 Canon 226, sec. 2.

1082 See, for example, *Collection and Recovery of Assets, Inc. v. Patel*, 276 So. 3d 494, 497 (Ct. App., Fla, 2019 ("Such a right without a remedy is no right at all"); *Commissioner of Highways v. West Dulles Properties, Inc.*, 86 Va. Cir. 284 (Fairfax Co., 2014) ("In short, a right without a remedy is no right at all"); *Foothills Federal Credit Union v. Superior Court*

And without doubt, the rights acknowledged by the Code were broad and far-reaching. They were also rights that could be negatively impacted by acts of administrative discretion. It goes without saying that the right of parents to educate their children in the faith might be adversely affected by the decision to close a parish school; or the right to participate actively in the faith could suffer where access to the liturgy, the sacraments, and the means to carry out one's faith in the world is frustrated by the decision to close a particular parish. The question arises: granted we have rights, how does one vindicate those rights?

5.10 *On Recourse against Administrative Acts*

Canons 1732 to 1739 is entitled *De Recursu Adversus Decreta Administrativa* – "On Recourse Against Administrative Acts," and its inclusion in the 1983 Code marks a substantial development from the 1917 law, which, it might be recalled, offered little in the way of protection from capricious administrative decision-making. And, as we shall see, the guiding spirit of this section of the Code, as revealed in a close study of its vocabulary and linguistic choices, very much favors the protection of rights from careless administrative deprivation and provides the mechanisms by which to ensure an appropriate review of acts of administrative discretion. But it is a section of the Code very much governed by the spirit of voluntariness that informed Pope Paul VI's *nihil obstat* back in 1972. Parties – including, most especially, the administrative decision-maker – choose whether and how much of the law they wish to implement, although the law-giver clearly states a preference that all affected parties avail themselves of the means of conciliation.

5.10.1 Canon 1732

We should begin with an understanding of the scope and application of canon 1732, which introduces the section on recourse. The Latin of canon 1732 reads as follows:

C. 1732: "Quae in canonibus huius sectionis de decretis statuuntur, eadem applicanda sunt ad omnes administrativos actus singulares, qui in foro externo extra iudicium dantur, iis exceptis, qui ab ipso Romano Pontifice vel ab ipso Concilio Oecumenico ferantur."

---

of Los Angeles County, 155 Cal. App. 4th 632, 644 (2007) ("As there is no right without a remedy ...") (Johnson, Acting P.J., concurring); *Cornett's Executor v. Rice*, 299 Ky. 256, 261, 187 S.W. 454 (App. Ct., 1945); ("A maxim of the law is that 'There is no wrong without a remedy'"); *Dodd v. Reese*, 216 Ind. 449, 462, 24 N.E. 2d 995 (1940) ("There is a maxim that: 'Equity will not suffer a wrong to be without a remedy"). Numerous other examples might be adduced.

C. 1732: "What is said about decrees in the canons of this section applies with the same force to every kind of administrative act which is taken in the external forum, with the exception of the judicial process, aside from those issued by the Roman Pontiff or promulgated by an Ecumenical Council."

Two terms of art need elaboration. The first is the word *decretis* (nominative singular, *decretum*, English "decree"). To speak of "decrees" might have an alien feel, I am guessing, for most American lawyers. It carries connotations of monarchs seated high upon their thrones disposing of the affairs of their kingdoms. In fact, the word "decree" has a precise meaning at canon law, and its definition is found in Canon 48: "An individual decree is an administrative act issued by a competent authority in which a decision is rendered or a provision is made."[1083]

Decrees, in other words, are the life blood of the administrative law of the Catholic Church.[1084] Whenever a bishop, or a religious superior, or some other competent ecclesiastical official makes a decision, the document that he or she issues is known as a "decree." (And if this term of art comes with a kind of antiquarian, monarchical flavor, then that is just a reminder that the Catholic Church retains significant monarchical elements in its governance).

The other term that we should notice, however, is *administrativos actus* (nominative singular, *administrativus actus*, English "administrative act"). Canon 1732 makes the rules governing "decrees" applicable to every type of administrative act, with exceptions. Canon 35 further defines what is meant by "administrative acts." These include the aforementioned "decrees," but also embrace "precepts" and "rescripts."[1085]

A word should be said about these other two terms of art. First, precepts (*praecepta*): "A singular precept is a decree which directly and legitimately enjoins a specific person (*imponitur*) to do or omit to do something, especially in order to urge the observance of law."[1086] An example might be given: Suppose a competent ecclesiastical authority has learned that a religious community has begun to observe customs contrary to canon law, say, by reverting to impermissible liturgical practices? That authority might choose to issue a precept ordering the community to return to a more lawful form of the liturgy. Precepts thus have a mandatory, imperative application. They seek to restore order, urge discipline, and promote lawful obedience.

1083 C. 48 (1983 Code).
1084 Robert Ombres, "Justice and Equity in the 1983 Code," *Law & Justice: The Christian Law Review* 96 (1988), pp. 23, 31.
1085 C. 35 (1983 Code).
1086 C. 49.

The second term of art to consider is "rescripts." A definition is found in Canon 59, sec. 1: "A rescript is an administrative act issued in writing by competent ecclesiastical authority; of its very nature, a rescript grants a privilege, dispensation, or other favor at someone's request."[1087] Again, an example illustrates the operation of a rescript: Suppose a Catholic high school basketball team traveling to play a game in a Sunday tournament. Since it might be difficult or impossible to satisfy the Sunday Mass obligation, competent authority – let's say, a pastor or other ecclesiastical official with jurisdiction over the school – can issue a dispensation, relaxing the obligation for Sunday Mass attendance because of the tournament.

Finally, there is the language about *extra iudicium* – "with the exception of the judicial process." This provision signifies that one may not utilize the canons on administrative recourse to appeal an adverse decision of an ecclesiastical tribunal. Administrative recourse and the judicial process, in other words, are meant to operate on parallel tracks, and one may not use administrative recourse to subvert the judicial process.

So, now let us return to the canons on recourse against administrative acts. These are canons 1732 to 1739. Of these, canons 1734 to 1739 establish the procedures to be utilized for a formal challenge to an administrative decree. It is a precisely defined juridic process that can necessitate reliance on counsel,[1088] the preparation of technical, legal arguments,[1089] and that may finally eventuate in the matter being appealed to the Apostolic Signatura.[1090]

What follows does not concern the operation of canons 1734 to 1739. Its focus, rather, is on canon 1733, which is intended to provide an alternative form of dispute resolution. Its concern is simply this: what does the law say about the possible use of the tools of conciliation and mediation to avoid the many drawbacks of formal, hierarchical recourse? It makes the point that the lawgiver's linguistic choices demonstrates a deep commitment to conciliation as the preferred method for resolving disputes concerning administrative acts.

5.10.2 Canon 1733, sec. 1

Canon 1733 consists of three sections. The significance of sections 2 and 3 can be briefly stated: Canon 1733, sec. 2 permits national conferences of bishops,

1087 C. 59, sec. 1.

1088 C. 1738.

1089 C. 1737, sec. 1.

1090 Thomas J. Paprocki, " The Method of Proceeding in Administrative Recourse and in the Removal or Transfer of Pastors," in John P. Beal, et al., eds., *New Commentary on the Code of Canon Law* (Mahwah, NJ, 2000), pp. 1818, 1818–1837; and Dino Cardinal Staffa, "Introductio: Praesupposita recursus ad Alterem Partem Signaturae Apostolicae," *Periodica* 67 (1978), pp. 524–534.

throughout the world, to mandate that individual dioceses establish "some office or council ... whose function is to find and suggest equitable solutions."[1091] Canon 1733, sec. 3 provides further directions to guide the operation of diocesan conciliation offices.[1092] Both of these provisions are important, but are limited to the day-to-day operation of offices of mediation and conciliation. Thus they are not the focus of what follows. Our focus, rather, is on canon 1733, sec. 1, which enshrines the principle of conciliation as a central canonical value.

Again, we might begin with the language of the canon:

C. 1733, sec. 1: "Valde optandum est ut, quoties quis gravatum se decreto putet, vitetur inter ipsum et decreti auctorem contentio atque inter eos de aequa solutione quarenda communi consilio curetur, gravibus quoque personis ad mediationem et studium forte adhibitis, ita ut per idoneam viam controversia praecaveatur vel dirimatur."

C. 1733, sec. 1: "It is strongly preferred that whenever someone believes [himself or herself] aggrieved by a decree, that *contentio* between them be avoided. Thus care should be taken to find an equitable resolution by common deliberation; or perhaps also through mediation by serious persons the controversy might be side-stepped or settled by a suitable means."[1093]

5.10.2.1 *Clause One*

For analytical purposes, we might divide canon 1733 into four clauses. The first clause can be seen as including: "valde optandum est ut, quoties quis gravatum, se decreto putet, vitetur inter ipsum et decreti auctorem contentio" ("It is strongly preferred that whenever someone believes [himself or herself] aggrieved by a decree, that *contentio* between them be avoided").

If we perform here the kind of linguistic analysis we conducted in Part 4, we notice first that the phrase *valde optandum*, which featured prominently in Canon 1925 of the old Code, has been retained. We analyzed the expression extensively in the previous chapter, so there is no need now to repeat that discussion. There is, however, one key comparison to make in the way this language was deployed in the two codes. In the 1917 Code, *valde optandum* was grammatically connected to the verb *adhibeat*. It established an obligation, binding on the judge, to urge litigants to settle their cases. In the 1983 Code, in contrast, *valde optandum* is not correlated with any verb of command. In contrast, it stands alone as a strongly stated preference of the law-giver's. It speaks equally to the judge, to the parties, to those parties' advocates, should they

1091 C. 1733, sec. 2 (1983 Code).
1092 C. 1733, sec. 3 (1983 Code).
1093 C. 1733, sec 1 (1983 Code).

have any, and to any other persons who may have an interest in the outcome. The obligation is more diffuse in two senses of that word: first, it does not create a binding obligation on any particular person; but, second, its indefiniteness of scope gives it a wider applicability.

Next, let us consider the phrase *quoties quis gravatum se decreto putet*, "whenever someone believes [himself or herself] aggrieved by a decree." We might begin with *quoties*. I have translated that word as "whenever." This adverb carries a truly expansive meaning. The *Oxford Latin Dictionary* makes this point well when it offers as a colloquial translation, "What a lot of times!"[1094] The Latin thus strongly encourages parties to resort to conciliation on every occasion a grievance arises.

And if the adverb *quoties* was chosen for its breadth, the same can be said for the pronoun *quis*. As a relative pronoun, the *Oxford Latin Dictionary* gives as its meaning "[a]nyone who or anything that, whoever, whatever."[1095] We might contrast this choice of words with the 1917 Code's use *inter fideles*. When the 1917 Code encouraged the use of alternative dispute resolution, it was directed at avoiding litigation among the faithful. *Quis* is considerably broader. Conceivably, it is directed at non-Catholics as much as Catholics. Suppose a non-Catholic student enrolled in a Catholic elementary school, who is impacted by an administrative decree, perhaps being held back a grade, or suspended, or expelled. That student's family would seem to have as much right as a Catholic family to seek remediation under canon 1733.

Now what about that adjective *gravatum*? It is the past participle of the verb *gravo, gravare*, which means "to make heavy, load, weigh down."[1096] It has as extended meanings "to make (troubles, etc.) more burdensome."[1097] Columella used the expression to describe the burning weight of a feverish condition.[1098] Quintus Curtius Rufus employed the term to describe the heavy burden of anxiety.[1099] Seneca the Younger coined the expression *vino gravatum* – "weighed down by wine" – as a clever way to say "drunk."[1100] It is not terribly

1094 Glare, ed., *Oxford Latin Dictionary, supra*, p. 1569.

1095 *Id.*, p. 1559.

1096 *Id.*, p. 776.

1097 *Id.*

1098 Columella, *De Agricultura*, VI.9 (= *Lucius Junius Moderatus Columella, On Agriculture, Books V–IX*, E.S. Foster and Edward H. Heffner, trs. (Cambridge, MA, 1954) (Loeb Classical Library) pp. 154–155).

1099 Quintus Curtius Rufus, *Historia Alexandri Magni*, IV.13.17 (= *Quintus Curtius, History of Alexander, Books I–V*, John C. Rolfe, tr. (Cambridge, MA, 1946) (Loeb Classical Library) pp. 282–283).

1100 Seneca the Younger, *Thyestes*, line 910 (= *Seneca, Oedipus, Agamemnon, Thyestes*, John G. Fitch, ed. and tr. (Cambridge, MA, 2018) (Loeb Classical Library), pp. 308–309.

significant as a term of art at Roman law. In legal Latin, Berger notes that the adjectival form *gravis* could carry the sense of laboring under "a burdensome, heavy debt."[1101] The term retained its meaning as an onerous debt in the writings of the medieval lawyers.[1102]

In its very generality, we should read the choice of *gravatum* as signifying an expansive understanding of the type of harm for which a party might seek relief. Anyone who is troubled by a decree is eligible to use the tools of alternative dispute resolution to seek its modification or revocation. To make this point, we might compare the adjective *gravatum* with the more specialized noun *iniuria*. *Iniuria* at Roman law was a "wrongful act."[1103] *Iniuria* offered grounds for a plaintiff to sue for damages.[1104] Historically, canon law retained this technical sense of *iniuria*, and so it was certainly open to the legislator to have used it here.[1105]

Gravatum – "burdened" – in contrast, carries a more open-ended, flexible, even subjective meaning. Persons experience burdens differently, and the law means to recognize this wide human variability. We should keep this meaning in mind, furthermore, when we turn to our next word, the verb *putet*.

Putet is derived from *puto, putare* – a verb that includes translations such as "to think," "suppose," "go over in the mind," "ponder."[1106] We must pay particular attention to the verb's ending. Recall that Latin is a heavily inflected language, in which the case endings of nouns and adjectives, and the conjugation forms of verbs matter greatly to meaning. And when we consider *putet*, we notice that it is placed in the present tense and the subjunctive mood. In context, it carries the sense of subjective perception. Whenever someone "feels" aggrieved, whenever she "believes" herself as having been wronged, at any time she "concludes" that she has been harmed – these are all possible translations of *putet*.

Notice, the emphasis is on the subjective perception of the person who has experienced the alleged grievance. This "subjectivist" interpretation of canon 1733 can be reinforced if we note that canon 1733 is missing what we might

1101 Berger, *Encyclopedic Dictionary*, *supra*, p. 483.

1102 Thomas Kuehn, *Patrimony and Law in Renaissance Italy* (Cambridge, UK, 2022), p. 178, note 60; and Thomas Kuehn, "'*Materia Est Valde Periculosa*:' Interpreting Testaments in Quattrocento Florence," in Maria Giglioa di Renzo Villata, ed., *Succession Law, Practice, and Society in Europe Across the Ages* (Cham, Switzerland, 2018), pp. 249, 255, note 18.

1103 Berger, *Encyclopedic Dictionary*, *supra*, p. 502.

1104 Cristina Rosillo-López, *Public Opinion and Politics in the Late Roman Republic* (Cambridge, UK, 2017), p. 31.

1105 Richard H. Helmholz, *The Spirit of Classical Canon Law* (Athens, GA, 2010), p. 388; Debora Shuger, *Censorship and Cultural Sensibility: The Regulation of Language in Tudor-Stuart England* (Philadelphia, 2006), pp. 103–105.

1106 Glare, ed., *Oxford Latin Dictionary*, *supra*, p. 1526.

consider to be an important, indeed, an indispensable element. There is no mention of rights in canon 1733. When we come to our discussion of implementation, we shall see that canon 1733 has been generally understood by practitioners as a mechanism for vindicating ecclesial rights. And of course, the lawyer adds, it only makes sense to limit canon 1733 to the vindication of rights, since the law demands precision, and we can obtain the assurance of precision by consulting canons 208 to 223, the charter of rights and obligations found in the Code. But the literal language of the canon omits all discussion of rights and this omission can be reasonably interpreted as an invitation to aggrieved persons to consult their perceptions of right and wrong.

Thus if we read what we have said about *putet* together with our discussion of *gravatum*, we can only conclude that the law-giver is taking seriously petitioners' subjective consciousness of harm. To draw a comparison with the American law of contracts or torts, there is no hypothetical reasonable objective person standing over the petitioner's shoulder telling her that her grievance does not pass the reasonableness test. If the person subjectively decides that she has been unfairly burdened by a decree, she has satisfied the threshold requirement of canon 1733, sec. 1.

Finally, there is the noun *contentio*. It is a word that carries a precise juristic meaning, and that is litigation.[1107] The second-century Gaius, in his *Institutes* used *contentio* to mean causes of action.[1108] Ulpian utilized the word to signify legal disputes.[1109] The canonists spoke of the *contentio iudicialis* – "legal proceedings."[1110] And *contentio* is a noun rich in non-juristic significance as well. St. Jerome deployed it to indicate disputes over the interpretation of Scripture.[1111] Erasmus, in his high neo-classical Latin, made use of *contentio* to denote stubborn, intractable conflict.[1112] *Contentio* is rivalry, it is competition, it is strife, and it leads to faction and division. *Contentio* is thus an evil very much to be avoided.

When we reassemble this clause, then, after this exercise in vivisection, we can draw a number of conclusions. First, the law-maker made plain his desire

1107 Berger, *Encyclopedic Dictionary*, *supra*, p. 412.

1108 Gaius, *Institutes*, Bk. 4:166 (cf., *The Institutes of Gaius*, W.M. Gordon and O.F. Robinson, trs. (Ithaca, NY, 1988), p. 251).

1109 *Digest* 11.6.1 (Ulpian).

1110 Michele Lega, *Praelectiones in Textum Iuris Canonici De Iudiciis Ecclesiasticis* (Rome, 1895), vol. I, p. 355; P. Joseph Noval, *Commentarium Codicis Iuris Canonici* (Turin, 1920), *Liber IV, De Processibus*, p. 146.

1111 St. Jerome, Letter 127.7 (= *Jerome Select Letters*, F.A. Wright, tr. (Cambridge, MA, 1933) (Loeb Classical Library) pp. 454–455).

1112 Jessica Wolfe, *Homer and the Question of Strife From Erasmus to Hobbes* (Toronto, 2015), pp. 92–93.

that *contentio* be avoided. Administrators, complainants, judges, litigants, are all alike so admonished. *Contentio* leads to hard feelings, to fractures and fissures in the community, and such division should have no place among Christians. Second, the Code takes the perspective of the aggrieved party in describing who may seek recourse against an administrative act. The use of *putet* in the subjunctive mood puts the reader squarely in the position of a party who is mulling over whether or not she has a grievance worth pursuing. This reading is further supported by the other word choices the legislator makes. The Code offers a sympathetic, even a subjective legal standard, and encourages such a petitioner both to seek a redress of grievances, and to make use of the tools of alternative dispute resolution to do so. Third, there is the *valde optandum* language. Reliance on the tools of conciliation is strongly encouraged – but it is not mandated.

5.10.2.2 *Clause Two*

Canon 1733's second clause of relevance reads: "atque inter eos de aequa solutione quarenda communi consilo curetur" ("Thus care should be taken to find an equitable resolution by common deliberation").[1113]

We might begin with the verb *curetur*. It stands in parallel construction with the previous verb, *putet*. *Curetur* is a form of the verb *curo, curare*, which means, most basically, "to watch over, look after, care for."[1114] The noun *cura* – "care," "concern" – was derived from this verb and was regularly used by the medieval lawyers to signify the responsibilities of a pastor to tend to his flock.[1115] As a verb, *curo, curare* also conveys a richly-inlaid series of connotations. It carries the extended meaning of devotion; of cultivation; of attentiveness; of zealous solicitude.[1116] We find the term used in legal sources, such as Gaius' *Institutes*, which speak of the vigilance (*curat*) the praetor must exercise in ensuring that

1113 C. 1733, sec. 1 (1983 Code).

1114 Glare, *Oxford Latin Dictionary*, *supra*, p. 475.

1115 See, for instance, C. Colt Anderson, "Ritual Purity and Pastoral Reform in the Thirteenth Century," in Ronald J. Stansbury, ed., *A Companion to Pastoral Care in the Late Middle Ages (1200–1500)* (Leiden, 2010), pp. 73, 73; and Heikki Pihlajamäki and Mia Korpiola, "Medieval Canon Law: The Origins of Modern Criminal Law," in Markus D. Dubber and Tatjana Hörnle, eds., *The Oxford Handbook of Criminal Law* (Oxford, UK, 2014), pp. 201, 208.

1116 Glare, *Oxford Latin Dictionary*, *supra*, p. 475.

guardians do not deplete or waste their wards' inheritance.[1117] The noun "curator" is derived from this root.[1118]

Parallel with *putet, curetur* is placed in the present tense and the subjunctive mood. *Putet* speaks to the petitioner's personal sense of grievance; *curetur*, on the other hand, expresses the wish that the parties will be able to take the steps necessary to bring their dispute to a peaceful and happy conclusion. Neither verb stands as a command. They speak rather to the sincere hope of the lawmaker that peace between the parties might be attained.

Now, what of the phrase *de aequa solutione* ("equitable resolution")? We have already commented extensively on the meaning of *aequo*, and that commentary is applicable here. And *solutione* – the ablative form of the noun *solutio* ("resolution") – can be easily summarized. As used here, "resolution" stands in contrast with *iudicium*, "judgment." At Roman law, *solutio* meant "any kind of liberation of the debtor from his debt,"[1119] or simply the payment of a purchase price.[1120] Here we should understand *solutio* in its non-technical sense as "the unfastening of knots" or "the solving (of a puzzle or dilemma)."[1121]

The parties, furthermore, are urged to resolve their disagreement through the exercise of *communi consilio*. This expression requires some close analysis. *Communi* is the ablative of the adjective *communis*. The word means "common," of course, but used in context it also carries the significance of "mutuality."[1122] Indeed, the *Oxford Latin Dictionary* proposes as one translation "mutual participation (in rights, ownership, etc.), association, sharing."[1123] And it is an entirely reasonable extension of this translation, well-grounded in the sources, to propose that mutuality also entails equality.[1124] In their dealings with one another – and even in their disputes – parties should maintain an equality – of

1117 Gaius, *Institutes*, Bk. I: 199 (Cf., *Institutes*, Gordon and Robinson, trs., p. 53).

1118 Judith Winter, "Coming Together Differently: Art, Anthropology, and the Curatorial Space," in Roger Sansi, ed., *The Anthropologist as Curator* (New York, 2020), pp. 115, 115.

1119 Berger, *Encyclopedic Dictionary of Roman Law, supra*, p. 710.

1120 Marcus Terentius Varro, *De Agricultura*, Bk. II.1.15 (= *Marcus Porcius Cato On Agriculture, Marcus Terentius Varro On Agriculture*, William Davis Hooper, tr. (Cambridge, MA, 1934) (Loeb Classical Library) pp. 320–321).

1121 Glare, ed., *Oxford Latin Dictionary, supra*, p. 369.

1122 María Pia Lara, "Reframing Perspectives on Evil: Accountability, Moral Responsibility, and Collective Judgment," in Andrea Veltman and Kathryn J. Norlock, eds., *Evil, Political Violence, and Forgiveness: Essays in Honor of Claudia Card* (Lanham, MD, 2009), pp. 195, 203.

1123 Glare, ed., *Oxford Latin Dictionary, supra, p. 369.*

1124 William H.F. Altman, *The Revival of Platonism in Cicero's Late Philosophy: Platonis Aemulus and the Invention of Cicero* (Lanham, MD, 2016), p. 48.

respect, of power, of willingness to compromise. One party must not impose a solution upon the other, for that is the very antithesis of mutuality.

Next we should examine *consilio*. In its translation of the 1983 Code, the Canon Law Society of America rendered this noun as "counsel."[1125] And while this translation is not plainly wrong, better word choices can be identified. I have myself translated the expression as "deliberation." The primary idea behind *consilium* is "debate" or "discussion."[1126] Secondarily, the expression includes "the exercise of judgment or discernment;"[1127] or purposeful planning or conscious design.[1128] Medieval lawyers invented a whole genre of literature known as the *consilium* (plural *consilia*) which constituted commentary by leading jurists that was intended to dispense learned advice to resolve particularly complex or ambiguous problems.[1129] When read together with its modifying adjective *communi*, the sense of a back-and-forth communication, an exchange among equals, seeking a good-faith outcome to some difficult controversy is the obvious meaning. "Conversation" is another possible rendering, as is "dialogue." "Conciliation" also suggests itself as a fine translation. Thoughtful, informal, intelligent, open-ended process-oriented resolution. That is settlement by *communi consilio*.

Settlement of a dispute by *communi consilio*, however, is only one of two alternative forms of resolution recommended in canon 1733, sec. 1. As we transition from clause two to clause three, we shall move from the informality of dialogue to a more structured process of mediation.

5.10.2.3 *Clause Three*

We ought next to consider the third clause, which reads: "gravibus quoque personis ad mediationem et studium forte adhibitis. …" My English paraphrase reads: "or perhaps also through thoughtful mediation by serious persons."

As noted, we have now moved to a second form of alternative dispute resolution, "mediation." But we should see precisely what the law-giver has in mind for this mediation, and, again, to do that, we should give careful scrutiny to language.

1125 *Code of Canon Law: Latin-English Edition* (new English translation) (Washington, DC, 2020), p. 486.

1126 Glare, ed., *Oxford Latin Dictionary*, *supra*, p. 415.

1127 *Id.*, p. 416.

1128 Ovid, *Tristia*, v.v., lines 32–33 (= *Ovid: Tristia, Ex Ponto*, Arthur Leslie Wheeler, tr. (Cambridge, MA, Loeb Classical Library, 1996), 2d ed. rev. by G.P. Goold, pp. 228–229).

1129 Thomas J. McSweeney, *Priests of the Law: Roman Law and the Making of the Common Law's First Professionals* (Oxford, UK, 2019), pp. 190–204.

Thus I shall dissect some of the text's Latin. First, the expression *gravibus personis*. *Gravibus* is the ablative plural of the adjective *gravis*. Among the definitions we find is that of "having weight or authority, respected, venerable, august, influential."[1130] Thus Cicero writes: "Xenocratem illum gravissimum philosophorum" ("Xenocrates ... that most influential of philosophers").[1131] Similarly, Ovid in the *Metamorphoses* has the legendary praetor Cipus refer to the Roman Senate as *gravemque Senatum* – "the authoritative Senate."[1132] The Code, in using a word like *gravibus*, wanted persons of stature, of seriousness, persons with the necessary skills – legal, social, interpersonal – to solve what might otherwise be intractable problems.

But notice what the Code does not say. There is no discussion of training or credentials. One does not have to be licensed to be a mediator, or a member of a professional association of arbitrators. Why? The law wishes to allow for maximum flexibility. The law-giver undoubtedly recognized that the Catholic Church is a world-wide community and that conditions vary greatly in different parts of the world. A mediator working in the Amazon Basin may have – and need – very different skills and background from someone working in an American diocese, or in the small but fervent Catholic Church in China. In using *gravibus*, the law-giver is signaling a desire that the mediator be well-qualified, but that these qualifications be adapted to the needs of the community. Thus it has been proposed in the commentaries that the legislator meant to entrust bishops' conferences with the responsibility of more carefully specifying whether and what further formal qualifications mediators should possess.[1133]

On the other hand, Kurt Martens is certainly correct to raise a concern that the very open-endedness of the expression *gravibus personis* is an invitation to abuse: "[T]here is a danger that the use of wise persons might become a caricature whereby any person can be asked to simply give his or her impression that a serious attempt for reconciliation was undertaken."[1134]

1130 Glare, ed., *Oxford Latin Dictionary*, *supra*, p. 775.

1131 Cicero, *Tusculan Disputations*, 5.51 (= *Cicero Tusculan Disputations*, J.E. King, tr. (Cambridge, MA, 1945) (Loeb Classical Library), pp. 476–477).

1132 Ovid, *Metamorphoses* 15: 590 (= Ovid, *Metamorphoses Books IX–XV*, Frank Justus Miller, tr. (Cambridge, MA, 1984) (Loeb Classical Library), 2d ed. rev. by G.P. Goold, pp. 406–407).

1133 Jorge Miras, "Commentary," (canon 1733), in Ángel Marzoa, et al., eds., *Exegetical Commentary on the Code of Canon Law* (Montreal, 2004), vol. IV/2, pp. 2057, 2060.

1134 Kurt Martens, "Administrative Procedures in the Roman Catholic Church: Difficulties and Challenges," *Ephemerides Theologicae Lovanienses* 76 (2000), pp. 354, 360.

Mediationem et studium is the next word-pair we should address. I have chosen a less literal reading, preferring to render the text as "thoughtful mediation," treating the noun *studium* as the virtual equivalent of an adjective. Alternatively, the expression might be rendered "serious mediation."

To appreciate this proposed translation, we should review more carefully the multiple meanings of these two words, *studium* and *mediatio*. First, the word *studium*. Its primary meaning, as found in the *Oxford Latin Dictionary*, is "earnest application of one's attention or energies to some specified or implied object."[1135] The *Dictionary* further recommends, as a secondary translation, "enthusiasm, eagerness."[1136] The word also signifies "an activity to which one devotes one's attention, a pursuit, a pastime."[1137]

The English nouns "study" and "student" have their roots in *studium*, but the Latin original only came to denote intellectual activity because of the presumed single-mindedness of the scholar in pursuit of knowledge. Thomas Aquinas neatly captured this duality of meaning when he characterized *studium* "as 'the vehement application of the mind to some thing.'"[1138] Cicero, too, managed to balance these meanings when he punned about his eagerness for intellectual pursuits.[1139]

The Latin noun *mediatio*, meanwhile, does not appear in the classical sources, but it can be found in the works of St. Augustine as a kind of intermediation or median between extremes.[1140] The noun *mediator*, on the other hand, does occasionally occur in late classical Latin, as in Apuleius' *Metamorphoses*, where it carried a kind of informal legal sense of a body of persons willing to assist a neighbor in need in a quarrel with a rich landowner.[1141] The word *mediator*, however, became a prominent feature of early Christian writers. Thus Tertullian spoke of Jesus as the *mediator* between God and humankind, that is, as a bridge between the divine and human worlds.[1142] Prudentius said

1135 Glare, ed., *Oxford Latin Dictionary*, *supra*, p. 1830.

1136 *Id.*, p. 1832.

1137 *Id.*

1138 John F. Boyle, "St. Thomas, Job, and the University Master," in Matthew Levering, et al., eds., *Reading Job With Thomas Aquinas* (Washington, DC, 2020), pp. 21, 22, and note 6 (quoting St. Thomas Aquinas, *Summa Theologiae*, II–II, q. 166, art. 1, resp).

1139 Katherina Volk, *The Roman Republic of Letters: Scholarship, Philosophy, and Politics in the Age of Cicero and Caesar* (Princeton, NJ, 2021), p. 37.

1140 St. Augustine, *De Civitate Dei*, 10.24 (= *Augustine: The City of God Against the Pagans, Books VIII–XI*, David S. Wiesen, tr. (Cambridge, MA, 1968) (Loeb Classical Library), pp. 358–359); and *id.*, 9.16 (pp. 216–217).

1141 Apuleius, *Metamorphoses*, 9: 36 (= *Apuleius, Metamorphoses, Books VII–XI*, J. Arthur Hanson, tr. (Cambridge, MA, 1989) (Loeb Classical Library), pp. 158–159.

1142 Tertullian, *De Carne Christi*, 15:11.

much the same thing.[1143] So also did St. Ambrose,[1144] Lactantius,[1145] Hilary of Poitiers,[1146] and a host of other writers.

Medieval jurists transposed this theological vocabulary onto the law. Thus we see lawyers writing about "Justice as a virtual deity, a holy mediator (*Justitia Mediatrix*) between natural and positive law."[1147] Aware of this history, when we render the Latin *mediationem* as "mediation," we should simultaneously keep in mind the many Latin texts in which *mediator* is used to describe the one who "stands between" or who "bridges differences," and also recall the underlying theological richness of the patristic sources. Nor should we lose sight of its association with the salvific mission of Jesus Christ.

We must also briefly comment on the adverbial phrases *quoque* and *forte*. The use of these two terms actually marks an important transition in the canon between two types of conciliation. The first type is less formal – settlement of the dispute through "common deliberation." The second type is more formal and makes use of the instruments of mediation. Hence the use of the noun *mediatio*. *Quoque* means "also,"[1148] and its use here facilitates the transition from one form of conciliation to the other. And *forte*, which I have translated as "perhaps,"[1149] simply heightens the sense that *consilium* and *mediatio* represent distinctly alternative means of dispute resolution.

We must finally, however, acknowledge that there is no means of compelling the parties to mediation. The Code speaks of *valde optandum* – an expression of desire, indeed, ardent desire, but the language is not imperative. It carries no obligatory force. Unlike the 1917 Code, the canon does not in the end even speak of an obligation binding on the judge. The language is purely precatory.

5.10.2.4 *Clause Four*

In Latin, the final clause reads: "ita ut per idoneam viam controversia praecavaeatur vel dirimatur." A good English paraphrase might be rendered as: "So that the controversy might be side-stepped or settled by a suitable means."

1143 Prudentius, *The Divinity of Christ*, line 174 (= *Prudentius, Volume 1*, H.J. Thomson, tr. (Cambridge, MA, 1949) (Loeb Classical Library), pp. 132–133).

1144 St. Ambrose, *Expositio Evangelii Secundum Lucam* 3: 256.

1145 Lactantius, *Divinae Institutiones*, 4: 25.

1146 Hilary of Poitiers, *De Trinitate*, 11: 20, line 3.

1147 Donald R. Kelley, "Lord Deliver Us From Justice," *Yale Journal of Law and the Humanities* 5 (1993), pp. 159, 160.

1148 Glare, ed., *Oxford Latin Dictionary*, *supra*, p. 1568.

1149 Domenico Pietropaolo, *Semiotics of the Christian Imagination: Signs of the Fall and Redemption* (London, 2021), p. 56.

Let us first inspect the expression *per idoneam viam*, "by a suitable means." In particular, let us look at the adjective *idoneam* (*idoneus*). The word is a fixture in the legal Latin of texts that Justinian's editors included in the *Digest*. Ulpian used this adjective in his discussion of the procedure by which to obtain the release of a wrongly-detained freedman.[1150] Paulus employed the term to establish criteria for the selection of plaintiffs in public-interest litigation.[1151] Similarly, Justinian's *Institutes* spoke of the necessity of appointing a "worthy guardian" ("tutor … idoneus") for a ward.[1152] Any number of other examples might be elicited.[1153]

The main point to bear in mind is that *idoneus* conveys the idea of suitability. But the phrase, as it appears in canon 1733, is deliberately open-ended. "Suitability" thus has a kind of subjective element to it – what is suitable is finally that which leaves the parties feeling satisfied that a good and just result has been obtained.

Then there is the verb *praecaveatur* (*praecaveo*). Its primary meaning is to "be on one's guard, to exercise foresight, beware."[1154] The verb also carries the meaning "take precautions against."[1155] Its past participial form is *praecautum*, the source of our noun, "precaution."[1156]

So why did I propose a translation like "side-step?" *Praecaveatur* is paired, in this clause, with the verb *dirimatur*, which should be translated as "settled." The Code intends a contrast between a case that is settled and a case that is averted by taking the proper precautionary steps. What I tried to do with my alliterative translation was to capture that contrast.

5.10.3 Canon 1733, sec. 1: Significance

There are elements to canon 1733 that are praiseworthy, and equally there are elements that invite strong criticism. Let us begin with what is praiseworthy. First, the law-giver recognizes that persons might be harmed by administrative decisions. Indeed, the law takes an extraordinarily capacious view of the matter with word choices like *gravatum* and *putet*. The law seeks to put the focus on the person experiencing the harm, and to see the harm subjectively, from the perspective of the individual who feels aggrieved.

1150 *Digest* 43.29.3.12 (Ulpian).

1151 *Digest* 48.23.3 (Paulus).

1152 *Institutes*, 1.23.5.

1153 See, for example, *Digest* 26.2.18 (Callistratus) (also on the appointment by will of the most suitable candidate to serve as guardian).

1154 Glare, ed., *Oxford Latin Dictionary*, *supra*, p. 1421.

1155 *Id.*

1156 *Id.*

Second, the law-giver provided aggrieved persons with a choice between two forms of alternative dispute resolution. The person might choose the path of *communi consilio* – what I have called "common deliberation," but which could just as easily be called "conciliation." It is a process that involves dialogue, conversation, and a thoughtful give-and-take in an effort directed at reaching a fair-minded compromise.

Or the person might opt for the path of mediation. Again, what we see, at the level of word-choice and vocabulary, is a commitment to installing a process that is respectful of aggrieved parties and that seeks to provide genuine relief. The Code calls specifically for "thoughtful mediation." That mediation, furthermore, is to be conducted by someone who is "serious" – in all the many dimensions of that word. Well-qualified, yes, but also wise, insightful, prudent, and fair-minded. The expectation is for a professional, disinterested, independent inquiry, followed by thoughtful recommendations on how best to resolve a distressing situation.

Third, the law favors flexibility. The law-giver recognizes that the Catholic Church is not a monolith but that it actually subsists in a wide variety of local cultures and traditions. The law is open to – indeed, it invites – parties to choose the methods that seem most sensitive to local conditions and most likely to result in a favorable outcome as that is understood in the local culture. It means to facilitate settlements that leave all parties satisfied that a wrong has been righted and that a breach in good relations has been repaired. It similarly invites bishops' conferences and local ordinaries to adapt canon 1733 in ways that satisfy the particular cultural and social expectations of the given region.

But we must also note that the system put in place under canon 1733 is deficient in key respects. The law lacks any means of compelling parties to mediation. The Code uses the language of *valde optandum* – rhetoric, in other words, of fervent wishes and devout hopes. To be sure, the Code warmly invites the parties to participate in some form of alternative dispute resolution, and it would be churlish to turn down an invitation so enthusiastically extended by the law-giver. But there is no means of compelling parties to submit to mediation.

The process, in the end, depends upon the good faith and good will of the parties. It relies on the administrator – almost always the stronger party in any process – to be willing to voluntarily agree to a review of his decision and then to revise or reverse it in light of subsequent conciliation or mediation. The language and the spirit of the Code tells the administrator that he should always remain open to rethinking his choices. But in the final analysis, it is the administrator's choice to make. And this discretion inevitably leads to a problem when highly aspirational language is met with inaction or indifference.

That is the danger that the law comes to be viewed cynically. Good intentions that lack follow-through can lead to curdled relations and to the silent shrug of those who think the game is rigged.

There is also a notable gap in the law. Although the Canon Law Society of America had proposed the creation within dioceses of permanent offices for conciliation and arbitration, the 1983 Code refrained from ordering their formation. The appointment and training of mediators and conciliators, their method of proceeding, their interrogation of the interested parties, their weighing and sifting of evidence – all of the functions we would associate with effective dispute resolution – was left to the discretion of local authorities. Again, one is left to rely on good faith, and the awareness that the administrators who are most likely to cause bruised feelings and trigger disputes may also be those least likely to establish or rely on such institutions.

Perhaps an outcome like this is unavoidable. Perhaps it is even necessary to the operation of the system. The process of mediation and conciliation is made to depend on the good will of the parties and a compelled will, so the reasoning might run, lacks the commitment to revisit a decision that he may have got wrong.

But that leads to the final observation. The great weakness at the heart of the system is the possibility that the rights of the Christian faithful – which the Code is pledged to protect – can be violated with impunity in at least some circumstances. No right without a remedy. We have already made note of that maxim. The Catholic Church has been an eloquent defender of human rights in the international arena. The world has been made a better place for the Church's many interventions. But the Church should do a better job of protecting the rights of members of the ecclesial community.

Has the Code thus betrayed its commitment to the rights of the faithful, a commitment made with so much enthusiasm at the Second Vatican Council? To speak of "betrayal" is too harsh. But the law's effectiveness is placed very much in the hands of individual administrators. Conscientious administrators, who by definition are the ones most likely to rethink their decisions and submit to conciliation and mediation, can certainly ensure that the system runs properly in at least some places. But the law has a harder time with unscrupulous administrators, or ideological ones, or the simply incompetent ones – those, in other words, who are most in need of the fraternal guidance that conciliation provides.

So in the end, perhaps it is well to say, "Two Cheers for Canon 1733!" It is a legal provision that would have been unthinkable under the old 1917 Code. It provides a mechanism for the peaceful resolution of a wide variety of disputes. And these are welcome developments. But canon 1733 can also be charged with failing to fully protect the rights of the People of God, and this is a defect that ought to be ameliorated.

5.11 *Conciliation, Mediation, and the Informal Resolution of Ecclesiastical Disputes Today*

Canon 1733 is a canon that declares a set of broad principles. Those principles might be summarized as: Rights are important and the law is committed to ensuring that they are respected. In doing so, it is vastly better to seek a peaceful reconciliation of a dispute than to pursue vindication through formal hierarchical recourse. Reconciliation should be achieved, if possible, through common consultation, or, if that fails, through the mediation of wise persons of great counsel. The canon, however, cries out for more specificity in its implementation. What is "consultation?" What is "mediation?" And who counts as "wise?" But implementation is entrusted to the local church – whether that be national bishops conferences, dioceses, or other types of Christian community.

It is only natural, therefore, to ask: in the forty years since the promulgation of the Code, how has canon 1733 been implemented? In what follows, we shall examine implementation in four very different parts of the Catholic world: the United States; the nation of India; the Benelux countries (particularly the Netherlands and Belgium); and Nigeria.

5.11.1 The United States

In 1983, following the promulgation of the new Code, the Canon Law Society of America established a task force to examine and ensure the implementation of norms governing the amicable reconciliation of administrative disputes that was to proceed in two phases: the hosting of a symposium to investigate the legal and theoretical issues involved in the resolution of administrative grievances; and the conducting of an empirical survey of what was actually occurring in American dioceses.[1157]

Let us look first at the symposium. The symposium's proceedings were published in the 1986 edition of the *Jurist*. Adapting the vocabulary of human rights, as regularly used by political theorists and international lawyers, the Jesuit ethicist John Langan argued that the Church, "as an anticipation and expression of [humankind's] universal ... destiny," must be particularly assiduous in

1157 Kurt Martens, "Protection of Rights: Experiences with Hierarchical Recourse and Possibilities for the Future," *Jurist* 69 (2009), pp. 646, 689–690; and Ricardo E. Bass, "Due Process: Conciliation and Arbitration," *Canon Law Society of America Proceedings* 53 (1991), pp. 63, 69.

defending the rights of its members.[1158] Other contributors sought to give specificity to this far-ranging moral obligation. Thus John Beal admonished that administrators with broad discretion ought always to take into account the "hardship" that they might "inflict[]" through the careless use of administrative power.[1159] Michael Moodie found the provisions for the protection of rights to be defective since "they urge but never absolutely require an equitable procedure."[1160] Elizabeth McDonough noted that religious life, with its jostling of personalities and its often deep insularity, requires special solicitude when it comes to the protection of rights.[1161]

We should turn next to the survey. The results of the survey were published one year after the symposium, in 1987.[1162] The survey strove for a comprehensive review of due process and administrative procedure in the years roughly between the 1969 publication of *On Due Process* and 1985. The task force charged with conducting the survey found that consciousness of the necessity for due process had taken hold in many dioceses. Thus: "Over 57% of the dioceses in the United States have some experience with diocesan 'due process,' either in developing materials or in actually processing a case."[1163] And the number of cases processed was not insignificant: "Since 1970 over 900 cases have been submitted for 'due process' consideration, and decisions have been reached in nearly 500 of these."[1164]

The task force further determined that not only dioceses, but religious institutes had been active in developing due process norms. Indeed, the task force concluded that the practices established by religious institutes hewed "closer to the ecclesial approach of *On Due Process* than the policies adopted by" diocesan agencies such as offices of education.[1165] Indeed, the task force concluded that "[d]iocesan due process can learn from the religious institutes a sensitivity that not every difficulty can be addressed adequately through 'due process'

1158 John Langan, "Can There Be a Human Rights Problem in the Church?" *Jurist* 46 (1986), pp. 14, 40.

1159 John Beal, "Confining and Structuring Administrative Discretion," *Jurist* 46 (1986), pp. 70, 103.

1160 Michael R. Moodie, "The Administrator and the Law: Authority and Its Exercise in the Code," *Jurist* 46 (1986), pp. 43, 67.

1161 Elizabeth McDonough, "The Protection of Rights in Religious Institutes," *Jurist* 46 (1986), pp. 164–204.

1162 James H. Provost, ed., *Due Process in Dioceses in the United States, 1970–1985: Report on a Survey Task Force to Survey Due Process Experience* (Washington, DC, 1987).

1163 *Id.*, p. 6.

1164 *Id.*

1165 *Id.*, p. 7.

procedures."[1166] In other words, by the latter 1980s, it was safe to conclude that although respect for due process was not universal, and that the methods for conciliation were far from uniform, it was nevertheless true that a reform-oriented *mentalité* could be found alive and well in many places. Rights might not have been respected everywhere, but substantial progress had nevertheless been made in the two decades since Vatican Council II's close.

In 1991, the Canon Law Society of America issued a substantially revised and updated version of the Report of the Ad Hoc Committee on Due Process that was originally published in 1969.[1167] It followed the same essential organizational structure found in the 1969 document, but its recommendations were far more specific and focused. Thus in the section on Conciliation, one finds a detailed identification of the sorts of controversies that could be amenable to this process. They involve: "disputes between a person and a parochial or diocesan administrator or administrative body within the diocese where it is contended that an act or decision (including administrative sanctions and disciplinary actions) has violated a right recognized as such in the law of the Church or in the documents of the magisterium."[1168]

The sorts of disputes envisioned in this document, in other words, are not large and bold challenges to episcopal authority, but the kinds of complaints one encounters in the management of any complex organization. And the complaints, furthermore, must involve "a right recognized as such" by the Church.

Where the 1969 document painted in bright primary colors, where the 1983 Code spoke in the subjunctive voice about grievances that afflicted parties might subjectively feel or perceive, the Canon Law Society took a different direction, narrowing considerably the subject-matter open to conciliation while making more specific the avenues by which disputes could be addressed. Under the proposed CLSA guidelines, parents might still be able to utilize these provisions where a pastor, let us say, restricted admission to the parish school to parishioners who made weekly contributions to the parish fund. Or where a diocesan administrator or a bishop merged parishes thus limiting the number of liturgies a particular neighborhood might be able to access. But a far-ranging challenge to policy? Say, about ecumenical relations within the diocese? Or the distribution of charitable resources? Inquiries into such matters were entirely out of bounds.

1166 *Id.*

1167 *Protection of Rights of Persons in the Church: Revised Report of the Canon Law Society of America on the Subject of Due Process* (Washington, DC, 1991), pp. 13–22.

1168 "Conciliation: Art. 1, sec. 1," *Protection of Rights of Persons, supra*, p. 13.

The revised document also left open some important questions. Thus, precisely how narrowly (or broadly) should we construe that phrase, "right recognized as such?" John Beal, in his introduction to the revised Report, paid particular attention to the rights of labor in construing this passage. Beal noted that Pope John Paul II, in his encyclical on labor, *Laborem Exercens*,[1169] insisted that employers protect the rights of those who work for their firms and companies. Beal now extended the logic. "Justice," he wrote, "requires this system of particular rights of workers be honored not only by secular employers but also by the Church in its own employment practices."[1170]

An argument can be made that employment disputes are quintessentially the sort of subject amenable to conciliation. An awareness of Catholic teaching on the subject confirms this intuition. The Magisterium contains robust teachings on the subject of workers' rights. *Laborem Exercens* made this clear, but so did earlier encyclicals like Pope Paul VI's *Populorum Progressio*[1171] and John XXIII's *Mater et Magistra*. John XXIII spoke eloquently of just wages and the guarantees of social security and pensions.[1172] But if we speak of rights recognized in the Magisterium, then how far do the 1991 norms extend? Can Church employees petition for conciliation as a means of insisting on the provision of adequate pensions? And what of the right to organize? The Magisterium has not only defended the right of workers to organize unions, but endorsed the many benefits labor organizations provide not only to workers but to society at large.[1173] So should a Catholic organization that evinces hostility to having its workers organize a union be subject to conciliation?[1174]

There are other provisions of the revised Report on Due Process deserving of comment. Thus the revised document on Conciliation goes on to declare that "[a] party shall not be represented by a civil lawyer during the conciliation

---

1169 John Paul II, *Laborem Exercens* (1981).

1170 John P. Beal, "*On Due Process*: The Third Decade," in *Protection of Rights*, *supra*, pp. 1, 7.

1171 Paul VI, *Populorum Progressio* (1967).

1172 John XXIII, *Mater et Magistra*, (1961), nos. 68–72 (just wage); and no. 135 (social security).

1173 Pius XI, *Quadragesimo Anno* (1931), no. 28 (endorsing the creation of labor law as vital to society); and no. 36 (praising the creation of unions that "maintain vigorously the rights and legitimate demands of Catholic workers and insist also on the salutary Christian principles of society").

1174 Mark Pattison, "Unions at Catholic Workplaces Called 'Magisterium in Word and Deed,'" *Crux*, August 21, 2016, cruxnow.com/church-in-the-usa/2016/08/unions-catholic-work places-called-magisterium-word-deed. Cf., *NLRB v. Catholic Bishop of Chicago*, 440 U.S. 490 (1979) (hostility of Cardinal John Cody of Chicago to labor organizing in the Chicago Archdiocese).

process."[1175] It is plain that the drafters of the revised Report feared that the retention of a lawyer by one or the other of the parties would have the effect of "escalating" the situation. Lawyers are seen as a proxy for adversariness, on this reading of the text, and the adversary process is antithetical to conciliation. Still, the prohibition on outside counsel may not be realistic. It is likely, especially in America's hyper-legalized environment, that administrators, prior to taking a decision that could impact the rights of third parties, had access to legal advice, and would remain well-positioned to receive further advice in any conflict with an aggrieved party. So why not permit the other side to "level the playing field?"

Following the section on Conciliation in the revised Report, one finds a section entitled "Arbitration." As in the older, 1969 document, arbitration is assumed to be adversarial. Each side may be represented by an "adviser," and there is no prohibition on the use of civil lawyers.[1176] The arbitrator's role, furthermore, fundamentally differed from that of the "conciliator." The conciliator's primary responsibility was to effect a reconciliation between the parties.[1177] The arbitrator, on the other hand, functioned much as a judge might. It was the arbitrator's responsibility to judge the relevance and probative value of evidence,[1178] examine documents,[1179] and come to a binding resolution of the disputed matter.[1180]

Much of the remainder of the revised Report was taken up with a set of proposed norms for the establishment of diocesan administrative tribunals empowered to resolve administrative disputes judicially.[1181] The document notes that two canons of the 1983 Code "presume the existence of such tribunals," and the Canon Law Society meant to address that legal need.[1182] It is an important document, but one that we shall not review since this book is devoted principally to the resolution of disputes outside of the standard judicial process.

The 1991 revised Report, in other words, provided a detailed set of norms to guide and govern the conciliation process. And in 1993, the Canon Law

1175 "Conciliation: Art. II, sec. 2," *Protection of Rights*, *supra*, p. 15.
1176 Arbitration, Art. I, sec. 4, *Protection of Rights*, *supra*, p. 19.
1177 Conciliation, Art. 2, sec. 4, p. 15.
1178 Arbitration, Art. 1, sec. 5, p. 20.
1179 *Id.*
1180 Arbitration, Art. 1, sec. 2, p. 19.
1181 *Protection of Rights*, *supra*, pp. 23–41.
1182 *Id.*, p. 23, note 25. Cf., canons 149, sec. 2; and 1400, sec. 2.

Society's Committee on Due Process proposed to conduct an experiment to see how well conciliation and mediation might work at the local level.[1183]

Two dioceses were selected to run pilot programs on conciliation – the Diocese of Dallas, Texas,[1184] and the Diocese of Portland, Maine.[1185] Both dioceses relied on local resources to give selected personnel specialized training in mediation techniques.[1186] In each diocese, a small number of disputes were successfully resolved,[1187] and each diocese promised to continue to utilize their systems after the expiration date of the experiment.[1188] Should the limited number of cases be seen as a success or failure? Thus posed, the question is impossible to answer and perhaps even unfair. They represent a start, and one can hope that bishops and diocesan administrators see the wisdom in the continued utilization of the tools of peaceful reconciliation.

5.11.2 India

In 1994, the Conference of Catholic Bishops of India (Latin Rite) promulgated a document known as the "Complementary Legislation to the Code of Canon Law."[1189] This document addressed "individual bishops" and "advise[d]" them "to provide for fitting conciliation measures in each diocese so as to avoid conflicts within the Christian community."[1190]

At a somewhat later point, Oswald Gracias, the President of the Canon Law Society of India and the future Cardinal Archbishop of Bombay, published a set of proposed norms to serve as guidelines to the Indian Church.[1191] The document proposed that each diocese should "have an office of Conciliation."[1192]

1183 Patricia McGreevy, et al., "The Final Report of the Committee on the Experiment in Due Process in the Church," *Proceedings of the Canon Law Society of America* 61 (1999), pp. 137–159.

1184 *Id.*, pp. 142–145, 154.

1185 *Id.*, pp. 142–146, 155.

1186 *Id.*, p. 142 (Dallas established "a working relationship with [Dispute Mediation Services of Dallas, a local business]" to provide training; while Portland looked to services offered by the University of Southern Maine. *Id.*

1187 *Id.*, p. 154 (Dallas resolved five cases, "three employment and two parish related"); and *id.*, p. 155 (Portland resolved between four and six cases).

1188 Dallas, however, indicated that it might in the future exempt personnel disputes from the conciliation process. *Id.*, p. 144.

1189 Conference of Catholic Bishops of India (Latin Rite), "Complementary Legislation to the Code of Canon Law," December 2, 1994, ccbi.in/wp-content/uploads/2015-12/Complementary-Legislations-to-the-Code-of-Canon-Law-1.pdf.

1190 *Id.*

1191 Oswald Gracias, "Solving Conflicts in the Church," canonlawsocietyofindia.org/research/solving-conflicts-in-the-church/.

1192 Conciliation Committees, 1 Structure.

Its head, known as the Conciliation Officer, is named by the bishop to serve "a three-year term."[1193] The types of disputes to be resolved through conciliation included: "Disputes between a person and a parochial or diocesan Official (including the Bishop) or administrative body, when it is contended that an act or decision has violated a right recognized as such in the Church or in documents of the Magisterium."[1194]

The procedure recommended by the document imposed on the conciliator "a two-fold role: the investigation of the case and the attempts at conciliation."[1195] The investigation would consist of interviews of the parties, and the collection and review of any other evidence submitted by the parties. The document continues: "The Conciliator(s) then attempt to motivate and assist the parties in settling the dispute themselves while discreetly suggesting possible areas of compromise or other suitable solutions."[1196]

It might be fair to say that this document reflects a certain amount of realism and may, in fact, have roots in actual practice. Clearly, it assigns to the conciliator an active role in seeing to the settlement of the dispute. And there is a level of structure and formality to it as well. Thus the conciliator is obligated, at the conclusion of the process, to "make[] a report which he gives to the Conciliation Officer saying Conciliation has been effected; or explaining that conciliation efforts have failed and giving the reasons for the same."[1197]

5.11.3 The Benelux Countries

In writing about conciliation and arbitration in the Benelux nations – Belgium, the Netherlands, and Luxembourg – we might best begin with the work of Rik Torfs, one of the most creative and insightful canonists working in that part of the world. Torfs has been variously a Professor of Canon Law at the University of Leuven, the Rector of that University, and a Senator in the Belgian Federal Parliament. He has hosted his own television show, and has also served as Dean of the Faculty of Canon Law at Leuven.[1198] He has written on church-state relations,[1199] as well on theories of justice,[1200] the sacrament of Holy

1193 *Id.*

1194 *Id.*, "III. Allowability of Disputes."

1195 *Id.*, "IV. Procedure to be Followed."

1196 *Id.*

1197 *Id.*

1198 "Rik Torfs," in Sam Muller, et al., eds., *The Law of the Future and the Future of Law* (The Hague, 2012), vol. II, p. 493.

1199 See, for example, Rik Torfs, "The Religion-State Relationship in Europe," *Review of Faith and International Affairs* 8 (Summer, 2010), pp. 15–20.

1200 Rik Torfs, "Justice: An Elusive Concept," *In die Skriflig* 54 (2020).

Orders,[1201] and the future of religion.[1202] He has explored in thoughtful and provocative ways the future of canon law now that Catholic ecclesiology has moved beyond the *societas perfecta* model.[1203]

Particular mention should be made of his work on rights since it is by focusing on rights that Torfs was led to the Canon Law's provisions on conciliation. His essay "Human Rights in the History of the Roman Catholic Church," is actually less an historical account of the Church's sometimes troubled relationship with secular rights-talk than it is a discussion of the foundation of rights in contemporary canon law.[1204] Are rights grounded specifically in an ecclesiological vision – like the *communio* theology so favored by the Second Vatican Council?[1205] Or do rights have some larger anthropological justification – that is, are they grounded in something ineradicable and fundamental about the human person?[1206] And finally, since canon 223 admonishes both the Christian faithful and ecclesiastical authority to be mindful of the common good in the exercise or regulation of rights,[1207] "is the common good eventually an enemy or an ally of individual rights?"[1208]

This discussion, then, serves a window into Torfs' book, *A Healthy Rivalry: Human Rights in the Church*, which offers a careful reading of canons 208–223, the Code of Canon Law's charter of rights and obligations.[1209] The canon law declares that "among all Christians, there prevails, as a result of their regeneration in Christ, a true equality respecting both dignity and action."[1210] But what does this language mean, Torfs asks, and how do we work towards actualizing authentic equality in ecclesial life?[1211] Or how do we make real the right

1201 Rik Torfs, "Holding Companies and Holy Orders: Reflections on a Number of Remarkable Similarities," in James H. Provost and Knut Walf, eds., *Studies in Canon Law Presented to P.J.M. Huizing* (Leuven, 1991), pp. 142–159.

1202 Rik Torfs, "Religion as a Utopia?" in Veerle Achten, et al., eds., *'A Truly Golden Handbook:' The Scholarly Quest for Utopia* (Leuven, 2016), pp. 210–22.

1203 Rik Torfs, "Church Tribunals, *secundum* and *praeter legem*," *Louvain Studies* 26 (2001), pp. 346–366; and Rik Torfs, "Legal Relevance of Canon Law," in Felix Wilfred, et al., eds., *Revision of Canon Law* (Concilium, 2016/5) (London, 2016), pp. 34–40.

1204 Rik Torfs, "Human Rights in the History of the Roman Catholic Church," in Hans-Georg Zieberts and Johannes A. Van der Ven, eds., *Human Rights and the Impact of Religion* (Leiden, 2013), pp. 55–74.

1205 *Id.*, pp. 59–60.

1206 *Id.*, pp. 62–63.

1207 Canon 223, sec. 1.

1208 Torfs, "Human Rights," *supra*, pp. 72–73.

1209 Rik Torfs, *A Healthy Rivalry: Human Rights in the Church* (Louvain, 1995), especially pp. 56–85.

1210 Canon 208.

1211 Torfs, *Healthy Rivalry*, *supra*, pp. 58–59.

to free expression? Torfs focuses in particular on free expression. It is a highly conditioned right, as defined by canon law.[1212] Thus the Christian faithful, depending upon their training, their skill, and even their high repute, have the right and sometimes even the obligation to make their views respecting the good of the Church known to "the sacred pastors" and even to other members of the Christian community, keeping in mind the requirements of the common good and due reverence.[1213] Wow. Every word of this canon, Torf notes, constitutes either a qualification or a condition.

Rights in canon law are all like this. Hedged in with conditional language. Torfs recommends the tools of alternative dispute resolution as the best means of developing these rights, giving them meaning, and thereby arriving at a fuller, more complete Christian practice. In many legal systems, one might look to the courts for answers to these problems, but the Code failed to create the administrative tribunals that could have served this function. Still, Torfs concludes, that is just as well.[1214] "In the Netherlands," Torfs writes, "another model has already been made operational."[1215] Dutch dioceses have created a method for "organized reconciliation."[1216] Relying, at least in general terms, on canon 1733, these dioceses have staffed "Bureaus of Dispute," which attempt "to prevent the escalation and the further juridicizing of a difference of opinion."[1217] These bodies, Torfs asserts, live out the spirit of the Code in the ways in which they defuse tensions, promote good feelings, and otherwise seek to reconcile persons who, in the best of good faith, may have very different, competing visions of how to fulfill a life of Christian responsibility.[1218]

If Torfs operates on the level of grand aspirations and high theory, Kurt Martens has also had a chance to survey the operations of reconciliation offices in the Benelux nations and focused more concretely on events on the ground. [1219] He found, like Torfs, that a number of Dutch dioceses have functioning offices of reconciliation, but that the Belgian situation is not as well developed.[1220] And within Belgium, the Flemish speaking dioceses have enjoyed greater success than the French-speaking ones.[1221]

1212 *Id.*, p. 59.

1213 Canon 212, sec. 3.

1214 Torfs, *Healthy Rivalry*, *supra*, pp. 78–79.

1215 *Id.*, p. 80.

1216 *Id.*

1217 *Id.*

1218 *Id.*, pp. 80–81.

1219 Martens, "Protection of Rights," *supra*, pp. 659–660.

1220 *Id.*, p. 660.

1221 Martens, "Administrative Procedures," *supra*, p. 367.

Regarding the episcopal reaction to the use of the tools of reconciliation, Martens writes: "[W]hereas some bishops were at first reluctant to establish such offices, they are now happy with their existence; they no longer have to deal with certain cases, as they are dealt with by the offices."[1222]

Martens makes two points about the overall effectiveness of the reconciliation offices. First, they arrive at an "equitable solution ... in only half of the cases."[1223] But, second, even where no resolution is reached, Martens concludes that they nevertheless fulfill an important pastoral function: "[I]t seems that parties are satisfied they could tell their story to some church official."[1224] The offices, in other words, furnish important emotional support to those who perceive themselves to have been harmed by some ecclesial action, and it might be said that a subjective reconciliation is attained even where the underlying problem has not been worked out. And perhaps, if we take our subjectivist interpretation of canon 1733 to its logical conclusion, this is exactly what the law-giver intended.

5.11.4 Nigeria

The modern history of Catholicism in Nigeria is traceable to the pontificates of Popes Pius IX and Leo XIII.[1225] Leo, in particular, entrusted proselytization to groups of missionaries, particularly from France and from Ireland, with significant results.[1226] The Catholic Church grew substantially in the early twentieth century, and it has been noted that "[b]y 1920, numerous missions had appeared throughout Igboland."[1227] In this early phase, Catholic schooling, too, made a profound contribution to the Christianization of large parts of Nigeria.[1228]

1222 Martens, "Protection of Rights," *supra*, p. 660.

1223 *Id.*

1224 *Id.*

1225 Jean-Marc Ela, *African Cry*, Robert J. Barr, tr. (Eugene, OR, 2005) (originally published 1986), p. 13; F. Anyika, "The Roman Catholic Mission and Traditional Rulers in Igboland and in the Nineteenth Century," *Africa: Rivista trimestrale di studi e documentazione dell-Istituto italiano per l'Africa e l'Oriente* 44 (1989), pp. 211–231.

1226 Eddie E. Okafor, "Francophone Catholic Achievements in Igboland, 1883–1905," *History in Africa* 32 (2005), pp. 307–319; Felix K. Ekechi, "The Holy Ghost Fathers in Eastern Nigeria, 1885–1920: Observations on Missionary Strategy," *African Studies Review* 15 (1972), pp. 217–239; and Augustine Senan Ogunyeremuba Okwu, *The Mission of the Irish Holy Ghost Fathers Among the Igbo of Southeastern Nigeria* (Ph.D. dissertation, Columbia University, 1977), pp. 164–214.

1227 "Catholicism in Nigeria," harvard.edu/faq/catholicism-nigeria.

1228 David W. Kling, *A History of Christian Conversion* (Oxford, UK, 2020), pp. 635–638.

The result, after decades of growth and flourishing, has been the emergence, in the first years of the twenty-first century, of a large and important Catholic Church in much of the nation of Nigeria. It is estimated that there are presently a little more than thirty million Catholics in Nigeria, and that Mass attendance among this population is close to ninety percent.[1229] It is a faith that remains under threat from hostile outsiders.[1230] But it remains nevertheless an active, thriving Church.

Among the Nigerian Church's leadership is Peter Okpaleke. According to the biographies that appear on the website of the Holy See and his home diocese, Okpaleke was born in March, 1963, "and was raised by his maternal grandmother."[1231] He entered Catholic seminary in 1982. Ordained a priest in 1992, he studied canon law at the Pontifical University Santa Croce, where "he obtained a doctorate."[1232] He was appointed bishop of the Ahiara Diocese by Pope Benedict XVI in 2012, but that nomination proved controversial when the diocese refused to accept him because he did not share their ethnic background.[1233] In 2020, Pope Francis resolved what had become an embarrassing situation by naming Okpaleke bishop of the newly-created Diocese of Ekwulobia,[1234] and, two years later, elevating him to the rank of Cardinal.[1235]

1229 John L. Allen, "Running the Numbers, Africa Isn't the Catholic Future – It's the Present," *Crux*, January 25, 2023, cruxnow.com/news-analysis/2023/01/running-the-numbers-africa-isnt-the-catholic-future-its-the-present.

1230 Tawanda Karombo, "As Nigerians Vote for New President, Catholics Hope for End to Violence Against Christians," *National Catholic Reporter*, February 23, 2023; Anthony Ailemen, "39 Catholic Priests Killed, 30 Abducted Across Nigeria in 2022 – Report," *Business Day*, January 24, 2023, businessday.ng/news/article/39/catholic-priests-killed-30-abducted-across-nigeria-in-2022-report/; Tawanda Karombo, "Church Killings in Nigeria Leave Catholics 'Confused, Afraid, and Sad,'" *National Catholic Reporter*, July 6, 2022.

1231 "Biography of +Peter Ebere Cardinal Okpaleke, Bishop of Ekwulobia Diocese," ekwulobia-diocese.org/bishop-bio.

1232 *Id.* Cf., "Okpaleke, Card. Peter Ebere," press.vatican.va/content/salastampa/en/documentation/cardinali_biografie/cardinali_bio_okpaleke_p.html.

1233 Inés San Martin, "Nigerian Bishop Rejected by Ahiara Diocese Installed as Bishop of Ekwulobia," *Crux*, May 5, 2020, cruxnow.com/church-in-africa/2020/05/nigerian-bishop-rejected-by-ahiara-diocese-installed-as-bishop-of-ekwulobia.

1234 Patrick Egwu, "Nigerian Bishop, Rejected by Former Diocese, Installed at New Diocese," *National Catholic Reporter*, May 2, 2020; Ken Briggs, "Francis Compromised Wisely in Protracted Drama of Bishop Okpaleke's Appointment," *National Catholic Reporter*, May 28, 2020.

1235 Christopher Parker, et al., "Meet the 16 New Cardinal Electors," *America*, August 26, 2022, americamagazine.org/faith/2022/08/26/pope-cardinal-electors-2022-243634; Michael Sean Winters, "Rome Consistory Showed Pope Francis' Vision Taking Root," *National*

Nearly two decades earlier, in 2004, then Fr. Okpaleke published a short book directly addressing the theme of reconciliation of conflict within the Church.[1236] He began with some basic premises about the nature of human relationships: "No organization is without conflict."[1237] "Conflict is usually difficult, often messy, and frequently painful."[1238] And he adds, this is as much true within the Church as in the larger secular world.[1239]

But if conflict is a sad and inevitable feature of the human condition, this does not mean that we must accept its presence and do nothing to ameliorate its harshness. On the contrary, especially within the Church, we should take measures to relieve its severity, and to soften its stridency. But before we can do that, we need to understand the sources of discord within the community. In answering this question, Okpaleke was led to propose a whole sophisticated anthropology of human conflict. Persons might suffer from low self-esteem. It is known that such persons feel threatened easily and react in defensive ways that others perceive as hostile.[1240] Or there might be money or financial issues that are the hidden main cause for some conflict.[1241] Much human anxiety is a displaced fear about how and where to pay the next round of bills. Finally, an administrator might simply be bad at communicating and so become the cause of needless division or strife.[1242]

Okpaleke added yet other causes of human strife, but one can derive certain insights from the list he produced. First, Okpaleke assumes the good faith of all of the parties. It is possible that a party has a bad-faith motive for objecting to a particular decision, but that should never be presumed absent compelling evidence. Second, entirely absent from his list is any sense of moral condemnation. Persons with grievances likely have reasons – maybe even good reasons – for their sense of affront. Third, although he did not quite say this, implicit in his list is the admonition that we should not judge. We should rather respectfully listen.

Catholic Reporter, August 29, 2022; Mike Lewis, "A Most Unlikely Cardinal," *Where Peter Is*, August 17, 2022, wherepeteris.com/a-most-unlikely-cardinal/.

1236 Peter Ebere Okpaleke, *Conflict Prevention, Management, and Resolution in the Church* (Amenyi, Nigeria, 2004).

1237 *Id.*, p. 2.

1238 *Id.*

1239 *Id.*, pp. 4–5.

1240 *Id.*, pp. 7–8. Cardinal Okpaleke added that one must always be sensitive to self-esteem issues in others since "a sense of lowered self-esteem is rarely expressed directly but is frequently manifested in indirect ways." *Id.*, p. 8.

1241 *Id.*, p. 8.

1242 *Id.*, pp. 9–10.

The devices Okpaleke proposes to resolve conflict have a familiar feel. First, there is "facilitation," which "is a collaborative process used to help a group of individuals or parties with divergent views reach a goal or complete a task to the mutual satisfaction of the participants."[1243] Then there is conciliation, by which Okpaleke means "an informal process" of conversation and communication meant to build trust and repair relationships.[1244] This was followed by "mediation" – a means by which parties seek to bridge differences caused by "distance, ignorance, disagreement, or hostility;"[1245] and arbitration – the resolution of the dispute by third parties.[1246] All of this, can be channeled and guided by reference to canon 1733.[1247]

"[A]rbitrariness in Church administration [must] be banished," and if it is not, the Church should prepare to deal with those "front page" stories about administrative failure.[1248] This is Okpaleke's solemn warning. Thus the goal, Okpaleke concludes, is the protection of rights, which he recognizes "has become central to the mission of the Church itself as the Church has become a prophetic voice on behalf of human rights for the poor and oppressed of the world."[1249]

5.11.5 Observations

Cardinal Okpaleke's dream, that rights be forcefully and consistently vindicated within the Church, remains a hopeful yet visionary possibility. The possibility of realizing this dream became the focus of a major study in 1986 by Fr. James Provost (1939–2000), for many years Professor of Canon Law at the Catholic University of America, and Executive Coordinator of the Canon Law Society of America.[1250]

Rights, Fr. Provost noted, ought not to be seen as claims opposed to good church order, but rather as flowing from the Church's mission and reflections of "coresponsibility, subsidiarity, and legitimate diversity."[1251] Properly

1243 *Id.*, p. 34.
1244 *Id.*
1245 *Id.*
1246 *Id.*, pp. 37–38.
1247 *Id.*, pp. 41–42.
1248 *Id.*, p. 59.
1249 *Id.*, p. 50.
1250 James H. Provost, "Promoting and Protecting the Rights of Christians: Some Implications for Church Structure," *Jurist* 46 (1986), pp. 289–342; cf., John P. Beal, "Provost, James H.," *encyclopedia.com*, encyclopedia.com/religion/encyclopedias-almanacs-transcripts-and-maps/provost-james-h.
1251 Provost, "Promoting and Protecting," *supra*, p. 300. Cf., James A. Coriden, "Reflections on Canonical Rights," in Provost and Walf, eds., *Studies*, *supra*, pp. 21, 22–23 ("Today

contextualized, one can identify any number of rights embodied in the canon law – in the charter of rights found in canons 208 to 223, of course, but also in other corners of the Code. There is a "right to a just family wage and the attendant benefits which the Church has been preaching to society since the time of Leo XIII."[1252] There are, furthermore, "rights of married persons and of the family."[1253] Associations "formed at the free initiative of Catholics" also "enjoy a proper autonomy" and must be seen as repositories of rights.[1254] In all of these ways, and in many more, the Catholic faithful possess rights, assume responsibilities, and might turn to the mechanisms of alternative dispute resolution should those rights be compromised.[1255]

Due process – which preeminently must include conciliation and other forms of alternative dispute resolution – has a major role to play in the protection of rights. The Catholic Church of the high middle ages was juridically a dense honeycomb of rights.[1256] Prelates, preachers, pastors, and others were zealous in claiming and safeguarding their rights. By including a charter of rights in the 1983 Code, the law-giver was doing something new, yes, in the sense that it has been a long time since the canon law was focused on the protection and promotion of rights. But it is in keeping with long-standing Church tradition. And conciliation, arbitration, mediation, and the peaceful, good-faith settlement of ecclesiastical disputes have a major role to play in the living out of this renewed commitment to rights.

Conclusion

In 1987, Robert Ian Moore published his provocative book, *The Formation of a Persecuting Society*.[1257] Twenty years later, in 2007, he published the second

the sacramental community must show that the rights of its members are actually respected"). *Id.*

1252 Provost, "Promoting and Protecting," *supra*, pp. 310–311.

1253 *Id.*, p. 312.

1254 *Id.*, p. 316.

1255 Working within principally the Anglican dispensation, James Behrens indicates that that Christian denomination has begun to make significant use of forms of mediation and conciliation but that much more could still be done. See James Behrens, *Church Disputes Mediation* (Leominster, UK, 2003), especially pp. 343–466.

1256 Charles J. Reid, Jr., "The Canonistic Contribution to the Western Rights Tradition: An Historical Inquiry," *Boston College Law Review* 33 (1991), pp. 37–92; Charles J. Reid, Jr., "Thirteenth-Century Canon Law and Rights: The Word *Ius* and Its Range of Subjective Meanings," *Studia Canonica* 30 (1996), pp. 295–342.

1257 Robert Ian Moore, *The Formation of a Persecuting Society: Power and Deviance in Western Europe, 950–1250* (Oxford, UK, 1987).

edition of this work.[1258] In both editions, he seeks to explain a phenomenon that became increasingly apparent across the twelfth and thirteenth centuries. Certain disfavored groups – particularly heretics, Jews, and lepers – were singled out and made to bear harsh treatment by their orthodox Christian neighbors. In many instances they were killed. Killed, indeed, in large and tragic numbers. And the persecution of these groups was not simply the result of some temporary flight of madness – the modern sociologist might use the expression "moral panic." That would be bad enough. But what Moore documented was far worse. The persecutions seemed sustained. Indeed, that is the point of Moore's use of the term "society."[1259] Persecution became, to the medieval society of the twelfth and thirteenth centuries something integral, something essential, much as the ownership of slaves had been central to both the ancient Roman Empire and the antebellum American South.[1260]

Particularly in his book's second edition, Moore is at pains to insist that neither "the persecutors themselves or the culture which produced them" should be identified with the Church.[1261] The story is more complex than that, and involves the consolidation of royal power by a number of European states, such as France and England.[1262] Still, it is also true that social categories such as "heretics" or "Jews," were transformed into legal categories and assigned the status they were precisely on the basis of Christian belief.

We can see this in the work of Thomas Aquinas. Thomas Aquinas, as I have written, left the philosophical category of the "common good" remarkably open-ended. There were, he insisted, only a few specific, positive obligations that rulers had to fulfill in satisfaction of the common good. But chief among these duties was the persecution and extirpation of heresy in the community. Heretics posed such a profound threat to the eternal well-being of the community's innocent members, that they had to be removed, indeed, executed if they remained pertinacious in their repudiation of the faith.[1263]

If all of this is true, then the question arises, how is it possible that I should begin a book on peacemaking and the canon law by situating it in the heart of this very unpromising territory? Not an easy question to answer. One might begin by noting that some of the religious texts central to medieval Christendom did

1258 Robert Ian Moore, *The Formation of a Persecuting Society: Power and Deviance in Western Europe, 950–1250*, 2d ed (Malden, MA, 2007).

1259 *Id.*, p. 147.

1260 *Id.*, pp. 147–148.

1261 *Id.*

1262 *Id.*, pp. 37–42.

1263 Charles J. Reid, Jr., "Thomas Aquinas (1225–1274)," in Orazio Condarelli and Rafael Domingo, eds., *Law and the Christian Tradition in Italy: The Legacy of the Great Jurists* (London, 2021), pp. 98, 108.

offer a quite positive vision of peacemaking. "Blessed are the peacemakers," Jesus proclaimed.[1264] "You have heard it said, 'An eye for an eye and a tooth for a tooth.' But I say to you offer no resistance to one who is evil. When someone strikes you on [your] right cheek, turn the other one to him as well."[1265] Or: "Beloved, let us love one another, because love is of God."[1266] Or, again: "I give you a new commandment. Love one another. As I have loved you, so you also should love one another."[1267]

These texts – and other similar ones – established principles: of non-violence; of social peace and concord; of patient forbearance and a willingness to conciliate. They are the raw materials that provide a foundation for peace-making, not only within the canon law but, I dare say, for the entire Christian tradition.

Why then begin this narrative with the middle ages? Because important institutions were then being formed. The papacy had certainly been around for a millennium by the time men like Innocent III and Innocent IV ruled from St. Peter's throne. But these two popes, and their many medieval contemporaries conferred on the papacy an important institutional character. The papacy became a leading international actor. This was not always a good thing. Far from it. But when St. John Paul II strove to his utmost to prevent the American war on Iraq, and when Pope Francis used every tool at his disposal to stop the violence in South Sudan, they were acting as legatees of an institution that had a deep memory about how to navigate global conflict. The same can be said for the canon law. Medieval canonists helped to define the law of heresy and were responsible for judging who fell afoul of its precepts. But the canonists also developed keen insights about the nature of equity, and these insights live on today in the Church's conciliation practices.

This book has investigated peacemaking in three different dimensions. The first of these dimensions was the development of diplomacy as a tool to be used to stop violence. Each of the episodes studied in Parts 2 and 3 had at its heart the desire to avert violence or at least cause it to cease. Humanity, the steady premise of these efforts can be understood, flourishes when nations do not go to war with other nations. Human beings, in conditions of peace, are free to pursue their pleasures, assume their responsibilities, and live out the fullness of their lives. War blights all of this. Steadily, the papacy has moved in the direction of seeing war as an unmitigated tragedy for the human

1264 *Matthew* 5: 9.
1265 *Matthew* 5: 38–39.
1266 1 *John* 4: 7.
1267 *John* 13: 34.

condition, and, equally steadily, the popes have tried their utmost to minimize the suffering.

But there were also two other dimensions to peacemaking that were explored in this volume. The first of these was the use of the tools of alternative dispute resolution to settle private cases and controversies. Litigation – persons facing off against each other as adversaries in courts of law – is also seen as a failure, if not of humanity, then at least of Christians. Not nearly on the scale of war, to be sure. But St. Paul asked his Corinthian correspondents, why do they go to court when they could – and should – settle their disputes amongst themselves?[1268] To that end, I reviewed carefully the provisions of the 1917 Code of Canon Law governing the non-judicial settlement of disputes. And I continue that discussion in the Appendix, where I briefly take up the place of arbitration and mediation in the 1983 Code.

Finally, there is the matter of reconciliation and the reconsideration of administrative decisions. If the Church is the Body of Christ and the People of God, then it must be characterized by solidarity. Administrative decision-makers must – must, it is their calling and their mandate – have foremost in their minds the good of the people entrusted to their care. And that responsibility carries with it, so it would seem, a responsibility to listen and to take seriously what those people have to say. Canon 1733 and its associated canons seem to rest on that premise. Where rights have been violated, where decision-makers have made a mistake, there should be a readiness to reexamine the choices they have made. In its open-endedness and its flexibility, canon 1733 reminds decision-makers that this is at the very least a moral obligation.

That finally is the meaning of that Latin phrase, found both in the 1917 and the 1983 Codes – *valde optandum*. "Really!" The law-giver means it. "Really!" It is hoped that all parties to have a controversy have both the self-awareness and the personal courage to reexamine their actions and to reconcile. Really.

Appendix: The Arbitration and Mediation of Private Disputes under the 1983 Code of Canon Law

Comparisons and Contrasts, 1917 and 1983

I should begin by calling attention to a contrast between Parts 4 and 5. Part 4 focused on the use by private parties of arbitration and mediation under the 1917 Code of Canon Law. Part 5, on the other hand, looked carefully at reconciliation and administrative acts. My choice in emphases, however, does not mean that the 1983 Code of

1268 1 *Corinthians* 6: 4–7.

Canon Law lacks mechanisms for the settlement of private disputes. In fact, canons 1713 to 1716 provide for just such a possibility.

We should concentrate in what follows especially on canons 1713 and 1714. The Latin of canon 1713 states: "Ad evitandas iudiciales contentiones transactio seu reconciliatio utiliter adhibetur, aut controversia iudicio unius vel plurium arbitrorum committi potest."

Or, a loose paraphrase in idiomatic English: "In order to avoid a judicial contest, a matter might either be profitably settled or reconciled, or the controversy entrusted to the judgment of one or several arbiters."

And again, the Latin of canon 1714: "De transactione, de compromisso, deque iudicio arbitrali serventur normae a partibus selectae vel, si partes nullas selegerint, lex ab Episcoporum conferentia lata, si qua sit, vel lex civilis vigens in loco ubi conventio initur."

And, again, a loose paraphrase in English: "The rules selected by the parties are to govern the settlement, the negotiated compromise, or the arbitration process; if the parties have not made a choice of law, then the law of the Episcopal conference governs, if there is any, or the civil law in effect at the place where the agreement was made."

Several comparisons between these two canons and their counterparts in the 1917 Code of Canon Law are in order:

First, canon 1925 of the 1917 Code expressed a strong preference for the non-judicial settlement of disputes. Surprisingly, the language of canon 1713 is essentially neutral. The law neither recommends nor discourages the use of the tools of alternative dispute resolution. The law-giver merely presents it as an option. That said, there is also continuity between the 1917 and 1983 Codes. Thus the phrase *ad evitandas iudiciales contentiones* – "in order to avoid a judicial contest" – is repeated word-for-word from canon 1929 of the 1917 Code.

Second, canon 1925 of the 1917 Code of Canon Law addressed the judge directly and imposed upon the judge an obligation to encourage litigants to pursue alternative dispute resolution wherever possible. Canon 1713, on the other hand, is not addressed to any particular person. The text, rather, states in a simple and matter-of-fact way, that arbitration and conciliation are available as means of settling contentious matters. The law places no obligation on anyone to seriously consider this method of proceeding.

Third, canon 1925 recommended that disputes "among the faithful" (*inter fideles*) be settled through arbitration or mediation. It is possible to read the language of "among the faithful" as a jurisdictional limitation – disputes of the non-faithful are to be excluded from consideration under the 1917 Code. It is interesting, therefore, to note that canon 1713 is not so limited. Could non-Catholics or even non-Christians avail themselves of canonical arbitration? Canon 1713 at least erects no jurisdictional barrier, express or implied, to that possibility. A nod to the ecumenism of the Second Vatican Council? Maybe.

Fourth, canon 1925 of the 1917 Code spoke of the possibility of a "peaceful" resolution to a dispute, using the noun *concordia* to signify "peaceful."[1269] The 1983 Code, on the other hand, uses the noun *conciliatio* – "conciliation." Is there a difference of meaning implicit in these differing word choices? Possibly. *Concordia* is a state of non-hostility. It is a state in which neither party is actively seeking to prevail against the other. *Conciliatio*, on the other hand, carries a richer, affective dimension. By using *conciliatio*, the law-giver is holding out hope that parties to a controversy might attain a meaningful, substantive renewal of what was presumably a broken relationship.

Fifth: now, let us turn our attention to canon 1714. This canon groups together terms the 1917 Code was at pains to keep separate and distinct. These are the words *transactio* and *compromissum*. Recall, that *De transactio* and *De compromisso* formed separate chapters in the 1917 Code. Recall also that these provisions looked to distinctive procedures, and sources of law. Recall as well the sharp distinction between the office *arbiter* and that of *arbitrator*. All of those sharp distinctions are much reduced in the 1983 Code. What is emphasized, instead, is the law's objective: and that is the desire to facilitate the fashioning of a peaceful settlement of disputes between a pair of litigants.

Sixth, we should notice the differences in the choice of law provisions between the 1917 and 1983 Codes. The 1917 Code, recall, established a strict rule governing choice of law. Canon 1926 of the old Code thus spoke of "the norms established by civil law in the place in which the settlement is undertaken" as governing the resolution of the dispute. The 1983 Code imposes no territorial requirement on choice of law. And this can be significant in certain classes of disputes.

Consider, for instance, the law of trusts. There are European nations in which the law of trusts is relatively under-developed. This is the case, for example, in the nation of Italy, where practitioners must turn to the Hague Convention of 1985 as a means of validating trust agreements.[1270] Canon 1714, by allowing the parties to a dispute to select the norms to govern the resolution of their dispute, are granted a similar degree of flexibility under canon law. If law is at least partly about the facilitation of parties' choices,

1269 Canon 1925, sec. 1 (1917 Code).

1270 Gregor Christandl, "Will-Substitutes in Italy," in Alexandra Braun and Anne Röthel, eds., *Passing Wealth on Death: Will-Substitutes in Comparative Perspective* (Oxford, UK, 2016), pp. 131, 148.

then choice of governing law must become part of the equation. And the canon recognizes this modern requirement for flexibility.

Seventh, and finally, the canon does not distinguish particularly well between procedural and substantive norms. The passage in the canon that speaks of "the law of the episcopal conference," might be a reference to procedural norms. But the canon is simply unclear on this point. And one could well imagine a situation in which parties may wish to avail themselves of the procedural norms from one state and substantive norms from another. Thus one may want the benefits of the law of evidence from State X, while seeking the expansive protections afforded, let us say, the trust corpus found in State Y. The canon simply does not speak to this level of complexity.

Finally, a few words about canons 1715 and 1716.

Canon 1715 restates the long-standing limitation that settlements and compromises are juridically impossible where the issue involves the public good or matters about which the parties lack the authority to settle.

Canon 1716, finally, states that where "the civil law refuses to recognize the validity of canonical arbitration"[1271] unless first confirmed by a judge, then approval by an ecclesiastical judge is required. The canon seems to have in mind principally nations in which an ecclesiastical judge can act with civil effect, most likely by means of concordat. The canon does not address the American situation, in which the judge who may asked to approve an arbitration award will invariably be someone from the secular court system.

Conciliation, Arbitration, Compromise, and the 1983 Code of Canon Law: Some Hypothetical Cases

What follows is a series of hypothetical scenarios. They are designed to test the limits of the canons we have reviewed. The first example involves conciliation under canon 1733. The second example is bifurcated. The first half looks to canon 1733, while the second half looks to canons 1713 to 1716. The third and fourth examples are meant as clear examples of arbitration of private matters – questions that are governed by canons 1713 to 1716. The final two examples are illustrations of arbitration that would require the intervention of the Holy See.

Closing Parish Schools

Let us suppose a Catholic parish and school named the Church of the Holy Grail. The parish and school have a long history, dating to the 1890s. The school in particular has graduated many thousands of persons, but it has now encountered financial problems,

1271 A loose paraphrase of "lex civilis arbitrali sententiae vim non agnoscat. …"

made far worse by the recent pandemic. The school is partially subsidized by the Archdiocese, and the Archbishop has indicated to Holy Grail's principal that the subsidy can no longer continue.

The principal – let's call him Galahad – notifies the parish and the alumni of the school's dire financial condition. Fund-raising is begun, but it soon becomes evident that the fund-raising will fail to fill the gap left by the Archdiocese's withdrawal of the subsidy. A parents' group is organized and its elected leadership seeks legal advice on what remedies are available at canon law.

Let's consider the legal landscape: Canon 793, section 1, recognizes that parents have both the right and the obligation to see to the religious upbringing of their children.[1272] Canon 217 declares that all of the Christian faithful "have the right to a Christian education."[1273] Canon 212, section 2, tells Catholics that they "are free to make known their needs, especially spiritual ones, and their desires to the pastors of the Church."[1274] Finally, canon 221, section 1, declares that the "Christian faithful can legitimately vindicate and defend the rights which they enjoy in the Church before a competent ecclesiastical court."[1275]

So, what are the parents' options? Let us add that the closure of the school is an act of administrative power. The first step is to seek administrative recourse through the canons governing that process. Thus the affected parties could appeal up the hierarchical chain of command. Such a step, however, is unlikely to succeed.[1276] The Archbishop is the chief teacher of the Archdiocese.[1277] Similarly, the Archbishop has the administrative authority to determine how archdiocesan resources are to be spent.[1278] His decision on which schools to subsidize and which schools should be cut loose is likely final and non-reviewable.

Still, the situation is not entirely hopeless for the parents. This is the sort of scenario that would seem to fit well under canon 1733, the provision on conciliation. The parents certainly feel themselves injured by the administrative decree issued by the Archbishop eliminating the school subsidy. They have had their right and obligation to see to the Christian upbringing of their children impacted if not impaired. An Archbishop might do well to act under the terms of this canon and hold a series

1272 Canon 793, sec. 1 (1983 Code).
1273 Canon 217 (1983 Code).
1274 Canon 212, sec. 2 (1983 Code).
1275 Canon 221, sec. 1 (1983 Code).
1276 Not that it hasn't been tried. See Jay Tokasz, "Parishioners Appeal Bishop's Decision to Close School in City of Tonawanda," *buffalonews.com*, January 23, 2014.
1277 Canon 375, sec. 2 (1983 Code); canon 386, sec. 1 (1983 Code).
1278 Canon 381, sec. 1 (1983 Code); canon 391, sec. 1 (1983 Code).

of meetings with the parents' association, perhaps even relying on a professional mediator.

It is a situation in which the Archbishop has the legal authority to take the actions he has taken. But it is best to try to find some creative resolution to the problem that protects the legitimate interest of the parents in the Christian education of their children. And, indeed, when we look at school closures from around the United States, we do see efforts to accommodate the interests of parents and children in precisely this way.[1279]

The Catholic Newspaper Editor

At-Will Employment

Now let us suppose the editor of a Catholic diocesan newspaper. Let's call her Joan d'Arché. As editor, she has kept the editorial pages open for the expression of divergent views, and has recently published guest editorials from writers who favor the ecclesiastical recognition of same-sex unions and the good-faith usage, by married Catholics, of contraceptives. In her own writings, however, she has always been careful to put distance between her views, and those of the newspaper, and the guest editorialists selected precisely because of their disagreement with other editorial content.

The Bishop under whom she has served, let us call him Robert Grosseteste, saw value in the maintenance of such an opinion page. He believed that wide-ranging conversation by Catholics, even on matters of doctrine and practice, was healthy for the Church and deserved to be promoted.

Joan's contract with the Diocese, furthermore, has always been "at-will." At-will contracts are the default form of employment contract in the United States. Under at-will

1279 See, for instance, Kenneth C. Crowe, "Catholic Central, St. Ambrose Schools to Merge," *Times Union* (Albany, NY), November 15, 2021; Dan Irwin, "New Castle Students Coming to Kennedy Catholic," *The Herald* (Sharon, PA), April 25, 2021; Jay Tokasz, "Two Buffalo Schools to Merge Next Fall," *The Buffalo News*, March 13, 2021; Susan Essoyan, "St. Ann School in Kaneohe to Close in June After 180 Years," *Honolulu Star-Advertiser*, January 26, 2021. And while conciliation is sometimes effective in achieving compromises that satisfy the interests of all concerned, it must also be acknowledged that public pressure can be an effective tool as well. See, for instance, Valerie Johnson, et al., "Does Archbishop Kurtz Care About the Struggling Black Catholic Parishes?" *Louisville Courier-Journal*, November 10, 2021; Hallie Lauer, "Large Group Appealing School Closure Holds March," *Pittsburgh Post-Gazette*, March 8, 2021. Since the process of conciliation is akin to the process of the good-faith negotiations one might see in collective bargaining situations, pressure and conciliation might sometimes be effective when used in conjunction.

doctrine, either party is free to terminate the relationship at any time, for any reason whatsoever,[1280] provided, however, that the reason is not unlawful (such as a violation of the Civil Rights laws).[1281] Joan, however, regarded her employment secure because she had always enjoyed a good working relationship with Bishop Grosseteste.

Bishop Grossteste, however, has now retired and is replaced by Bishop Pierre Cauchon. Bishop Cauchon has a very different view of what a Catholic newspaper should look like. Without offering an explanation, Bishop Cauchon fires Joan summarily. Does Joan have any recourse?

Again, let us look at her rights under the Code of Canon Law. Joan might seek support in canon 218, which provides that "those who are engaged in the sacred disciplines enjoy a lawful freedom of inquiry and of prudently expressing their opinions on matters in which they have expertise."[1282] She might argue that the maintenance of an open forum constituted a legitimate form of inquiry. Her claim, however, would be weak, since it is highly unlikely a diocesan newspaper would count among the "sacred disciplines." It is also the case that the canon law "canonizes" the law of contracts of the jurisdictions in which the Church is active, at least insofar as it is not a violation of the divine law.[1283] While the doctrine of at-will employment is certainly a harsh rule,[1284] it is probably not a violation of divine law.

All that said, Bishop Cauchon might still wish to engage in a process of conciliation with Joan. Why? To preserve harmony within the diocese. The diocese, after all, is canonically defined as "a portion of the People of God … entrusted for pastoral care to a bishop."[1285] And while Joan may be lacking in rights, it may still be advisable for the bishop to offer her a real and visible opportunity at conciliation, if only because this would be pastorally and politically wise. No doubt, Joan's guest editorialists enjoyed a significant readership and publicly healing a rift with a former editor-in-chief might assist with broader reconciliation efforts within the diocese.

1280 Donald Rutherford, ed., *Routledge Dictionary of Economics*, 3d ed. (New York, 2012), p. 23.

1281 Charles J. Muhl, "The Employment At-Will Doctrine: Three Major Exceptions," *Monthly Labor Review*, January 2001, pp. 3–11, bls.gov/opub/mlr/2001/01/artıfull.pdf.

1282 Canon 218 (1983 Code).

1283 Canon 22 (1983 Code).

1284 Julia Tomassetti, "Power in the Employment Relationship: Why Contract Law Should Not Govern At-Will Employment," *Economic Policy Institute*, November 19, 2020, epi.org/unequal power/publications/the-legal-understanding-and-treatment-of-an-employment-rela tionshi-versus-a-contract.

1285 Canon 369 (1983 Code).

Three-Year Employment Contract with Liquidated-Damages Clause

Now, let us vary the hypothetical situation somewhat. Suppose that Joan recently signed a three-year contract as editor during the final days of Bishop Grosseteste's tenure. Let us suppose further that the contract contains a liquidated-damages provision that permits termination for cause, but holds that should she be fired absent good cause, she is entitled to eighteen months of full salary, plus benefits.

Joan is now no longer an at-will employee. Unless Bishop Cauchon can demonstrate cause – a difficult standard to meet – Joan would be entitled to her eighteen months of salary. But now suppose that Bishop Cauchon has refused to meet Joan's demand for payment of the liquidated damages.

Joan may choose to litigate the matter before the civil courts. But she might also choose to have the case handled under the alternative dispute resolution canons of the 1983 Code. She would not proceed, however, under canon 1733. She is not, after all, seeking the reversal or review of an administrative decision. Rather, she would proceed under canons 1713 to 1716. Her complaint is essentially a private-law contractual matter – she is seeking the satisfaction of a liquidated-damages clause in her contract.

Under canons 1713 and 1714, she and the Bishop might seek a settlement (*transactio*) or a compromise (*compromissum*) under the law. The procedure might take place before arbiters, but conceivably it could also look to the older equity jurisprudence (*de bono et aequo*) that we discussed in Part 4 under canon 1929 (1917 Code). In such circumstances, the parties might choose to arbitrate for all of the reasons typically cited by those litigants who prefer arbitration to adjudication – lower costs, more efficient procedure, a speedier outcome.

The Seriously Catholic Couple and Their Tragic Divorce

Catholic monasticism has for centuries permitted laypersons to associate closely with their missions by seeking the status either of lay oblates or tertiary ("third-order") membership. This is a practice with deep medieval roots. St. Catherine of Siena (1347–1380), for instance, wrote major works of theology, practiced a rigorously ascetic life, was proclaimed a doctor of the Church, but affiliated with the Dominican Order only as a tertiary member, and not as a nun.[1286] Recent years have seen a considerable growth in interest among Catholic laypersons in such affiliations.[1287] Although Catholic oblates and tertiaries are expected to follow the

1286 Heather Webb, "Catherine of Siena's Heart," *Speculum* 80 (2005), pp. 802, 802.

1287 See, for instance, Judith Valente, "The Laypeople Seeking a Monastic Life in the Modern World," *U.S. Catholic*, June 4, 2019; Elizabeth Scalia, "She's a Tertiary? He's an Oblate? What Is That All About?" *Aleteia*, January 20, 2016. Cf., Tom Gjelten, "Catholics Build 'Intentional' Community of Like-Minded Believers," *National Public Radio*, April 10,

spiritual disciplines of the orders with which they are affiliated, they may live in the world, and are not forbidden from marriage.[1288]

Let us suppose now a young couple who have met in college. Let's call them Louisa and Dmitri. They became acquainted with one another at the university Catholic Center, where they frequently attended Mass. Following college graduation, Louisa and Dmitri attended elite law schools and embarked upon prestige legal practices. They eventually marry. In keeping with their intense Catholicism, Louisa becomes a Dominican tertiary, while Dmitri affiliates with the Benedictine Oblates.

Louisa and Dmitri own two homes, both in joint tenancy. Their primary residence is located in a separate-property jurisdiction. They maintain joint investment accounts. Their financial resources are thoroughly intermingled. But marital problems eventually creep in. Dmitri works in the London office of a major international law firm, while Louisa becomes a partner in a major law firm headquartered in Cleveland, Ohio. They begin to neglect one another's emotional needs and seek out marriage counseling. The counseling, however, proves to be ineffective, and the parties conclude that they must divorce. They are both grieved in their hearts that their marriage has failed. But even though they have experienced the profound personal disappointment of divorce, they nevertheless remain loyal to their calling as Catholics, and as members, respectively, of the Dominicans and the Benedictines.

Thus Louisa and Dmitri properly seek a divorce under the law of their home jurisdiction. And they also petition for the nullity of their marriage under the matrimonial provisions of the 1983 Code of Canon Law. They are fully aware that a petition for nullity is not something that can be resolved through informal processes, but something that must proceed with full judicial formality.

But they decide that they want to do something that is both novel for their property settlement and in keeping with their faith. They thus conclude that Catholic arbitrators appointed under the terms of canons 1713 to 1716 might do a better – or at least a more faith-appropriate job – than the civil courts in managing their property settlement.

2017 (detailing the creation of a community of like-minded Catholics in suburban Washington, DC).

1288 See, for example, "Become an Oblate," *St. Benedict's Abbey*, Atchison, Kansas, kansasmonks.org/oblates; "Third Order (Brothers and Sisters of Penance and Tertiaries)/Secular Franciscan Order – OFS)," *Franciscan Friars, Province of Santa Barbara*, sbfranciscans.org/who-are-we/franciscan-spirituality/third-order-brothers-and-sisters-of-penance-and-tertiaries-secular-franciscan-order-ofs/; "The Lay Fraternities of St. Dominic," *Dominican Province of the Assumption* (serving Australia, New Zealand, the Solomon Islands, and Papua New Guinea), op.org.au/about-the-dominicans/the-dominican-family/the-lay-fraternities-of-st-dominic.

Can this be done under the canon law? Indeed, it can. A property settlement consequent upon a divorce is classically a private matter, not a matter of public right. The parties are acting, in the words of canon 1713 – *ad evitandas iudiciales contentiones* – "to avoid judicial contentions." Arbitration of property disputes is a regular feature of American divorce law, and has been for a long time.[1289] Provided that the state's civil law is complied with, there would seem to be no obstacle to relying on Church-appointed arbitrators in this matter.

The Case of the Two Protestant Pastors

Suppose two Protestant ministers, the Reverend Wesley Iliff, who is chief pastor at a large suburban Methodist church in the upper Midwest; and the Reverend Mason Knox, who holds a similar position at a suburban Presbyterian church. Suppose further that the two Protestant churches are large and adjacent to one another, occupying a total of two city blocks. Separating their properties is a line of ash trees.

Both Reverend Iliff and Reverend Knox are civically-engaged, community-oriented, public personalities. Reverend Iliff thus serves as a board member for Good Samaritan Hospital, a non-denominational Christian medical facility. Reverend Knox, meanwhile, is a member of the Board of Governors for the Center for Sacred Music and Dance – an organization that promotes awareness of religious song and ritual through education and performance.

Now let us add a third personality, Bishop Terry Hanratty. The Most Reverend Hanratty, like his Protestant colleagues, is civically-minded and happens to belong to the boards of both the Good Samaritan Hospital and the Center for Sacred Music and Dance. Through their joint memberships, Bishop Hanratty has become a good friend of each Protestant minister. They see one another socially, and have even hosted ecumenical events at Christmas and at Easter.

The upper Midwestern community where the three religious leaders are situated, however, has recently identified a large number of emerald ash borers in its urban canopy. Emerald ash borers are an invasive species in the upper Midwest and are wreaking havoc in communities that have over-relied on ash trees in their urban landscape.

1289 See, for example, Anne E. Meroney, "Mediation and Arbitration of Separation and Divorce Agreements," *Wake Forest Law Review* 15 (1979), pp. 467–486; Robert D. Benjamin, "Formal Mediation in the Settlement of Divorce and Other Family Conflicts," *St. Louis Bar Journal* 32 (Spring, 1986), pp. 43–51. Cf., M.A. Ansaripour, "Arbitration in Divorce Proceedings Under Islamic and Iranian Law," *Yearbook of Islamic and Middle Eastern Law* 15 (2009/2010), pp. 37–52 (giving an example of another religious tradition that relies on arbitration in divorce settlements).

Notified by the authorities to have their trees inspected, the Reverends Iliff and Knox discover that the tree line separating their two congregations has become badly infested, and that the trees will therefore have to be removed at considerable expense.

Not sure how to share the costs of the removal, the two pastors turn to Bishop Hanratty, who suggests that they might make use of diocesan arbitrators to take evidence and apportion the costs accordingly. The two pastors agree contractually to be bound by the results of the arbitration process. Evidence is gathered and it is concluded that Reverend Iliff should bear 60% of the cost, and Reverend Knox 40%, in part on the non-legal but equitable ground that Reverend Iliff's congregation is in a superior position to bear the costs of abatement.

Notice in particular two features that I have introduced in this hypothetical scenario; and the ways in which the canons are accommodative. First, this arbitration is not, strictly speaking, the settlement of some dispute. The parties are on good terms and have no intention of litigating the matter. What they sought from arbitration was expert fact-finding, and a neutral mediator. These objectives were satisfied, and the matter was amicably resolved. But also notice, secondly, that the parties are not Catholic. As I previously indicated, canons 1713–1716 do not draw a jurisdictional boundary between Catholics and non-Catholics. Members of other religious faiths or, presumably, of no religious faith, may avail themselves of arbitration in circumstances such as these.

Litigation between Two Catholic Institutions in an International Context

Let us suppose the existence of two purely hypothetical major Catholic institutions of Catholic higher learning, one located, say, in a Western Canadian province, like British Columbia; and the other on the Eastern seaboard of the United States. The Canadian institution has an internationally well-regarded medical school. The American university has strong research and development laboratories in the biological sciences. The two institutions have entered into a partnership agreement to pool resources over a ten-year period. Research physicians from the Canadian university may use the American laboratories; while American researchers may teach and hold positions at the Canadian center.

Let us suppose, further, a worsening geopolitical climate. Thus the Canadian institution employs researchers from nations that have come to be viewed unfavorably by the United States – particularly, let us say, China. The American State Department, fearing Chinese access to biological information, thus takes steps to restrict access on the basis of national origin to laboratories doing cutting-edge research.

Suppose then matters come to a head when the American institution, acting under the belief that it is required to do so by the Department of State, chooses to bar a group of Chinese researchers from the laboratories that they are contractually entitled to use. The Canadian institution brings suit in British Columbia, claiming breach of contract. The American university raises the defense of force majeure.

We are left with an unseemly situation. Two Catholic institutions facing off in a Canadian courtroom over a dispute precipitated by American geopolitical anxieties. This is the sort of situation in which the Holy See is likely to become involved. The Holy See continues to take seriously St. Paul's injunction that Christians should not sue Christians in a secular court of law.[1290] This is especially so when the Christian entities involved are highly visible, major institutions of learning.

It is at this point that the papacy would likely to put its diplomatic offices to good use in the dispute. The Holy See maintains a diplomatic presence in both Canada[1291] and the United States.[1292] One might speculate that the first move would be made by the papal nuncio to the United States, who would attempt to negotiate with the State Department favorable treatment for the affected researchers. Failing that, however, one would expect that the papal nuncios to Canada and the United States would collaborate on the naming of an arbitrator empowered to hear the dispute, reach a decision on the merits, and determine whether damages are warranted.

The Trail Smelter Case Revisited in the Light of *Laudato Sí*

My final hypothetical scenario builds on the facts of the famous *Trail Smelter* case that resolved through international arbitration awards in 1938 and 1941.[1293] The case involved a lead and zinc smelter operated by the LeRoi Mining and Smelting Company and several successor corporations, most notably the Consolidated Mining and Smelting Company of Canada, Ltd., in Trail, British Columbia, beginning in the year 1896.[1294] Located near the boundary with the United States, the smelting operation caused substantial harm to lumber and agricultural interests in the State of Washington.[1295]

Private litigation proved unavailing, as did several steps taken by the Consolidated Company to ameliorate the cross-border damage it was causing. Finally, in "December 1927, the United States Government proposed to the Canadian Government that

1290 1 *Corinthians* 6:1–8.

1291 About Apostolic Nunciature (Canadian Conference of Catholic Bishops), cccb.ca/about/apostolic-nunciature/.

1292 Apostolic Nunciature United States of America, nuntiususa.org.

1293 *Trail Smelter Case*, April 16, 1938; and March 11, 1941, *Reports of International Arbitral Awards* 3 (2006), pp. 1905–1982.

1294 *Id.*, pp. 1915 and 1917.

1295 *Id.*, pp. 1916–1917.

problems growing out of the Smelter at Trail should be referred to the International Joint Commission, United States and Canada, for investigation and report."[1296]

The Arbitration Commission eventually ruled in favor of the United States, declaring that "'under the principles of international law ... no State has the right to use or permit the use of its territory in such or the properties or persons therein, when the case is of serious consequence and the injury is established by clear and convincing evidence.'"[1297] The case is famous today as "the first arbitral award in international environmental law."[1298]

What I want to do is to imagine a contemporary *Trail Smelter* case, arising between two historically Catholic nations. A quarrel, say, between Chile and Argentina, over mining; or perhaps a dispute among the nations of Ecuador, Peru, and Brazil over the management of the resources of the upper Amazon River Basin.

Pope Francis has written extensively on environmental issues and in his encyclical *Laudato Sí* he proclaimed his intent "to enter into dialogue with all people about our common home."[1299] In this encyclical, he described the earth and all within it as "our common home."[1300] "Climate," he has asserted, "is a common good."[1301] The Pope chose the name Francis, he indicated, in part because of St. Francis of Assisi's solicitude for "an integral ecology lived out joyfully and authentically."[1302]

What would be the result if these nations of the Amazon Basin requested Pope Francis to mediate their dispute? How far would a decision issued by the Holy See reach? And what effect would such an award enjoy at international law? These are questions. Speculations. Nothing more. But it is perhaps suitable to end this book with a set of questions pointing to the vast possibilities offered by the prospect of papal mediation of the world's most intractable, insoluble problems.

1296 *Id.*, p. 1918.

1297 *Trail Smelter Case* (quoted in Ralph C. D'Arge and Allen V. Kneese, "State Liability for International Environmental Degradation: An Economic Perspective," *Natural Resources Journal* 20 (1980), pp. 427, 429–430.

1298 Mara Tignino and Christian Bréthaut, "The Role of International Case Law In Implementing the Obligation Not to Cause Significant Harm," *International Environmental Agreements: Politics, Law, and Economics* 20 (2020), doi: 10.1007/s10784-020-09503-6.

1299 *Laudato Sí*, no. 3.

1300 *Id.*, no. 13.

1301 *Id.*, no. 23.

1302 *Id.*, no. 10.

Bibliography

Primary Sources

Ambrose, *Expositio Evangelii secundum Lucam* (Corpus Christianorum, series latina, vol. 14).

Apuleius, *Metamorphoses* (= Apuleius, *Metamorphoses,* J. Arthur Hanson, tr., Cambridge, MA, Loeb Classical Library).

Augustine, *Quaestiones et Locutiones in Heptateuchum* (Corpus Christianorum series latina, vol. 33).

Augustine, *De Civitate Dei* (= Augustine, *The City of God Against the Pagans*, David S. Wiesen, tr., Cambridge, MA, Loeb Classical Library) 7 volumes.

Benedict XV (Pope), *Ad Beatissimi Apostolorum* (1914).

Benedict XV, *Providentissma Mater Ecclesia* (1917).

Benedict XV, *Quod Iam Diu* (1918).

Benedict XV, *Pacem, Dei Munus Pulcherrimum* (1918).

(Bernard of Parma), *Decretales D. Gregorii papae ix: suae integritati una cum glossis restitutae* (Rome, 1582).

"Birgitta's Reply to Pope Gregory IX's Request for a Sign," February, 1373 in *The Revelations of St. Birgitta of Sweden*, Searby, Denis, tr. (Oxford, 2008), vol. II, pp. 256–257.

Böcking, Eduard, ed., *Corpus Legum sive Brachylogus Iuris Civilis* (Berlin, 1829).

Boethius, *Consolatio Philosophiae* (= Boethius, *The Theological Tractates*, S.J. Tester, tr., Cambridge, MA, Loeb Classical Library).

Christus Dominus (Vatican II) (1965).

Cicero, *De Officiis* (= Cicero, *De Officiis*, Walter Miller, tr., Cambridge, MA, Loeb Classical Library).

Cicero, *De Oratore* (= Cicero, *De Oratore*, E.W. Sutton and H. Rackham, trs. Cambridge, MA, Loeb Classical Library, 2 volumes).

Cicero, *Pro Caecina* (= Cicero, *Pro Lege Manilia, Pro Caecina, Pro Cluentio, Pro Rabirio Perduellionis*, H. Grose Hodge, tr., Cambridge, MA, Loeb Classical Library).

Cicero, *Tusculan Disputations* (= Cicero, *Tusculan Disputations*, J.E. King, tr., Cambridge, MA, Loeb Classical Library).

Code of Canon Law: Latin-English Edition (Washington, DC, 2020).

Codex Iuris Canonici (Westminster, MD, 1961) (1917 Code of Canon Law).

Columella, *De Agricultura* (= Lucius Junius Moderatus Columella, *On Agriculture*, E.S. Foster and Edward H. Heffner, trs. Cambridge, MA, Loeb Classical Library) 3 volumes.

Commercial Arbitration Rules and Mediation Procedures: Including Procedures For Large, Complex Commercial Disputes (American Arbitration Association), adr.org /commercial.

Commission on Human Rights in South Sudan, "Conflict-Related Sexual Violence Against Women and Girls in South Sudan," Human Rights Council, United Nations, March, 21, 2022.

Concordat Between the Holy See and Spain, August 27, 1953.

Concordat Between the Holy See and the Dominican Republic, June 16, 1954.

Conference of the Catholic Bishops of India (Latin Rite), "Complementary Legislation to the Code of Canon Law," December 2, 1994, ccbi.in/wp-content/uploads/2015-12/Complementary-Legislations-to-the-Code-of-Canon-Law-1.pdf.

Corpus Iuris Civilis, 3 vols. Paul Krueger, Theodor Mommsen, Rudolph Schoell, and Wilhelm Kroll, eds. (Berlin, 1904–1911).

"Due Process in Canon Law," *Catholic Lawyer* 15 (1969), 278–307.

Durandus, William, *Speculum Iudiciale*, 2 vols. (Basil, 1574) (reprinted, Aalen, 1975).

Francis (Pope), *Laudato Sí* (2015).

Francis, "Address of His Holiness Pope Francis to the General Assembly of the United Nations," September 25, 2015.

Francis, "Urbi et Orbi Message," December 25, 2013.

Francis, "Address of His Holiness Pope Francis to the Members of the Diplomatic Corps Accredited to the Holy See," January 13, 2014.

Francis, "Address of His Holiness Pope Francis to Members of the Diplomatic Corps Accredited to the Holy See," January 9, 2023.

Francis, "Address of His Holiness Meeting With Internally Displaced Persons," February 4, 2023.

Francis, "Ecumenical Prayer," February 4, 2023.

Francis, "General Audience," February 8, 2023.

Francis, "In-Flight Press Conference," February 5, 2023.

Francis, "Meeting With Authorities, Civil Society, and the Diplomatic Corps, Address of His Holiness," February 3, 2023.

Francis, "Urbi et Orbi Message of Pope Francis," April 20, 2014.

Francis, "Urbi et Orbi Message of Pope Francis," December 25, 2022.

Gracias, Oswald, "Solving Conflicts in the Church," canonlawsocietyofindia.org/research/solving-conflicts-in-the-church/.

Les Grands Traités de la Guerre de cent ans, Cosneau, E., ed. (Paris, 1889).

(Gratian), *Decretum Magistri Gratiani, Corpus Iuris Canonici*, vol. 1, Emil Friedberg, ed. (Leipzig, 1879).

Gregory XVI (Pope), *Mirari Vos* (1832).

Greneck, Adam Joseph, *Theses sive Controversiae Juridicae ex Selectissimis Juris Universi tum Publici, tum Canonici, tum Privati* (Vienna, 1718).

Hilary of Poitiers, *De Trinitate*, Corpus Christianorum series latina, vol. 62.

Horack, Samuel Johann, *Controversiae canonico-morales de restitutione et poenitentia* (Olmütz, Czech Republic, 1737).

Hostiensis, *Summa* (Lyon, 1537) (reprinted, Aalen, 1962).
International Theological Commission, "In Search of a Universal Ethic: A New Look at the Natural Law" (Vatican City, 2009).
Institutes of Gaius, W.M. Gordon and O.F. Robinson, trs. (Ithaca, NY, 1988).
Jerome, St., Letter 127 (= Jerome, *Select Letters*, F.A. Wright, tr., Cambridge, MA, Loeb Classical Library).
John XXIII (Pope), *Pacem in Terris* (1963).
John XXIII, *Mater et Magistra* (1961).
John Paul II (Pope), *Sacrae Disciplinae Leges* (1983).
John Paul II, *Laborem Exercens* (1983).
John Paul II, "Message of His Holiness John Paul II to the Presidents of Argentina and Chile."
John Paul II, "Pacem in Terris: A Permanent Commitment," Message of His Holiness Pope John Paul II for the Celebration of the World Day of Peace, January 1, 2003.
John Paul II, "Message of His Holiness John Paul II on the Occasion of the Fiftieth Anniversary of the Beginning of the Second World War," August 27, 1989.
John Paul II, "Address of His Holiness John Paul II to the Diplomatic Corps Accredited to the Holy See," January 12, 1985.
John Paul II, "Address of His Holiness John Paul II to the Diplomatic Corps, January 13, 2003."
John Paul II, "Homily of the Holy Father, Midnight Mass, Christmas, 24 December, 2002."
John Paul II, "Urbi et Orbi Message of His Holiness Pope John Paul II," December 25, 2002.
Lactantius, *Divinae Institutiones*, Samuel Brandt, ed., *Corpus Scriptorum Ecclesiasticorum Latinorum* 19.
Leo XIII (Pope), *Rerum Novarum* (1891).
Leo XIII, *Catholicae Ecclesiae* (1890).
Leo XIII, *Diuturnum* (1881).
Leo XIII, *Sapientiae Christianae* (1890).
Leo XIII, "Allocution *Etsi Res* to the College of Cardinals," in *Principles for Peace* (= *Acta Sedis Sanctae* 18 (1886)), 309–311.
Leo XIII, "Letter *Cum de Carolinis Insulis* to Prince Bismarck of Germany," in *Principles for Peace*.
Leo XIII, "Letter, *Nous ne Pouvons*, to Queen Wilhelmina of the Netherlands" (May 29, 1999), in *Principles for Peace*.
Leo XIII, "Proposal of His Holiness, Leo XIII, in the Question of the Caroline Archipelago and the Palaos," in *Principles for Peace*.
(Liber Extra), *Decretales Gregorii P. IX*, in *Corpus Iuris Canonici*, vol. II, Emil Friedberg, ed. (Leipzig 1881).

Liguori, Alphonsus de, *Guide For Confessors* (Morrisville, NC, 2018).

Livy, *Ab Urbe Condita* (= Livy, *History of Rome*, Evan T. Sage and Alfred C. Schlesinger, trs., Cambridge, MA, Loeb Classical Library), vol. 12.

Lumen Gentium (Vatican II, 1964).

Menke, Lüder, *Gymnasium polemicum juris comlectens plures quam DCXX selectas controversias juris naturalis et gentium, Juris Publici Romano-Germanici, juris civilis, et canonici* (Leipzig, 1689).

"Nihil Obstat for Due Process," *Jurist* 32 (1972), 291–292.

On Due Process, rev. ed. (Washington, DC, 1972).

Ovid, *Metamorphoses* (= Ovid, *Metamorphoses*, Frank Justus Miller, tr., rev. by G.P. Goold, Cambridge, MA, Loeb Classical Library).

Ovid, *Tristia* (= Ovid, *Tristia, Ex Ponto*, Arthur Leslie Wheeler, tr. Cambridge, MA, Loeb Classical Library) (2d ed., rev. by G.P. Goold).

Pastor Aeternus (Vatican I) (1870).

Paul VI (Pope), *Populorum Progressio* (1967).

Peters, Edward N., *The 1917 Pio-Benedictine Code of Canon Law: In English Translation with Extensive Scholarly Apparatus* (San Francisco, CA, 2001).

Pius IX (Pope), *Syllabus of Errors* (1864).

Pius X (Pope), *Arduum Sane Munus* (1904).

Pius X, *Pascendi Dominici Gregis* (1907).

Pius X, *Sapienti Consilio* (1908).

Pius XI (Pope), *Quadragesimo Anno* (1931).

Pius XII (Pope), *Mystici Corporis* (1943).

Pliny the Younger, *Panegyricus* (= Pliny, *Letters*, Betty Radice, tr., Cambridge, MA, Loeb Classical Library), vol. II.

Principles for Peace: Selections From Papal Documents, Leo XIII to Pius XII (Washington, DC, 1943).

Prosper of Aquitaine, *Epitoma Chronicon*, in *Monumenta Germaniae Historica, Auctores Antiquissimi*, vol. 9.

Protection of Rights of Persons in the Church: Revised Report of the Canon Law Society of America on the Subject of Due Process (Washington, DC, 1991).

Provost, James H., ed., *Due Process in Dioceses of the United States, 1970–1985: Report on a Survey Task Force to Survey Due Process Experience* (Washington, DC, 1987).

Prudentius, *The Divinity of Christ* (= *Prudentius*, H.J. Thomson, tr. Cambridge, MA, Loeb Classical Library) 2 volumes.

Quebec Civil Code.

Quintilian, *The Orator's Education* (= Quintilian, *The Orator's Education*, Donald A. Russell, tr., Cambridge, MA, Loeb Classical Library) 5 volumes.

Quintilian, *The Lesser Declamations* (= Quintilian, *The Lesser Declamations*, D.R.B. Shckleton-Bailey, tr. Cambridge, MA, Loeb Classical Library) 2 volumes.

Quintus Curtius Rufus, *Historia Alexandri Magni* (= Quintus Curtius, *History of Alexander*, John C. Rolfe, tr., Cambridge, MA, Loeb Classical Library) 2 volumes.

"Report of the Ad Hoc Committee on Due Process to the Canon Law Society of America," *Canon Law Society of America Proceedings* 31 (1969), 18–51.

Report of the Commission on Human Rights in South Sudan, United Nations General Assembly (2018).

Rhetorica ad Herennium (= [Cicero], *Rhetorica ad Herennium*, Harry Caplan, tr., Cambridge, MA, Loeb Classical Library).

Sallust, *Bellum Jugurthinum* (= Sallust, *The War With Cataline, the War With Jugurtha*, J.C. Rolfe, tr.rev. by John T. Ramsey, Cambridge, MA, Loeb Classical Libary).

Schmalzgrueber, Franciscus, *Jus Ecclesiasticum Universum Brevi Methodo ad Discentium* 5 vols. (Rome, 1843–1845).

"Second Diplomatic Note of Cardinal Rampolla, Secretary of State, to Count Mouraviev, Secretary of Foreign Affairs of Russia," in *Principles for Peace*.

Seneca the Elder, *Controversiae* (= Seneca the Elder, *Declamations*, M. Winterbottom, tr., Cambridge, MA, Loeb Classical Library) 2 volumes.

Seneca the Younger, *De Clementia* (= Seneca, *Moral Essays*, John W. Basore, tr. Cambridge, MA, Loeb Classical Library) 3 volumes.

Seneca the Younger, *Thyestes* (= Seneca, *Oedipus, Agamemnon, Thyestes*, John G. Fitch, tr., Cambridge, MA, Loeb Classical Library, 2018).

Sidonius, *Letters* (= Sidonius, *Poems, Letters*, W.B. Anderson, tr., Cambridge, MA, Loeb Classical Library), 2 volumes.

"Statement on Iraq From Bishop Gregory, February 26, 2003," United States Conference of Catholic Bishops.

Suetonius, *Lives of the Twelve Caesars* (= *Suetonius*, J.C. Rolfe, tr. Cambridge, MA, Loeb Classical Library), 2 volumes.

Tancred, *Ordo iudiciarius*, in Friedrich Christian Bergmann, ed., *Pilii, Tancredi, Gratiae Libri de Iudiciorum Ordine* (Aalen, 1965).

Terence, *Adelphoi* (= Terence, "The Brothers," in *Terence*, John Barsby tr., Cambridge, MA, Loeb Classical Library) vol. II.

Tertullian, *De Carne Christi* (= Tertullian, *La chair du Christ, Sources chrétiennes*, Paris), vols. 216–217.

"Towards a Declaration of Christian Freedom," *Jurist* 29 (1969), 1–9.

United Nations Security Council Resolution no. 678 (November 29, 1990).

Secondary Sources

Abbo, John A., "The Revision of the Code," *Jurist* 20 (1960), 371–397.

Adams, Gwenfair Walters, "Visions of the Otherworlds in the Late Middle Wages, *c.*1300–*c.*1500," in Richard Matthew Pollard, ed., *Imagining the Medieval Afterlife* (Cambridge, UK, 2020), 115–130.

Adams, Tracy, "Christine de Pizan and Jehanne d'Arc: Above All Heroes Past," in Cecile Thérèse Tougas and Sara Ebenreck, eds., *Presenting Women Philosophers* (Philadelphia, 2000), 188–199.

Adler, Gary J., *Secularism, Catholicism, and the Future of Public Life: A Dialogue with Ambassador Douglas W. Kmiec* (Oxford, UK, 2015).

Aguilar, Susan L., "Jewish-Christian Relations in Teruel, Aragon: 1391 and Its Aftermath," in Kim Bergkvist, et al., eds, *Conflict and Collaboration in Medieval Iberia* (Newcastle-Upon-Tyne, 2020), 249–268.

Aguilera-Barchet, Bruno, *A History of Western Public Law: Between Nation and State* (Cham, Switzerland, 2015).

Alesandro, John, "One Hundred Years Since the 1917 Code of Canon Law," *Studia Canonica* 51 (2017), 357–389.

Alesandro, John, "General Introduction," in James A. Coriden, et al., eds., *The Code of Canon Law: A Text and Commentary* (New York, 1985), 1–22.

Altman, William H.F., *The Revival of Platonism in Cicero's Late Philosophy: Platonis Aemulus and the Invention of Cicero* (Lanham, MD, 2016).

Alvarez, David, *The Pope's Soldiers: A Military History of the Modern Vatican* (Lawrence, KS, 2011).

Alvarez, David, *Spies at the Vatican: Espionage and Intrigue From Napoleon to the Holocaust* (Topeka, KS, 2002).

Alvarez, David, "The Holy See and the First Hague Peace Conference (1899)," *Archivum Historiae Pontificiae* 26 (1988), 431–438.

Anderson, C. Colt, *The Great Catholic Reformers: From Gregory the Great to Dorothy Day* (New York, 2007).

Anderson, C. Colt, "Ritual Purity and Pastoral Reform in the Thirteenth Century," in Ronald J. Stansbury, ed., *A Companion to Pastoral Care in the Late Middle Ages (1200–1500)*, (Leiden, 2010), 73–94.

Ansaripour, M.A., "Arbitration in Divorce Proceedings Under Islamic and Iranian Law," *Yearbook of Islamic and Middle Eastern Law* 15 (2009/2010), 37–52.

Anthony, Francis-Vincent, et al., "Impact of Religion on Socioeconomic Rights: An Empirical Study of Italian Students' Attitudes," in Hans-Georg Ziebart, ed., *International Empirical Studies on Religion and Socioeconomic Human Rights* (Cham, Switzerland, 2020), 63–100.

Anykia, F., "The Roman Catholic Mission and Traditional Rulers in Igboland and in the Nineteenth Century," *Africa: Revista trimestrale di studi e documentazione dell-Istituto italiano per l'Africa e l'Oriente* 44 (1989), 211–231.

Araujo, Robert John, "The Holy See: International Person and Sovereign," *Ave Maria International Law Journal* 1 (2011), 1–66.

Ascher, Abraham, "Introduction," in Jonathan D. Smele and Anthony Heywood, eds., *The Russian Revolution of 1905: Centenary Perspectives* (New York, 2005), 1–12.

Augustine, Charles, *A Commentary on the New Code of Canon Law*, 2d. ed., 8 volumes (St. Louis, 1918–1924).

Avis, Paul, *Beyond the Reformation: Authority, Primacy, and Unity in the Conciliar Tradition* (London, 2006).

Aydinyan, Anna, *Formalists Against Imperialism: The Death of Vazir-Mukhtar and Russian Orientalism* (Toronto, 2022).

Baer, James A., *Anarchist Immigrants in Spain and Argentina* (Urbana, IL, 2015).

Baldwin, John W., "The Medieval Theories of the Just Price: Romanists, Canonists, and Theologians in the Twelfth and Thirteenth Centuries," *Transactions of the American Philosophical Society* 49 (1959), 1–92.

Bargilliat, Michel, *Praelectiones Juris Canonici*, 3d ed. (Paris, 1915) 2 volumes.

Bartlett, C.J., "After Palmerston: Britain and the Iberian Peninsula, 1865–76," *English Historical Review* 109 (1994), 74–88.

Bartlett, Kenneth R., and McGlynn, Margaret, *The Renaissance and Reformation in Northern Europe* (Toronto, 2014).

Bartolini, Giulio, ed., *A History of International Law in Italy* (Oxford, UK, 2020).

Bass, Ricardo E., "Due Process: Conciliation and Arbitration," *Canon Law Society of America Proceedings* 53 (1991), 63–76.

Batiza, Rodolfo, "Origins of the Modern Codification of the Civil Law: The French Experience and Its Implications for Louisiana Law," *Tulane Law Review* 56 (1981–1982), 477–601.

Batiza, Rodolfo, "The French Revolution and Codification – Comment on the Enlightenment, the French Revolution, and the Napoleonic Code," *Valparaiso University Law Review* 18 (1984), 675–682.

Bauer, Nancy, "The 1983 *Codex Iuris Canonici*: a Holiness Code?" in Kurt Martens, ed., *A Service Beyond All Recompense: Essays Offered in Honor of Monsignor Thomas J. Green* (Washington, DC, 2018), 61–84.

Bauer, Stefan, *The Invention of Papal History: Onofrio Panvinio Between Renaissance and Catholic Reform* (Oxford, 2020).

Bay-Hansen, C.D., *Power Geopolitics in the Pacific Age: East Asia, the United Nations, the United States, and Micronesia at the Edge of the 21st Century, 1991–2001* (Portland, OR, 2011).

Beal, John P., et al., eds., *New Commentary on the Code of Canon Law* (Washington, DC, 2000).

Beal, John P., "Confining and Structuring Administrative Discretion," *Jurist* 46 (1986), 70–106.

Beal, John P., "*On Due Process*: The Third Decade," in *Protection of Rights of Persons*, 1–12.

Beal, John P., "Provost, James H.," *encyclopedia.com*, encyclopedia.com/religion/encyclopedias-almanacs-transcripts-and-maps/provost-james-h.

Beals, Derek, and Biagini, Eugenio F., *The Risorgimentio and the Unification of Italy*, 2d ed. (London, 2013).

Beattie, Blake, *Angelus Pacis: The Legation of Cardinal Giovanni Gaetano Orsini, 1326–1334* (Leiden, 2007).

Behr, Thomas C., "The Nineteenth-Century Historical and Intellectual Context of Catholic Social Teaching," in Gerard V. Bradley and E. Christian Brugger, eds., *Catholic Social Teaching: A Volume of Scholarly Essays* (Cambridge, UK, 3019), 34–65.

Behrens, James, *Church Disputes Mediation* (Leominster, UK, 2003).

Beneduzi, Renato, *Equity in the Civil Law Tradition* (Cham, Switzerland, 2021).

Benham, Jenny, *Peacemaking in the Middle Ages: Principles and Practice* (Manchester, UK, 2011).

Benjamin, Robert D., "Formal Mediation in the Settlement of Divorce and Other Family Conflicts," *St. Louis Bar Journal* 32 (Spring, 1986), 43–51.

Bennett, Scott H., and Howlett, Charles F., *Antiwar Dissent and Peace Activism in World War I America: A Documentary Reader* (Lincoln, NE, 2014).

Berger, Adolf, *Encyclopedic Dictionary of Roman Law* (Philadelphia, 1953).

Berger, Stefan, "Building the Nation Among Visions of German Empire," in Stefan Berger and Alexei Miller, eds., *Nationalizing Empires* (Budapest, 2015), 247–308.

Berman, Harold J., *Law and Language: Effective Symbols of Community*, John Witte, Jr., ed. (Cambridge, UK, 2013).

Berman, Harold J., *Law and Revolution: The Formation of the Western Legal Tradition* (Cambridge, MA, 1983).

Bernardin, Joseph L., "The NCCB on the Subject of Due Process," in *On Due Process* (1972).

Berti, Emanuele, "Law in Declamation: The *status legales* in Senecan *Controversiae*," in Eugenio Amato, et al., eds., *Law and Ethics in Greek and Roman Declamation* (Berlin, 2015), 7–34.

Beste, Udalricus, *Introductio in Codicem: Quam in usum et utilitatem scholae et cleri ad promptam expeditamque canonum interpretationem* (Naples, 1956).

Binchy, Daniel, "The Papacy in a Changing World," *Studies: An Irish Quarterly Review* 26 (December, 1937), 641–647.

"Biography of +Peter Ebere Cardinal Okpaleke, Bishop of Ekwulobia Diocese," ekwulo bia.org/bishop-bio.

Bjorge, Eirik, *The Evolutionary Interpretation of Treaties* (Oxford, UK, 2014).

Bloch, Herbert, *Monte Cassino in the Middle Ages*, 2 vols. (Rome, 1986).

Blumenfeld-Kosinski, Renate, *Poets, Saints, and Visionaries of the Great Schism, 1378–1417* (University Park, PA, 2006).

Boersma, Hans, *Nouvelle Théologie and Sacramental Ontology: A Return to Mystery* (Oxford, UK, 2009).

Bonner, Stanley, *Education in Ancient Rome: From the Elder Cato to the Younger Pliny* (New York, 2012) (reprint of 1977 edition).

Borgman, Erik, "Retrieving God's Contemporary Presence: The Future of Edward Schillebeeckx's Theology of Culture," in Lieven Boeve, et al., eds., *Edward Schillebeeckx and Contemporary Theology* (London, 2012), 235–251.

Boyle, John F., "St. Thomas, Job, and the University Master," in Matthew Levering, et al., eds., *Reading Job with Thomas Aquinas* (Washington, DC, 2020), 21–41.

Boyle, Marjorie O'Rourke, *Petrarch's Genius: Pentimento and Prophecy* (Berkeley, CA, 1991).

Brandmüller, Walter, *Das Konzil von Pavia-Siena, 1423–1424* (Münster, 1968).

Brasington, Bruce C., *Order in the Court: Medieval Procedural Treatises in Translation* (Leiden, 2016).

Breyer, Stephen, et al., *Administrative Law and Regulatory Procedure: Problems, Text, and Cases*, 8th ed. (New York, 2017).

Briggs, Charles F., "Life, Works, and Legacy," in Charles F. Briggs and Peter Eardley, eds., *A Companion to Giles of Rome* (Leiden, 2016), 6–33.

Broad, Jacqueline, and Green, Karen, *A History of Women's Political Thought in Europe, 1400–1700* (Cambridge, UK, 2009).

Brown, Elizabeth A.R., "Moral Imperatives and Conundrums of Conscience: Reflections on Philip the Fair of France," *Speculum* 87 (2012), 1–36.

Brucker, Gene, *Living on the Edge in Leonardo's Florence: Selected Essays* (Berkeley, CA, 2005).

Brüggemeyer, Gert, "Constitutionalisation of Private Law – the German Perspective," in Tom Barkhuysen and Siewert Lindenbergh, eds., *Constitutionalisation of Private Law* (Leiden, 2006), 59–82.

Brundage, James A., *The Profession and Practice of Medieval Canon Law* (New York, 2004).

Brundage, James A., *The Medieval Origins of the Legal Profession: Canonists, Civilians, and Courts* (Chicago, 2008).

Brundage, James A., "Canon Law as an Instrument for Ecclesial Reform: An Historic Perspective," *Canon Law Society of America Proceedings* 45 (1983), 1–17.

Brundage, James A., "The Learned Judge: The Development of an Ideal," *University of St. Thomas Law Journal* 1 (2003), 434–446.

Brundage, James A., "Full and Partial Proof in Classical Canon Law," *The Jurist* 67 (2007), 58–71.

Brydon, Steven R., *American Propaganda From the Spanish-American War to Iraq* (Lanham, MD, 2022).

Bryson, David Morrow, "Clement v and the Road to Avignon, 1304 to 1309," in Helen J. Nicholson, ed., *On the Margins of Crusading: The Military Orders, the Papacy, and the Christian World* (London, 2016), pp. 61–74.

Buckland, W.W., *Equity in Roman Law* (London, 1911).

Bull, Beate, and Tostensen, Arne, "Bolstering Human Rights by Means of 'Smart' Sanctions?" in Hugo Stokke and Arne Tostensen, eds., *Human Rights in Development: Yeabook 1999/2000* (The Hague, 2001), 83–135.

Burkle-Young, Francis A., *Papal Elections: In the Age of Transition, 1878–1922* (Lanham, MD, 2000).

Burr, David, "History as Prophecy: Angelo Clareno's *Chronicle* as a Spiritual Franciscan Apocalypse," in Michael F. Cusato and Guy Geltner, eds., *Defenders and Critics of Franciscan Life: Essays in Honor of John V. Fleming* (Leiden, 2009), 119–138.

Bushlack, Thomas J., *Politics for a Pilgrim Church: A Thomistic Theory of Civic Virtue* (Grand Rapids, MI, 2015).

Byfield, Ted, *The Christians: Their First Two Thousand Years*, vol. VIII, *The Renaissance: God in Man, A.D. 1300–1500* (Edmonton, AB, 2010).

Caine, Barbara, "'My Vast Empire and All Its Many Peoples:' Queen Victoria's Imperial Family," in Sarah Carter and Maria Nugent, eds., *Mistress of Everything: Queen Victoria in Indigenous Worlds* (Manchester, UK, 2016), 125–143.

Caldwell, Peter C., "The Weimar Constitution," in Nadine Rossol and Benjamin Ziemann, eds., *The Oxford Handbook of the Weimar Republic* (Oxford, UK, 2022), 119–140.

Calenza, Christopher S., "The Will of Cardinal Giordano Orsini (OB. 1438)," *Traditio* 51 (1996), 257–286.

Candelaria, Michael R., *Popular Religion and Liberation: The Dilemma of Liberation Theology* (Albany, NY, 1990).

Canning, Joseph, *Ideas of Power in the Late Middle Ages, 1296–1417* (Cambridge, UK, 2011).

Capello, Felix, *Summa Iuris Canonici in Usum Scholarum*, 3 volumes (Rome, 1940).

Capponi, Niccolo, *The Day the Renaissance Was Saved: The Battle of Anghiari and Da Vinci's Lost Masterpiece*, Andre Naffis-Sahely, tr. (Brooklyn, 2015).

Carson, Mike T., *Archaeology of Pacific Oceania: Inhabiting a Sea of Islands* (London, 2018).

Carter, Alexander, "Introduction," in Coriden, ed., *We the People of God*, vii–xii.

Carucci, Lawrence M., "Book Review," *American Anthropologist* 87 (1985), 428–430 [reviewing Hezel, *First Taint of Civilization*].

Cassese, Emilio, "The Russian Secret Mission in the Vatican Between 1887 and 1906: Historical Dynamics and New European Alliances," in Antonello Biagini and Giovanna Motta, eds., *Empires and Nations From the Eighteenth Century to the Twentieth* (Newcastle-Upon-Tyne, 2014), vol. I, 96–104.

Casteen, Elizabeth, *From She-Wolf to Martyr: The Reign and Disputed Reputation of Johanna I of Naples* (Ithaca, NY, 2015).

Castillo, Dennis A., *Papal Diplomacy From 1914 to 1989: The Seventy-Five Years War* (Lanham, MD, 2019).

Castillo, Dennis A., *The Santa Marija Convoy: Faith and Endurance in Wartime Malta, 1940–1942* (Lanham, MD, 2012).
"Catholicism in Nigeria," harvard.edu/faq/catholicism-nigeria.
Cessario, Romanus, "Non Possumus," *First Things* (February, 2018).
Chadwick, Owen, *The Popes and European Revolution* (Oxford, UK, 1981).
Chadwick, Owen, *A History of the Popes, 1830–1914* (Oxford, 1998).
Chelini-Pont, Blandine, "Papal Thought on Europe and the European Union in the Twentieth Century," in Lucian N. Leustean and John T.S. Madely, eds., *Religion, Politics, and Law in the European Union* (New York, 2010), 125–140.
Cheyette, Fredric L., "*Suum Cuique Tribuere*," *French Historical Studies* 6 (1970), 287–299.
Chiam, Madeleine, *International Law in Public Debate* (Cambridge, UK, 2021).
Christandl, Gregor, "Will-Substitutes in Italy," in Alexandra Braun and Anne Röthel, eds., *Passing Wealth on Death: Will-Substitutes in Comparative Perspective* (Oxford, UK, 2016), 131–157.
Ciampani, Andrea, "Rethinking the Origins of the Catholic Party in Liberal Italy (The *Unione Romana*) (1877–1887)," in Jan de Maeyer and Vincent Viaene, eds., *World Views and Worldly Wisdom: Religion, Ideology, and Politics, 1750–2000* (Leuven, 2016), 105–124.
Clarke, Peter D., *The Interdict in the Thirteenth Century: A Question of Collective Guilt* (Oxford, UK, 2007).
Cocchi, Guido, *Commentarium in Codicem Iuris Canonici ad Usum Scholarum* (Turin, 1930), 4 volumes.
Coleman, Gerald D., "Discerning the Meaning of *Humanae Vitae*," *Theological Studies* 79 (2018), 864–878.
"Colonna, Landolfo," *Treccani Enciclopedia* (online), treccani.it/enciclopedia/landolfo-colonna/.
Comparato, Guido, *Nationalism and Private Law in Europe* (Oxford, UK, 2014).
Conrad, Joseph, *Heart of Darkness* (London, 1902).
Considine, Kevin P., *Salvation for the Sinned-Against: Han and Schillebeeckx in Intercultural Dialogue* (Eugene, OR, 2015).
Constable, Giles, *Monastic Tithes: From Their Origins to the Twelfth Century* (Cambridge, UK, 1964).
Conte a Coronata, Matteo, *Institutiones iuris canonici ad usum utriusque cleri et scholarum* (Rome, 1941) 5 volumes.
Coppa, Frank, *The Modern Papacy Since 1789* (London, 1998).
Coppa, Frank, "Pio Nono and the Jews: From 'Reform' to 'Reaction,' 1846–1878," *Catholic Historical Review* 89 (2003), 671–695.
Corfield, Justin, "Leo XIII (1810–1903)," in Kenneth E. Hendrickson, ed., *The Encyclopedia of the Industrial Revolution in World History* (Lanham, MD, 2015), 539–557.

Coriden, James A., *An Introduction to Canon Law*, rev. ed. (London, 2004).

Coriden, James A., ed., *We the People of God: A Study of Constitutional Government for the Church* (Huntington, IN, 1968).

Coriden, James A., "Diplomatic Recognition of the Holy See," *Jurist* 48 (1988), 483–498.

Coriden, James A., "Editor's Preface," in Coriden, ed., *We the People of God*, xiii–xvi.

Coriden, James A., "Reflections on Canonical Rights," in Provost and Walf, eds., *Studies in Canon Law*, 21–36.

Coriden, James A., "Nihil Obstat," *Encyclopedia.com*, encyclopedia.com/religion/encyclopedias-almanacs-transcripts-and-maps/nihil.obstat.

Cortright, David, and Lopez, George, *The Sanctions Decade: Assessing U.N. Strategies in the 1990s* (Boulder, CO, 2000).

Coss, Peter, *The Aristocracy in England and Tuscany, 1000–1250* (Oxford, UK, 2020).

Crawford, Neta C., "Blood and Treasure: United States Budgetary Costs and Human Costs of 20 Years of War in Iraq and Syria, 2003–2023," Watson Institute for International and Public Affairs, Brown University, March 15, 2023.

Cronin, Sonya Shetty, *Raymond Brown, 'The Jews,' and the Gospel of John: From Apologia to Apology* (London, 2015).

Cummings, Owen F., *Popes, Councils, and Theology: From Pope Pius IX to Pope Francis* (Eugene OR, 2021).

Cunningham, Richard G., "The Principles Guiding the Revision of the Code of Canon Law," *Jurist* 30 (1970), 447–455.

Curran, Charles E., *The Origins of Moral Theology in the United States: Three Different Approaches* (Washington, DC, 1997).

Curran, Charles E., "Churches and Human Rights: From Hostility/Reluctance to Acceptability," in Charles E. Curran, ed., *Change in Official Catholic Moral Teaching* (New York, 2003), 38–61.

Curry, Anne, *The Hundred Years War Revisited* (London, 2019).

Curry, Anne, "Two Kingdoms, One King: The Treaty of Troyes (1420) and the Creation of a Double Monarchy of England and France," in Glenn Richardson, ed., *'The Contending Kingdoms:' France and England, 1420–1700* (Aldershot, UK, 2008), 23–42.

Dadrian, Vahakn N., "The Armenian Genocide as a Dual Problem of National and International Law," *University of St. Thomas Journal of Law and Public Policy* 4 (2010), 60–82.

Daileader, Philip, *Saint Vincent Ferrer, His World and Life: Religion and Society in Late Medieval Europe* (New York, 2016).

Daileader, Philip, "Local Experiences of the Great Western Schism," in Rollo-Koster and Izbicki, eds., *Companion to the Great Western Schism*, 89–121.

David, René, and Brierly, John E.C., *Major Legal Systems in the World Today: An Introduction to the Comparative Study of Law*, 2d ed. (New York, 1978).

Decock, Wim, "Neo-Thomism, Law, and Society: A Prolegomenon to Further Study," in Wim Decock, et al., eds., *Neo-Thomism in Action: Law and Society Reshaped by Neo-Scholastic Philosophy, 1880–1960* (Leuven, 2021), 7–26.

Delany, Douglas E., *The Imperial Army Project: Britain and the Land Forces of the Dominions and India, 1902–1945* (Oxford, UK, 2018).

Delogu, Daisy, *Theorizing the Ideal Sovereign: The Rise of the French Vernacular Royal Biography* (Toronto, 2008).

De Mey, Peter, "The Bishop's Participation in the Threefold *Munera*: Comparing the Appeal to the Pattern of the *Tria Munera* at Vatican II and in the Ecumenical Dialogues," *Jurist* 69 (2009), 31–58.

Democopoulos, George E., *Gregory the Great: Ascetic, Pastor, and First Man of Rome* (South Bend, IN, 2015).

Denery, Dallas, G., "Christine de Pizan on Gossip, Misogyny, and Possibility," in Jason Glenn, ed., *The Middle Ages in Text and Texture: Reflections on Medieval Sources* (Toronto, 2011), 309–321.

Denis, Philippe, *The Genocide Against the Tutsi, and the Rwandan Churches: Between Grief and Denial* (Woodbridge, UK, 2022).

Descantes, Christophe, "The Martyrdom of Father Juan Cantova on Ulithi Atoll: The Hegemonic Struggle Between Spanish Colonialism and a Micronesian Island Polity," *Missionalia* 32 (2004), 394–418.

Desilva, Jennifer Mara, "Articulating Work and Family," *Renaissance Quarterly* 69 (2016) 1–39.

Dijk, Kees van, *Pacific Strife* (Amsterdam, 2015).

Ditchfield, Simon, "Catholic Reformation and Renewal," in Peter Marshall, ed., *The Oxford Illustrated History of the Reformation* (Oxford, 2015), pp. 152–185.

Donahue, Charles, "Equity in the Courts of Merchants," *Tijdschrift voor Rechtsgechiedenis* 72 (2004), 1–35.

Donahue, Charles, "Medieval and Early Modern *Lex Mercatoria*: An Attempt at the *Probatio Diabolica*," *Chicago Journal of International Law* 5 (2004), 21–37.

Douglas, Bruce, *A Companion to Anglican Eucharistic Theology*, vol. I, *The Reformation to the Nineteenth Century* (Leiden, 2012).

Drescher, Seymour, "From Consensus to Consensus: Slavery in International Law," in Jean Allain, et al., eds., *The Legal Understanding of Slavery: From the Historical to the Contemporary* (Oxford, UK, 2012), 85–104.

Dreuzy, Agnes de, *The Holy See and the Emergence of the Modern Middle East: Benedict XV's Diplomacy in Greater Syria (1914–1922)* (Washington, DC, 2016).

Duchesne, Louis, *Early History of the Christian Church: From Its Foundation to the End of the Fifth Century*, Claude Jenkins, tr. 3 volumes (London, 1909–1924).

Duchesne, Louis, *The Churches Separated From Rome*, Arnold Harris Mathew, tr. (London, 1907).

Duchesne, Louis, *Christian Worship: Its Origin and Evolution: A Study of the Latin Liturgy Up to Charlemagne*, M.L. McClure, tr. (London, 1903).

Duerksen, Darren, and Dyrness, William A., *Seeking Church: Emerging Witnesses to the Kingdom* (Downer's Grove, IL, 2019).

Dulles, Avery, *Princeps Concordiae: Pico della Mirandola and the Scholastic Tradition* (Cambridge, MA, 1941).

Dulles, Avery, *A Testimonial to Grace* (New York, 1946).

Dulles, Avery, *The Dimensions of the Church; A Postconciliar Reflection* (Westminster, MD, 1967).

Dulles, Avery, "The Sacramental Ecclesiology of *Lumen Gentium*," *Gregorianum* 86 (2005), 550–562.

Dullin, Sabine, "L'entre-voisins en période de transition étatique (1917–1924): La frontiére épaisse des bocheviks à l'Est de l'Europe," *Annales, Histoire, Sciences Sociales* 69 (2014), 383–414.

Eckhardt, Carl Conrad, *The Papacy and World Affairs: As Reflected in the Secularization of Politics* (Eugene, OR, 2016) (reprint of 1937 edition).

Edelstein, David M., *Over the Horizon: Time, Uncertainty, and the Rise of Great Powers* (Ithaca, NY, 2017).

Ekechi, Felix K., "The Holy Ghost Fathers in Eastern Nigeria, 1885–1920: Observations on Missionary Strategy," *African Studies Review* 15 (1972), 217–239.

Ela, Jean-Marc, *African Cry*, Robert J. Barr, tr. (Eugene, OR, 2005) (originally published 1986).

Ellis, John Tracy, "The Catholic Church and Peace Efforts," *Notre Dame Lawyer* 9 (1934), 173–214.

Engelstein, Laura, *Russia In Flames: War, Revolution, Civil War, 1914–1921* (Oxford, UK, 2018).

Esmark, Kim, "Disputing Property in Zealand: The Records of the Sorø Donation Book," in Kim Esmark, et al., eds., *Disputing Strategies in Medieval Scandinavia* (Leiden, 2013), 181–218.

Evangelista, Matthew, and Reppy, Judith, "Much Ado About Democracy: Some Skeptical Observations on Democracies and War," in Matthew Evangelista, et al., eds., *Democracy and Security: Preferences, Norms, and Policy-Making* (London, 2008), pp. 167–186.

Exegetical Commentary on the Code of Canon Law, 8 volumes (Montreal, 2004).

Faggioli, Massimo, *John XXIII: The Medicine of Mercy* (Collegeville, MN, 2014).

Faggioli, Massimo, *A Council for the Global Church: Receiving Vatican II in History* (Minneapolis, MN, 2015).

Falkeid, Una, *The Avignon Papacy-Contested: An Intellectual History from Dante to Catherine of Siena* (Cambridge, MA, 2017).

Famiglietti, R.C., *Royal Intrigue: Crisis at the Court of Charles VI, 1392–1420* (New York, 1986).

Fedele, Dante, *The Medieval Foundations of International Law: Baldus de Ubaldis (1327–1400), Doctrine and Practice of the Ius Gentium* (Leiden, 2021).

Fletcher, Stella, *The Popes and Britain: A History of Rule, Rupture, and Reconciliation* (London, 2017).

Fluehr-Lobban, Carolyn, "Protracted Civil War in the Sudan – Its Future as a Multi-Religious, Multi-Ethnic State," *Fletcher Forum of World Affairs* 16 (1992), 67–80.

Flynn, Gabriel, "*Ressourcement* and Theologies of Communion," in Lewis Ayres and Medi Ann Volpe, eds., *The Oxford Handbook of Catholic Theology* (Oxford, UK, 2015), 683–700.

Follesdal, Andreas, "The Principle of Subsidiarity as a Constitutional Principle in International Law," *Global Constitutionalism* 2 (2013), 37–62.

Forbes, Frances Alice, *Life of Pius X* (New York, 1918).

Forclaz, Amalia Ribi, *Humanitarian Humanism: The Politics of Anti-Slavery Activism, 1880–1940* (Oxford, UK, 2015).

Fraher, Richard M., "Conviction According to Conscience: The Medieval Jurists' Debate Concerning Judicial Discretion and the Law of Proof," *Law and History Review* 7 (1989), 23–88.

Fraioli, Deborah A., *Joan of Arc and the Hundred Years War* (Westport, CT, 2005).

Fudge, Thomas A., *The Trial of Jan Hus: Medieval Heresy and Criminal Procedure* (Oxford, UK, 2013).

Gaillardetz, Richard R., *The Cambridge Companion to Vatican II* (Cambridge, UK, 2020).

Garrett, James L., "The Beagle Channel Dispute: Confrontation and Negotiation in the Southern Cone," *Journal of Interamerican Studies and World Affairs* 27 (1985), 81–109.

Gasparri, Pietro, *Tractatus canonicus de sacra ordinatione* (Paris, 1893/1894).

Gasparri, Pietro, *Tractatus canonicus de sanctissima Eucharistia* (Paris, 1897).

Gasparri, Pietro, *Tractatus canonicus de matrimonio* (Paris, 1904).

Gaudemet, Jean, "Le role de la papauté dans le réglement des conflicts entre états aux XIIIe et XIVe siécles," *Recueils de la Société Jean Bodin* 15 (1961), 79–106.

Gblerkpor, William Narteh, and Gavua, Kodzo, "South Sudan, Republic of," in Toyin Falola and Daniel Jean-Jacques, eds., *Africa: An Encyclopedia of Culture and Society* (Santa Barbara, 2016), vol. III, 1128–1142.

Geary, Patrick, *Living With the Dead in the Middle Ages* (Ithaca, NY, 1994).

Gerhard, B.C., "Woywod, Stanislaus," *Encyclopedia.com.*

Gerhard, B.C., "Woywod, Stanislaus," *New Catholic Encyclopedia* 14 (2003), 860.

Gerosa, Libero, *Canon Law* (New York, 2002).

Gibbons, Rachel, "'The Limbs Fail When the Head Is Removed:' Reactions of the Body Politic of France to the Madness of Charles VI (1380–1422)," in Sean McGlynn and

Elena Woodacre, eds., *The Image and Perception of Monarchy in Medieval and Early Modern Europe* (Newcastle-Upon-Tyne, 2014), 48–69.

Gibran, Daniel K., *The Falklands War: Britain Versus the Past in the South Atlantic* (Jefferson, NC, 2008).

Gibson, Bryan, *Law, Justice, and Mediation: The Legend of St. Yves* (Hook, UK, 2008).

Gill, Joseph, "The Representation of the *Universitas Fidelium* in the Councils of the Conciliar Period," in *Councils and Assemblies* (Cambridge, UK, 1971) 177–195.

Glare, P.G.W., *Oxford Latin Dictionary* (Oxford, UK, 1982).

Glenn, H. Patrick, *The Cosmopolitan State* (Oxford, 2013).

Glenn, H. Patrick, "The Grounding of Codification," *U.C. Davis Law Review* 31 (1998), 765–782.

Glowczewski, Barbara, *Indiginising Anthropology With Guattari and Deleuze* (Edinburgh, 2020).

Godfrey, Andrew M., *Civil Justice in Renaissance Scotland: The Origins of a Central Court* (Leiden, 2009).

Goeschel, Christian, *Mussolini and Hitler: The Forging of the Fascist Alliance* (New Haven, CT, 2018).

Goodenough, Ward H., "Navigation in the Western Carolines: A Traditional Science," in Sandra Harding, ed., *The Postcolonial Science and Technology Studies Reader* (Durham, NC, 2011), 159–174.

Goodwine, John A., "Problems Respecting the Censorship of Books," *Jurist* 10 (1950), 152–183.

Gordon, Ignacio, "Normae Speciales Supremi Tribunalis Signaturae Apostolicae: Editio Aucta Introductione, fontibus et notis," *Periodica* 59 (1970), 75–166.

Gordon, Michelle, *British Colonial Violence in Perak, Sierra Leone, and the Sudan* (Ph.D. dissertation, Royal Holloway, University of London, 2017).

Granfield, Patrick, "The Church as *Societas Perfecta* in the Schemata of Vatican I," *Church History* 48 (1979), 431–446.

Gray, Janette, "Marie-Dominique Chenu and Le Saulchoir: A Stream of Catholic Renewal," in Gabriel Flynn and Paul D. Murray, eds., *Ressourcement: A Movement for Renewal in Twentieth-Century Theology* (Oxford, UK, 2012), pp. 205–212.

Greeley, Andrew M., "A Social Organizational View of the Catholic Church," in Coriden, ed., *We the People of God*, 81–89.

Green, Garrett, "Modernity", in Gareth Jones, ed., *The Blackwell Companion to Modern Theology* (Malden, MA, 2004), 162–179.

Green, Karen, *Joan of Arc and Christine de Pizan's Ditié* (Lanham, MD, 2021).

Grewe, Wilhelm G., *The Epochs of International Law*, Michael Byers, tr. (Berlin, 2013).

Griffin, Miriam, "The Elder Seneca and Spain," *Journal of Roman Studies* 62 (1972), 1–19.

Groppe, Elizabeth Teresa, *Yves Congar's Theology of the Holy Spirit* (Oxford, UK, 2004).

Gumbleton, Thomas J., "Due Process in the Church," *Canon Law Society of America Proceedings* 31 (1969), 1–9.

Hage, Per, "Was Proto-Oceanic Society Matrilineal?" *Journal of the Polynesian Society* 107 (1998), 365–379.

Halberstam, Daniel, "Federalism: Theory, Practice, Law," in Michael Rosenfeld and András Sajó, eds., *Oxford Handbook of Comparative Constitutional Law* (Oxford, UK, 2012), 576–608.

Hall, Jon, *Politeness and Politics in Cicero's Letters* (Oxford, UK, 2009).

Hallenbeck, Jan T., "Pavia and Rome: The Lombard Monarchy and the Papacy in the Eighth Century," *Transactions of the American Philosophical Society* 72 (1982), 1–186.

Hanlon, David, *Upon a Stone Altar: A History of the Island of Pohnpei to 1890* (Honolulu, HI, 1988).

Hanlon, David, *Making Micronesia: A Political Biography of Tosiwo Nakayama* (Honolulu, HI, 2014).

Hanlon, David, "The 'Sea of Little Lands:' Examining Micronesia's Place in 'Our Sea of Islands,'" *Contemporary Pacific* 21 (2009), 91–110.

Harriman, Edward Avery, *The Law of Contracts*, 2d ed. rev. and enlarged (Boston, 1901).

Harris, John, "Hiding the Bodies: The Myth of the Humane Colonisation of Aboriginal Australia," *Aboriginal History* 27 (2003), 79–104.

Harris, Lester, "Recognition of the Holy See," *Dickinson Law Review* 55 (1950), 235–245.

Harte, Liam, *The Literature of the Irish in Britain: Autobiography and Memoir, 1725–2001* (New York, 2009).

Harvey, Margaret, *England, Rome, and the Papacy, 1417–1464: The Study of a Relationship* (Manchester, UK, 1993).

Harvey, Margaret, "Martin v and the English, 1422–1431," in Christopher Harper-Bill, ed., *Religious Belief and Ecclesiastical Careers* (Woodbridge, UK, 1991), 59–86.

Harvey, Margaret, "Martin v and Henry v," *Archivum Historiae Pontificiae* 24 (1986), 49–70.

Harvey, Philip, "Aspirational Law," *Buffalo Law Review* 52 (2004), 701–726.

Havely, Nick, *Dante and the Franciscans: Poverty and the Papacy in the 'Commedia,'* (Cambridge, UK, 2004).

Hebblethwaite, Peter, *Pope John Paul II and the Church* (Kansas City, MO, 1995).

Hedeman, Anne D., "Constructing Memories: Scenes of Conversation and Presentation in Pierre Salmon's 'Dialogues,'" *Journal of the Walters Art Gallery* 54 (1996), 119–134.

Hehir, J. Bryan, "The Modern Catholic Church and Human Rights: The Impact of the Second Vatican Council," in John Witte, Jr., and Frank Alexander, eds., *Christianity and Human Rights*, 113–134.

Hein, James R., "Caroline Islands," in Rosemary Gillespie and David Clague, eds., *Encyclopedia of Islands* (Berkeley, CA, 2009), 148–150.

Helmholz, Richard H., *The Spirit of Classical Canon Law* (Athens, GA, 2010).

Helmholz, Richard H., "Pope Innocent III and the Annulment of *Magna Carta*," *Journal of Ecclesiastical History* 69 (2018), 1–14.

Herghelegiu, Moncia-Elena, *Reservatio Papalis: A Study on the Application of a Legal Prescription According to the 1983 Code of Canon Law* (Berlin, 2008).

Herzog, Tamar, *A Short History of European Law: The Last Two and Half Millennia* (Cambridge, MA, 2018).

Hezel, Francis X., *The First Taint of Civilization: A History of the Western Caroline and Marshall Islands in Pre-Colonial Days* (Honolulu, HI, 1983).

Hezel, Francis X., *Strangers in Their Own Land: A Century of Colonial Rule in the Caroline and Marshall Islands* (Honolulu, 1995).

Hezel, Francis X., "The Beginnings of Foreign Contact With Truk," *Journal of Pacific History* 8 (1973), 51–73.

Hezel, Francis X., "Early European Contact With the Western Carolines, 1525–1750," *Journal of Pacific History* 7 (1972), 26–44.

Hiery, Herman Joseph, *Fa'a Siamani: Germany in Micronesia, New Guinea, and Samoa, 1884–1914* (Wiesbaden, 2020).

Hill, Felicity, *Excommunication in Thirteenth-Century England: Communities, Politics, Publicity* (Oxford, UK, 2022).

Hill, Harvey, "Leo XIII, Loisy, and the 'Broad School:' An Early Round of the Modernist Crisis," *Catholic Historical Review* 89 (2003), 39–51.

Himes, Kennneth, "Papal Thinking About Peace Since *Pacem in Terris*: The World Day of Peace Messages, 1967–2013," *Journal of Catholic Social Thought* 11 (2014), 9–32.

Hittinger, Russell, "Pope Leo XIII (1810–1903)," in John Witte, Jr., and Frank S. Alexander, eds., *The Teachings of Modern Roman Catholicism on Law, Politics, and Human Nature* (New York, 2007), pp. 39–75.

Hochschild, Adam, *Lessons From a Dark Time and Other Essays* (Berkeley, CA, 2018).

Hochschild, Adam, *King Leopold's Ghost: A Story of Greed, Terror, and Heroism in Colonial Africa* (New York, 2019).

Hoffman, Morris B., *The Punisher's Brain: The Evolution of Judge and Jury* (Cambridge, UK, 2014).

Hoffmann, Henryk, *Latin In Modern Fiction: Who Says It's a Dead Language?* (Wilmington, DE, 2021).

Hofmann, Andreas R., "Reweaving the Urban Fabric: Multiethnicity and Occupation in Łódź, 1914–1918," in Marcus Funck and Roger Chickering, eds., *Endangered Cities: Military Power and Urban Societies in the Eras of the World Wars* (Leiden, 2004), 81–94.

Holland, Joe, *Catholic Social Teaching: The Popes Confront the Industrial Age, 1740–1958* (Mahwah, NJ, 2003).

Homan, Gerlof D., "Catholic Emancipation in the Netherlands," *Catholic Historical Review* 52 (1966), 201–211.

Hooper, J. Leon, ed., *Bridging the Sacred and the Secular: Selected Writings of John Courtney Murray* (Washington, DC, 1994).

Hudock, Barry, *Struggle, Condemnation, Vindication: John Courtney Murray's Journey Toward Vatican II* (Collegeville, MN, 2015).

Hughes, Kevin L., "The Spiritual Interpretation of Scripture," in Jordan Hillebert, ed., *T & T Companion to Henri de Lubac* (London, 2017).

Hunt, Nigel, *Landscapes of Trauma: The Psychology of the Battlefield* (London, 2020).

Huzzey, Richard, *Freedom Burning: Anti-Slavery and Empire in Victorian Britain* (Ithaca, NY, 2012).

Hyams, Paul R., *Rancor and Reconciliation in Medieval England* (Ithaca, NY, 2003).

Hyland, William Patrick, "Book Review" *Catholic Historical Review* 89 (2003) 770–771 [reviewing Walter Brandmüller, *Das Konzil von Pavia-Siena, 1423–1424*].

Ivereigh, Austen, *The Great Reformer: Francis and the Making of a Radical Pope* (New York, 2014).

Izbicki, Thomas M., "The Canonists and the Treaty of Troyes," in Stephan Kuttner and Kenneth Pennington, eds., *Proceedings of the Fifth International Congress of Medieval Canon Law* (Vatican City, 1980), 425–434.

Jacobson, Stephen, "Law and Nationalism in the Nineteenth Century: The Case of Catalonia in Comparative Perspective," *Law and History Review* 20 (2002), 307–348.

Jalata, Asafa, "The Impacts of English Colonial Terrorism and Genocide on Indigenous/ Black Australians," *Sage Open* vol. 3, no. 3 (July–September, 2013).

Johnson, Darin E.W., "Revolution, Peace, and Justice in Sudan," *University of Pennsylvania Journal of International Law* 43 (2021), 187–240.

Johnson, Douglas H., *The Root Causes of Sudan's Civil Wars: Old Wars and New Wars*, expanded 3d ed. (Woodbridge, UK, 2016).

Johnston, William M., *The Austrian Mind: An Intellectual and Social History, 1848–1938* (Berkeley, CA, 1972).

Jolowicz, J.A., "Adversarial and Inquisitorial Models of Civil Procedure," *International and Comparative Law Quarterly* 52 (2003), 281–295.

Jolowicz, J.A., "Civil Procedure in the Common and Civil Law," in Guenther Doeker-Mach and Klaus A. Ziegert, eds., *Law, Legal Culture, and Politics in the Twenty-First Century* (*Essays in Honor of Alic Erh-Soon Tay*) (Stuttgart, 2004), 55–78.

Jones, Colin, *The Cambridge Illustrated History of France* (Cambridge, UK, 1994).

Justenhoven, Heinz-Gerhard, "Peace Through a Public Global Authority in Papal Teaching From Leo XIII to John XXIII," in Heinz-Gerhard Justenhoven and James Turner, eds., *Rethinking the State in the Age of Globalisation: Catholic Social Thought and Contemporary Political Theory* (New Brunswick, NJ, 2003), 167–194.

Justenhoven, Heinz-Gerhard, "The Peace Ethics of Pope John Paul II," *University of St. Thomas Law Journal* 3 (2005), 110–138.

Karsh, Efraim, and Rautsi, Inari, "Why Saddam Hussein Invaded Kuwait," *Global Politics and Strategy* 33 (1991), 18–30.

Kaye, Bruce N., *Frozen Institutions: Questions for the Church After Christendom* (Eugene, OR, 2022).

Keating, Kevin T., *Papal Teaching in the Age of Infallibility, 1870 to the Present: A Critical Evaluation with Historical Illustrations* (Eugene, OR, 2018).

Keith, Charles, *Catholic Vietnam: A Church From Empire to Nation* (Berkeley, CA, 2012).

Keith, Jeanette, *Rich Man's War, Poor Man's Fight: Race, Class, and Power in the Rural South During the First World War* (Chapel Hill, NC, 2004).

Kelley, Donald R., "Lord Deliver Us From Injustice," *Yale Journal of Law and the Humanities* 5 (1993), 159–168.

Kelly, J.N.D., and Walsh, Michael, eds., *A Dictionary of the Popes*, 3d ed. (Oxford Reference) (online).

Kerr, Fergus, "Chenu's Little Book," *New Blackfriars* 66 (1985), 108–112.

Kertzer, David I., *The Kidnaping of Edgardo Mortara* (New York, 1997).

Kertzer, David I., *Prisoner of the Vatican: The Popes, the Kings, and Garibaldi's Rebels in the Struggle to Rule Modern Italy* (Boston, 2004).

Kertzer, David I., "The Lost Cause: Failed French Ultimata and the Restoration of Papal Rule in Rome in 1849," *Journal of Modern Italian Studies* 22 (2017), 555–570.

Keyser, Richard L., "Agreement Supersedes Law, and Love Judgment: Legal Flexibility and Amicable Settlement in Anglo-Norman England," *Law and History Review* 30 (2012), 37–88.

Kirch, Patrick Vinton, *On the Road of the Winds: An Archaeological History of the Pacific Islands Before European Contact*, rev. and expanded (Berkeley, 2017).

Kizhakkeparampil, Isaac, *The Invocation of the Holy Spirit as Constitutive of the Sacraments According to Cardinal Yves Congar* (Rome, 1995).

Klaiber, Jeffrey, *The Church, Dictatorships, and Democracy in Latin America* (Eugene, OR) (reprint of 1998 edition).

Kling, David W., *A History of Christian Conversion* (Oxford, UK, 2020).

Köhler, Oskar, "The World Plan of Leo XIII: Goals and Methods," Margit Resch, tr., in Hubert Jedin and John Dolan, eds., *History of the Church*, vol. IX, *The Church in the Industrial Age* (London, 1981), 3–25.

Kuehn, Thomas, *Patrimony and Law in Renaissance Italy* (Cambridge, MA, 2022).

Kuehn, Thomas, "*Materia Est Valde Periculosa*: Interpreting Testaments in Quattrocento Florence," in Maria Giglioa di Renzo Villata, ed., *Succession Law, Practice and Society in Europe Across the Ages* (Cham, Switzerland, 2018), 249–270.

Kuttner, Stephan, "The Code of Canon Law in Historical Perspective," *Jurist* 28 (1968), 129–148.

Lagrange, Marie-Joseph, *La méthode historique: La critique biblique et l'Église* (Paris, 1904).

Lagrange, Marie-Joseph, *La judaisme avant Jésus Christ* (Paris, 1931).

Lagrange, Marie-Joseph, *Évangile selon saint Jean* (Paris, 1936).

Lamb, Matthew, and Levering, Matthew, eds., *The Reception of Vatican II* (Oxford, UK, 2017).

Lambertini, Roberto, "Giles of Rome," *Stanford Encyclopedia of Philosophy* (online).

Lambertini, Roberto, "Political Prudence in Some Medieval Commentaries on the Sixth Book of the *Nichomachean Ethics*," in István Bejczy, ed., *Virtue Ethics in the Middle Ages: Commentaries on Aristotle's Nichomachean Ethics, 1200–1500* (Leiden, 2008), 223–246.

Landau, Peter, "*Aequitas* in the *Corpus Iuris Canonici*," *Syracuse Journal of International Law and Commerce* 20 (1994), 95–104.

Langan, John, "Can There Be a Human Rights Problem in the Church?" *Jurist* 46 (1986), 14–42.

Laqua, Daniel, "The Tensions of Internationalism: Transnational Anti-Slavery in the 1880s and 1890s," *International History Review* 33 (2011), 705–726.

Lara, María Pia, "Reframing Perspectives on Evil: Accountability, Moral Responsibility, and Collective Judgment," in Andrea Veltman and Kathryn J. Norlock, eds., *Evil, Political Violence, and Forgiveness: Essays in Honor of Claudia Card* (Lanham, MD, 2009), 195–211.

Larner, John, "The Church and the Quattrocento Renaissance in Geography," *Renaissance Studies* 12 (1998), 26–39.

Laureys, Marc, "Antiquarianism and Politics in Fourteenth-Century Avignon: The Humanism of Giovanni Cavallini," in Jan Papy and Karl A.E. Enenkel, eds., *Petrarch and His Readers* (Leiden, 2006), 31–52.

Lay, Stephen, *The Reconquest Kings of Portugal: Political and Cultural Reorientation on the Medieval Frontier* (New York, 2009).

Lease, Gary, "Vatican Foreign Policy and the Origins of Modernism," in Darrell Jodock, ed., *Catholicism Contending with Modernity: Roman Catholic Modernism and Anti-Modernism in Historical Context* (Cambridge, UK, 2000), 31–55.

Lefebvre, Charles, "Natural Equity and Canonical Equity: Note," *Natural Law Forum* 8 (1963), 122–136.

Lega, Michele, *Praelectiones in textum iuris canonici de iudiciis ecclesiasticis* (Rome, 1896–1901), 4 volumes.

Legrand, Pierre, "'Strange Power of Words:' Codification Situated," *Tulane European and Civil Law Forum* 9 (1994), 1–34.

Legrand, Pierre, "Codification and the Politics of Exclusion: A Challenge for Comparativists," *UC Davis Law Review* 31 (1998), 799–808.

Leng, Felicity, *Smiles of God: The Flowers of Saint Thérèse of Lisieux* (London, 2003).

Leontovitsch, Victor, *The History of Liberalism in Russia* (Pittsburgh, PA, 2012).

Lessa, William A., "An Evaluation of Early Descriptions of Carolinian Culture," *Ethnohistory* 9 (1962), 313–403.

Lessa, William A., "Drake in the South Seas," in Norman J.W. Thrower, ed., *Sir Francis Drake and the Famous Voyage, 1577–1580: Essays Commemorating the Quadricentennial of Drake's Circumnavigation of the Earth* (Berkeley, CA, 1984), 60–77.

Leustean, Lucian N., *The Ecumenical Movement and the Making of the European Community* (Oxford, UK, 2014).

Levasseur, Alain A., "Portalis and Pound: A Debate on 'Codification,'" *Louisiana Law Review* 81 (2021), 1113–1128.

Levasseur, Alain A., "The Boundary of Property Rights: La Notion de Biens," *American Journal of Comparative Law* 54 (2006), 145–165.

Levering, Matthew, "Christus Dominus," in Matthew Lamb and Matthew Levering, eds., *The Reception of Vatican II* (Oxford, UK, 2017), 147–169.

Levin, Maureece J., et al., "A Partial Chronological Sequence of Human Habitation for Pingelap Atoll (Pohnpei State, Federated States of Micronesia)," *Radiocarbon* 61 (2019), 765–776.

Lewin, Allison Williams, *Negotiating Survival: Florence and the Great Schism, 1378–1417* (Madison, WI, 2003).

Lienhard, Joseph T., "'Faith of Our Fathers:' The Fathers of the Church and Vatican II," in Kevin McMahon, ed., *Divine Promise and Human Freedom in Contemporary Catholic Thought* (Lanham, MD, 2015), 1–14.

Lindberg, Carter, *The European Reformations*, 2d ed. (Malden, MA, 2010).

Lindsley, Lisa, "The Beagle Channel Settlement: Vatican Mediation Resolves a Century-Old Dispute," *Journal of Church and State* 29 (1987), 435–455.

Llewellyn, Peter, "The Popes and the Constitution in the Eighth Century," *English Historical Review* 101 (1986), 42–67.

Lobingier, Charles Sumner, "Napoleon and His Code," *Harvard Law Review* 32 (1918–1919), 114–134.

Loisy, Alfred, *Les Évangiles synoptiques* (Paris, 1907).

Loisy, Alfred, *My Duel With the Vatican: The Autobiography of a Catholic Modernist*, Richard Wilson Boynton, tr. (New York, 1924).

Lopez, Bianca, "Between Court and Cloister: The Life and Lives of Margherita Colonna," *Church History* 82 (2013), 554–575.

Lorente, Marta, "Historical Titles v. Effective Occupation: Spanish Jurists on the Caroline Islands Affair (1885)," *Journal of the History of International Law* 20 (2018), 303–344.

"Louis Duchesne," *Catholic Historical Review* 9 (1922), 214–216.

Lovell-Hoare, Sophie and Max, *South Sudan: The Bradt Travel Guide* (Guilford, CT, 2013).

Lubet, Stephen, "Judicial Kidnaping, Then and Now: The Case of Edgardo Mortara," *Northwestern University Law Review* 93 (1998/1999), 961–1008.

Luca, Mariano de, *De Iudiciis Ecclesiasticis Civilibus Compendium Iuxta Ordinem Decretalium*, 2d ed. (Rome, 1902).

Lupano, Alberto, "Pietro Gasparri (1852–1934)," in Orazio Condarelli and Rafael Domingo, eds., *Law and the Christian Tradition in Italy: The Legacy of the Great Jurists* (London, 2021), 348–361.

Madar, Martin, *The Church of God and Its Human Face: The Contribution of Joseph A. Komonchak to Ecclesiology* (Eugene, OR, 2019).

Madigan, Kevin, *Medieval Christianity: A New History* (New Haven, CT, 2015).

Magraw, Roger, *France 1800–1914: A Social History* (New York, 2014) (reprint of 2002 edition).

Maher, Anthony M., *The Forgotten Jesuit of Catholic Modernism: George Tyrell's Prophetic Theology* (Minneapolis, MN, 2018).

Maida, Adam, "Rights in the Church," in George J. Dyer, ed., *A Pastoral Guide to Canon Law* (Dublin, 1977), 30–45.

Malia, Martin, *History's Locomotives: Revolutions and the Making of the Modern World* (New Haven, CT, 2006).

Mamdani, Mahmood, "Beyond Nuremberg: The Historical Significance of the Post-Apartheid Transition in South Africa," in Karen Engle, et al., *Anti-Impunity and the Human Rights Agenda* (Cambridge, UK, 2016), 329–360.

"March 25th: Servant of God (SG), Felix Maria Capello, S.J.," jesuit.org.sg/mar-felix-maria-capello-sj/.

Margolis, Nadia, "The 'Joan Phenomenon' and the French Right," in Bonnie Wheeler and Charles T. Wood, eds., *Fresh Verdicts on Joan of Arc* (New York, 1966), 265–288.

Margolis, Oren, *The Politics of Culture in Quattrocentro Europe: René of Anjou in Italy* (Oxford, UK, 2016).

Marrone, John, and Zuckerman, Charles, "Cardinal Simon of Beaulieu and Relations Between Philip the Fair and Boniface VIII," *Traditio* 31 (1975), 195–222.

Martel, William C., *Victory in War: Foundations of Modern Strategy*, rev. and expanded (Cambridge, UK, 2011).

Martens, Kurt, "The Position of the Holy See and Vatican City State in International Relations," *University of Detroit Mercy Law Review* 83 (2006), 729–760.

Martens, Kurt, "The Law That Never Was: The *Motu Proprio Administrativae Potestatis* on Administrative Procedures," *Jurist* 68 (2008), 178–222.

Martens, Kurt, "Protection of Rights: Experiences with Hierarchical Recourse and Possibilities for the Future," *Jurist* 69 (2009), 646–702.

Martens, Kurt, "Administrative Procedures in the Roman Catholic Church: Difficulties and Challenges," *Ephemerides Theologicae Lovanienses* 76 (2000), 354–380.

"Martin V," *Brittanica Academic*, academic-eb-ezproxy.stthomas.edu/levels/college/article/Martin-V/51150.

Martin, Randolph, "Sudan's Perfect War," *Foreign Affairs* 81, no. 2 (March–April 2002), 111–127.

Martin, Thomas Owen, "The Present Status of Canon Law," *Ohio State Law Journal* 20 (1959) 388–411.

Martinez, H. Salvador, *Alfonso x, the Learned: A Biography*, Odile Cisneros, tr. (Leiden, 2010).

Maschke, Timothy H., *Called to Be Holy in the World: An Introduction to Christian History* (Eugene, OR, 2016).

Massaro, Thomas J., "The Social Question in the Papacy of Leo xiii," in James Corkery and Thomas Worcester, eds., *The Papacy Since 1500: From Italian Prince to Universal Pastor* (Cambridge, UK, 2010), 143–161.

Massaro, Thomas J., "The First Jesuit Pope: The Contribution of His Jesuit Charism to His Political Views," in Alynna J. Lyon, et al., eds., *Pope Francis as a Global Actor: Where Politics and Theology Meet* (New York, 2018), 41–57.

Mastnak, Tomaž, *Crusading Peace: Christendom, the Muslim World, and Western Political Order* (Berkeley, CA, 2002).

Matusiak, John, *Henry v* (London, 2013).

Maxson, Brian Jeffrey, "Visual and Verbal Portraits of Cardinals in Fifteenth-Century Florence," in Piers Baker-Bates and Irene Brooks, eds., *Portrait Cultures of the Early Modern Cardinal* (Amsterdam, 2021), 69–89.

May, John D'Arcy, *"The Heaviest Blow:" The Catholic Church and the East Timor Issue* (Münster, 2004).

McBrien, Richard, "The Church (*Lumen Gentium*)," in Michael A. Hayes and Liam Gearon, eds., *Contemporary Catholic Theoloy: A Reader* (New York, 1999), 279–293.

McCahill, Elizabeth, *Reviving the Eternal City: Rome and the Papal Court, 1420–1447* (Cambridge, MA, 2013).

McCarthy, Justin, *Pope Leo xiii*, 2d. ed. (New York, 1899).

McCarthy, Timothy G., *The Catholic Tradition: The Church in the Twentieth Century*, 2d ed. (Eugene, OR, 2012).

McDannell, Colleen, *The Spirit of Vatican ii: A History of Catholic Reform in America* (New York, 2011).

McDonough, Elizabeth, "The Protection of Rights in Religious Institutes," *Jurist* 46 (1986), 164–204.

McGreevy, John T., *Catholicism: A Global History From the French Revolution to Pope Francis* (New York, 2022).

McGreevy, Patricia, et al., "The Final Report of the Committee on the Experiment in Due Process in the Church," *Proceedings of the Canon Law Society of America* 61 (1999), 137–159.

McNamee, Colm, "Britain (Narrative) (1300–1500)," in Clifford J. Rogers, *The Oxford Encyclopedia of Medieval Warfare and Military Technology* (Oxford, 2010), vol. 1 (online).

McPartlan, Paul, "The Church," in Ayres and Volpe, eds., *Oxford Handbook of Catholic Theology*, 198–213.

McSweeney, Thomas J., *Priests of the Law: Roman Law and the Making of the Common Law's First Professionals* (Oxford, UK, 2019).

Mendelson, Michael, "*De Oratore* and the Development of *Controversia*," in Richard O. Brooks, ed., *Cicero and Modern Law* (New York, 2016), 123–164.

Mendelson, Michael, "Everything Must Be Argued: Rhetorical Theory and Pedagogical Practice in Cicero's *De Oratore*," *Journal of Education* 179 (1997), 15–47.

Menache, Sophia, *Clement V* (Cambridge, UK, 1998).

Meron, Theodor, "The Authority to Make Treaties in the Late Middle Ages," *American Journal of International Law* 89 (1995), 1–20.

Meroney, Anne E., "Mediation and Arbitration of Separation and Divorce Agreements," *Wake Forest Law Review* 15 (1979), 467–486.

Meszeros, John C., "Procedures of Administrative Recourse," *Jurist* 46 (1986), 107–141.

Mettepenningen, Jürgen, *Nouvelle Théologie – New Theology: Inheritor of Modernism, Precursor of Vatican II* (London, 2010).

Metz, René, "Pouvoir, centralisation, et droit: La codification du droit de l'Église catholique au début du XXe siécle," *Archives de sciences sociales de religions* 26 (1981), 49–64.

Miller, William Ian, "Avoiding Legal Judgment: The Submission of Disputes to Arbitration in Medieval Iceland," *American Journal of Legal History* 28 (1984), 95–134.

Minnerath, Roland, "The Position of the Catholic Church Regarding Concordats From a Doctrinal and Pragmatic Perspective," *Catholic University Law Review* 47 (1998), 467–476.

Miras, Jorge, "Commentary" (canon 1733), in Ángel Maroza, et al., eds., *Exegetical Commentary on the Code of Canon Law* (Montreal, 2004), vol. IV/2, 2057–2069.

Mirow, Matthew C., "International Law and Religion in Latin America: The Beagle Channel Dispute," *Suffolk Transnational Law Review* 28 (2004), 1–25.

Misner, Paul, *Catholic Labor Movements in Europe: Social Thought and Action, 1914–1965* (Washington, DC, 2015).

Mode, Robert L., "Masolino, Uccello, and the Orsini 'Uomini Famosi,'" *The Burlington Magazine* 114, no. 831 (June, 1972), 368–378.

Moodie, Michael R., "The Administrator and the Law: Authority and Its Exercise in the Code," *Jurist* 46 (1986), 43–69.

Moons, Jos, *The Holy Spirit, the Church, and Pneumatological Renewal* (Leiden, 2022).

Moore, John Bassett, ed., *A Digest of International Law*, vol. V (Washington, DC, 1906).

Morrall, John B., *Gerson and the Great Schism* (Manchester, UK, 1960).

Morris, Michael A., *The Strait of Magellan* (Dordrecht, 1989).

Morrison, Wayne, "Atrocity and the Power of the Image," *Social Justice* 36 (2009–2010), 61–77.

Morss, John R., "International Legal Status of the Vatican/Holy See Complex," *European Journal of International Law* 26 (2015), 927–946.

Movsesian, Mark, "Elusive Equality: The Armenian Genocide and the Failure of Ottoman Legal Reform," *University of St. Thomas Journal of Law and Public Policy* 4 (2010), 1–17.

Mudimbe, V.Y., *The Idea of Africa* (Bloomington, IN, 1994).

Muhl, Charles J., "The Employment-At-Will Doctrine: Three Major Exeptions," *Monthly Labor Review*, January 2001, 3–11, bls.gov/opub/mlr/2001/01/art1full.pdf.

Murphy, Edward F., *St. Thomas' Political Doctrine and Democracy* (Washington, DC, 1921) (Ph.D. dissertation, Catholic University of America).

Murray, John Courtney, *We Hold These Truths: Catholic Reflections on the American Proposition* (Lanham, MD, 2005) (reprint of 1960 edition).

Murray, John Courtney, "Freedom, Authority, Community," in Coriden, ed., *We the People of God*, 145–157.

Murray, Paul D., "Expanding Catholicity Through Ecumenicity in the Work of Yves Congar: *Ressourcement*, Receptive Ecumenism, and Catholic Reform," *International Journal of Systematic Theology* 13 (2011), 272–302.

Musto, Ronald G., *Catholic Peace Tradition* (New York, 2002).

Musto, Ronald G., *Apocalypse in Rome: Cola di Rienzo and the Politics of the New Age* (Berkeley, CA, 2003).

Nartey, Emmanuel K., *Accountability and Corporate Human Rights Violations in Tort and International Law* (Newcastle-upon-Tyne, 2021).

Natarajan, Usha, "Accounting for the Absence of the Rule of Law: History, Culture, and Causality,"in Jeremy Farrall and Hilary Charlesworth, eds., *Strengthening the Rule of Law Through the U.N. Security Council* (London, 2016) 43–57.

Neff, Stephen C., *Justice Among Nations: A History of International Law* (Cambridge, MA, 2014).

Neil, Bronwen, *Leo the Great* (New York, 2009).

Nester, William R., *Theodore Roosevelt and the Art of American Power: An American For All Time* (Lanham, MD, 2019).

Nichols, Terence L., *That All May Be One: Hierarchy and Participation in the Church* (Collegeville, MN, 1997).

Noble, Thomas F.X., *The Republic of St. Peter: The Birth of the Papal State* (Philadelphia, 1984).

Noonan, John T., Jr., *The Scholastic Analysis of Usury* (Cambridge, MA, 1957).

Noonan, John T., Jr., *Contraception: A History of Its Treatment by the Catholic Theologians and Canonists* (Cambridge, MA, 1968).

Noonan, John T., Jr., *Power to Dissolve: Lawyers and Marriages in the Courts of the Roman Curia* (Cambridge, MA, 1972).

Noonan, John T., *The Lustre of Our Country: The American Experience of Religious Freedom* (Berkeley, CA, 1998).

Norte, Armando, "Literati in the Court of King Afonso III of Portugal (1248–1279)," *Royal Studies Journal* 1 (2015), 1–12.

Novacovitch, Mileta, *Les Compromis et les arbitrages internationaux du XIIe au XVe siécles* (Paris, 1905).

Noval, Joseph, *Commentarium Codicis Iuris Canonici Liber IV. De processibus* (Turin, 1920).

Oakley, Francis, *The Conciliarist Tradition: Constitutionalism in the Catholic Church, 1300–1700* (Oxford, UK, 2008).

Oakley, Francis, "History and the Return of the Repressed in Catholic Modernity: The Dilemma Posed by Constance," in Michael J. Lacey and Francis Oakley, eds., *The Crisis of Authority in Catholic Modernity* (Oxford, UK, 2011), 29–56.

O'Brien, Brendan P., "'Our System:' Father Robert T. Kennedy, the American Legal Tradition, and the Development of Administrative Law in the Revision of the Code of Canon Law," *Jurist* 77 (2021), 361–406.

O'Brien, Emily, *The "Commentaries" of Pope Pius II (1458–1464) and the Crisis of the Fifteenth-Century Papacy* (Toronto, 2015).

O'Brien, Thomas W., *John Courtney Murray in a Cold War Context* (Lanham, MD, 2004).

O'Donohoe, James A., "Administrative Aids to the Bishop," *Jurist* 30 (1960), 13–29.

Office of Chief of Naval Operations, *Civil Affairs Handbook, East Caroline Islands* (Washington, DC, 1944).

Offler, H.S., "Book Review," *Journal of Theological Studies* 20 (1969), 685–688 [reviewing Walter Brandmüller, *Das Konzil von Pavia-Siena, 1423–1424*].

Okafor, Eddie E., "Francophone Catholic Achievements in Igboland, 1883–1905," *History in Africa* 32 (2005), 307–319.

"Okpaleke, Card. Peter Ebere," press.vatican.va/content/salastampa/en/documentation/cardinal_biografie/cardinali_bio_okpaleke_p.html.

Okpaleke, Peter Ebere, *Conflict Prevention, Management, and Resolution in the Church* (Amenyi, Nigeria, 2004).

Okwu, Augustine Senan Ogunyeremuba, *The Mission of the Irish Holy Ghost Fathers Among the Igbo of Southeastern Nigeria* (Ph.D. dissertation, Columbia University, 1977).

Olson, James S., ed., *Historical Dictionary of European Imperialism* (New York, 1991).

O'Malley, John W., *A History of the Popes: From Peter to the Present* (Lanham, MD, 2010).

Ombres, Robert, "Justice and Equity in the 1983 Code," *Law & Justice: The Christian Law Review* 96 (1988), 23–33.

O'Meara, Thomas F., "Dominican and Jesuit Theologians at an Ecumenical Council: Yves Congar and Karl Rahner," *Journal of Jesuit Studies* 7 (2020), 459–471.

Omer, Reem, "South Sudan: From Independence to a Detrimental Civil War," *Harvard International Review* 37, no. 3 (2016), 11–12.

Oppenheimer, Mark, *Knocking on Heaven's Door: American Religion in the Age of Counterculture* (New Haven, CT, 2003).

Orsy, Ladislas, "The Spirit of Common Law and the Reform of Canon Law," *Catholic Lawyer* 15 (1969), 65–76.

Osheim, Amanda C., "The Christian Faithful," in Gaillardetz, ed., *Cambridge Companion to Vatican II*, 211–231.

Otu, Idara, *Communion Ecclesiology and Social Transformation in African Catholicism: Between Vatican II and African Synod II* (Eugene, OR, 2020).

"Our Founder, Father Marie-Joseph Lagrange, O.P.," *École biblique archéologie française de Jérusalem*, ebaf.edu/ecole-biblique/father-marie-joseph-lagrange-op/.

Owens, Karen, *Franz Joseph and Elisabeth: The Last Great Monarchs of Austria-Hungary* (Jefferson, NC, 2014).

Pace, Paul, "Francisco Suárez and Justice: A Common Good Perspective," *Gregorianum* 93 (2012), 497–525.

Padoa-Schioppa, Antonio, *A History of Law in Europe: From the Early Middle Ages to the Twentieth Century* (Cambridge, UK, 2007).

Padovano, Anthony, *The Estranged God: Man's Search for Belief* (New York, 1966).

Padovano, Anthony, *Who Is Christ?* (Notre Dame, IN, 1967).

Parsons, Gerald, *The Cult of Saint Catherine of Siena: A Study in Civil Religion* (Aldershot, UK, 2008).

Paulson, Lex, *Cicero and the People's Will: Philosophy and Power at the End of the Roman Republic* (Cambridge, UK, 2023).

Pennington, Kenneth, "The Jurisprudence of Procedure," in Wilfred Hartmann and Kenneth Pennington, eds., *The History of Courts and Procedure in Medieval Canon Law* (Washington, DC, 2016), 125–159.

Perkins, J. Blake, *Hillbilly Hellraisers: Federal Power and Populist Defiance in the Ozarks* (Urbana, IL, 2017).

Peters, Edward, *The Shadow King: Rex Inutilis in Medieval Law and Literature, 751–1327* (New Haven, CT, 2010).

Peters, Walter H., *The Life of Benedict XV* (Milwaukee, WI, 1959).

Peterson, Glenn, "Micronesia's Breadfruit Revolution and the Evolution of a Culture Area," *Archaeology in Oceania* 41 (2006), 82–92.

Pfanze, Otto, "Bismarck and German Nationalism," *American Historical Review* 60 (1955), 548–566.

Pfau, Aleksandra, *Medieval Communities and the Mad: Narratives of Crime and Mental Illness in Late Medieval France* (Amsterdam, 2021).

Philibert, Paul J., "Yves Congar: Theologian, Ecumenist, Visionary," *U.S. Catholic Historian* 17 (1999), 116–120.

Phillimore, John George, *Principles and Maxims of Jurisprudence* (Union, NJ, 2001) (reprint of 1856 edition).

Pihlajamäke, Heikke, and Korpiola, Mia, "Medieval Canon Law: The Origins of Modern Criminal Law," in Markus D. Dubber and Tatjana Hörnle, eds. *Criminal Law: A Comparative Perspective* (Oxford, UK, 2014), 201–224.

Pietropaolo, Domenico, *Semiotics of the Christian Imagination: Signs of the Fall and Redemption* (London, 2021).

Plovanich, Patricia, "Chenu, Marie-Dominique (1895–1990)," in Orlando Espin and James B. Nickhoff, eds., *An Introductory Dictionary of Theology and Religious Studies* (Collegeville, MN, 2007), 228.

"Points From the Discussions," in Coriden, ed., *We the People of God*, 19–23.

Pollard, John F., *The Papacy in the Age of Totalitarianism, 1914–1958* (Oxford, UK, 2014).

Pollard, John F., *Money and the Rise of the Modern Papacy: Financing the Vatican, 1850–1950* (Cambridge, UK, 2005).

Pollard, John F., *Benedict XV: The Unknown Pope and the Pursuit of Peace* (New York, 1999).

Pollard, John F., *The Vatican and Italian Fascism, 1929–1932: A Study in Conflict* (Cambridge, UK, 1985).

Pollard, John F., "Papal Diplomacy and the Great War," *New Blackfriars* 96 (2015), 147–157.

Polzenhagen, Frank, and Dirven, René, "Rationalist or Romantic Model in Globalisation?" in Gitte Kristiansen and René Dirven, eds., *Cognitive Sociolinguistics: Language Variation, Cultural Models and Social Systems* (Berlin, 2008), 237–300.

Porter, Jean, "From Natural Rights to Human Rights: Or, Why Rights Talk Matters," *Journal of Law and Religion* 14 (1999/2000), 77–90.

"Position Paper: Towards Constitutional Development Within the Church," in Coriden, ed., *We the People of God*, 5–23.

Post, Gaines, "Book Review," *Speculum* 49 (1974), 762–765 [reviewing Brian Tierney, *Origins of Papal Infallibility*].

Postema, Gerald J., "The British Tradition of Legal Positivism," in Torben Spaak and Patricia Mindus, eds., *The Cambridge Companion to Legal Positivism* (Cambridge, UK, 2021), 176–200.

Posthumus-Meyjes, G.H.M., *Jean Gerson – Apostle of Unity: His Church Politics and Ecclesiology* (Leiden, 1999).

Potworowski, Christophe F., *Contemplation and Incarnation: The Theology of Marie-Dominique Chenu* (Montreal, QB, 2001).

Poujol, A., *Le Différend entre Haïti et Saint Domingue au sujet de leurs frontières nationales* (Paris, 1900).

Poujol, A., "Haiti el arbitraje de suas fronteras," *Revista Nacional* 28 (Argentina, 1899), 169–180.

Pound, Roscoe, "The French Civil Code and the Spirit of Nineteenth Century Law," *Boston University Law Review* 35 (1955), 77–98.

Powell, Edward, "Settlement of Disputes by Arbitration in Fifteenth-Century England," *Law and History Review* 2 (1984), 21–43.

Prentiss, Craig R., *Debating God's Economy: Social Justice in America on the Eve of Vatican II* (University Park, PA, 2008).

Pril, Ward de, "Modernism and the Problematic Relation Between History and Theology: The Search for a Compromise by Louvain Historians and Theologians (1870–1910)," *Church History and Religious Culture* 91 (2011), 377–396.

Princen, Thomas, "International Mediation – The View From the Vatican," *Negotiation Journal* 3 (1987), 347–366.

Provost, James H., and Walf, Knut, eds., *Studies in Canon Law: Presented to P.J.M. Huizing* (Leuven, 1991).

Provost, James H., "Promoting and Protecting the Rights of Christians: Some Implications For Church Structure," *Jurist* 46 (1986), 289–344.

Puas, Gonzaga, *The Federated States of Micronesia's Engagement with the Outside World: Control, Self-Preservation, and Continuity* (Canberra, Australia, 2021).

Queller, Donald E., *The Office of Ambassador in the Middle Ages* (Princeton, NJ, 1967).

Raedts, Peter, "The Church as Nation State: A New Look at Ultramontane Catholicism (1850–1900)," *Dutch Review of Church History* 84 (2004), 476–496.

Ragazzoni, David, and Urbinati, Nadia, "Theories of Representative Government and Parliamentarism in Italy from the 1840s to the 1920s," in Pasi Ihalainen, et al., eds., *Parliament and Parliamentarism: A Comparative History of a European Concept* (New York, 2016), 243–261.

Ragnau, Edmond Hugues de, *The Vatican: The Center of Government in the Catholic World* (New York, 1913).

Rainbird, Paul, *The Archaeology of Micronesia* (Cambridge, UK, 2004).

Ralf, Malte, *Imperial Russian Rule in the Kingdom of Poland, 1864–1915* (Pittsburgh, PA, 2021).

Ralston, Jackson H., *International Arbitration From Athens to Locarno* (Stanford, CA, 1929).

Rapp, Claudia, *Holy Bishops in Late Antiquity: The Nature of Christian Leadership in an Age of Transition* (Berkeley, CA, 2005).

Rasilla, Ignacio de la, *In the Shadow of Vitoria: A History of International Law in Spain (1770–1953)* (Leiden, 2018).

Rech, Walter, "International Law as a Political Language, 1600–1859," in Giulio Bartolini, ed., *A History of International Law in Italy* (Oxford, UK, 2020), 48–78.

Reid, Charles J., Jr., "The Rights of Self-Defence and Justified Warfare in the Writings of the Twelfth- and Thirteenth-Century Canonists," in Kenneth Pennington and Melodie Harris Eichbauer, eds., *Law as Profession and Practice: Essays in Honor of James A. Brundage* (Burlington, VT, 2011), 73–92.

Reid, Charles J., Jr., "Thomas Aquinas (1225–1274)," in Orazio Condarelli and Rafael Domingo, eds., *Law and the Christian Tradition in Italy: The Legacy of the Great Jurists* (London, 2021), 98–127.

Reid, Charles J., Jr., "The Canonistic Contribution to the Western Rights Tradition: An Historical Inquiry," *Boston College Law Review* 33 (1991), 37–92.

Reid, Charles J., Jr., "Thirteenth-Century Canon Law and Rights: The Word *Ius* and Its Range of Subjective Meanings," *Studia Canonica* 30 (1996), 295–342.

Renzi, Francesco, "The Crisis of Power: Otto IV, Kings of Léon-Castile, the Cistercian Order," in Flocel Sabaté, ed., *Life and Religion in the Middle Ages* (Newcastle-Upon-Tyne, 2015), 103–124.

Riall, Lucy, *Garibaldi* (New Haven, CT, 2007).

Riccards, Michael P., *Faith and Leadership: The Papacy and the Roman Catholic Church* (Lanham, MD, 2012).

Ricciardi, Matthew M., "Title to the Aouzou Strip: A Legal and Historical Analysis," *Yale Journal of International Law* 17 (1992), 301–488.

Richardson, Carol M., *Reclaiming Rome: Cardinals in the Fifteenth Century* (Leiden, 2009).

Richardson, Carol M., "The Allure of Rome," in Carol M. Richardson, ed., *Locating Renaissance Art* (New Haven, CT, 2007), 25–61.

Risk, James E., "*Arduum Sane Munus*: A Retrospective," *Theological Studies* 5 (1944), 184–197.

Rodimer, Frank J., *Canonical Effects of Infamy in Fact: A Historical Synpopsis and Commentary* (Washington, DC, 1954).

Roebuck, Derek, *Medieval and Arbitration in the Middle Ages: England, 1154–1558* (Oxford, UK, 2013).

Rollo-Koster, Joëlle, *Avignon and Its Papacy, 1309–1417: Popes, Institutions, and Society* (Lanham, MD, 1015).

Rollo-Koster, Joëlle, "Civil Violence and the Initiation of the Schism," in Rollo-Koster and Izbicki, eds., *Companion to the Great Schism*, 9–65.

Rollo-Koster, Joëlle, and Izbicki, Thomas, eds., *Companion to the Great Schism (1378–1417)* (Leiden, 2009).

Rosales, Luis, and Olivera, Danile, *Francis, a Pope for Our Time: The Definitive Biography* (Boca Raton, FL, 2013).

Rosillo-López, Cristina, *Public Opinion and Politics in the Late Roman Republic* (Cambridge, UK, 2017).

Rubenstein, Joshua, *Leon Trotsky: A Revolutionary's Life* (New Haven, CT, 2011).

Ruddy, Christopher, "Yves Congar and Hans Küng at Vatican II: Differing Paths of Church Reform," *Ecclesiology* 10 (2014), 159–185.

Rush, Ormond, "Roman Catholic Ecclesiology from the Council of Trent to Vatican II and Beyond," in Paul Avis, ed., *The Oxford Handbook of Ecclesiology* (Oxford, UK, 2018), 263–292.

Russell, Frederick H., *The Just War in the Middle Ages* (Cambridge, UK, 1975).

Rutherford, Donald, ed., *Routledge Dictionary of Economics*, 3d ed. (New York, 2012).

Rutler, George William, *The Curé D'Ars Today: St. John Vianney* (San Francisco, CA, 1988).

Ryan, John A., and McGowan, R.A., *A Catechism of the Social Question* (New York, 1921).

Ryngaert, Cedric, "The Legal Status of the Holy See," *Göttingen Journal of International Law* 3 (2011), 829–859.

Saak, Erik Leland, *Highway to Heaven: The Augustinian Platform Between Reform and Reformation, 1292–1524* (Leiden, 2002).

Sacco, Ugo Colombo, *John Paul II and World Politics: Twenty Years of Search for a New Approach, 1978–1998* (Leuven, 1999).

Sambanis, Nicholas, et al., "Nation-Building Through War," *American Political Science Review* 109 (2015), 279–296.

Sanguineti, Sebastiano, *Iuris Ecclesiastici Institutiones in Usum Praelectionum*, 4th ed. (Rome, 1901).

Santos, Boaventura de Sousa, *Toward a New Legal Common Sense: Law, Globalization, and Emancipation*, 3d ed. (Cambridge, UK, 2020).

Savell, Stephanie, "How Death Outlives War: The Reverberating Impact of the Post-9/11 Wars on Human Health," Watson Institute for International and Public Affairs, May 15, 2023.

Schatz, Klaus, *Papal Primacy: From Its Origins to the Present* (Collegeville, MN, 1996).

Schelkens, Karim, et al., *Aggiornamento? Catholicism From Gregory XVI to Benedict XVI* (Leiden, 2013).

Schelkens, Karim, "Papal Leadership in the First Half of the Twentieth Century: Resistance and Renewal," in Richard R. Gaillardetz, ed., *The Cambridge Companion to Vatican II* (Cambridge, UK, 2020), 41–60.

Schillebeeckx, Edward, *Jesus: An Experiment in Christology*, Hubert Hoskins, tr. (New York, 1979).

Schillebeeckx, Edward, *Christ, the Sacrament of the Ecounter with God* (New York, 1963).

Schillebeeckx, Edward, *The Problem of Eschatology*, Boniface A. Willems, tr. (New York, 1969).

Schillebeeckx, Edward, *The Sacraments in General: A New Perspective*, Boniface A. Willems, tr. (New York, 1968).

Schillebeeckx, Edward, *Sacramental Reconciliation* (New York, 1971).

Schillebeeckx, Edward, *Man as Man and Believer*, Boniface A. Willems, tr. (New York, 1967).

Schillebeeckx, Edward, *A Personal God?*, Bastian von Iersel, tr. (New York, 1973).

Schillebeeckx, Edward, *God Among Us: The Gospel Proclaimed* (New York, 1983).

Schoof, Ted, ed., *The Schillebeeckx Case*, Matthew J. O'Connell, tr. (Ramsey, NJ, 1984).

Schram, Albert, *Railways and the Formation of the Italian State in the Nineteenth Century* (Cambridge, UK, 1997).

Schuyler, Eugene, "The African Slave-Trade: American Interest in Its Suppression," *The Anti-Slavery Reporter* 9 (January, 1889), 38–39.

Schwartzman, Micah, and Wilson, Jocelyn, "The Unreasonableness of Catholic Integralism," *San Diego Law Review* 56 (2019), 1039–1067.

Scirocco, Alfred, *Garibaldi, Citizen of the World: A Biography* (Princeton, NJ, 2007).

Scott, James Brown, *The Spanish Origin of International Law: Francisco de Vitoria and His Law of Nations* (Oxford, UK, 1932).

Selosse, Louis, *L'affaire des Carolines: Étude de droit internationale* (Paris, 1886).

Sereni, Angelo Piero, "The Code and the Case Law," in Bernard Schwartz, ed., *The Code Napoleon and the Common Law World* (New York, 1956), 55–79.

Seyerstad, Finn, "Jurisdiction Over Organs and Officials of States, the Holy See, and Intergovernmental Organizations," *International and Comparative Law Quarterly* 14 (1965), 31–82.

Shanley, Brian J., *The Thomist Tradition* (Dordrecht, 2002).

Shirley, Kevin L., *The Secular Jurisdiction of Monasteries in Anglo-Norman and Angevin England* (Woodbridge, UK, 2004).

Shuger, Debora, *Censorship and Cultural Sensibility: The Regulation of Language in Tudor-Stuart England* (Philadelphia, 2006).

Simpson, A.W.B., "The Agincourt Campaign and the Law of War," *Michigan Journal of International Law* 16 (1995), 653–666.

Simpson, W.A., "Cardinal Giordano Orsini (+1438) as a Prince of the Church and a Patron of the Arts: A Contemporary Panegyric and Two Descriptions of the Lost Frescoes in Monte Giordano," *Journal of the Warburg and Courtald Institutes* 29 (1966), 135–159.

Singer, Julie, *Representing Mental Illness in Late Medieval France: Machines, Madness, Metaphor* (Woodbridge, UK, 2018).

Sohrabi, Nader, "Global Waves, Local Actors: What the Young Turks Knew About Other Revolutions, and Why It Mattered," *Comparative Studies in Society and History* 44 (2002), 45–79.

Soth, Amelia, "The French King Who Believed He Was Made of Glass," *JStor Daily*, March 29, 2018, daily.jstor.org/french-king-who-believed-made-glass.

Soukop, Pavel, *Jan Hus: The Life and Death of a Preacher* (West Lafayette, IN, 2020).

Sperber, Jonathan, *The European Revolutions, 1848–1851*, 2d ed. (Cambridge, UK, 1994).

"Stanislaus, Woywod, O.F.M.," *Franciscan Friars of Holy Name Province*, "Deceased Friars," hnp.org/about-us/our-friars/deceased-friars/stanislaus-woywod/.

Stantchev, Stefan, and Weber, Benjamin, "*In Coena Domini*: A Hierocratic Weapon or a Pastoral Staff?" *Bulletin of Medieval Canon Law* 38 (2021), 361–419.

Stearns, Jason K., "Rebels Without a Cause: The New Face of African Warfare," *Foreign Affairs* 101, no. 3 (May–June, 2022), 143–156.

Stegherr, Marc, "'Kings By the Grace of the People Are No Grace for the People:' The Post-World War One Order and Its Conservative Critics," in Ioan Bolovan and Oana

Mihaela Tămaş, eds., *World War I and the Birth of a New World Order: The End of an Era* (Newcastle-Upon-Tyne, 2020), 256–263.

Stephenson, Charles, *Germany's Asia-Pacific Empire: Colonialism and Naval Policy, 1885–1914* (Woodbridge, UK, 2009).

Steuart, A. Francis, "Scotland and the Papacy During the Great Schism," *Scottish Historical Review* 14 (1907), 144–158.

Staffa, Dino, "Introductio: Praesupposita recursus ad Alteram Partem Signaturae Apostolicae," *Periodica* 67 (1978), 524–534.

Stiphout, Maurice van, "On the Roles of the State and Canon Law in the Nineteenth and Early Twentieth Centuries," in Martin Schermeier, et al., eds., *De rebus divinis et humanis: Essays in Honour of Jan Hallebeek* (Göttingen, 2019), 427–440.

Strandmann, Hartmut Pogge von, "Domestic Origins of Germany's Colonial Expansion Under Bismarck," *Past and Present* 42 (1969), 140–159.

Strayer, Joseph, *The Reign of Philip the Fair* (Princeton, NJ, 1980).

Suenens, Leon-Joseph, *Coresponsibility in the Church*, Francis Martin, tr. (New York, 1968).

Sullivan, Maureen, *The Road to Vatican II: Key Changes in Theology* (New York, 2007).

Suny, Ronald Grigor, *"They Can Live in the Desert But Nowhere Else:" A History of the Armenian Genocide* (Princeton, NJ, 2015).

Sussman, Lewis A., *The Elder Seneca* (Leiden, 1978).

Swafford, Andrew Dean, *Nature and Grace: A New Approach to Thomistic Ressourcement* (Eugene, OR, 2014).

Talar, C.J.T., "The Synthesis of All Heresies – 100 Years On," *Theological Studies* 68 (2007), 491–514.

Tanaka, Yoshifumi, *The Peaceful Settlement of International Disputes* (Cambridge, UK, 2018).

Taylor, Craig, "Henry V, Flower of Chivalry," in Gwilym Dodd, ed., *Henry V: New Interpretations* (York, UK, 2013), 217–247.

Taylor, Leonard Francis, *Catholic Cosmopolitanism and Human Rights* (Cambridge, UK, 2020).

Taylor, Miles, *Empress: Queen Victoria and India* (New Haven, CT, 2018).

Templeman, Geoffrey, "Edward III and the Beginnings of the Hundred Years War," *Transactions of the Royal Historical Society* 2 (1952), 69–88.

Thompson, Augustine, *Revival Preachers and Politics in Thirteenth-Century Italy* (Eugene, OR, 2010) (reprint of 1992 edition).

Thorne, Samuel E., "The Assize *Utrum* and Canon Law in England," *Columbia Law Review* 33 (1933), 428–436.

Tierney, Brian, *Foundations of the Conciliar Theory: The Contributions of the Medieval Canonists, From Gratian to the Great Schism*, enlarged new edition (Leiden, 1997) (originally published, 1955).

Tierney, Brian, *Origins of Papal Infallibility, 1150–1350: A Study on the Concepts of Infallibility, Sovereignty, and Tradition in the Middle Ages* (Leiden, 1972).

Tierney, Brian, "Roots of Western Constitutionalism in the Church's Own Tradition: The Significance of the Council of Constance," in Coriden, ed., *We the People of God*, 113–128.

Timby, Kim, *3D and Animated Lenticular Photography: Between Utopia and Entertainment* (Berlin, 2015).

Tomassetti, Julia, "Power in the Employment Relationship: Why Contract Law Should Not Govern At-Will Employment," *Economic Policy Institute*, November 19, 2020, epi.org/unequalpower/publications/the-legal-understanding-and-treatment-of-an-employment-relationship-versus-a-contract.

Tomassini, Carlo, "Vecchiotti, Settimio Maria, serviglianese vescovo, nunzio apostolico, docente," *luoghifermani.it/?p=4960* (2015).

"Torfs, Rik," in Sam Muller, et al., eds., *The Law of the Future and the Future of Law* (The Hague, 2012), vol. II, 493.

Torfs, Rik, *A Healthy Rivalry: Human Rights in the Church* (Leiden, 1995).

Torfs, Rik, "The Religion-State Relationship in Europe," *The Review of Faith and International Affairs* 8 (Summer, 2010), 15–20.

Torfs, Rik, "Justice: An Elusive Concept," *In die Skrifling/In Luce Verbi* 54 (2020), indieskrifling.org.za/index.php/skrifling/article/view/2612/6787.

Torfs, Rik, "Holding Companies and Holy Orders: Reflections on a Small Number of Remarkable Similarities," in James H. Provost and Knut Walf, eds., *Studies on Canon Law Presented to P.J.M. Huizing* (Leuven, 1991), 142–159.

Torfs, Rik, "Religion as a Utopia?" in Veerle Achten, et al., eds., *'A Truly Golden Handbook:' The Scholarly Quest for Utopia* (Leuven, 2016), 210–222.

Torfs, Rik, "Church Tribunals *secundum* and *praeter legem*," *Louvain Studies* 26 (2001).

Torfs, Rik, "Legal Relevance in the History of the Roman Catholic Church," in Hans-Georg Zieberts and Johannes A. Van der Ven, eds., *Human Rights and the Impact of Religion* (Leiden, 2013), 55–74.

Tunc, Andre, "Grand Outlines of the Code Napoleon," *Tulane Law Review* 29 (1954–1955), 431–452.

Turvasi, Francesco, *The Condemnation of Alfred Loisy and the Historical Method* (Rome, 1979).

Uginet, Francois-Charles, "Martin v," in Phillippe Levillain and John W. O'Malley, eds., *The Papacy: An Encyclopedia* (New York, 2002), vol. II, 974–977.

Vallejo, Eduardo Aznar, and González Zalacain, "Maritime Conflicts and Their Resolution in Late Medieval Castile," in Louis Sicking and Alain Wijffels, eds., *Conflict Management in the Mediterranean and the Atlantic, 1000–1800: Actors, Institutions, and Strategies of Dispute Settlement* (Leiden, 2020), 109–124.

Vecchiotti, Septimio, *Institutiones Canonicae: ad usum seminariorum accommodatae* (Turin, 1875).

Vermeersch, Arthur, and Creusen, Joseph, *Epitome Iuris Canonici cum Commentariis* (Rome, 1928), 3 volumes.

Verzijl, J.H.W., *International Law in Historical Perspective*, part VIII, *Inter-State Disputes and Their Settlement* (Leiden, 1976).

Viaene, Vincent, *Belgium and the Holy See From Gregory XVI to Pius IX (1831–1859): Catholic Revival, Society, and Politics in Nineteenth-Century Europe* (Leuven, 2001).

Viaene, Vincent, "A Pope's Dilemma: Temporal Power and Moral Authority in the History of the Modern Vatican," in Jan de Maeyer and Vincent Viaene, eds., *World Views and Worldly Wisdom: Religion, Ideology, and Politics, 1750–2000* (Leuven, 2016), pp. 245–255.

Vine, David, et al., "Creating Refugees: Displacement Caused by the United States' Post-9/11 Wars," Watson Institute for International and Public Affairs, Brown University, September 21, 2020.

Vivarelli, Roberto, "1870 in European History and Historiography," *Journal of Modern History* 53 (1981), 167–188.

Volk, Katherina, *The Roman Republic of Letters: Scholarship, Philosophy, and Politics in the Age of Cicero and Caesar* (Princeton, NJ, 2021).

Waal, Alex de, "When Kleptocracy Becomes Insolvent: Brute Causes of the Civil War in South Sudan," *African Affairs* 113 (2014), 347–369.

Waddy, Patricia, "Cardinals' Palaces: Architecture and Decoration," in Mary Hollingsworth, et al., eds. *A Companion to the Early Modern Cardinal* (Leiden, 2020), 351–371.

Wagner, Wienczyslaw J., "Codification of Europe and the Codification Movement in the Middle of the Nineteenth Century," *St. Louis University Law Journal* 2 (1953), 335–359.

Waldman, Thomas, "Politics and War: Clausewitz's Paradoxical Equation," *Parameters* 40 (2010), 1–13.

Ward, James E., "Leo XIII: 'The Diplomat Pope,'" *Review of Politics* 28 (1966), 47–61.

Ward, James E., "Leo XIII and Bismarck: The Kaiser's Vatican Visit of 1888," *Review of Politics* 24 (1962), 392–414.

Ward, John O., *Classical Rhetoric in the Middle Ages: The Medieval Rhetors and Their Art, 400–1300: With Manuscript Survey to 1500 CE* (Leiden, 2019).

Warninck, Hildegard, "The Roman Catholic Church and Church Autonomy," in Hildegard Warninck, ed., *Legal Position of Churches and Church Autonomy* (Leuven, 2001), 251–264.

Warwick, Donald P., "Personal and Organizational Effectiveness in the Roman Catholic Church," in Coriden, ed., *We the People of God*, 91–110.

Waterman, A.M.C., "The Intellectual Context of 'Rerum Novarum,'" *Review of Social Economy* 49 (1991), 465–482.

Watson, Alan, "The Hidden Origins of Enorm Lesion," *Journal of Legal History* 2 (1981), 186–193.

Webb, Heather, "Catherine of Siena's Heart," *Speculum* 80 (2005), 802–817.

Weiss, Gunther A., "The Enchantment of Codification in the Common-Law World," *Yale Journal of International Law* 25 (2000), 435–532.

Weiss, Stefan, "Luxury and Extravagance at the Papal Court in Avignon and the Outbreak of the Great Schism," Charlotte Masemann, tr., in Joëlle Rollo-Koster and Thomas M. Izbicki, eds., *A Companion to the Great Western Schism (1378–1417)* (Leiden, 2009), 67–87.

Wernz, Franciscus Xavier, and Vidal, Pietro, *Jus Canonicum* (Rome, 1927–1946) 7 volumes.

Wesemann, Paul, "Fora Arbitrii Conciliationis et Tribunalia Adminstrativa in Germania," *Monitor Ecclesiasticus* 100 (1975), 189–194.

Wesemann, Paul, and Lüdicke, Klaus, "De Organis Iustititiae Administrativae in Dioecesibus Reipublicae Foederalis Germaniae Statutis: Fora Arbitrii Conciliationis, Tribunalia Administrativa," *Periodica* 67 (1978), 731–736.

Westlake, John, *International Law*, Part 1, *Peace* (Cambridge, UK, 1904).

Whelan, Brett Edward, *Dominion of God: Christendom and Apocalypse in the Middle Ages* (Cambridge, MA, 2009).

Whelan, Brett Edward, *The Two Powers: The Papacy, the Empire, and the Struggle for Sovereignty in the Thirteenth Century* (Philadelphia, 2019).

White, Stephen D., "'Pactum … Legem Vincit, et Amor Judicium:' The Settlement of Disputes By Compromise in Western France," *American Journal of Legal History* 22 (1978), 281–308.

Whitman, James Q., *The Origins of Reasonable Doubt: Theological Roots of the Criminal Trial* (New Haven, CT, 2008).

Whitman, James Q., *The Legacy of Roman Law in the German Romantic Era: Historical Vision and Legal Change* (Princeton, NJ, 1990).

Williman, Daniel, "Schism Within the Curia: The Twin Elections of 1378," *Journal of Ecclesiastical History* 59 (2008), 29–47.

Wilson, Jacqueline, *The Religious Landscape in South Sudan: Challenges and Opportunities for Engagement* (Washington, DC, 2019).

Winter, Judith, "Coming Together Differently: Art, Anthropology, and the Curatorial Space," in Roger Sansi, ed., *The Anthropologist as Curator* (New York, 2020), 115–132.

Witte, John, Jr., and Alexander, Frank S., eds., *Christianity and Human Rights: An Introduction* (Cambridge, UK, 2010).

Witte, John, Jr., and Alexander, Frank S., eds., *The Teachings of Modern Roman Catholicism on Law, Politics, and Human Nature* (New York, 2007).

Wolfe, Jessica, *Homer and the Question of Strife From Erasmus to Hobbes* (Toronto, 2015).

Wolowyna, Ola, "A Demographic Framework for the 1932–1934 Famine in the Soviet Union," *Journal of Genocide Research* 23 (2021), 501–526.

Wood, Jacob, *To Stir a Restless Heart: Thomas Aquinas and Henri de Lubac on Nature, Grace, and the Desire for God* (Washington, DC, 2019).

Wortman, Richard S., *Scenarios of Power: Myth and Ceremony in Russian Monarchy From Peter the Great to the Abdication of Nicholas II* (Princeton, NJ, 2006).

Woywod, Stanislaus, *A Practical Commentary on the Code of Canon Law* (New York, 1925), 2 volumes.

Wright, Nicholas, *Knights and Peasants: The Hundred Years War in the French Countryside* (Rochester, NY, 1998).

Wright, O.J., *Great Britain and the Unifying of Italy: A Special Relationship?* (London, 2019).

Young, Robin Darling, "'A Soldier of the Great War:' Henri de Lubac and the Patristic Sources for a Premodern Theology," in James L. Heft, ed., *After Vatican II: Trajectories and Hermeneutics* (Grand Rapids, MI, 2012), 134–163.

Zelenietz, Martin, and Kravitz, David, "Absorption, Trade, and Warfare: Beachcombers on Ponape, 1830–1854," *Ethnohistory* 21 (1974), 223–249.

Zimmermann, Reinhard, *The Law of Obligations: Roman Foundations of the Civilian Tradition* (Oxford, UK, 1996).

Zimmermann, Reinhard, "The German Civil Code and the Development of Private Law in Germany," *Oxford Comparative Law Forum* 1 (2006), at oulf.ac.uk.

Zollmann, Jakob, "Interstate Mediation and Arbitration: Concepts, Cases, and Actors of Third Party Dispute Resolution (Seventeenth to Nineteenth Century)," in Karl Härter, et al., eds., *On Mediation: Historical, Legal, Anthropological, and International Perspectives* (New York, 2020), 153–183.

Zürcher, Erik Jan, "The Young Turk Revolution: Comparisons and Connections," *Middle Eastern Studies* 55 (2019), 481–498.

Journalistic Sources

About Apostolic Nunciature (Canadian Conference of Catholic Bishops), cccb.ca/about/apostolic/-nunciature/.

"Across Europe, Millions Protest a War in Iraq," *Washington Post*, March 15, 2003.

Agnew, Paddy, "Blair Set for Tough Talks With Pope," *The Irish Times*, February 22, 2003.

Ailemen, Anthony, "39 Catholic Priests Killed, 30 Abducted Across Nigeria – Report," *Business Day*, January 24, 2023.

Akwei, Ismail, "Pope Francis Donates Over $500,000 to South Sudan After Failed Visit," *Africanews*, June 22, 2017.

Allam, Lorena, and Evershed, Nick, "The Killing Times: The Massacres of Aboriginal People Australia Must Confront," *The Guardian*, March 3, 2019.

Allen, Elise Ann, "Church Encourages Women in South Sudan to Break Through Cultural Barriers," *Crux*, February 6, 2023.

Allen, John L., Jr., "Vatican Diplomat, Pio Laghi, Dead at 86," *National Catholic Reporter*, January 12, 2009.

Allen, John L., Jr., "Resilient Pope Presides Over a Decidedly Multilateral Holy Week," *Crux*, April 10, 2023.

Allen, John L., Jr., "Running the Numbers, Africa Isn't the Christian Future – It's the Present," *Crux*, January 25, 2023.

Apostolic Nunciature United States of America, nuntiususa.org.

Applebaum, Anne, "The New New World Order: America and the New Geopolitics," *Hoover Institution* 2001.

Aquilino, Giada, "Spiritual Retreat With South Sudan Leaders in Vatican: Time to Choose Life," *Vatican News*, April 11, 2019.

"At Least 200,000 Protest in Australia," *Los Angeles Times*, February 17, 2003.

Axelsson, Pelle, "Hans Blix: The Search for Weapons of Mass Destruction," *Global Policy*, March 17, 2023 (online blog).

Bates, Stephen, "Blair to Have Private Audience with Pope," *The Guardian*, February 19, 2003.

"Become an Oblate," *St. Benedict's Abbey*, Atchison, KS, kansasmonks.org/oblates.

Bordoni, Linda, and Morley, Nathan, "Pope Francis Prays For Peace in South Sudan," *Vatican News*, December 11, 2022.

Bordoni, Linda, "Ecumenical Leaders to South Sudan's Rulers: Peace Is In Your Hands," *Vatican News*, February 3, 2023.

Briggs, Ken, "Francis Compromised Wisely in Protracted Drama of Bishop Okpaleke's Appointment," *National Catholic Reporter*, May 28, 2020.

"Cardinal de Lubac, 95, of France, An Architect of Church's Renewal," *New York Times*, September 5, 1991.

"Cardinal Turkson Brings Pope's Good Wishes to South Sudan," *Catholic Radio Network*, March 18, 2014.

Chavez, Lydia, "Argentina and Chile in Accord on Beagle Channel," *New York Times*, October 5, 1984.

Christiansen, Drew, "A Vision of Peace: How the Prophetic 'Pacem in Terris' Helped Change the World," *America*, March 27, 2013.

Chute, Eleanor, "George H. Tavard, February 6, 1922–August 13, 2007, Respected Theology Professor at Mount Mercy College," *Pittsburgh Post-Gazette*, August 15, 2007.

Clemetson, Lynette, "Protest Groups Using Updated Tactics to Spread Antiwar Message," *New York Times* January 15, 2003.

Clemetsen, Lynette, "Thousands Converge in Capital to Protest Plans for War," *New York Times*, January 19, 2003.

Conason, Joe, "The Case for War Has Not Been Made," *Salon* February 5, 2003.

Conason, Joe, "'Seven Countries in Five Years:' Wesley Clark's New Memoir Casts More Light on the Bush Administration's Secret Strategies for Regime Change in Iran and Elsewhere," *Salon*, October 12, 2007.

Crowe, Kenneth C., "Catholic Central, St. Ambrose Schools to Merge," *Times-Union* (Albany, NY), November 15, 2021.

Daalder, Ivo H., "The Coalition That Isn't," *Brookings Institution*, March 24, 2003.

D'Emilio, Frances, "Pope Deplores 'Senseless Spiral of Blind Violence:' Thousands Hear Pontiff's Plea For Peace," *Calgary Herald* December 26, 2002.

De Stradis, Susanna, "Not Quite Silenced: Understanding the Censoring of John Courtney Murray," *Commonweal*, December 9, 2021.

DiMassa, Cara Mia, and Hayasaki, Erika, "Tens of Thousands March in Opposition to War in Iraq," *Los Angeles Times* February 17, 2003.

Donlon, Lorna, "South Sudan Visit With Pope Francis 'Not Cancelled' But Postponed Until It Can Best Effect Peace, Says Welby," *The Tablet*, June 1, 2017.

"Editorial: Saving South Sudan," *America*, February 3, 2014.

Egwu, Patrick, "Nigerian Bishop, Rejected by Former Diocese, Installed at New Diocese," *National Catholic Reporter*, May 2, 2020.

Elie, Paul, "The Reinvention of the Catholic Church," *The Atlantic*, December 11, 2022 (January/February 2023 print issue).

Emling, Shelley, "U.N. Split on Iraq War: France, Russia, China Say Facts Don't Support Call for Military Action," *Atlanta Journal Constitution* February 15, 2003.

Essoyan, Susan, "St Ann School in Kaneohe to Close in June After 180 Years," *Honolulu Star-Advertiser*, January 26, 2021.

Esteves, Junno Arocho, "War and Greed: Rome Events Shed Light on Conflict in South Sudan, Congo," *National Catholic Reporter*, November 21, 2017.

Faloyin, Dipo, "6 Journalists Arrested Over Video of South Sudan President 'Urinating on Himself,'" *Vice*, January 11, 2023.

Farley, Maggie, "Showdown With Iraq: Inspection Report Firms Up Council's Opposition to War," *Los Angeles Times* February 15, 2003.

Flegenheimer, Matt, "Pride is Tinged With Sadness as a Nation is Born," *New York Times*, July 13, 2011.

Fortin, Jacey, and Kron, Josh, "Factional Fighting Breaks Out in South Sudan's Capital," *New York Times*, July 9, 2016.

Fortin, Jacey, and Kron, Josh, "New Wave of Violence Ripples Across South Sudan's Capital," *New York Times*, July 11, 2016.

Freedland, Jonathan, "Turning Towards Iraq," *The Guardian* November 20, 2001.

Gallagher, Delia, and Dixon, Emily, "Pope Francis Kisses Feet of Once-Rival Sudan Leaders," CNN, April 12, 2019.

Gettleman, Jeffrey, "Newest Nation is Full of Hope and Problems," *New York Times*, July 8, 2011.

Gettleman, Jeffrey, "Struggle Over, Independent South Sudan Rejoices," *New York Times*, July 10, 2011.

Gjelten, Tom, "Catholics build 'Intentional' Community of Like-Minded Believers," *National Public Radio*, April 10, 2017.

Gramer, Robbie, "U.S. Quietly Gives Up on South Sudan War Crimes Court," *Foreign Policy*, July 20, 2021.

Greenwald, Glenn, "Wes Clark and the Neocon Dream," *Salon*, November 26, 2011.

Gross, Terry, "Why Pius IX Might be 'the Most Important Pope' in Modern Church History," *NPR*, April 24, 2018 (interview with David Kertzer) (online).

Harlan, Chico, and Houreld, Katharine, "Pope Francis Tells Leaders of Troubled South Sudan: 'Enough!'" *Washington Post*, February 3, 2023.

Hehir, J. Bryan, "From Leo XIII to John Paul II: The Evolution of Catholic Social Thought," *Commonweal* 118 (May 3, 1991), 281–282.

Herlinger, Chris, "Crisis Grips a Fragile New South Sudan," *National Catholic Reporter*, February 25, 2014.

Hooper, John, "Pope Francis and the Vatican Played Key Roles in U.S.-Cuba Thaw, Leaders Reveal," *The Guardian*, December 17, 2014.

Horowitz, Jason, and Walsh, Declan, "Hopes for Peace in South Sudan Are Pinned on a Papal Visit," *New York Times*, February 4, 2023.

Houlihan, Patrick J., "Pope Benedict XV and the Forgotten Campaign to End World War I," *America* (August 3, 2017).

"Hunger and Malnutrition Being Driven by Climate Crisis and Conflict in South Sudan," *Unicef*, November 3, 2022.

"In Memory of William W. Bassett, Jr.," mooreandsnear.com/tribute/details/9059/william-bassett-jr/obituary.html.

Irwin, Dan, "New Castle Students Coming to Kennedy Catholic," *The Herald* (Sharon, PA), April 25, 2021.

Jasanoff, Maya, "How *Heart of Darkness* Revealed the Horror of Congo's Rubber Trade," *Literary Hub*, December 7, 2017 (online).

Jasanoff, Maya, "With Conrad on the Congo River," *New York Times*, August 18, 2017.

Jeffrey, Paul, "Bishop: South Sudan Has Become 'The Place Where God Weeps,'" *National Catholic Reporter*, April 23, 2014.

Jerome-Cohen, Deborah, "A Case for Iraq Inspections," *Newark Star-Ledger*, February 16, 2003.

Johnson, Valerie, et al., "Does Archbishop Kurtz Care About the Struggling Black Catholic Parishes?" *Louisville Courier-Journal*, November 10, 2021.

Jones, Nigel, "Britain's Bloody History in Sudan," *The Spectator*, April 25, 2023.

"Juba Welcomes Establishment of Vatican Consulate in South Sudan," *Catholic Radio Network*, June 12, 2018.

Justin, Tito, "Vatican Envoy Urges South Sudan Peace," *Voice of America*, July 19, 2016.
Kamm, Henry, "Cardinal Samoré Vatican Mediator," *New York Times* February 3, 1983.
Karombo, Tawanda, "As Nigerians Vote for New President, Catholics Hope for End to Violence Against Christians," *National Catholic Reporter*, February 23, 2023.
Karombo, Tawanda, "Church Killings in Nigeria Leave Catholics 'Confused, Afraid, and Sad,'" *National Catholic Reporter*, July 6, 2022.
Kenney, Peter, "Pope Francis Meets Sudan Bishops as UN Documents Atrocities in the South," *ecunews.com*, January 22, 2016.
Kessler, Glenn, and Lynch, Colum, "Powell Lays Out Case Against Iraq: Evidence Shows Hussein Foiled Inspections, Secretary Tells U.N.," *Washington Post*, February 6, 2003.
Koo, Samuel, "Argentina and Chile Sign Treaty on Beagle Channel," *Associated Press*, May 2, 1985.
Kornbluth, Jesse, "Judith Miller Carried Water for the USA's Worst Debacle Since Vietnam," *Observer*, April 8, 2015.
Lauer, Hollie, "Large Group Appealing School Closure Holds March," *Pittsburgh Post-Gazette*, March 8, 2021.
Lewis, Mike, "A Most Unlikely Cardinal," *Where Peter Is*, August 17, 2022.
Lubov, Deborah Castellano, "Pope To South Sudan's Clergy: We Need Courageous Souls Ready to Die for Africa," *Vatican News*, February 4, 2023.
Machol, Deng, "Explosion of Violence in South Sudan,Threatens Peace Pact," *A.P. News*, July 18, 2022.
MacKaskill, Ewan, and Borger, Julian, "Iraq War Was Illegal and Breached U.N. Charter, Says Annan," *The Guardian*, September 15, 2004.
Maddox, J.D., "The Day I Realized I Would Never Find Weapons of Mass Destruction in Iraq," *New York Times*, January 29, 2020.
Manning, Maurice, "The Lives of Daniel Binchy: Irish Scholar, Diplomat, Public Intellectual," *The Irish Times*, June 18, 2016 (online).
McClory, Robert, "Why Yves Congar is Relevant Today," *National Catholic Reporter*, June 6, 2013.
Mena, Adelaide, "Churches Critical to Development of South Sudan," *National Catholic Reporter*, March 6, 2014.
Merchant, Nomaan, "Iraq WMD Failures Shadow U.S. Intelligence 20 Years Later," *AP*, March 23, 2023.
Moses, Paul, "Vatican Diplomacy and the Iraq War: Unheeded Warnings," *Commonweal*, January 13, 2020.
Newman, Johanna, "Pope's Emissary Meets With Bush, Calls War 'Unjust,'" *Los Angeles Times* March 6, 2003.
Nieves, Evelyn, "Worldwide, Civil Disobedience; Protesters Speak and Act Out Against War," *Washington Post* March 21, 2003.

Nieves, Evelyn, "From Sea to Sea, Rallies For, Against the War; One of the Largest Shows of Civil Disobedience Since Vietnam War Results in About 420 Arrests," *Washington Post*, March 22, 2003.

O'Grady, Robert M., "Father Robert T. Kennedy, Civil and Canon Lawyer, Canon Law Professor," *Boston Pilot*, April 12, 2019.

Onyulo, Tonny "'He Is the Only Hope We Have,' Say Refugees in South Sudan About Pope's Visit," *Detroit Catholic*, January 30, 2023.

Paprocki, Thomas J., "The Method of Proceeding in Administrative Recourse and in the Removal and Transfer of Pastors," in John P. Beal, et al., eds., *New Commentary on the Code of Canon Law* (Mahwah, NJ, 2000), 1818–1852.

Parker, Christopher, et al., "Meet the 16 New Cardinal Electors," *America*, August 26, 2022.

Patel, Dinyar, "Viewpoint: How British Let One Million Indians Die of Famine," *BBC News*, June 11, 2016.

Pattison, Mark, "Unions at Catholic Workplaces Called 'Magisterium in Word and Deed,'" *Crux*, August 21, 2016.

"People Eating Leaves to Survive in South Sudan as Aid Fails to Keep Pace with Spiraling Hunger Crisis – Oxfam," *Oxfam International*, December 1, 2022.

Philpott, Terry, "World War I's Pope Benedict XV and the Pursuit of Peace," *National Catholic Reporter*, July 19, 2014.

"Pope in New Note to Ban Conscription; Gasparri Decries Wilson Peace Plan; Allies Scoff at Berlin Professions," *New York Times*, September 23, 1917.

"Pope Meets With Annan; Blair to Visit Next; Pontiff and British Leader are at Odds on the Issue of A Potential U.S.-Led War on Iraq," *Los Angeles Times* February 19, 2003.

"Pope Urges End to War and Spiral of Violence," *Daily Telegraph*, December 26, 2002.

"Pope Calls For Peace in South Sudan," *Catholic Radio Network*, January 21, 2014.

"Pope Calls For Peaceful End to S. Sudan Conflict," *Sudan Tribune*, February 11, 2014.

"Pope Francis Receives Rousing Welcome in Uganda," *Nation* (Kenya), November 28, 2015.

"Pope Francis Blesses South Sudan and Sudan, Says Bishop Loku," *Catholic Radio Network*, January 26, 2016.

"Pope Francis Accepts Church Leaders' Invitation to Visit South Sudan," *Reuters*, October 27, 2016.

"Pope Francis' Christmas Day Message: Hope in the Darkness," *Washington Post*, December 25, 2019.

"Pope's Envoy in South Sudan in Pursuit of Peace-Building," *Vatican Radio*, July 21, 2016.

Pulella, Philip, "Protect, Advance Women for a Better South Sudan, Pope Says," *Reuters*, February 4, 2023.

Pur, Nyagoah Tut, "Has South Sudan's Conflict Really Ended? Accountability for Conflict Related Abuses Key," *Human Rights Watch*, December 14, 2022.

Ramesh, Randeep, "India's Secret History: 'A Holocaust, One Where Millions Disappeared,'" *The Guardian*, August 24, 2007.

Reid, Charles J., Jr., "War Begets War, Violence Begets Violence," *Huffington Post*, September 4, 2013.

Reid, Charles J., Jr., "The Modern Papacy and War," *Huffington Post*, April 13, 2015.

Riedel, Bruce C., "9/11 and Iraq: The Making of a Tragedy," *Brookings Institution*, September 18, 2021.

Roberts, Dan, and Carroll, Rory, "Obama and Raúl Castro Thank Pope for Breakthrough in U.S.-Cuba Relations," *The Guardian*, December 17, 2014.

"Salva Kiir: South Sudan's President in a Cowboy Hat," *BBC News*, June 21, 2018.

Samusano, Paul, "Salva Kiir: 'I Trembled When the Pope Kissed Our Feet,'" *Vatican News*, May 16, 2019.

San Martin, Inés, "Top Christians in South Sudan Urge Pope to Visit to Foster Peace," *Crux*, October 29, 2016.

San Martin, Inés, "Nigerian Bishop Rejected by Ahiara Diocese Installed as Bishop of Ekwulobia," *Crux*, May 5, 2020.

Saxon, Wolfgang, "William Ball Is Dead at 82; Defended Religious Rights," *New York Times*, January 18, 1999.

Scalia, Elizabeth, "She's a Tertiary? He's an Oblate? What Is That All About?" *Aleteia*, January 20, 2016.

Schuster, Beth, "World Has Edgy Little Christmas," *Los Angeles Times* December 26, 2002.

Sherwood, Harriet, and Mwesigwa, Alon, "Pope Francis Uses Mass in Uganda to Preach Reconciliation and Peace," *The Guardian*, November 28, 2015.

Simons, Marlise, "In the Street, Across Europe, a Weekend of Antiwar Rallies," *New York Times* January 20, 2003.

Simpson, Victor L., "Iraqi Official Gets an Audience with Pope, Hears Plea; the Pontiff Urged Deputy Prime Minister Tariq Aziz's Government to Comply with U.N. Demands," *Philadelphia Inquirer* February 15, 2003.

"Sociology Lecturer Warwick Dies at 63," *The Harvard Crimson*, December 11, 1997.

"South Sudan at Crossroads Say Its Bishops," *Caritas*, February 4, 2014.

"South Sudan Violence Has Killed 166 Civilians, Displaced Over 20,000 – U.N.," *Reuters*, December 14, 2022.

Specia, Megan, "383,000 Estimated Death Toll in South Sudan's War," *New York Times*, September 27, 2018.

Starr, S. Frederick, "You Can't Murder History," *New York Times Book Review*, July 19, 1992.

"Statement by Yasmin Sooka, Chair of the Commission on Human Rights in South Sudan, to the Human Rights Council," Office of the High Commissioner for Human Rights (March 18, 2022).

"The Czar's Death," *New York Times*, August 1, 1918.
"The Lay Fraternities of St. Dominic," *Dominican Province of the Assumption* (serving Australia, New Zeland, the Solomon Islands, and Papua, New Guinea), op.org.au/about-the-dominicans/the-dominican-family/the-lay-fraternities-of-st-dominic.
"Third Order (Brothers and Sisters of Penance and Tertiaries) (Secular Franciscan Order – OSF)," *Franciscan Friars, Province of Santa Barbara*, sbfranciscans.org/who-are-we-franciscan-spirituality/third-order-brothers-and-sisters-of-penance-and-tertiaries-secular-franciscan-order-ofs/.
Tokasz, Jay, "Parishioners Appeal Bishop's Decision to Close School in City of Tonawanda," *buffalonews.com*, January 23, 2014.
Tokasz, Jay, "Two Buffalo Schools to Merge Next Fall," *The Buffalo News*, March 13, 2021.
Tornielli, Andrea, "The Gesture of the Servant of the Servants of God," *Vatican News*, April 12, 2019.
Tulloch, Joseph, and Tumusiime, John Baptist, "'Great Sense of Hope' Ahead of Pope's Visit to South Sudan," *Vatican News*, January 28, 2023.
Tumusiime, John Baptist, "Pope Francis Concludes Ecumenical Visit to South Sudan," *Vatican News*, February 6, 2023.
Updike, Robin, "'Prisoner of the Vatican:' A Pope's Last Stand and the Birth of the New Italy," *The Seattle Times*, January 9, 2005 (online).
"U.S. Papal Nuncio Gets Vatican Post," *Los Angeles Times* April 14, 1990.
Valenti, Judith, "The Laypeople Seeking a Monastic Life in the Modern World," *U.S. Catholic*, June 4, 2019.
"Vatican Backs Efforts to Prevent Iraq War, Disarm Saddam," *America*, March 3, 2003.
"Violence in South Sudan's Upper Nile Displaces 9,000 – U.N. Delegate," *Reuters*, December 7, 2022.
Walsh, Declan, et al., "In South Sudan, Pope Recounts Troubles of Young, Fractured Nation," *New York Times*, February 4, 2023.
Wemple, Erik, "A Journalist's Defense of Her Flawed Reporting," *Washington Post*, April 12, 2015.
White, Christopher, "Pope Francis' Plea for Trip to Congo and South Sudan: No More Bloodshed," *National Catholic Reporter* January 30, 2023.
White, Christopher, "Pope, Archbishop of Canterbury Beg For Peace in Historic Joint Visit to South Sudan," *National Catholic Reporter*, February 3, 2023.
White, Christopher, "Francis Urges Divided South Sudan Christians to Reject Tribalism, Embrace Nonviolence," *National Catholic Reporter*, February 4, 2023.
Winfield, Nicole, and Machol, Deng, "Pope Heads to South Sudan to Urge Peace as Fighting Kills 27," *The Independent*, February 3, 2023.
Winfield, Nicole, and Machol, Deng, "Pope Encourages South Sudanese, Will Raise the Plight of Women," *The Independent*, February 4, 2023.

Winfield, Nicole, and Machol, Deng, "Pope Makes Final Bid for Peace, Forgiveness in South Sudan," *The Independent*, February 5, 2023.

Winters, Michael Sean, "Rome Consistory Showing Pope Francis' Vision Taking Root," *National Catholic Reporter* August 29, 2022.

Wright, George, "South Sudan: Journalists Held Over Film of President Appearing to Wet Himself," *BBC News*, January 7, 2023.

Zengarini, Lisa, "Abp. Welby Asks for Prayers Ahead of Ecumenical Pilgrimage to South Sudan," *Vatican News*, January 30, 2023.

Zengarini, Lisa, "Pope to Displaced South Sudanese: Be Seeds of Hope and Rebirth," *Vatican News*, February 4, 2023.

Cases Cited

Collection and Recovery of Assets, Inc. v. Patel, 276 So. 3d 494 (Ct. App., Fla, 2019).

Commissioner of Highways v. West Dulles Properties, Inc., 86 Va. Cir. 284 (Fairfax Co., 2014).

Cornett's Executor v. Rice, 299 Ky. 256, 187 S.W. 454 (Ky. App., 1945).

Dodd v. Reese, 216 Ind. 449, 24 N.E. 2d 996 (1940).

Foothills Federal Credit Union v. Superior Court of Los Angeles County, 155 Cal. App. 4th 632 (2007).

Goldberg v. Kelly, 397 U.S. 254 (1970).

NLRB v. Catholic Bishop of Chicago, 440 U.S. 490 (1979).

Trail Smelter Case, April 16, 1938; and March 11, 1941; *Reports of International Arbitral Awards* 3 (2006) 1905–1982.

www.ingramcontent.com/pod-product-compliance
Lightning Source LLC
Chambersburg PA
CBHW031322230926
51848CB00001B/56
9789004681446